89-2570

DS
832.7
.K6
W45
1989

BERGEN COMMUNITY COLLEGE LIBRARY

THE ORIGINS OF THE KOREAN COMMUNITY IN JAPAN
1910 – 1923

Michael Weiner

Centre for Japanese Studies
University of Sheffield

Studies on East Asia

HUMANITIES PRESS INTERNATIONAL, INC
Atlantic Highlands, NJ

First published in 1989 by
HUMANITIES PRESS INTERNATIONAL, INC.,
Atlantic Highlands, NJ 07716

Not for sale outside North America

Copyright © Michael A. Weiner, 1989

Editorial responsibility for *Studies on East Asia* rests with the East Asia Centre,
University of Newcastle upon Tyne, England, which promotes publications
on the individual countries and culture of East Asia,
as well as on the region as a whole.

All rights reserved. No reproduction, copy or transmission
of this publication may be made without written permission.

Library of Congress Cataloging-in-Publication Data
Weiner, Michael A.
The origins of the Korean community in Japan, 1910-1923—
   (Studies on East Asia)
   Bibliography: p.
   1. Koreans—Japan—History. 2. Japan–Ethnic relations.
   I. Title II. Series: Studies on East Asia
      (Atlantic Highlands, N.J.)
   DS832.7.K6W45 1989   952′.004957   86-27548
   ISBN 0-391-03494-4

Printed in Great Britain

Table of Contents

Introduction 1

Chapter 1   Japanese Images of Korea: 1868–1910 7

Chapter 2   From Korea to Chōsen:
                       The First Phase of Colonial Rule 30

Chapter 3   The Immigration of Korean Workers to Japan,
                       1910–1923 49

Chapter 4   Korean Workers and the Formation of
                       Labour Organizations in Japan 99

Chapter 5   The Korean Student Movement in Japan:
                       From Nationalism to Socialism 117

Chapter 6   Myth and Reality:
                       The Great Kantō Earthquake 164

Conclusion 201

Appendices 205

Bibliography 226

Index 247

Acknowledgements

A great many people have given freely of their time and knowledge to assist and advise me in the preparation of this manuscript. I would like to take this opportunity to thank them all. Special thanks are due to Professor R P Dore who first suggested the topic of this study. I am also indebted to Professor Nimura Kazuo of Hosei University who aided me in my search for materials, and to the entire staff of the Ohara Social Problems Institute for the kindness and courtesy they extended to me throughout my stay in Japan. I would also like to thank Dr Gordon Daniels and Mr Colin Holmes of the University of Sheffield, and Dr Ian Neary of the University of Newcastle, who read all or part of this manuscript, and whose suggestions and criticisms were gratefully received. A note of thanks is also due to the Japan Foundation Endowment Committee which financed an eighteen month stay in Japan.

Finally I would like to express my gratitude to two people without whose support, advice and encouragement this work would never have been completed. My greatest debt is to Dr R M V Collick, friend and respected teacher, who has always given far too generously of his time. Above all I would like to thank my wife Fiona, for her patience and encouragement.

For my parents

Introduction

> Racial discrimination and racial prejudice are phenomena of colonialism. It was as a result of the conquest of poor and relatively under-developed countries by the technologically advanced nations during the nineteenth century, that new kinds of economy, new forms of social relations of production involving both conqueror and conquered were brought into being. The inequalities between men of different nations, ethnic groups, or religions, or between men of different skin colours which resulted, were often justified in biological racist theories or some functional equivalent.[1]

At present there are approximately 700,000 Koreans residing in Japan. Although the vast majority were born in Japan and speak Japanese as their first language, relatively few possess Japanese citizenship. Most are classified by the Ministry of Justice as aliens, and Koreans comprise more than 85% of the total foreign resident population.[2] This limits not only their legal rights in the broadest sense, but also access to employment, particularly in the public sector, and to a wide range of social services.

Koreans are subject to equal taxation under the law, but welfare benefits and access to public subsidized housing programmes and national health insurance schemes are severely circumscribed by their status as foreigners. Although some Koreans have achieved notable success in business, the arts, music and sports, success for most is limited by the presence of discrimination in virtually all fields of endeavour. Korean entrepreneurs experience great difficulty in obtaining bank loans, while employment opportunities and the prospect of promotion for Koreans in Japan's largest and most prestigious institutions are reduced by discriminatory employment practices.[3] Relatively few Koreans are able to enter the 'professions', and Korean residents are, in principle, barred from taking up employment in government service, public corporations and, with few exceptions, in the public school system. For most, therefore, employment is confined to the lower stratum of the labour market.

Japanese ambivalence towards the legal rights and status of Korean residents can be traced back to the period between 1910 and 1945 when Korea was administered as a Japanese colony. Although the people of Korea were regarded as Japanese nationals by virtue of the act of annexation, the basic legal and political rights of citizenship contained in the Meiji Constitution were never extended to Korea. Koreans were therefore free, at least in principle, to take up employment anywhere within the empire, but beyond that nationality was an empty gesture which offered little to them 'in terms of civil liberties and racial equality which nationality was supposed to guarantee'.[4]

Similarly, many of the negative characteristics attributed to Korean residents today are identical to those which were ascribed to them during or immediately before the colonial period. School textbooks currently in use in Japan contain pejorative images of Korea which have their origins in the past, while surveys of public opinion have consistently shown that the negative stereotypes associated with Korean residents are no different from those which existed before the Second World War. Clearly therefore any study of the Korean minority in either the prewar or postwar setting must consider the specific historical context in which these negative images first arose, and how they have come to colour Japanese perceptions of the Korean community. One question, however, is how far back in history one must venture before the roots of current attitudes are exposed.

The popular view in Japan, and one which has largely been accepted by Western scholars, holds that the prejudice and discrimination encountered by Korean residents can be attributed in part to 'traditional' animosity, and in part to certain unique aspects of Japanese culture and society which militate against either assimilation or an ethnically pluralistic definition of what constitutes being Japanese.[5] The present study, however, starts from an entirely different set of premises.

First, the origins of the prejudice encountered by Korean immigrants in the early part of the twentieth century are to be found in the tumultuous years following the Meiji Restoration of 1868. Before this time there is little to suggest that the sense of ethnic or racial uniqueness, which has been such a dominant feature of Japanese life since Meiji, was a factor determining either relations with Korea or the acceptance of immigrants from the peninsula.[6] Rather, it was confrontation with the wealth and power of the West which necessitated a new concept of a nation based largely upon racial mythology, and generated an equally new sense of national unity and purpose. The symbol of a semi-divine Emperor served as an important psychological prop, while the foundation myths which comprise a large part of Japan's earliest written records were accepted and taught as faithful records of early Japanese history. Scholars who criticized the new orthodoxy risked official censure, and the sense of racial superiority engendered by this mythology was reinforced by the introduction of a national education system which promoted nationalism.[7] Throughout the pre-1945 period the Japanese people were socialized into accepting a view of the world in which their country was portrayed as the only Asian nation capable of creating a viable alternative to Western civilization. Such beliefs, implying also a considerable degree of backwardness and inferiority on the part of their neighbours, were encouraged by the inability of either Korea or China to resist Western aggression. The annexation of Korea in 1910 was, for many Japanese, the final confirmation that their country had not only achieved Great Power Status, but had also become the 'Leader of Asia'.

The first chapter of this study, therefore, examines the context in which a particular set of stereotypes concerning Korea developed after 1868. It is not my intention to provide either a political history of Meiji Japan or a history of Japanese-Korean relations between 1868 and 1910, but rather to trace the evolution of attitudes towards Korea within a historical framework. Consequently, certain important aspects of Japanese-Korean relations, such as trade and Japanese investment in Korea, receive only cursory treatment, while the views expressed by prominent Japanese statesmen, journalists and educators are considered in greater detail. This should not be taken to imply that economic issues exerted no influence upon the men who determined the course and direction of Japanese activities in Korea. As Peter Duus has argued:

> If one looks not at foreign policy debates among the late Meiji leaders but at the context of economic thinking within which they took place, it becomes clear that 'economic matters' were very much on their minds.[8]

Nevertheless, in the context of the present study, other factors such as security, national aggrandizement and the acceptance of Darwinist theories of natural selection as applied to the international order of the late nineteenth century were of far greater importance in shaping popular perceptions of Korea during the Meiji period.

Second, throughout the pre-1945 period relations between Korean residents and the majority Japanese society were determined by the former's status as immigrant/colonial workers who were assigned a clearly defined position at the base of the economic and social order. Any study of the pre-1945 Korean community must, of course, consider the colonial context in which immigration to Japan occurred. There are at least three reasons for this.

There is, firstly, a need to understand the economic and other pressures which encouraged Koreans to leave their homes and even their families in order to offer themselves as industrial labour in Japan. These 'push' and 'pull' factors were, however, neither discreet nor unconnected, but were the logical outgrowth of both the economic and social policies implemented by the colonial administration in Korea, and of capitalist development in Japan. As Cheng and Bonacich in their recent study of Asian workers in the United States have noted, the migration of workers from colonial territories to the metropolitan society 'is not fortuitous; it is systemic'.[9]

The subordination and exploitation of immigrant Korean labour in Japan was, moreover, justified by the same racist ideology which informed Japanese rule in Korea. Throughout the colonial period Japanese cultural and social policy was underpinned by the doctrine of *dōka* (assimilation). Although, as Peatie has pointed out, the Japanese concept of assimilation was 'distinctly Asian in origin and character', it rested upon a belief in the racial and cultural superiority of the colonizing power.[10] For Koreans, assimilation implied the abandonment, either voluntarily or involuntarily, of their identity as Koreans, while for the Japanese, assimilation meant no change at all. Moreover, as is discussed in chapter two of this study, the realities of Japanese colonial rule made it impossible for Koreans to take an informed and equal role in either their own or Japanese society.

Finally, much of the postwar literature produced in Japan on this subject has tended to reflect the political cleavages which deeply divide the Korean community, so that very often the past has been discussed in the light of much more recent events, thus lessening the overall value of such studies. While Western scholarship has, for the most part, managed to avoid the political rhetoric so evident in studies published in Japan, earlier research was handicapped by the unavailability of contemporary materials. More recent studies have focussed upon the present-day Korean community, and have made even less use of the rich harvest of prewar materials recently published in Japan. This has led to oversimplification and generalization about the nature of the prewar immigrant community and the events which shaped its future development. The most striking example of this has been the use of the term 'holocaust' to describe the persecution of Koreans following the Great Kantō Earthquake of 1923.[11] The inappropriate use of such labels not only distorts our understanding of what actually took place, but imposes yet another layer of stereotypes on what remains a sensitive issue among Korean residents.

The next three chapters are given over to an examination of the immigration of Koreans to Japan during the first fifteen years of colonial rule. Since contract and other workers made up the bulk of the immigrant community, particular emphasis is placed upon conditions of recruitment and employment, the growth and distribution of the Korean community, relations with indigenous Japanese workers, and the attempts made by Korean workers to create labour organizations. Wherever possible the views expressed by those Japanese who were involved, either directly or indirectly, in the management of immigrant Korean workers are cited – since it is they who most clearly revealed the source and function of prejudice against Koreans. As Castles and Kosack have remarked:

In reality the relationship between discrimination and prejudice is a dialectical one: discrimination is based on economic and social interests and prejudice originates as an instrument to defend such discrimination. In turn, prejudice becomes entrenched and helps to cause further discrimination.[12]

Chapter six, which examines the events surrounding the persecution of Koreans following the Great Kantō Earthquake, stands as the centrepiece of this study. The actions taken against Koreans during the first week of September, 1923, and the tone of subsequent accounts which appeared in the Japanese press, visibly demonstrated not only the cosmetic nature of 'assimilation', but also how deeply entrenched prejudice against Koreans had become. The events of 1923 are therefore regarded by the author as a water-shed in the history of this minority group. Although the Korean community continued to grow after this time, reaching a peak of just over two million during the Second World War when hundreds of thousands of Koreans were mobilized for work in Japan as part of the war effort, the pattern of relations between its members and those of the majority Japanese society had been firmly fixed.

With the exception of the first two chapters, which should be regarded as a preamble to the main part of this work, I have relied almost exclusively upon official reports and other contemporary Japanese materials since they provide the most reliable and consistent sources of information concerning the immigrant community. Except where the authors of works cited have chosen to do otherwise, all Japanese, Korean, and Chinese names appearing in this study are presented with the family name first. Macrons have also been used except in the case of place names such as Tokyo, Osaka, and Kyoto. With regard to the romanization of Korean names and proper nouns, except where otherwise stated, the McCune Reischauer system has been adhered to throughout.

Notes:
1. John Rex, *Race, Colonialism and the City*, Routledge and Kegan Paul, London, 1973, p. 75
2. George A. DeVos and William O. Wetherall, 'Japan's Minorities: Burakumin, Koreans, Ainu and Okinawans', *Minority Rights Group*, Report No 3, London, 1983, p. 10.
3. A typical example of this is the case involving Pak Chong-Sok and Hitachi Industries. Pak was initially employed by the company under his Japanese name (Arai Shōji), but Hitachi's offer of employment was withdrawn when his nationality was revealed. Pak filed suit against the company alleging that he had been unfairly discriminated against on the basis of his nationality. The Yokohama District Court ruled in his favour and found the company guilty of violating both the Labour Standard Act and the Civil Code of Japan. See Changsoo Lee and George DeVos, eds., *Koreans in Japan: Ethnic Conflict and Accommodation*, University of California Press, Berkeley and Los Angeles, 1982, pp. 277–278, and Robert W. Northup, The Case of 'Park Chong Sok and Hitachi Industries', *IDOC*, No. 65, September 1974, pp. 25–28.
4. Edward I-te Chen, 'The Attempt to Integrate the Empire: Legal Perspectives', in Ramon H. Myers and Mark R. Peattle, eds., *The Japanese Colonial Empire, 1895–1945*, Princeton University Press, Princeton, New Jersey, 1984, p. 246.
5. This is certainly the view taken in Lee and DeVos, op. cit., pp. 356–358.
6. A survey of relations between Korea and Japan, as well as Korean immigration to Japan before 1868 can be found in Michael Weiner, *The Origins and Early Development of the Korean Minority in Japan: 1910–1925*, unpublished Doctoral Dissertation, The University of Sheffield, 1982, pp. 1–33
7. Tsuda Sōkichi's critical analysis of early Japanese history brought him into direct conflict with state orthodoxy. Several of his books were banned in 1940, and he was subsequently forced to resign from Waseda University. See Gari Ledyard, 'Galloping Along with the Horseriders: Looking for the Founders of Japan', *The Journal of Japanese Studies*, Vol. 1, No 2, Spring, 1975, p. 218, and Saeki Arikiyo, 'Studies on Ancient Japanese History, Past and Present', *Acta Asiatica*, No. 31, January, 1977, pp. 115–116. With regard to education and the moulding of attitudes toward Asia, an excellent account can be found in John Caiger, 'The Aims and Content of School Courses in Japanese History, 1872–1945', Edmund Skrypczak, ed., *Japan's Modern Century*, Sophia University, Tokyo, 1968, pp. 51–81.
8. Peter Duus, 'Economic Dimensions of Meiji Imperialism: The Case of Korea, 1895–1910', in Myers and Peattie, op. cit., p. 137.
9. Lucie Cheng and Edna Bonacich, eds., *Labor Immigration Under Capitalism: Asian Workers in the United States Before World War II*, University of California Press, Berkeley, Los Angeles, London, 1984, p. 2.
10. Mark R. Peattie, 'Japanese Attitudes Toward Colonialism, 1895–1945, in Myers and Peattie, op. cit., p. 96.
11. Lee and DeVos, op. cit., p. 21.
12. Stephen Castles and Godula Kosack, *Immigrant Workers and Class Structure in Western Europe*, Oxford University Press, London, New York, Toronto, 1973, p. 430.

Chapter 1

Japanese Images of Korea: 1868–1910

After nearly a century and a half of self imposed isolation there were very few Japanese who held realistic views about either the international community or Japan's place in it. Of course, this isolation had never been complete and limited trade had been maintained with both Korea and China, while the existence of a Dutch commercial mission on the island of Deshima had permitted some access to information about the West. There had also been irregular contacts with other European nations from as early as the eighteenth century, but it was not until the *bakufu* was confronted with the overwhelming military power of the West that Japan was compelled to open its doors to diplomatic and commercial intercourse. The arrival of an American flotilla in the middle of the nineteenth century not only visibly demonstrated Japan's vulnerability to foreign aggression, but stirred a debate over national security which contributed to the eventual collapse of the Tokugawa regime. The issue of Japan's survival as an independent nation in a world dominated by the rivalries of the Western powers was not, however, resolved by the restoration of Imperial rule in 1868.

Even before the Restoration there had been few individuals who had advocated a redefinition of Japan's role in Asian affairs. For Yoshida Shōin, whose vision of a powerful nation united under the Emperor was a major influence within the Restoration movement, Japan's security could best be preserved through territorial expansion.[1] But one must be careful not to overstate the importance of Tokugawa expansionists like Yoshida, since, as Marius Jansen has remarked:

> Tokugawa expansionists were reacting against a long period of seclusion and torpor, and there was little likelihood that they would be called upon to implement their suggestions. To a considerable degree they were only legitimating their proposals for opening the country to trade and proving that their patriotism should not be questioned.[2]

Moreover, by the end of the Tokugawa period there also existed support for the creation of an Asian alliance, which would defend the region from Western encroachment. This view was well summarized by Katsu Rintarō, a *bakufu* official who after the Restoration served as a member of the Council of State. In marked contrast to the expansionism advocated by Yoshida, he argued that Japan should persuade both Korea and China to cooperate in the construction of a modern navy which would prevent their 'being trampled underfoot by the West'.[3] With relatively little reliable information concerning conditions abroad, proposals such as these were largely based on abstract speculation. Nevertheless, elements of both Yoshida's expansionism and Katsu's vision of an Asian alliance were to become a feature of both Meiji foreign policy and the writings of influential journalists and educators.

The attitude of the new Meiji government towards the establishment and maintenance of relations with the outside world paralleled its determination to transform Japan into a modern industrial state along Western lines. In 1868 the government announced that 'intercourse with foreign countries shall be carried on in accordance with the public law of the whole world', and that all treaties concluded by the *bakufu* would be renegotiated.[4] Relations with Korea, however, began under a cloud of suspicion when Korean officials at Pusan refused either to acknowledge the legitimacy of the Meiji government, or to receive its representatives.[5] This refusal to consider the establishment of 'modern' relations caused considerable consternation within the Japanese Government, and there were some, like Kido Kōin, a former disciple of Yoshida Shōin, who advocated the immediate and forcible opening of Korean ports.[6] More moderate views, however, prevailed and the Government elected to persuade the Koreans through diplomacy rather than the use of force. During the next four years a series of diplomatic missions were sent to Korea which, though unsuccessful, did illustrate Japan's determination to conduct foreign policy in accordance with accepted international practice.[7] The first of these missions departed for Korea in January 1870, and after failing to reach agreement with Korean officials at Pusan returned to Japan in the spring of that year. Upon its return, Sada Hakubo, the leader of the mission, submitted a private memorandum which revealed the growing impatience among a hardline minority within Japan. In his view the Government should no longer tolerate these insults to the 'Imperial dignity', and he urged the immediate despatch of a special envoy accompanied by a strong military force. He also warned that failure to do so could result in Western (in particular Russian) intervention in Korean affairs.[8]

Sada's views were not, however, representative of contemporary official thinking, and there is no evidence to suggest that an invasion of Korea was seriously contemplated. Moreover, as Jansen has noted:

> Samurai advocates of punishment of Korea or of Taiwanese aborigines were expressing long-pent-up aspirations to greatness and action, and the urgency of their advocacy was the greater because hopes that had been noised in late Tokugawa rhetoric were not being realised.[9]

But, by the summer of 1873, the continued obstinacy of the Korean Government, coupled with the reported mistreatment of Japanese residents in Pusan, led to a revival of arguments in favour of a punitive expedition. The ensuing debate over war with Korea – known as *Seikanron* – and the political crisis it precipitated, have been discussed elsewhere in great detail.[10] Nevertheless, the arguments expressed by the principal protagonists in the debate are worthy of brief mention here, since they shed some light on contemporary attitudes toward Korea.

Saigō Takamori, the leading military figure within the Council of State and the acknowledged champion of *samurai* interests, was the chief spokesman for the pro-war element. Like Sada Hakubo three years earlier, Saigō's advocacy of military force was dictated by both the intransigence of the Korean court and the threat of Russian expansion in the area. Saigō's views need also to be considered against a background of serious civil unrest in Japan and his conviction that a foreign expedition would not only prevent further disturbances, but also foster national unity.[11]

Ōkubo Toshimichi, a member of the Iwakura Mission and Minister of Finance, who emerged as Saigō's principal adversary, issued his opinion in a memorandum typical of the pragmatism which was to characterize Meiji foreign policy. Ōkubo insisted that the admittedly provocative behaviour of the Koreans could not be permitted to interfere with or endanger the ultimate objective of national reconstruction. He also doubted whether the people would support an invasion of Korea, and warned his colleagues that such an undertaking could easily invite foreign intervention.[12]

Despite the intensity of the debate, it is extremely difficult to identify specific attitudes toward Korea among the participants. The arguments on both sides tended to emphasize the need to alleviate domestic tensions while preserving Japan's position in the international community. For some, like Saigō, Japan's immediate interests could best be served by a war with Korea, which would offer the disgruntled and increasingly troublesome *samurai* an opportunity to restore their prestige. But for others, like Kido Kōin, who had reversed his earlier position on Korea, the benefits of such a war were outweighed by the hazards it might entail.[13] Iwakura Tomomi, recently returned from a European tour, argued that the frontier dispute with Russia presented the more serious threat to Japan's security,[14] and even Yamagata Aritomo, a later proponent of Asian expansionism, withheld his support, since he believed that Japan did not yet possess the necessary military strength.[15]

With the eventual defeat of the pro-war faction, the Government resumed its attempt to establish relations with the Yi court through active diplomacy. Encouraged by an optimistic report submitted by Moriyama Shigeru, further missions were sent to Pusan, and Moriyama himself spent much of 1874 in Korea negotiating with Korean officials. His efforts, however, failed to produce any tangible results, and Japanese impatience was clearly evident in the decision to send warships into Korean territorial waters in 1875.[16] Although the Government maintained that it was merely surveying the Korean coastline, there is little doubt that this decision was taken with a view to exerting pressure on Korea in much the same way that Perry's 'show of force' twenty years earlier had compelled the *bakufu* to enter into treaty negotiations with the United States. Given the determination of the Meiji leadership to model their international behaviour on that of the leading Western powers, this course of action was hardly surprising. In an era when gunboat diplomacy was regarded as a legitimate means of conducting foreign policy, the Japanese response was both appropriate and predictable.

When news that members of the expedition had been fired upon by Korean soldiers reached Tokyo, a pro-war faction, this time led by Itagaki Taisuke, urged a vigorous response, but rumours of an imminent war were stilled by the Government's decision to send a high level mission to Korea. With the tacit approval of both the American Minister to Japan and the Chinese Government, General Kuroda Kiyotaka and Inoue Kaoru, accompanied by a formidable display of military might, arrived at Inchon in February 1876 to open direct negotiations with the Korean court.[17] The Treaty of Kanghwa which resulted consisted of twelve articles, the most important of which were: (a) the recognition of Korea as a sovereign and independent nation; (b) the opening of three ports to Japanese trade; and (c) the extension of the principle of extraterritoriality to Japanese citizens in Korea. In August 1876 a supplementary treaty was signed which permitted Japanese nationals to lease land in Korea, employ Korean nationals for work in Korea, and to pay for goods purchased in Korea with Japanese currency.[18]

The implementation of these treaties, however, was delayed by the Korean authorities, and it was not until 1882 that Hanabusa Yoshimoto was permitted to take up residence at Seoul as permanent representative of the Japanese Government.[19] At the same time, the treaty's failure to solve the question of Korea's international status brought Chinese and Japanese differences over this issue to the fore. In fact, Japanese relations with and attitudes toward Korea after 1876 were dominated by the continual conflict of Chinese and Japanese interests in the peninsula. It is also from about this time that the chauvinism which was to dominate Japanese perceptions of Asia began to crystallize.

Unlike Japan, whose contact with the West had stimulated the creation of a dynamic new state which vigorously pursued an ambitious programme of economic development and industrialization, Korea's response more closely resembled that of Imperial China. While in theory there existed a strong centralized state in the form of the monarchy and a

Confucian-style bureaucracy, the governing capacity of the Yi dynasty had almost always been limited by the power of the landed aristocracy, which also dominated the state bureaucracy. These internal pressures were brought into sharper relief by external forces in the form of French, American and Japanese warships, whose repeated appearances in Korean coastal waters posed an obvious threat to that country's policy of exclusion.[20] Further indications of administrative and economic decay were also evident in the increasing frequency of peasant uprisings during the final decades of Yi rule. In 1862, for example, there were serious disturbances in the Provinces of Kyŏngsang and Ch'ungch'ŏng, and by the end of that year there was civil disorder throughout the country.[21]

The *Tonghak* (Eastern Learning) movement arose not only in opposition to foreign encroachment, but also as an expression of rural discontent with maladministration and bureaucratic corruption. Although its founder was executed in 1864 and its adherents persecuted, the movement continued to draw widespread support from among both the peasantry and impoverished members of the gentry class. By 1890 it had spread throughout the country and when, in 1894, a major rebellion was triggered by further official incompetence and corruption, the enfeebled monarchy was compelled to rely on outside assistance to suppress the *Tonghaks*.[22]

Increased confidence in their own abilities, coupled with a growing sense of unease over the vulnerability of their neighbours to both internal disorder and external aggression, gradually convinced many Japanese that Japan was destined to become the leader of Asia. At its best, this attitude was translated into a determination to provide assistance and encouragement to progressive elements in Korea and elsewhere, and at its worst revealed a thinly disguised contempt for their neighbours' inability to manage their own affairs. In this respect, the views expressed by Fukuzawa Yukichi are of particular importance, not only because of his influence on the intellectual life of the Meiji period, but also because his intimate association with the Korean reform movement was reflected in many of his later writings.

In common with many of his contemporaries, Fukuzawa's views on Asia and, in particular, his preoccupation with Korea were moulded by the 'special historical circumstances of the late Tokugawa period.'[23] It was through the unease generated by China's humiliation during the middle of the nineteenth century that the concepts of Asian unity and the Japanese mission in Asia were developed by Fukuzawa and others. But, in Fukuzawa's view, notions of solidarity with the rest of Asia (China and Korea) were useful only in so far as they furthered Japan's own national interests.[24] A factor that tempered Fukuzawa's utilitarian view of foreign relations, however, was his close association with and commitment to the early reform movement in Korea. His initial contact with this movement was brought about by the arrival in May 1881 of the first *Sinsa Yuramdam* (Gentlemen's Touring Group) to be sent by the Korean government. The members of this mission were introduced to Fukuzawa, and two of their number, Yun Ch'i-ho and Yu Kil-chun, enrolled at *Keiō Gijuku* (now Keiō University) under his sponsorship.[25] Both of these students were associated with the nascent reform movement led by Kim Ok-kyun, Pak Yŏng-hyo and Sŏ Kwang-bŏm.[26]

It was also from this time that Fukuzawa began to develop the theme of Japan as *Tōyō no Meishu* (the Leader of Asia). The first occasion was in a lengthy article entitled 'My views on our relations with Korea'. In it he likened Japan's situation to that of a man whose neighbour's house was in danger of being destroyed by fire, and reminded his readers that, 'the momentum with which the Westerners are now advancing eastward is like a spreading fire.' Should Korea and China fall under the control of the Western powers, argued Fukuzawa, 'it would be as if we had invited the burning of our own house by allowing our neighbour's house to be consumed.' It was therefore natural that Japan, in the interests of its own security, should concern itself with conditions in China and intervene in Korean affairs.[27]

For Fukuzawa the continuing advance of the West had gradually transformed the concept of Asian unity from a vague ideal into a political imperative. But his vision of an Asian alliance did not imply equality for the nations concerned; in fact, his conclusion was that 'the only country which can be entrusted with the leadership of East Asia is Japan.'[28] In comparison with Japan, which had made great progress toward 'civilization', wrote Fukuzawa, Korea had remained weak and backward. Moreover, since Japan was the country which had 'opened' Korea, it was only natural that Japan should deal with Korea as she herself had been treated by the United States before the Meiji Restoration.[29] This belief in Japan's destiny to become the leader of Asia was to become 'the keynote of Japanese thinking concerning Asia,'[30] and, as we shall see, the basis for Japanese expansionism.

Fukuzawa's views on Korea were undoubtedly hardened by the *Imo Kullan* (military riot) of July 1882 in Seoul which resulted in the deaths of Japanese military advisers and the forced evacuation of the Japanese legation. That order was restored only after the arrival of a large Chinese army under the command of Yüan Shih-K'ai, who immediately assumed control over civil and military affairs, could only have deepened the humiliation felt by Fukuzawa and other Japanese.

While the Japanese leadership could take some consolation from the fact that the crisis was speedily resolved, the events of July and August 1882 highlighted the tenuous nature of Korean independence and restored Chinese influence in the peninsula. At home the Government's cautious handling of the affair was subjected to constant criticism from

Fukuzawa in particular.³¹ In an article in the July 31 edition of the *Jiji Shimpō*, he demanded the immediate despatch of a punitive expedition,³² and in a second article published on the following day Fukuzawa elaborated on his plans for the modernization of Korea:

> After putting down the present troubles, Minister Hanabusa ought to be appointed supervisor for Korea's internal affairs, and he should also supervise all matters of administration.³³

Equally angered by China's intervention in the affair, Fukuzawa urged the Government to adopt a firm position which would preserve Japanese interests in Korea. Moreover, were these interests to be endangered by Chinese interference, wrote Fukuzawa, the Japanese should not hesitate to 'cut down the big old decaying tree of the Orient with one stroke.'³⁴ In somewhat more restrained language, Enomoto Takeaki, the Japanese Minister in Peking, expressed official concern over China's actions. In a conversation with his American counterpart, Enomoto said that 'his government would never consent to see Korea a Chinese province, and capable at any time of becoming a base of attack upon Japan.'³⁵

There is little doubt that the sudden restoration of Chinese influence in Korea after 1882 brought about a fundamental change in the political and strategic situation in the Far East. China's determination to re-establish itself as a major power almost inevitably came into conflict with Japanese interests in the area, in particular over the question of Korean independence.³⁶ Nevertheless, the Meiji leadership, while recognizing the need to resolve Japan's differences with China, remained convinced that a direct confrontation with China might jeopardize the revision of the unequal treaties which Japan had signed with the Western powers. Voicing his own uncertainty over Japan's future role in Asia, Iwakura Tomomi suggested that Japan should restrict its activities to seeking a guarantee of Korean independence from the Western powers, and warned his colleagues that a lack of restraint might undermine Japan's respectability in the eyes of the West.³⁷ Consequently, official Japanese policy toward Korea during the decade after 1882 remained non-interventionist.

The 1880s also witnessed a broadening of interest in Korean affairs among a wide range of groups within Japan. Itagaki Taisuke's Liberal Party, for example, consistently supported Korean independence from China, and radicals like Ōi Kentarō were prepared to employ extreme methods in order to prevent Korea from becoming a Chinese dependency.³⁸ Expansionist societies like the *Gen'yōsha* (Black Ocean Society) and later the *Kokuryūkai* (Amur River Society) also became increasingly involved in Korean affairs, but for the most part it was the Japanese liberals, and, in particular, Fukuzawa Yukichi, who were most concerned with Korea during this period.³⁹ Under Fukuzawa's patronage *Keiō*

Gijuku welcomed a growing number of Korean students, and between 1882 and 1884 he not only supervised their studies but acted as an unofficial adviser for the Korean reform movement. Whether Fukuzawa was merely using Kim Ok-kyun and the other members of the reform movement in Korea to further Japanese interests there, as some have suggested, is unclear, but there is little doubt that he exerted considerable influence over them.[40]

The rapid diminution of Japanese influence in Korea following the *Imo Kullan* was also reflected in the deepening sense of isolation felt by Japanese and Korean liberals alike. Throughout the winter of 1882–1883 Fukuzawa continued to press for military expansion which, in his view, was fully justified by the existence of a new set of circumstances in Asia.[41] Fearful that Japan's position as 'the leader of civilization in East Asia' might be endangered by a resurgent China, Fukuzawa argued that, 'In culture we should become a leader of enlightenment, and in military arts we should become the leader of Asia.'[42]

By now firmly convinced that international relations were governed by the law of the jungle, Fukuzawa wrote:

> From time immemorial the rapacity of national rivals has been no different from birds and animals devouring one another . . . Japan too is like one of those birds and animals, and whether we will be devoured by others or whether we will devour them will ultimately be determined solely by the animal strength we possess.[43]

As China strengthened its position in Korea, the desperation of the Korean progressives and their Japanese supporters mounted until finally on December 4, 1884, the reform party, led by Kim and assisted by members of the Japanese legation guard, attempted to overthrow the Government. But the poorly planned coup lacked any substantial popular support, and within days Chinese troops had forced the conspirators and their allies to seek the protection of the Japanese legation. Eventually the legation was attacked, and its staff, accompanied by Kim and the other surviving members of the reform party, were compelled to flee to Inchon where they boarded a Japanese ship and returned to Japan.[44]

Despite the involvement of the Japanese Minister to Korea in the attempted coup, the Japanese Government itself appears to have played no part in Kim's attempt to wrest political control from the conservatives. Although dismayed by China's intervention in the affair, the Japanese Government restated its policy of avoiding a direct confrontation with China over the issue of Korean independence. The cabinet's position was outlined by Prime Minister Ito Hirobumi in the following way:

> We want to avoid hostilities with China . . . We cannot yet decide whether to risk war with China for Korean independence in the future. But for now we must avoid it.[45]

Foreign Minister Inoue Kaoru was immediately despatched to Korea to demand an official apology from the Korean authorities and to negotiate compensation for losses suffered by Japanese nationals. Inoue, on behalf of his Government, disavowed any responsibility for the actions taken by members of the legation staff during the uprising and refused to consider the Korean Government's demands for the extradition of Kim and the other conspirators who had escaped to Japan. The Korean Government, anxious not to provoke the Japanese, had no alternative but to accede to Inoue's demands. The treaty of Hansong, which resulted from these negotiations, was signed in January 1885 and stipulated that the Korean Government would, in addition to giving compensation for Japanese losses, take steps to punish those Koreans who had killed or injured Japanese nationals during the riots.[46]

In an attempt to resolve the issue of Korean independence, Itō Hirobumi was sent to Tientsin where he met with Li Hung-chang who was acting on behalf of the Chinese Government. Although Itō was unable to obtain Chinese recognition of Korea's independence, both parties agreed to withdraw their respective forces from Korea, and promised that any subsequent military intervention in Korea by either country would be preceded by formal notification to the other.[47] While the Treaty of Tientsin (often referred to as the Li-Itō Convention), signed in April 1885, went some way toward restoring Japanese influence in Korea, public opinion in Japan throughout this period was generally critical of the Government. In an editorial published in January, Fukuzawa advised the Government to prepare for war with China,[48] and later in the same month a student demonstration calling for the adoption of strong measures was held in Tokyo. Anticipating further displays of popular discontent, the Government censored all press accounts relating to the negotiations then underway at Tientsin, and the terms of the treaty itself were not made public until the end of May.[49]

Another result of the attempted coup of December 1884 was that it stimulated reappraisal of Japan's identity as an Asian nation. To many Japanese liberals the failure of the Korean reform movement reinforced their own growing sense of estrangement from the rest of Asia. Following his return from a trip to Europe in 1883, Itagaki Taisuke wrote:

> Consider, for example, a primitive (yaban) country. Some of its people are intelligent, but because the majority are not, the country is inevitably called primitive. In the same way, no matter how far Japan progresses, no matter how enlightened she becomes, just

because the great majority of people in other Asian countries are ignorant and primitive, the whole of Asia is considered primitive.[50]

This sense of frustration with and alienation from other Asian nations was given fuller, expression in Fukuzawa's famous article, *Datsu-A ron*, published in March 1885. Disillusionment with the Korean reform movement led him to conclude that Japan had no choice but to reject the bad company of East Asia' and align itself with the civilized nations of the West'. In Fukuzawa's view, geographical proximity did not warrant special treatment, and Japan should therefore emulate the West in its relations with both Korea and China. He concluded: People who keep bad company cannot avoid a bad name themselves. In my heart I believe that we must reject the bad company of East Asia.'[51] While support for an Asian alliance was not completely extinguished by the events of 1882 and 1884, there were many in Japan who shared the opinion that, if Asia were to be divided up among the European powers it would be in the national interest if Japan were to become a guest at the table rather than meat at the banquet.'[52] With the partitioning of China and the demise of the Korean kingdom not only inevitable but imminent, Fukuzawa reasoned that:

> Since as citizens of Korea they have nothing to live for they would, if anything, be happier to allow their country to be taken over by, for example, Russia or Britain and to become their subjects. To have one's country destroyed by the government of another and thus become a people without a country is by no means a happy fate. Yet rather than living in hopeless misery . . . as the object of the scorn of others, it would be better to have one's life properly protected securely.[53]

Despite the criticisms voiced by Fukuzawa and others outside the Government, official policy towards Korea remained one of restraint. In a letter outlining his Government's attitude toward the Korean issue, Foreign Minister Inoue Kaoru wrote:

> Unlike three years ago many complications have arisen in Korea and we must not lightly intervene. Our policy toward that nation is to avoid interference as much as possible and merely to watch the development of its national fortune with attention.[54]

Gradually, however, even Inoue became convinced that Korea was incapable of transforming itself into a modern civilized' state. In 1887 he conceded that he saw little hope of Korea's preserving its autonomy, while Yamagata Aritomo, expressing a view which was to characterize Japanese attitudes toward Korea during the colonial period, felt that its inability to modernize stemmed from defects in the national character' of its people.⁵⁵ Sharing Yamagata's fear of third party intervention in Korean affairs, Foreign Minister Aoki Shūzō, in a memorandum written in 1890 and entitled 'The Balance of Power among the East Asian Nations', argued that Korea should be made part of the Japanese map.⁵⁶

Attitudes toward Korea during the decade after 1884 were also being moulded by a resurgence of nationalist sentiment in Japan. By the early 1890's the failure of successive governments to secure a revision of the unequal treaties had generated a growing distrust of the Western powers, and, by extension, of the 'Westernization' of Japan. For some, like the young journalists and intellectuals who established the *Seikyōsha* (Society for Political Education) in 1888, Japan's cultural and political survival would best be served by the preservation of what they termed the *kokusui* (National Essence).⁵⁷ One of their leading members, Shiga Shigetaka, believed that Japan's national essence had given her a historic mission. He proposed that:

> Every year on the anniversary of Emperor Jimmu's accession . . . and on the anniversary of his passing . . . we should ceremonially increase the territory of the Japanese Empire, even if it be only in small measure. Our naval vessels should on each of these days sail to a still unclaimed island, occupy it, and hoist the Rising Sun . . . ⁵⁸

The search for a national identity, which fired the imagination of the *Seikyōsha*, led others still further down the imperialist path. Abandoning his earlier belief in pacifism, Tokotomi Sohō, the founder and editor of *Kokumin no Tomo* (The Nation's Friend), embraced the tenets of imperialism. For him, and other writers associated with the *Min'yūsha* (Friends of the Nation Society), Japan would regain the respect of the West by reviving its military and expansionist heritage.⁵⁹ An article which appeared in *Kokumin no Tomo* in June 1893 expressed bitter regret that 'the most progressive, developed, civilized, intelligent and powerful nation in the Orient still cannot escape the scorn of white people'. The author argued further that, having lost its martial spirit, Japan was now ranked alongside countries like Egypt and Korea 'which lacked both civilization and barbarian strength'.⁶⁰ And soon after the outbreak of the Sino-Japanese War in 1894, Tokutomi himself wrote:

> We must remember that we are fighting before the whole world. Why do some people say we fight in order to reform Korea, or to vanquish Peking, or to establish a huge indemnity? They should realize that we are fighting to determine once and for all Japan's position in the world . . . If our country achieves a brilliant victory, all previous misconceptions will be dispelled . . . ⁶¹

The decade of Chinese dominance in Korean affairs was abruptly ended by *Tonghak* rebellion which culminated in the Sino-Japanese War of 1894–1895. Japan's victory not only strengthened its position in Korea, but also served to broaden the appeal of the type of nationalism advocated by Tokutomi and others. During the war, the *Yomiuri Shimbun* sponsored a competition for war songs which would inspire hatred of China,[62] while Yosano Hiroshi glorified the war in a series of *tanka*, the last of which invoked memories of Hideyoshi's ruinous invasion of Korea:

> What need we yield
> to ancient glories?
> The time is near
> when again we shall build
> a mound of ears.[63]

The euphoria of victory was, however, soon followed by the humiliation of the Triple Intervention. With its interests in Korea now threatened by Czarist Russia's imperial ambitions, Japanese sensitivities were stung further by the overthrow of the pro-Japanese government in Seoul and the subsequent rise of Russian influence. Although Russian dominance was relatively brief, Japanese policy toward Korea after 1896 was shaped almost entirely by the threat of Russian expansionism.[64]

Japanese fear of Russia and disillusionment over the consistent failure of their attempts to bring 'civilization' to Korea also bred contempt for the Korean people. The failure to negotiate rights to the proposed Seoul-Inchon railway in 1896, for example, was attributed to the bigotry, ignorance, prejudice and stubbornness of the Korean people,[65] while the prestigious *Tōyō Keizai Shimpō* (Asia Economic Bulletin) described the situation in Korea at the end of the century in the following way:

> By and large, when people look at Korea, they think of it as an infirm and weak country whose sources of wealth have already all been exploited, but in fact it is rich in minerals and cereals and other natural resources . . . The only reason why Korean industry is today not greatly flourishing is that the Korean people are on the whole weak and lazy, and lacking the spirit of enterprise; . . . [66]

That the Koreans were now regarded as incapable of managing their own affairs was borne out by the establishment of a Japanese semi-protectorate immediately after the outbreak of the Russo-Japanese War in 1904. This was followed by a decision 'to take possession of the real powers of protection' in Korean political and military matters, and to 'promote the development of Japanese economic rights and interests in Korea'.[67] Through a series of defeats inflicted on Russia in 1905 Japan was ensured of eventual victory, and in July the Russian government agreed to enter into peace negotiations.

With the exception of a small number of Christian-Socialists grouped around Kōtoku Shūsui and Sakai Toshihiko, support for the war had been universal. Only the *Heimin Shimbun* (Commoner's Newspaper), which represented the views of the nascent socialist movement, had been prepared to criticize the Government's conduct of the war. It condemned official policy in Korea as an attempt to 'sell civilization by force',[68] while the chauvinistic attitude of many Japanese was also challenged:

> Japanese, despising the Korean people, are always saying that Koreans have no idea of nation, no idea of patriotism . . . Some say the Korean people are idle and cunning with no ability to be anything but slaves. They are not so by nature. In fact they are diligent and patient.

Given the extremely limited circulation of the *Heimin Shimbun*, however, such views were representative of only a small minority. Nevertheless, the members of the *Heiminsha*, the group publishing this paper, were themselves subject to almost continuous police harrassment. In April 1904 Sakai was sentenced to three months imprisonment for violation of the Press Laws, and in January 1905 he and Kōtoku were forced to suspend publication of the *Heimin Shimbun* altogether.[70]

The treaty which ended the war in 1905 ensured that Japanese interests in Korea would no longer be subject to outside interference. Consequently the Korean Government had no alternative but to agree in November 1905 to the establishment of a Japanese protectorate to be administered by a *Tōkan* (Resident-General).[71] This was followed by a tersely-worded declaration which noted that 'the experience of recent years has demonstrated the insufficiency of measures of guidance alone', and made clear the Government's intention to exercise complete control over the internal affairs of Korea.[72]

Itō Hirobumi's arrival in Korea as Resident-General was preceded by a press conference in Tokyo at which he summarized the policy objectives of the Japanese Government. In his view the most immediate concerns were institutional reforms coupled with the elimination of official corruption and poverty in Korea. Itō also emphasized that these objectives could only be achieved if a spirit of cooperation between Koreans and Japanese were firmly established, but conceded that, 'Unfortunately, many Japanese have had attitudes toward Koreans . . . We must watch ourselves and get rid of these bad attitudes.'[73] His speech was enthusiastically received by the assembled representatives of the Japanese press. The *Mainichi Shimbun* welcomed his appointment as 'a glorious climax to his long and useful career', while the *Tōkyō Nichi Nichi Shimbun* regarded the Government's attitude toward Korea as an enlightened one.[74] Both the *Asahi* and *Mainichi* newspapers also acknowledged the existence of a certain degree of animosity between Koreans and Japanese residents in Korea. This, they agreed, was due in large part to the arrogance shown by some Japanese in their dealings with Korea, and both papers urged Itō to promote better understanding and cooperation between the two peoples.[75]

Although Itō avoided discussing the possible annexation of Korea, and is thought to have opposed annexation until his death in 1909, there were others within the Government who regarded this as the most appropriate answer to Japan's security needs.[76] In February 1907, Motono Ichirō, the Japanese Minister in St. Petersburg, wrote:

> We have to gradually move toward the goal of annexing Korea since there is no other way of insuring the establishment of tranquility in Korea.[77]

Even after Itō had presided over the dissolution of the Korean army, and had forced the abdication of Emperor Kojong, his policies were subjected to consistent criticism by the more bellicose members of the Japanese government.[78] Members of the Yamagata faction were particularly critical of Itō's approach, and regarded him as 'the most weak-kneed among the weak-kneed party'.[79] But, however conciliatory Itō's policies may have appeared to the expansionists within the War Ministry or the extremists of the *Kokuryūkai*, the final years of his Residency were characterized by increasing opposition from within Korea itself. According to records compiled by the Residency-General, more than twenty thousand Koreans were killed, wounded or captured during clashes with Japanese police or military units between 1907 and 1909.[80] Due to the enforcement of press censorship in Korea the activities of the anti-Japanese *Ŭibyŏng* (Righteous Army) received little attention in the Japanese press, and when they did were referred to as the actions of rebels or law-breakers.[81]

By the summer of 1909 it was evident that Itō's gradualist approach had failed, and his assassination by a Korean while visiting the city of Harbin in Manchuria in October of that year brought annexation even closer. In December, the pro-Japanese *Ilchinhoe* (Renovation Society) petitioned the Japanese Government in support of annexation, but this was criticised by many of Japan's most influential newspapers.[82] Both the *Tōkyō Mainichi* and *Asahi* newspapers, for example, argued that Japan was not capable of supporting the economic burden which annexation would entail,[83] while an editorial on the *Jiji Shimpō* commented:

> We can understand why the *Ilchin* Society made such a proposal, but its opinion is not the opinion of the majority of Koreans

... We cannot know the future, but for the time being we hope there will be no change in present conditions.[84]

The arrival of the new Resident-General, Army Minister General Terauchi Masatake, in Seoul in July 1910, however, signalled an end to even the pretence of Korean independence. The Treaty of Annexation was signed on August 22, and General Terauchi was subsequently appointed to the post of *Chōsen Sōtoku* (Governer-General of Korea). Within days he made clear the tenor of the new administration by prohibiting the use of any materials in schools which would encourage independance and incite rebellion against the Japanese empire. The consequences of such a rebellion, he warned, would not hurt Japan; 'only Koreans would suffer'.[85]

In contrast to their earlier opposition to annexation, Japan's leading newspapers were unanimous in their support of Government policy. The *Jiji Shimpō* endorsed the annexation with a special commemorative issue containing the views of many statesmen and politicians. Ōkuma Shigenobu, the founder of Waseda University, wrote that the 'peaceful annexation' of Korea was 'like a dream', while others like Moriyama Shigeru and Hanabusa Yoshimoto, who had been involved with Korean affairs since the early years of Meiji, contributed equally supportive articles.[86] The *Tokyo Mainichi Shinbun*, in an editorial entitled 'The Happiness of the World', concluded that no one could oppose the policy now pursued by the Government since:

> The world can enjoy peace only when all countries reach the same level of civilization . . . It cannot permit such a thing as low civilization countries.[87]

Even the Japanese Congregational Church, which numbered among its members Yoshino Sakuzō and other prominent liberals, expressed its support for the annexation. In an editorial entitled 'The Annexation of Korea and the Evangelization of Koreans', which appeared in the September issue of *Kirisuto-Kyō Sekai*, (The Christian World), evangelization was identified with assimilation:

> ... We are not without sympathy for the feelings of the Koreans, but such sympathy is more suitable in women and children. On the contrary it is to the advantage of the Korean people to be part of a powerful empire. The choice they should make at this juncture is to assimilate to and identify themselves with, the Japanese nation in terms of political thought and feeling. If this is not like the gospel of Jesus Christ's resurrection, what is?[88]

It is of course, impossible to provide a completely reliable assesment of popular attitudes in Japan towards Korea at the time of the annexation.

But given the type of coverage which Korea had received in the popular press throughout the previous two decades, and the unsympathetic image this had generated, it is likely that most Japanese regarded Korea as socially stagnant, its people as ignorant, and the Government as corrupt. With its own security ultimately in the balance, Japan, they almost certainly felt, was therefore fully justified in managing the affairs of its weaker neighbour. This view was later embodied in the so-called 'stagnation theory' which held that social, economic and political development in Korea had been arrested several centuries earlier, and that this accounted for that country's inability to modernize. Such self-consciously imperialist sentiments as these were not however, uniquely Japanese. As Jansen has remarked; if late nineteenth century Japanese imperialism is to be judged, reference must be made to the international context in which it developed. In modelling their international behaviour on that of the Western powers, he argues, the Japanese 'could not have been expected to overlook the expansive drive that was such a prominent feature of all modernizing states in the last decades of the nineteenth century'.[89] Moreover:

> Even in the West, it must be remembered, voices critical of these new developments were relatively few, for the 'moral' face of imperialism's expansive urge was the promise of bringing civilization and Christianity to backward races.[90]

A second and equally compelling justification for the annexation, which gradually gained widespread acceptance, was the belief, based upon an orthodox interpretation of early Japanese history, that the union of the two countries represented a return to a relationship which had existed in ancient times. This re-affirmation of a common heritage implied that the annexation was not only politically necessary, but culturally possible.[91] In practice, however, Korea was to be regarded as a colonial possesion, and its people as culturally and politically inferior to the Japanese. This was clearly evident in an article in the *Ōsaka Asahi Shimbun* in October 1910:

> The purpose for which a country has a colony is not for the interests of the inhabitants of the colony but for the interest of the mother country. Seeing this, it is natural that the rights of the inhabitants of the colony should not be equal to those of the mother country.[92]

Notes:

1. See David Margary Earl, *Emperor and Nation in Japan*, University of Washington Press, Seattle, 1964, p. 173.
2. Marius B. Jansen, 'Japanese Imperialism: Late Meiji Perspectives', in Myers and Peattie, op. cit., p. 70.
3. Cited in Marius B. Jansen, *Sakamoto Ryōma and the Meiji Restoration*, Princeton University Press, Princeton, 1961, pp. 164–165.
4. Cited in Meiji Japan Through Contempory Sources, Vol. 2, The Centre for East Asian Cultural Studies, Tokyo, 1970, pp. 69–70.
5. A fuller treatment of the theoretical and political basis of Korea's relations with China and Japan during this period can be found in George M. McCune, op. cit., pp. 308–325, and Im Kwan Hwang, *The Korean Reform Movement of the 1880's and Fukuzawa Yukichi*, Unpublished Doctoral Dissertation, Washington University, 1975, pp. 69–73. Also see Watanabe Manabu, 'The Concept of *Sadae Kyorin* in Korea', *Japan Quarterly*, Vol. XXIV, No. 4, October–December, 1977, pp. 411–420, and Marius B. Jansen, 'Modernization and Foreign Policy in Meiji Japan', Robert E. Ward, ed., *Political Development in Modern Japan*, Princeton University Press, Princeton, New Jersey, pp. 168–169. For a detailed discussion of Sino-Korean relations see Chong Hae-Jong, 'Sino-Korean Tributary Relations in the Ch'ing Period', in the John K. Fairbank ed., *The Chinese World Order*, Harvard East Asian Series, No 32, Cambridge, Massachusetts, 1968, pp.90–111.
6. W. G. Beasley, *The Meiji Rastoration*, Stanford University Press, Stanford, California, London: Oxford University Press, 1973, p. 373. Also see Nobutaka Ike, *The Beginnings of Political Democracy in Japan*, The Johns Hopkins Press, Baltimore, 1952, p. 51. Both Beasley and Nobutaka cite letters written by Kido in 1868–1869 (one to Omura Masajiro and a second letter to Sanjō Sanetomi and Iwakura Tomomi on March 13, 1869) as evidence of Japan's aggressive intentions. Beasley goes on to say (p. 373) that at the height of the debate over Korea in 1873, 'there was no real question whether [an attack on Korea was desirable, only whether] it was wise'. While the Korean crisis of 1873 is still the subject of considerable controversy among historians, the use of these letters as proof of Japanese aggression is of dubious value, since by 1873 Kido, for reasons which will be discussed below, had completely reversed his previous views. See Marlene J. Mayo, 'The Korean Crisis of 1873 and Early Meiji Foreign Policy', *The Journal of Asian Studies*, Vol. XXXI, No. 4, August 1972, pp. 814–816.
7. Hilary Conroy, *The Japanese Seizure of Korea: 1868–1910*, University of Pennsylvania Press, Philadelphia, 1974, pp. 25–
8. Cited in Ching Young Choe, *The Rule of the Taewon'gun 1864–1873: Restoration in Yi Korea*, East Asia Research center, Harvard University, Cambridge, 1972, pp. 155–156.
9. Marius B. Jansen, '*Japanese Imperialism: Late Meiji Perspectives*', in Myers and Peattie, op. cit., p. 70.
10. Conroy, op. cit., pp. 17–77. The Meiji leadership were also confronted with other external disputes (notably with Russia over the harrassment of Japanese settlers on Sakhalin, and with China due to the murder of Okinawan sailors by Taiwanese aborigines) which added to the deepening

national crisis. Also see Mayo, op. cit., pp. 795–801, Roger F. Hackett, *Yamagata Aritomo in the Rise of Modern Japan, 1838–1922*, Harvard University Press, Cambridge, Mass., 1971, pp. 73–76, Masakazu Iwata, *Ōkubo Toshimichi – The Bismarck of Japan*, University of California Press, Berkeley and Los Angeles, 1964, pp. 179–224, and John K. Fairbank, Edwin O. Reischauer, Albert M. Craig, *East Asia the Modern Transformation*, Houghton Mifflin Company, Boston, 1965, pp. 238–239. (Cited hereafter as East Asia the Modern Transformation.)

11. Saigo's views were well summarized in a letter to his friend Itagaki Taisuke in which he concluded that a war with Korea would 'divert abroad the attention of those who desire civil strife, and thereby benefit the country'. Cited in Tsunoda Ryusaku, et al., *Sources of Japanese Tradition*, Vol. II, Columbia University Press, New York and London, 1958, pp. 149–150. The principal participants in the *Seikanron* debate can roughly be broken down into a peace party comprised of Iwakura Tomomi, Kido Kōin, Ōkubo Toshimichi and Itō Hirobumi (all of whom had been associated with the Iwakura mission to Europe – 1871–1873), and a pro-war faction which included Saigō Takamori, Itagaki Taisuke, Soejima Taneomi, Etō Shimpei and Gotō Shōjiro. Etō Shimpei was executed in April 1874 due to his involvement in a rebellion against the Government over the Korean issue. Saigō died in 1877 after leading an unsuccessful rebellion against the Government. For further information concerning these and other *samurai* rebellions during this period see Iwata, op. cit., pp. 243–251, Roger F. Hackett, op. cit., pp. 72–73, 76–81, and Conroy, op. cit., pp. 51–53.

12. Tsunoda, op. cit., pp. 151–155. Also see Conroy, op. cit., pp. 47–49, Iwata, op. cit., pp. 168–170, and Joseph Pittau, *Political Thought in Early Meiji Japan*, Harvard University.

13. Marlene J. Mayo, op. cit., p. 813.

14. Nobutaka Ike, op. cit., p. 52.

15. Marlene J. Mayo, op. cit., p. 815. Also see Roger F. Hackett, op. cit., p. 70.

16. Conroy, op. cit., pp. 60–61. Some commentators have suggested that this decision was part of a long-term policy whose ultimate object was the conquest and annexation of Korea. This is the view put forward by Chon Dong, *Japanese Annexation of Korea: A Study of Korean Japanese Relations to 1910*, Unpublished Doctoral Dissertation, University of Colorado, 1955, pp. 84–95. Chon's analysis of Japanese-Korean relations after 1905, for example rests almost entirely on the evidence provided in the *Nikkan Gappō Hishi (Secret History of the Merger of Japan and Korea)* published by the *Kokuryukai* (Amur River Society), an early expansionist society. This, as Conroy has argued (pp. 369–382), is a source which 'must be used with great care', since it was designed to underline (exaggerate) the role played by it and other expansionist organizations.

17. Martina Deuchler, *Confucian Gentlemen and Barbarian Envoys: The Opening of Korea, 1875–1885*, University of Washington Press, Seattle and London, 1977, pp. 35–38.

18. Cited in Chon Dong, op. cit., pp. 93–94. Also see Han Woo-Keun, op. cit., pp. 374–375. The importance of Article X is that while granting Japanese subjects extra-territorial rights in Korea, no such provision was made to cover the rights of Koreans residing in Japan. See *Meiji Japan Through Contemporary Sources*, Vol II, pp. 122–126, and Kim, *Korea and the Politics of Imperialism*, pp. 17–18. Also see Deuchler, op. cit., pp. 45–49, and William E. Henthorn, *A History of Korea*, The Free Press, New York, 1971,

pp. 199-200. Both Henthorn and Deuchler point out that the Korean acceptance of Japanese demands for extra territoriality was not inconsistent with the situation which had existed at the *Wakan* (Japan House) during the Tokugawa period. Although nominally under the jurisdiction of the local administrative officer at Tongnae the Japanese settlement had its own magistrates and police.
19. Conroy, op. cit., pp. 86-97. Also see Deuchler, op. cit., pp.54-57.
20. Han Woo-Keun, *The History of Korea*, Eul-Yoo Publishing Company, Seoul, 1971, pp. 336-354.
21. Ibid.
22. The best account (in English) of the *Tonghak* Movement is contained in Kim Han-gu, *Tonghak: Revitalization Movement in Korea*, Unpublished Doctoral Dissertation, University of Toronto, 1970, pp. 64-213. A briefer account can be found in Han Woo-Keun, op. cit., pp. 403-415, and James K. Ash, 'The Tonghak Rebellion: Problems and Interpretations', *Journal of Social Sciences and Humanities*, No. 30, June 1969, pp.89-106.
23. Sannosuke Matsumoto, 'Yukichi Fukuzawa, His Concept of Civilization and View of Asia', *The Developing Economies*, Vol. V, No. 1, March 1967, p. 165.
24. Ibid., pp.165-166.
25. Abe Hiroshi, '*Kaihōmae Nihon Ryugaku no Shiteki Tenkai Katei to no Tokushitsu*' ('A Historical Review of Korean Students in Japan Before 1945: Development and Special Characteristics'), *Kan (The Han)* Vol. 5, No. 12, November 1976, p. 22. (Cited hereafter as Abe, 'Korean Students in Japan before 1945'.) A similar mission was sent to Tientsin in 1882 but was handicapped both by a lack of finance and by language difficulties. See Deuchler, op. cit., pp. 100-101.
26. Also involved in the early reform movements was So Chae-p'il (1863-1951), whose anglicized name was Philip Jaisohn. His involvement in the attempted coup of 1884 forced him into exile in the United States where he later took American citizenship. So returned to Korea in December 1895 where he began publishing the *Tongnip Shinmum* (The Independent) and subsequently established the *Tongnip Hyohoe* (Independence Club). See Lee Kwang-Rin, 'On the Publication of the Independent by Suh Jae-Pil (Philip Jaisohn)', Journal of Social Sciences and Humanities, No. 43, June 1976, pp. 1-43. For a fuller treatment of the influence exerted by Fukuzawa on the views of Kim Ok-kyun and Yu Kil-chun respectively, see Harold F. Cook, 'Kim Ok-kyun's Second Visit to Japan', *Journal of Social Sciences and Humanities*, No. 33, December 1970, pp. 37-60, and Harold F. Cook, 'Kim Ok-kyun's Early Career', *Journal of Social Sciences and Humanities*, No. 35, December 1971, pp. 49-63.
27. '*Chōsen no Kōsai wo ronzu*' ('My views on our relations with Korea'), *Jiji Shimpō*, March 11, 1882. In Keiō University, ed., *Fukuzawa Yukichi Zenshu (The Complete Works of Fukuzawa Yukichi*, Iwanami Shoten, Tokyo, 1960, Vol. 8, pp. 30-31. (Cited hereafter as FYZ.)
28. Ibid., p. 30.
29. Ibid., pp. 28-29. Fukazawa wrote ' . . . there are xenophobes in Korea too, and it is clear that opinion there is not tranquil. It is unclear what they might do, and if they do start something beyond the control of the Korean Government it is quite clear that it is the Japanese that they will turn on. Are those Japanese now living in Korea prepared to defend themselves? I am convinced they are not sufficiently so prepared.'

30. Matsumoto Sannosuke, op. cit., p. 167
31. In August alone Fukuzawa contributed twenty-three articles dealing with the Korean crisis. The background to this incident and its resolution is discussed in Conroy, op. cit., pp. 100-103, Han Woo-Keun, op. cit., pp. 381-382. Also see Deuchler, op. cit., pp. 103-107, 130-135, and Hatada Takashi, *A History of Korea*, translated and edited by Warren. W. Smith, Jr., and Benjamin H. Hazard, Clio Press, Santa Barbara, California,1969, p. 95. (Cited hereafter as Hatada *A History of Korea*.) The persistent criticism of the cautious foreign policy pursued by the oligarchs which was voiced by journalists and intellectuals throughout this period is discussed in Shumpei Okamoto, *The Japanese Oligarchy and the Russo-Japanese War*, Columbia University Press, New York, and London, 1970, pp. 42-46.
32. 'Chōsen no Henji' ('The Korean Emergency'), *Jiji Shimpō*, July 31, 1882. *FYZ*, Vol. 8, p.246.
33. 'Chōsen no Henji', *Jiji Shimpō*. August 1, 1882. *FYZ*, Vol. 8, p. 249.
34. 'Nichi-Shi-Kan Sankoku no Kankei' ('Relations between Japan, China and Korea'), *Jiji Shimpō*. August 25, 1882. *FYZ*, Vol. 8, p. 305.
35. Cited in Conroy, op. cit., p. 118.
36. Marius B. Jansen, 'Modernization and Foreign policy in Meiji Japan', p. 82. As Jansen suggests in this article, " 'Independence' for Korea gradually became altered to 'dependence' as the Meiji leaders became convinced that Korea's backwardness and weakness made it too inviting a prey for other powers". Korean Independence also meant different things to different people and organizations at different times. This important issue is discussed in Shumpei Okamoto, op. cit., pp. 46-47, and Conroy, op. cit., pp. 122-220. The Self-Strengthening Movement is the name given to the modernization of the Chinese army during the period of the T'ung-Chih Restoration (1862-1874). For a fuller treatment of this and other aspects of the restoration movement see Mary Clabaugh Wright, *The Last Stand of Chinese Conservatism: The T'ung-Chih Restoration, 1862-1874*, Stanford University Press, Stanford, 1972, pp. 68-95, 125-251, Joseph R. Levenson, *Confucian China and Its Modern Fate: A Trilogy*, Volume One: *The Problem of Intellectual Continuity*, University of California Press, Berkeley and Los Angeles, 1965, pp. 49-78, and W. G. Beasley, 'Self Strengthening and Restoration: Chinese and Japanese Responses to the West in the Mid Nineteenth Century', *Acta Asiatica*, No. 26, March 1974, pp. 91-107.
37. Im Kwan Hwang, op. cit., p. 184.
38. Ōi Kentarō's involvement in the Osaka Incident in 1885 is discussed in Conroy, op. cit., pp. 162-168. Of special relevance is a speech made by Ōi at his trial following an abortive attempt to restore the Korean progressives to power (p. 167). Also see Marius B. Jansen, 'Ōi Kentarō: Radicalism and Nationalism', *The Far Eastern Quarterly*, Vol. XI, No. 3, May 1952, pp. 306-312.
39. Both the *Gen'yōsha* (founded 1881) and the *Kokuryūkai* (founded 1901) were dominated by extreme nationalists like Toyama Mitsuru, Hiroaka Kōtarō and Uchida Ryōhei. Their advocacy of Japanese expansionism did not however preclude support for nationalists and other organizations in both Korea and China. The activities of these organizations are discussed in greater detail in: Conroy, op. cit., pp. 215-216, 230-233, 370-378, 400-439; E. Herbert Norman, 'The Genyōsha: A Study in the Origins of Japanese Imperialism', Pacific Affairs, Vol. XVII, No. 3, 1944, pp.261-284; Shumpei Okamoto, op. cit., pp. 50-52; Marius B. Jansen, *The Japanese and*

Sun Yat-Sen, Stanford University Press, Stanford, California, 1970, pp. 35–40, 110–112, 181–188; and John Wayne Sabey, *The Gen'yōsha, The Kokuryukai, and Japanese Expansionism*, unpublished Doctoral Dissertation, University of Michigan, 1972. The best account of the activities of Uchida Ryōhei is contained in Han Sang Il, *Uchida Ryōhei and Japanese Continental Expansion, 1874–1916*, unpublished Doctoral Dissertation, Claremont Graduate School, 1974, pp. 46-108, 152-219.

40. See, for example, the memorial on modernization presented by Kim to the King of Korea following the former's visit to Japan in 1882. Fukuzawa's influence is clearly evident in many of Kim's proposals, particularly those concerning the improvement of agriculture, the legal system and transport. This memorial is cited in its entirety in Harold F. Cook, 'Kim Ok-kyun's Second Visit to Japan', op. cit., pp. 38–42. Fukuzawa's involvement with the Korean progressives is also discussed in Conroy, op. cit., pp. 124–158, and Im Kwan Hwang, op. cit., pp. 154–203.
41. '*Tōyō no Seiryaku Hatashite Ikan-sen*' ('Just how should we pursue our diplomacy in the Orient?'), *Jiji Shimpō*, December 7, 1882, *FYZ*, Vol. 8, p. 427.
42. '*Tōyō no Seiryaku Hatashite Ikan-sen*', *Jiji Shimpō*, December 9, 1882, *FYZ* Vol. 8, p. 434. Also cited in Kimitada Miwa, 'Fukuzawa Yukichi's Departure from Asia, A Prelude to the Sino-Japanese War', in Edmund Skrzypczak, op. cit., p. 13.
43. '*Gaikō ron*' ('On Foreign Relations'), *Jiji Shimpō*, September 29, 1883, *FYZ*, Vol. 9, p. 192. Also see Seong-rae Park, 'Fukuzawa Yukichi on Korea', *Journal of Social Sciences and Humanities*, No. 45, June 1977, p. 40.
44. Im Kwan Hwang, op. cit., pp. 142–143, 191–196. Also see Conroy, op. cit., pp. 144–157, Deuchler, op. cit., pp. 205–210, and Han Woo-Keun, op. cit., pp. 393–395.
45. Cited in Conroy, op. cit., p. 159.
46. Han Woo-Keun, op. cit., p. 384. Also referred to as the Treaty of Seoul. See Deuchler, op. cit., p. 211.
47. Conroy, op.cit., pp.172–184. Also see Han Woo-Keun, op. cit., p. 395, and Deuchler, op. cit., pp. 213–215.
48. '*Otakara*' ('The Treasure Ship'), *Jiji Shimpō*, January 2, 1885, *FYZ*, Vol. 10, pp. 179–181. Also see Miwa, op. cit., pp. 16–17.
49. Conroy, op. cit., p. 170.
50. As cited in Kenneth B. Pyle, *The New Generation in Meiji Japan*, Stanford University Press, Stanford, 1969, pp. 148–149.
51. '*Datsu-A ron*' ('Shedding Asia'), *Jiji Shimpō*, March 16 1885, *FYZ*, Vol. 10, p. 240.
52. Statement attributed to Sugita Teiichi (1851–1920) in Oka Yoshitake, in Prologue to Marlene J. Mayo, ed., *The Emergence of Imperial Japan*, D. C. Heath and Company, Lexington, Mass., 1970, p. 6.
53. '*Chōsen Jimmin no tame ni Sono Kuni no Metsubō wo gasu*' (Congratulations to the people of Korea on the Occasion of the Destruction of their Country'), *Jiji Shimpō*, August 13, 1885, *FYZ*, Vol. 10, p. 381. Publication of this article was prohibited by government censors.
54. As cited in Eugene C. Kim and Han-Kyo Kim, *Korea and the Politics of Imperialism, 1876–1910*, University of California Press, Berkeley and Los Angeles, 1967, p. 63.
55. Marius B. Jansen, 'Modernization and Foreign Policy in Meiji Japan', pp. 174, 182–183.

56. Cited in Kim, *Korea and the Politics of Imperialism*, p. 79.
57. Kenneth B. Pyle, op. cit., p. 67.
58. Cited in ibid., p. 158.
59. Ibid., pp. 168, 172–179.
60. Cited in ibid., pp. 167–168.
61. Cited in ibid., p. 173.
62. Donald Keene, 'The Sino-Japanese War of 1894–5 and its Cultural Effects in Japan', Donald H. Shively, *Tradition and Modernization in Japanese Culture*, Princeton University Press, Princeton, 1971, p. 133.
63. Cited in ibid., p. 127.
64. The inevitability of a conflict between Japan and Russia had, in fact, been predicted some years earlier by Yamagata Aritamo. In a memorial to the Emperor written in 1893, he warned that, with the completion of the Trans-Siberian railway, Russia would be capable of invading Mongolia and possibly even China. Cited in Janet Hunter, 'Japanese Government Policy, Business Opinion on the Seoul-Pusan Railway, 1884–1906', *Modern Asian Studies*, Vol. II, Part 4, October 1977, p. 575. The effects of the Triple Intervention in Japan and the emergence of Russia as Japan's principal adversary in Asia is discussed in Sumpei Okamoto, op. cit., pp.47–92. Also Kim, *Korea and the Politics of Imperialism*, pp.83–96.
65. Cited in Hunter, op. cit., p. 577.
66. Cited in ibid., p. 585.
67. Cited in Kim, Korea and the Politics of Imperialism, p. 123.
68. *Heimin Shimbun*, April 3, 1904. Cited in Conroy, op. cit., pp. 396–397.
69. *Heimin Shimbun*, June 19, 1904. Cited in ibid., pp. 397–398.
70. F. G. Notehelfer, *Kōtoku Shusui, Portrait of a Japanese Radical*, Cambridge University Press, London, 1971, p. 107. Notehelfer (p. 97) gives the following as the circulation figures for the *Heimin Shimbun* during April and June 1904 respectively: 4,500, 3,700. It is estimated that by 1904 there were approximately 700,000 newspaper subscribers in Tokyo alone. See Okamoto Shumpei, op. cit., p. 53.
71. See Andrew C. Nahm, 'Introduction', Andrew C. Nahm, ed., *Korea Under Japanese Colonial Rule*, The Center for Korean Studies, Western Michigan University, 1973, pp.30–33. (Cited hereafter as Nahm, *Korea Under Japanese Rule*.) For a more detailed account of the establishment of the Residency-General see Wonmo Dong, *Japanese Colonial Policy and Practice in Korea, 1905–1945: A Study in Assimilation*, unpublished Doctoral Dissertation, Georgetown University, 1965, pp. 75–127. (Cited hereafter as Wonmo Dong, *Japanese Colonial Policy and Practice in Korea*.) Also see Chon Dong, op. cit., p. 281, and Han Woo-Keun, op. cit., pp. 447–448.
72. Cited in Conroy, op. cit., p. 334.
73. Cited in ibid., p. 339.
74. Cited in Kim, *Korea and the Politics of Imperialism*, pp. 136–137.
75. Ibid., p. 138.
76. This is the view put forward in Conroy, op. cit., pp. 370–378. Others have not been nearly so charitable in their assessment of Ito's role. See Wonmo Dong, *Japanese Colonial Policy and practice in Korea*, pp.101–117.
77. As cited in Kim, *Korea and the Politics of Imperialism*, p. 142.
78. The Hague Affair, as it is commonly referred to, occurred in the summer of 1907. King (now Emperor) Kojong despatched representatives to the Paris Peace Conference in an attempt to expose Japan's activities in Korea. His representatives failed to gain admission to the conference, and Kojong was

subsequently forced to abdicate. See Han Woo-Keun, op. cit., pp. 450–451, and Conroy, op. cit., pp. 345–352, 361–362.
79. Conroy, op. cit., p. 372.
80. This is discussed in Chong-Sik Lee, *The Politics of Korean Nationalism*, University of California Press, Berkeley and Los Angeles, 1963, pp. 79–85. Also see Kim, *Korea and the Politics of Imperialism*, pp. 196–205, Conroy, op. cit., pp. 364–369, and F. A. McKenzie, *Korea's Fight for Freedom*, reprinted by Yonsei University Press, Seoul, 1969, p. 151.
81. Kim, *Korea and the Politics of Imperialism*, p. 201.
82. The *Ilchinhoe* was prominent in Korean affairs between 1905 and 1910, but was dissolved, along with all other Korean political organizations, by order of Governor-General Terauchi immediately after the annexation. Although led by Song Pyong-chun, one of its principal advisers was Uchida Ryōhei, the founder of the *Kokuryukai*. The role of the *Ilchihoe* during the five years preceding the annexation is examined in Conroy, op. cit., pp. 415–438, and Han Sang Il, op. cit., pp. 158–219.
83. *Tōkyō Mainichi*, December 8, 1909 and *Tōkyō Asahi*, December 7, 1909. Cited in Conroy, op. cit., p. 388.
84. *Jiji Shimpō*, December 8, 1909. As cited in ibid.
85. Cited in E. Patricia Tsurumi, *Japanese Colonial Education in Taiwan, 1895–1945*, Harvard University Press, Cambridge, Massachusetts and London, 1977, p. 164.
86. Cited in Conroy, op. cit., pp. 388–390.
87. Cited in ibid., pp. 390–391.
88. *Kirisuto-Kyō Sekai* (The Christian World), September 1, 1910. As cited in Takayoshi Matsuo, 'The Japanese Protestants in Korea, Part One', *Modern Asian Studies*, Volume 13, Part 3, July 1979, p.404.
89. Marius B. Jansen, 'Japanese Imperialism: Late Meiji Perspectives', in Myers and Peattie, op. cit., p. 64.
90. Ibid.,
91. The views of the leading exponents of both the *Teitairon* and the *Dōso Ron* are discussed at length in Bang Hung Kyu, *Japan's Colonial Education Policy in Korea*, unpublished Doctoral Dissertation, University of Arizona, 1972, pp. 65–80. A briefer discussion of these theories can be found in Hatada Takashi, 'The Significance of Korean History', *The Japan Interpreter*, Vol. 9, No. 2, Summer-Autumn, 1974, pp. 167–176. Both Bang and Hatada acknowledge that Japanese attitudes toward Korea were largely determined by an 'Imperial view of history' which not only regarded the annexation as historically justifiable but necessary since it was Japan's mission to bring civilization to Korea.
92. As cited in Conroy, op. cit., p.392.

Chapter 2

From Korea to Chōsen: The First Phase of Colonial Rule

A feature of all colonial societies is the disruptive effect which the introduction of new market relations and changes in the system of land tenure have on the lives of the peasantry. While bearing in mind that distinctions need to be made between farmers who owned part or all of the land they worked and those who were 'pure' tenants, the commercialization of agriculture in colonial Korea led to the displacement of enormous numbers of peasant farmers who, once separated from the land, became available for wage labour elsewhere in the economy. The process by which 'great masses of men are suddenly and forcibly torn from their means of subsistence and hurled as free and 'unattached' proletarians on the labour market'[1] is depressingly familiar, but, in colonial Korea, it is the speed, and above all, the scale of this transformation which deserves special attention. As Bruce Cumings has observed:

> The effects of the new market relations, the rise of industry in the 1930s, and the mobilization policies of the colonial regime were so powerful that we can say with little hesitation that few if any societies ever were subject, in such a relatively short time period, to the immense population shifts and dislocations that Korea was under the Japanese.[2]

While colonial economic policy was of critical importance in the creation of a vast reservoir of labour in Korea, it cannot be looked at in isolation from a range of other factors which stimulated labour migration to Japan after 1910. A crucial factor was, of course, the increased demand for labour in Japan brought on by a period of rapid economic growth during and immediately after World War 1. The demands of the Japanese labour market are, however, treated in detail in Chapter 3, and the task here is confined to a discussion of those aspects of colonial rule which facilitated migration. This is preceded by a brief description of the colonial regime and an examination of the views of the men who were responsible for its creation. There are three reasons for this. First, the attitudes which informed colonial rule in Korea were equally prevalent in Japan itself. Second, the events which punctuated the first decade of

Japanese rule had a direct bearing on the way Korean immigrants were regarded in Japan. Third, an examination of the careers of many of the high-ranking officials who served in the colonial administration reveals that a significant number of them went on to hold high office in Japan. Of the eight men who held the post of Governor-General between 1910 and 1945, for example, no less than four served as premier, and only one failed to rise to ministerial level within the home government.[3] On their return to Japan these, and other, officials carried with them experiences and memories which would greatly affect the treatment of Korean residents.

Rule by the Military: The Terauchi and Hasegawa Administrations

By 1910 there already existed in Japan a large body of informed opinion concerning colonial policy and practice. The acquisition of Taiwan in 1895 had generated considerable interest in colonial theory, and many official and unofficial observers of the administration there had 'been students of comparative colonialism'.[4] Significantly, virtually all of them had rejected immediate assimilation in favour of a more gradual approach. Although few doubted that it was Japan's responsibility, as the colonizing power, to bring civilization and progress to its dependent peoples, there was agreement among colonial theorists that this process would take considerable time. This, it was thought, was particularly relevant in the case of Korea, whose people possesed a history and culture as old as Japan's.[5] An over-ambitious programme of enforced modernization, argued Takekoshi Yosaburō, ran counter to 'all laws of sociology and biology',[6] while Mizuno Rentarō, an authority in local self-government who served as *Seimu Sōkan* (Civil Governor) of Korea from 1919 to 1922, cautioned against a policy of immediate assimilation. He argued that, despite racial and cultural affinities, there was a need to consider the two-thousand year history of Korea before assimilation could be contemplated.[7] Like others in the mainstream of colonial thinking, Mizuno favoured policies which acknowledged the separate and subordinate identity of the Korean people, and suggested 'a benevolent system of administration' which would encourage passive submission to Japanese control.[8] The harsh realities of Japanese military government under Governor-General Terauchi, however, were soon to dispel paternalistic notions of Imperial benevolence.

With the exception of Yamagata Isaburō, who was the adopted son of Yamagata Aritomo and served as Civil Governor of Korea from 1910 until 1919, Terauchi and his principle aides (Hasegawa Yoshimichi and Akashi Motojirō) were all products of the Japanese military establishment. General Hasegawa commanded the Japanese garrison in Korea from 1905 until he succeeded Terauchi as Governor-General in 1916. Hasegawa's views on assimilation are not known, though he is reported to have remarked at the time of his appointment 'I do not know much about politics, all I intend to do is to follow the way established by Terauchi'.[9] Lieutenant-General Akashi, however, held strong views concerning the administration of Korea. In 1907 Akashi was appointed commander of the Japanese gendarmerie in Korea, and from 1910 until 1914 held the office of Director of Police Affairs. In that capacity he 'dealt mercilessly with Korean insurgents and suspected rebels alike, killing and torturing with little regard for legal process'.[10] Akashi later served as Governor-General of Taiwan where he pursued a vigorous programme of assimilation, but, as E. P. Tsurumi, in her study of colonial education in Taiwan, has made clear:

> To Akashi then assimilation did not mean equality with the Japanese . . . Although warnings to his subordinates suggest that Akashi believed that some day the Taiwanese and Japanese must become one, he undertook to assimilate Taiwanese at the bottom and at the lower-middle portions of the social pyramid where he thought they belonged.[11]

Although Tsurumi's study is confined to Japanese policies on Taiwan, there is no evidence to suggest that Akashi's attitude toward the assimilation of the Korean people was substantially different from that which characterized his administration of Taiwan.

Ultimately, however, responsibility for the formulation and implementation of colonial policy rested with Governor-General Terauchi, a man not known to possess any expertise in colonial matters. Unlike Gotō Shimpei who, as Civil Governor of Taiwan, had referred to a 'hundred year plan' for the transformation of Taiwanese society,[12] Terauchi was a staunch advocate of rapid assimilation. His views are well summarized in the following extract from the Proclamation of Annexation:

> It is a natural and inevitable course of things that two peoples, whose countries are in close proximity with each other, whose interests are identical and who are bound together with brotherly feelings should amalgamate and form one body.[13]

But as Tsurumi has suggested, 'assimilation meant many things to many men and was espoused for a variety of motives'.[14] In contrast to Ōishi Masami, a spokesman for the Constitutional National Party who equated assimilation with political integration,[15] for Terauchi, assimilation implied little more than submission to Japanese rule. In Mark Peattie's words:

> To justify a policy of enforced conformity to Japanese institutions and values, Terauchi marshalled all the classic arguments of Meiji times for Japanese rule over Korea: geographic proximity between

the two countries, shared ethnic, Japanese 'special understanding' of Korea's history and character, as well as the need to protect Korea from the corrosive influence of Western liberal ideas.[16]

Administration and the Establishment of the Chōsen Sōtokufu

The most immediate task confronting Terauchi and his aides was the establishment of absolute political control in Korea. With this in mind he ordered the dissolution of all political parties and associations, and prohibited all meetings, public debates and speeches.[17] Thereafter, Koreans were actively discouraged from organizing any type of association or club with the exception of those which were sponsored and controlled by the Government-General. All Korean-owned newspapers were forcibly purchased, and until 1919 there existed only one Korean language newspaper, the *Maeil Sinbo* (Daily News), which was operated by the Government-General.[18] Japanese and foreign newspapers alike were subjected to strict censorship, and between 1910 and 1912 alone more than 150,000 newspapers and other publications were confiscated by the police.[19] Criticized by the press in Japan for this suppression of all free speech, the Government-General maintained that while interference with the press and freedom of speech in a 'civilised' society was unacceptable, this was necessary in Korea since 'in a country like Korea, where public knowledge is yet backward and where insurrection and assassination are often provoked by seditious literature, proper measures of newspaper control and censorship are essential to the maintenance of peace and order'.[20]

Under the terms of an Imperial Rescript issued in 1910, Terauchi and his successors were invested with enormous discretionary powers which effectively made them the most powerful officials within the Japanese empire. Until 1919 the Governors-General of Korea were responsible to the Emperor alone, and even after that time were never fully subordinate to either the Japanese cabinet or the prime minister. In addition to exercising complete control over all civilian and military affairs, the Governor-General was authorized to issue *Seirei* (executive ordinances) which carried the same effect as laws passed by the Imperial Diet.[21]

The only area of government in which the outward appearance of self-government was maintained was in a consultative body known as the Chūsūin (Central Council). Members of the Council were chosen exclusively 'from among native Koreans of ability and reputation', but the post of President of the Council was filled by the Japanese Civil Governor and all Korean appointees were subject to the approval of the Governor-General.[22] The Chūsūin exercised no restraint over the administrative or legislative authority of the Governor-General, and during the first fifteen years of its existence the Council was never consulted on any substantive issue.[23]

The colonial civil service too was dominated by Japanese officials despite promises to recruit Koreans 'in accordance with their talent and ability'.[24] In fact, the proportion of Korean civil servants of all ranks within the Government-General actually declined between 1915 and 1925, and in 1935 the percentage of Korean officials was still lower than it had been in 1915.[25] It was only in the police force that Koreans were well represented, but few held a rank above that of assistant policeman.

The function of the police force in colonial Korea closely resembled that of the police system in Meiji Japan. In addition to the maintenance of public law and order, the colonial police were intimately involved in the administration of Korea. Their responsibilities included the collection of taxes, the enforcement of sanitary regulations, the promotion of industrial and agricultural programmes, the suppression of dangerous ideologies, and the enforcement of censorship laws. It was with good reason that the police were regarded as 'the hands and feet' of the colonial regime.[26] In contrast to the police system in metropolitan Japan, however, the police in Korea were not subject to civilian control. Under a system of dual-appointment, the Director-General of Police Affairs also commanded the *Kempeitai* (gendarmerie). Similarly, the post of Provincial Police Director was usually held by the commandant of the local gendarmerie garrison, thus subordinating the authority of the police to that of the military.[27] This use of the military to enforce public law and order was justified by Terauchi on the grounds that it was 'easier to use the gendarmes than police to control a primitive people'.[28]

Local police chiefs in Korea were also empowered to render summary judgements in minor criminal cases. This was regarded by the Government-General as an extremely effective legal device since Koreans, *by nature*, had little understanding of their legal rights, and because they could not be expected to appreciate the difference between 'being arraigned before a law court or before an ordinary administrative office'.[29] The most common form of summary judgement was the beating of prisoners with a bamboo cane or whip. This type of punishment was reserved for Koreans, since, according to Director-General Akashi:

> Flogging is an old Korean custom which we . . . look upon as a barbarous method of punishment, but if we were immediately to do away with such a custom, it would cause much agitation and unrest among the Korean people. You must remember that those who govern must govern in accordance with the will and desire of those whom they govern.[30]

In the absence of any external restraints on the power exercised by the police, abuses were inevitable. Deprived of legal counsel, there was often little opportunity for suspects to establish their innocence, and in 1916 alone, of more than eighty-thousand instances where the police rendered summary judgements, only thirty defendants were found innocent and released from custody.[31]

The Independence Movement of 1919 and Administrative Reforms

Backed by the full coercive power of the army and the gendarmerie, the authority of the colonial regime remained unchallenged until the spring of 1919. When such a challenge did materialize it came in the form of mass peaceful demonstrations which spread from Seoul throughout the country. Although the Government-General was clearly taken unawares by the initial demonstration on March 1, it was the scale of the movement which visibly shook the colonial establishment. Depending upon the source, official estimates of the number of persons participating throughout the country range from a low of nearly 600,000 to well over 1.3 million, while nationalist sources (which include figures for Koreans in Manchuria) give a figure of over 2 million.[32] By the end of April more than 26,000 arrests had been made, over 500 Koreans had been killed and nearly 1,500 injured. Japanese casualties, including civilians, were limited to one killed and thirty injured.[33] The savagery with which the authorities suppressed the movement created a wave of international revulsion and criticism to which the home government responded by announcing its intention to reform the colonial administration.[34]

This liberalization took the form of *Bunka Seiji (Cultural Rule)* under which it was promised that a new spirit of cooperation between Government and people would be pursued.[35] Under the new Governor-General, Admiral Saitō Makoto, the hated gendarmerie system was dismantled and replaced by an exclusively civilian police force, regulations governing the appointment and promotion of Korean officials were revised in order to expand employment opportunities for qualified Koreans, and all officials were advised to become more responsive to local needs and conditions.[36] In his first major address on September 3, 1919, Saitō also announced that in future the post of Governor-General would be open to civilian appointees.[37]

Although this appeared to signal a marked departure from the policies and style of his predecessors, actual reforms were far less substantial. The authority of the Governor-General to control political, legislative and judicial matters remained virtually unchanged, as did his ability to formulate and implement policies independently of the Japanese Cabinet.[38] Moreover, although the Governor-General's authority to command all military forces would in future be subject to certain legal limitations, the fact that high-ranking military officers continued to occupy this post right up until 1945 ensured their facto control of the Japanese garrison.[39]

Many of the other reform measures introduced by Saitō and the new Civil Governor, Mizuno Rentarō, followed a similar pattern.[40] Attempts by the new administration to eliminate some of the more obvious forms of discrimination and oppression need also to be considered against the background of a greatly expanded police force. Many former members of the gendarmerie were absorbed into the new civilian police system and a further 5,000 Japanese police officers and recruits were imported from Japan. Under the supervision of the new Director-General of Police Affairs, Akaike Atsushi, more efficient methods of political control were introduced, and by 1921 the independence movement had been suppressed.[41]

Although the reforms of 1919 were successful in subduing nationalist resistance to Japanese rule, the fundamental objectives of colonial policy remained unaltered. The resources of Korea, both human and material, were to be mobilized in the interests of metropolitan Japan. *Chōsen*, as it was referred to throughout the colonial period, was governed by a military administration which, even after 1919, tolerated little opposition to either its objectives or methods. Korean political associations were subject to constant surveillance and sources of potential dissent were ruthlessly suppressed. The Government-General made a determined effort to eradicate any expression of Korean national identity, but far from encouraging assimilation its policies tended to underline ethnic and cultural differences between colonizer and colonized. For the most part, the Japanese who came to Korea maintained themselves as a race apart; they lived in tight urban enclaves from which Koreans were excluded, and were provided by the state with a separate educational system for their children.

Education

Throughout the colonial period education was regarded as the principal instrument of assimilation. Yet it was also within the colonial education system that the contradictions in the policy of assimilation were most clearly evident. The ultimate objective of education, as enshrined in the Educational ordinance for Korea (issued in 1911), was the 'making of loyal and good subjects' in accordance with the Imperial Rescript on Education. It was also emphasized, however, that education needed to be 'adapted to the needs of the times and the condition of the people'.[42] Assimilation was, therefore, equated with the cultivation of loyalty, while education would qualitatively differ from that in Japan. This was underlined several years later when the Government-General cautioned that:

The educational policy is pursued fundamentally in conformity with the national policy of Japan, without losing sight, however, of the delicate fact that some differences exist between the habits of the Japanese and the Koreans, as well as in degree of civilization of the two peoples; and it aims ultimately at the realization of a greater empire by the thorough amalgamation of them.[43]

Consequently, a dual system of education, which acknowledged these supposed differences, was established. Except for minor modifications in the school curriculum, the education offered to Japanese residents was identical to that in Japan.[44] Korean students, however were provided with a truncated version of the Japanese school system. Although primary education was made compulsory for Japanese and Korean children alike, the Common School programme for Koreans was two years shorter than in the Japanese Elementary Schools. A similar situation existed in the Higher Common Schools, which offered a curriculum roughly equivalent to that of the Middle Schools for Japanese pupils, while educational opportunities for Korean students beyond the secondary level were extremely limited.[45] The educational ordinance of 1911 made no provision for university level education in Korea, and strenuous efforts were made to restrict the expansion of *Senmon Gakkō* (Professional Schools) which offered programmes of three to four years in duration. Including the Professional Schools, the maximum number of school years available to Koreans was eleven or twelve. This was roughly equivalent to a Japanese Middle School education.[46]

While conceding that a minimum number of Professional Schools were essential for the proper development of Korea, it was always emphasized that the education provided should conform to the immediate needs of society.[47] In common with other parts of the state sector, the acquisition of practical vocational skills was encouraged, while degree programmes in the social sciences were discouraged. Under the Regulations for Professional Schools, issued in 1915, only four public Professional Schools were officially recognized and permitted to offer degree courses.[48] All of these had been founded by the Korean government before the annexation, and by 1933 only one further such school had been established.[49]

Education in the private sector, though not prohibited, was subjected to constant monitoring by the state. Under regulations enacted by the Residency General, and retained by the colonial regime, all private schools were required to obtain a government licence before they could offer instruction. Any school judged to be meddling in politics, encouraging anti-Japanese attitudes, or refusing to use textbooks approved by the authorities was subject to immediate closure.[50] So stringent were the controls that during the decade after 1910 the number of private schools (excepting the *Sodang* – traditional Confucian academies) decreased from nearly 2,000 to less than 700.[51] Private education at the post-secondary level was subject to similar restraints, and as of 1920 only two private Professional Schools were permitted to operate.[52]

Despite promises made in 1919 to expand higher education, only one new public Professional School came into existence between 1922 and 1932, while attempts by Koreans to found a private university were continually thwarted by the authorities. Even after the establishment of Keijō Imperial University in 1926, access to higher education remained extremely limited for Koreans.[53]

Under an educational system which not only devalued their own language, history and culture, but also emphasized elementary and vocational skills at the expense of academic and post-secondary education, it is hardly surprising that increasing numbers of Korean students were compelled to complete their studies abroad. Drawn by the more liberal atmosphere which then existed in Japan, most entered Professional Schools and Universities in Tokyo, and by 1935 nearly half of all Korean students enrolled in such schools were in Japan.[54]

Agricultural Policy

The objectives of Japanese economic policy in Korea were determined by the needs of the home economy. During the initial phase of colonial rule this implied the development of Korea as a source of food (particularly rice) and raw materials, and as a market for Japanese manufactured goods. But before Korea could be developed as a granary, a new economic environment consistent with these objectives had to be created.

Economic life during the Yi period (1392–1910) had been dominated by agriculture, and as late as 1910 nearly 85% of all Korean households were engaged in farming.[55] In the absence of either a strong entrepreneurial class, or a market economy, the primary source of wealth lay in the possession and acquisition of land. Although all land was, in theory, owned by the state, by the end of the Yi period government control had been substantially eroded by the expansion of privately-owned estates in the hands of *Yangban* landlords. *Yangban* control over rural life was furthered by the maintenance of aristocratic privilege and the virtual monopolization of political power by the members of this class.[56] Tenant farmers, who comprised the bulk of the agricultural population, lived at, or only marginally above, subsistence level. High rents in kind were extracted by the landlords and, although there were exceptions, the tenancy system did not provide security of tenure.[57] The harsh conditions of peasant life were to a certain extent modified by the traditional network of social obligations which lubricated landlord-tenant relations, but, as is evident from the frequency of peasant rebellions, the livelihood of the tenant farmer was extremely precarious.[58]

During the Japanese protectorate, the Korean government, on the advice of its Japanese advisers, undertook a reorganization of the system of land ownership. By 1910 laws had been enacted which: recognized the rights of individuals and organizations to own land (this included Koreans and foreign nationals alike); legalized the transfer of land; and permitted the issuance and foreclosure of mortgages.[59] Following the annexation, the Government-General, acting through the newly-created Temporary Land Survey Bureau, accelerated the pace of land reform. Under the supervision of the Civil Governor, this agency carried out an extensive cadastral survey, which lasted eight years and cost more than 50 million yen. In addition to the identification, codification, and registration of all lands, the purposes of the land survey were to determine and safeguard ownership rights, simplify the commercial transfer of landholdings, reform the tax system, provide the data necessary for planned agricultural development, and rationalize landlord-tenant relations.[60]

New titles of ownership were issued to those who were able to provide sufficient evidence that they had possessed 'rent collection rights' prior to the annexation.[61] Landowners were required to submit documentation concerning the size, type and location of their holdings within a fixed period of time. Failure to do so resulted in immediate confiscation by the Government-General.[62] Other properties expropriated by the authorities included, all state and royal lands belonging to the former Korean Government, lands for which sufficient evidence of ownership was not provided, and lands forfeited due to failure to pay the land tax.[63] It has been estimated that by the end of 1912, the amount of land expropriated by the Government-General as a direct result of these measures was in excess of 130,000 Chōbu (1 Chōbu 2.45 acres). This accounted for approximately 5% of all the land under cultivation in Korea at that time.[64] As Bruce Cumings has argued, however, these reforms did not seriously disturb the pre-existing pattern of land ownership. Although stripped of their political power, *Yangban* landlords were permitted to establish legal title to their holdings, while thousands of officials associated with the *ancien régime* invested their state pensions in land.[65]

If the land survey was beneficial to the landlord class and other privileged sections of Korean society, it was the peasantry who paid the price of Japanese largesse. Many thousands lost their land through ignorance of the new laws, while others who had previously farmed state or royal lands were reduced to tenancy by the expropriation of these lands by the Government-General.[66]

Accompanying this rise in tenancy (see Table 1) was a redefinition of landlord-tenant relations. Whereas contracts between tenants and landlords during the Yi period had ranged from three to five years in duration, under the new laws contracts were subject to annual renewal – a change which clearly strengthened the position of landlords.[67] Moreover, the level of rent was not fixed by law but was left to the discretion of individual landlords.[68] Normally rent was paid in kind on a share-cropping basis and averaged between 50 and 60% of the crop.[69] In addition, tenant farmers were commonly required to share the burden of the land tax, irrigation fees (normally paid to irrigation associations), charges for seeds, fertilizer, and land improvement, as well as paying for various services, such as rice inspection and delivery. As a result, in certain areas the tenant's share of the annual yield frequently fell below 25%.[70]

TABLE 1

Distribution of Farm Households in Korea by Type of Ownership: 1914–1930

Year	(1) Landlord	Owner-Farmer	Owner-Tenant	Tenant	(2) Kadenmin	Total
1914	46,754	569,517	1,065,705	911,261	—	2,592,237
1919	90,386	525,830	1,045,606	1,003,003	—	2,664,825
1920	89,020	529,177	1,017,780	1,082,842	—	2,720,819
1922	99,083	534,907	971,877	1,106,598	—	2,712,465
1924	102,183	525,689	934,208	1,142,192	—	2,704,272
1926	104,614	525,747	895,721	1,193,099	34,316	2,753,497
1928	104,601	510,983	894,381	1,255,954	33,269	2,799,188
1930	104,004	504,009	890,291	1,334,139	37,514	2,869,957

Source: Yamabe Kentarō, op.cit., p. 45.
Notes: (1) Includes figures for both first and second class landlords. (Those possessing over 100 *chōbu*, 1 *chōbu* = 2.45 acres.)
(2) Lit. 'fire-field people'. Refers to farmers or squatters who possess no land of their own, and who cultivate (slash and burn) publicly owned forest or wasteland.

Industrial Development

In keeping with the policy of developing Korea as a protected market for Japanese manufactured goods, the Government-General issued the company Regulations of 1911. Thereafter, the establishment and conduct of all enterprises in Korea were carefully regulated by the Government, and all new companies were reguird to obtain a licence before they could begin trading. These regulations were vigorously enforced, and between 1910 and 1918 only 105 new companies (93 of which were Japanese-owned) were granted operating licences.[71] In addition to retarding industrial development in Korea, these regulations had several important effects on the economy as a whole. First, they prevented the establishment of potentially competitive companies in Korea, thus ensuring for Japanese manufactured goods a dominant position in the Korean market. Second, they preserved the predominance of Japanese concerns outside agriculture. Third, the absence of incentives for investment in industry, coupled with low levels of taxation and high land rents, guaranteed that investment would be directed toward the expansion of land-holdings in Korea. Finally, the failure to provide employment opportunities in non-agricultural industries had the effect of increasing the control exercised by landlords over their tenants.[72]

Under the conditions described above it was inevitable that both landlordism and the amount of land under Japanese control would expand rapidly. Of course not all landlords were Japanese, but, as Table 2 indicates, the largest landholdings were predominantly Japanese.

TABLE 2

Landlords by size of Holding and Nationality: 1921–1935

Year	Over 200 Chūngbo		100–200 Chūngbo	
	Korean	Japanese	Korean	Japanese
1921	65	169	360	321
1925	45	170	344	360
1930	50	187	304	361
1935	45	192	315	363

Source: Sang-Chul Suh, op.cit., p. 80.

Despite official claims to the contrary, the bulk of all Japanese landholdings in Korea was accounted for by large-scale commercial enterprises like the Oriental Development Company.[73] If changes in the land-tenure system provided the necessary structural changes, it was the activities of these large commercial corporations which provided the means by which agricultural production could be accelerated and exports to Japan increased. This was particularly true in the fertile rice-producing areas of the south where many large Japanese holdings were concentrated. As B. F. Johnston later wrote:

> A large proportion of the rice land in Korea was owned by large scale commercial owners, principally Japanese, who collected heavy land rents payable in kind. Most of the rice collected as rent moved into the export trade, and about 60% of Korea's exports came from these large scale farms. The heavy burden of rent in kind tended to increase the cash stringency of the small farmers, which in turn had the effect of increasing the percentage of the crop which was commercialized.[74]

In 1910, only 17,000 tons of Korean rice had been exported to Japan, but by 1919 this figure had increased to 400,000 tons, and by the mid 1930s had reached nearly 1.5 million tons – more than 50% of the annual crop.[75] As Table 3 illustrates, an increase in rice production of approximately 40% between 1912 and 1936 was more than offset by a 600% increase in the level of rice exports.

TABLE 3

Korean Rice Production and Exports: 1912–1936
(figures in thousand metric tons)

Year	Production	Index	Exports	Index	Exports as Percent of Production
1912–1916	1,840	100	208	100	11.3
1917–1921	2,115	115	366	176	17.3
1922–1926	2,175	117	656	315	30.2
1927–1931	2,370	128	993	477	41.9
1932–1936	2,550	138	1,310	630	51.4

Source: Bruce F. Johnston, op.cit., p. 54.

The principal victims of these forced exports were the poorer tenant families, for whom the circle of degradation was now complete. Stripped of what little protection they had possessed prior to the annexation, the mass of the Korean peasantry found itself confronted with forces it could neither comprehend nor control. While the cost of increased productivity was borne largely by the tenant-farmer, he enjoyed none of the benefits. In debt to both landlords and moneylenders, who charged as much as 70% in annual interest, lacking security of tenure, and required to perform various types of unpaid labour, thousands of tenant-farmers abandoned their farms and sought employment elsewhere.[76] This migration was both internal and external, but the most dramatic development was the rapid emergence of a Korean immigrant community in Japan. In 1910 Korean residents in Japan accounted for only a fraction of the total foreign community, yet within twenty years of the annexation the Korean immigrant population was in excess of 400,000, and by the end of the Second World War numbered more than 2 million.[77]

Notes:
1. Karl Marx.*Capital,* Vol 1, p. 716. Cited in Bruce Cumings, *The Origins of the Korean War: Liberation and the Emergence of Separate Regimes, 1945-1947,* Princeton University Press, Princeton, New Jersey, 1981, p. 50.
2. Ibid.
3. This is discussed in detail in Edward I-Te Chen, 'Japanese Colonialism in Korea and Formosa: A Comparison of the Systems of Political Control', *Harvard Journal of Asiatic Studies,* Vol. 30, 1970, pp. 129–132.
4. E. Patricia Tsurumi, op. cit., p. 47.
5. Mark R. Peattie, 'Japanese Attitudes Toward Colonialism', in Myers and Peattie, op. cit., pp. 90–96.
6. Cited in ibid., p. 95.
7. The Term *Seimu Sōkan* has at times been translated as Administrative Assistant, but given the enormous authority vested in the office, Civil Governor provides a more accurate translation.
8. See *The Japan Chronicle,* September 8, 1910. Also cited in Wonmo Dong, 'Assimilation and Social Mobilization in Korea', in Nahm, *Korean Under Japanese Colonial Rule,* p. 155.
9. Cited in Chong-Sik Lee, op. cit., p. 92.
10. E. Patricia Tsurumi, op. cit., p. 83.
11. Ibid., p. 90.
12. Mark R. Peattie, 'Japanese Attitudes Toward Colonialism', in Myers and Peattie, op. cit., p. 95.
13. Cited in Government-General of Chōsen, *Annual Report on Reforms and Progress in Chōsen,* 1910–1911, Keijō, 1911, p. 242. (Cited hereafter as *Annual Report* followed by the appropriate year and page number.) These reports (published in English) were compiled annually from 1907 (by the Residency-General and after 1910 by the Governor-General) until 1938. Except where otherwise noted (in the case of obvious mistranslations) all quotations from these reports are as they appear in the original.
14. E. Patricia Tsurumi, op. cit., p. 81.
15. *Taiyō,* October, 1910, p. 89. An extract from this article appears in Conroy, op. cit., p. 329.
16. Mark R. Peattie, 'Japanese Attitudes Toward Colonialism', in Myers and Peattie, op. cit., p. 105.
17. A list of those organizations specifically banned appears in *Annual Report,* 1910–1911, p. 86.
18. Wonmo Dong, *Japanese Colonial Policy and Practice in Korea,* pp. 202–203.
19. This figure was compiled from the *Annual Report,* 1910–1911, pp. 86–87, and the *Annual Report,* 1911–1912, pp. 54–55. The vast majority of the newspapers confiscated by the police were in fact Japanese newspapers published by anti-Japanese emigre groups in the United States and Russia.
20. Cited in *Annual Report,* 1910–1911, p. 86. Also see Chong-Sik Lee, op. cit., p. 91.
21. The authority of the Governor-General was set down in the *Chōsen Sōtokufu Kansei* (Organic Regulations of the Government-General of Korea) issued in October 1910 by Imperial Ordinance No. 354. These are cited in their entirety in *Annual Report,* 1910–1911, pp. 248–250.
22. *Annual Report,* 1910–1911, pp. 28–29.

23. Andrew J. Grajdanzev, *Modern Korea*, Institute of Pacific Relations, New York, 1944, pp. 46–47.
24. This report is taken from the Proclamation of Annexation as cited in *Annual Report*, 1910–1911.
25. Wonmo Dong, 'Assimilation And Social Mobilization in Korea', in Nahm, *Korea Under Japanese Colonial Rule*, p. 164.
26. Cited in Ching-chih Chen, 'Police and Community Control Systems in the Empire', in Myers and Peattie, op. cit., p. 239. A complete list of police functions can be found in Yamabe Kentarō *Nihon Tōjika no Chōsen (Korea Under Japanese Rule)*, Iwanami Shinsho, Tokyo, 1978, pp. 17–18. See also Han Woo-Keun, op. cit., p. 466.
27. Jong Hae Yoo, 'The System of Korean Local Government', in Nahm, *Korea under Japanese Colonial Rule*, p. 55.
28. Ching-chih Chen, 'Police and Community Control Systems in the Empire', in Myers and Peattie, op. cit., p. 221.
29. Annual Report, 1910–1911, p. 70.
30. Cited in Doretha E. Mortimore, 'Dr Frank W. Schofield and the Korean National Consciousness', in C. I. Eugene Kim and Doretha E. Mortimore, eds., *Korea's Response to Japan: The Colonial Period 1910–1945*, Center for Korean Studies, Western Michigan University, 1975, p. 225.
31. Henry Chung, *The Case of Korea*, Fleming H. Revell Co., New York and London, p. 1921, p. 71.
32. Chong-Sik Lee, op. cit., pp. 114–118.
33. Ibid., See also Gregory Henderson, *Korea the Politics of the Vortex*, Harvard University Press, Cambridge, 1968, pp. 80–86.
34. Mark R. Peattie, 'Japanese Attitudes toward Colonialism', in Myers and Peattie, op. cit., pp. 105–107. An excellent account of the demonstrations in Seoul and the subsequent decision to reform the colonial administration can be found in Frank Prentiss Baldwin, Jr., *The March First Movement: Korean Challenge and Japanese Response*, Unpublished Doctoral Dissertation, Columbia University, 1969, pp. 78–185.
35. *Seoul Press*, September 10, 1919, in Kondō Ken'ichi, ed., *Banzai Sōjō Jiken (san-ichi Undō), (The Manse Disturbances: March the First Movement)*, Yūhō Kyōkai, Tokyo, 1964, Vol. III, pp. 171–172. (Cited hereafter as Kondō *Banzai Sōjō Jiken.*)
36. Taken from Saitō's first major address on September 3, 1919. Cited in Kondō, *Banzai Sōjō Jiken*, Vol. III, p. 173.
37. Ibid.
38. A general outline of the reforms introduced in 1919 are contained in the *Annual Report*, 1918–1921, pp. 6–11.
39. This was particularly true in the case of Governors-General Minami Jirō and Koiso Kuniaki who had served as garrison commanders prior to their appointment. See Wonmo Dong, *Japanese Colonial Policy and Practice in Korea*, p. 154. Under the revised regulations, the Governor-General was required to apply to the garrison commander for the mobilization of the armed forces.
40. See, for example, Wonmo Dong, *Japanese Colonial Policy and Practice in Korea*, pp. 270–277, 295–303, 354–361, 379–380.
41. Ibid., p. 254. Also see Andrew J. Grajdanzev, op. cit., p. 63, and Frank Prentiss Baldwin, Jr., op. cit., pp. 209–213.
42. Issued as Imperial Ordinance No. 229, and promulgated on August 23, 1911. Cited in the *Annual Report*, 1911–1912, pp. 226–228.

43. Cited in *Annual Report*, 1917–1918, p. xii.
44. *Annual Report*, 1911–1912, p. 8. Classes in the Korean language were offered as an elective in Japanese schools.
45. Abe Hiroshi, 'Higher Learning in Korea Under Japanese Rule', *The Developing Economics*, Vol. 9, No. 2, June, 1971, pp. 175–176. (Cited hereafter as Abe, 'Higher Learning in Korea'.)
46. Ibid., p. 176. This was in marked contrast to the system which existed in Japan. Grajdanzev, for example, notes that even during the late 1930s, the number of students (Japanese) in primary schools in Japan per thousand of the population was three times as great as the number of Korean students per thousand of the population in primary schools in Korea. In Middle Schools (in Japan) and Higher Common Schools (in Korea) the difference was even greater, and at university level the number of Japanese students per thousand of the population was one hundred and eleven times greater than that of their Korean counterparts (per thousand of the population). See Andrew J. Grajdanzev, op. cit., pp. 261–265.
47. From a speech made by the Director of the Education Bureau Director at a training course for Common School teachers in August 1911. He went on to say that if this were ignored it would result in the production of 'educated idlers', who were 'aloof from the conditions of society'. Cited in Abe, 'Higher Learning in Korea', p. 176.
48. Ibid.
49. Ibid., p. 180.
50. *Annual Report*, 1910–1911, p. 230.
51. Abe, 'Higher Learning in Korea', p. 178.
52. See Wonmo Dong, *Japanese Colonial Policy and Practice in Korea*, pp. 415–428.
53. Ibid., pp.411–432.
54. Ibid., p. 427.
55. Sang-Chul Suh, *Growth and Structural Changes in the Korean Economy, 1910–1940*, Council on East Asian Studies, Harvard University, 1978, pp. 7–8, 33–35. Also see James I. Nakamura, 'Incentives, Productivity Gaps, and Agricultural Growth Rates in Prewar Japan, Taiwan and Korea, (Cited hereafter as Nakamura, Agricultural Growth Rates in Japan, Taiwan and Korea'), in Silberman and Harootunian, *Japan in Crisis*, pp. 345–346, Shannon McCune, *Korea's Heritage: A Regional & Social Geography*, Charles E. Tuttle Company, Rutland, Vermont and Tokyo, 1963, pp. 37–38, 84–86, and William W. Lockwood, *The Economic Development of Japan*, Princeton University Press, Princeton, New Jersey, 1961, p. 386.
56. Yunshik Chang, 'Colonization as Planned Change: The Korean Case', *Modern Asian Studies*, Vol. 5, Part 2, April 1971, pp. 166–167. Also see Bruce Cumings, op. cit., pp. 39–40.
57. Bruce Cumings, op. cit., pp. 40–41.
58. Ibid p. 39.
59. *Annual Report*, 1910–1911, p. 70.
60. Ibid., pp. 12–16, 41–42. Also see Sang-Chul Suh, op. cit., p. 9, and Nakamura, 'Growth Rates in Japan, Taiwan and Korea', pp. 333–352. Both Suh and Nakamura acknowledge that the land reform policies implemented in Korea and Taiwan during the colonial period were similar to those introduced in Japan early in the Meiji period, the implication being that although Japanese policies were anti-cultivator, they were not necessarily anti-Korean or anti-Taiwanese. Nevertheless, Nakamura (p. 334) points to

several differences between the land surveys carried out in Japan and the colonies – not the least of which was the fact that 'officials were armed with the coercive power of a colonial government which did not hesitate to use police power to obtain more accurate statements'.
61. Yamabe Kentarō, op. cit., pp. 32–36. Also see Yunshik Chang, op. cit., p. 168.
62. Han Woo Keun, op. cit., pp. 467–468. Also see Choy-youn Bong, *Korea, A History*, Charles E. Tuttle Company, Inc., Tokyo and Rutland, Vermont, 1971, pp. 153–155.
63. Yunshik Chang, op. cit., p. 168. See also Han Woo-Keun, op. cit., pp. 467–469. Han notes that in 1912 less than one hundred Korean farmers forfeited their ownership rights due to non-payment of taxes. By 1914, however, this figure had risen to more than thirteen thousand, and thereafter did not drop below six thousand per year.
64. Matsumura Takao, '*Nihon Teikokushugi ka ni okeru Shokuminchi Rōdōsha*', ('Colonial Workers under Japanese Imperialism'), *Keizaigaku Nenpō*, No. 10, 1967, pp. 109–110. (1 *chōbu* = approx. 2.45 acres.)
65. Bruce Cumings, op. cit., pp. 41–42, 45–48.
66. David Brudnoy, 'Japan's Experiment in Korea', *Monumenta Nipponica*, Vol. 25, No. 1–2, 1970, p. 168.
67. Sang-Chul Suh, op. cit., p.81.
68. Ibid., pp. 81–83.
69. Ibid. In certain areas, particularly in the rice-producing areas of southern Korea, annual rents were as high as 80% of the yield.
70. Andrew J. Grajdanzev, op. cit., p. 114.
71. Daniel Sungil Juhn, 'The Development of Korean Entrepreneurship', in Nahm, *Korea Under Japanese Colonial Rule*, p.119.
72. Sang-Chul Suh, op. cit., pp. 9–10.
73. Andrew J. Grajdanzev, op. cit., pp. 106–107. Grajdanzev concludes that, including public and royal lands expropriated by the Government-General, more than half the land in Korea was under Japanese control. He also refers to an independent study of agricultural conditions in Korea which highlighted the difficulties in assessing land ownership in Korea by nationality. If, for example, a company or other such organization possessing land in Korea was operating under a Korean charter, then those lands were listed in official documents as being Korean owned, despite the fact that the owner or owners may have been Japanese. Also see Shannon McCune, op. cit., pp. 172–173. Sang-Chul Suh, op. cit., p. 80, estimates that by 1921 Japanese landlords accounted for more than 50% of all large holdings (over 100 chungbō), and by 1934 owned more than 60% of such holdings.
74. Bruce F. Johnston, *Japanese Food Management in World War II*, Stanford University Press, Stanford, 1953, p. 55.
75. Ibid, pp. 51–52.
76. For about the first five years after the annexation the number of Koreans migrating to southern Manchuria and the Chientao region exceeded that moving to Japan. There were a number of reasons for this. First, due to earlier migrations, the Chientao region supported a predominantly Korean population. New arrivals were therefore assured by the presence of a well-established Korean community of a certain degree of support. The Chientao region was, moreover, a relatively undeveloped agricultural zone well suited to the needs of Korean immigrants, most of whom were farmers. Finally,

and perhaps most important, is the fact that the demand for Korean labour in Japan did not really begin until about 1916. See Setsure Tsurushima, 'Korean Immigrants in Kandō in the 1920s', *The Kansai University Review of Economics and Business*, Vol. 7, Nos. 1, 2, 1978, pp 48–52.

77. Tamura Toshiyuki, *'Zainichi Chōsenjin Jinkō no Suikei: 1910–1945'*, ('Estimates of the Korean Population in Japan: 1910–1945'), Kokumin Keizai, No. 138, November 1977, p. 27.

Chapter 3

The Immigration of Korean Workers to Japan, 1910–1923

Under Governor-General Terauchi and his successors, who governed Korea between 1910 and 1945, economic policies were pursued which led to the impoverishment of increasing numbers of Korean farmers, and created an environment in which a massive rural exodus became inevitable. But just as it has been necessary to place earlier Japanese attitudes toward Korea in their proper historical context, the emergence of a Korean community in Japan can only be fully understood with reference to the economic environment of Taishō Japan; an environment which attracted the immigrant, moulded his responses to the host community, and fostered specific attitudes toward him among the Japanese.

With the outbreak of World War 1 Japanese industry was given a tremendous boost and the demand for industrial labour accelerated rapidly. Between 1914 and 1919 the number of factories employing ten or more workers increased from approximately 17,000 to 24,000, while the number of workers employed in these factories increased from 850,000 to nearly 1.5 million.[1] The war boom not only encouraged the development of new industries to compensate for the loss of manufactured goods which had previously been imported from Europe, but stimulated production in older, more established industries like coal mining, cotton spinning and silk manufacturing.[2] Annual levels of coal production, for example, increased steadily from just under 7.5 million tons in 1900 to nearly three times that amount in 1914, and by 1919 the figure stood at more than 30 million tons. Stimulated by wartime demand and inflation the price of coal in 1919 was nearly three times its 1915 level, while the number of miners employed by the industry nearly doubled during the same period.[3]

Much of this industrial expansion was largely dependent upon the availability of cheap labour drawn principally from rural areas.[4] But, even before the war, factory and mine owners had not always found it easy to exploit these reservoirs of labour. In textiles, for example, where Japan's industrial revolution began, expansion had been so rapid that local supplies of labour in many areas had been exhausted by the turn of the century.[5] Moreover, as Koji Taira has argued, 'the majority of

Japanese workers were only partially committed to industrial labour', and as a result, the Japanese labour market was characterized by a shortage of labour for factory employment, excessive competition for labour among employers and high levels of labour turnover.[6] During the war this situation was exacerbated and the demand for unskilled industrial labour quickly outstripped local supplies. In an effort to alleviate this labour shortage, Japanese entrepreneurs, acting either through their own agents or through local labour brokers in Korea, began to recruit Koreans for work in Japan. Textiles and coal mining were areas in which the recruitment of labour presented particular difficulties, and it was in these two industries that Korean immigrants were first employed. These factors necessitate a brief discussion of recruitment practices in textiles and coal mining.

Although other industries expanded more rapidly during the war, the textile industry was the largest employer of factory labour, and accounted for more than half of the industrial labour force in Japan as late as 1930.[7] The vast majority of textile workers were young unmarried women drawn primarily from rural areas where poverty and overpopulation encouraged their families to offer them as temporary industrial workers.[8] By the mid-1890s the demand for mill workers in certain areas had begun to exceed local supplies, and as labour shortages developed employers came to rely increasingly on professional labour recruiters.[9]

Typically, recruiting agents were paid according to the number of workers recruited, and it was estimated that the cost of recruiting female operatives for cotton spinning rose sevenfold between 1907 and 1917.[10] In an attempt to reduce the impact of these expenses on overall production costs it was common for employers to shift the burden on to their employees, through wage reductions, the extension of working hours, or the curtailment of welfare benefits.[11] Even before such economies were introduced working and living conditions in most factories had been poor, and as William Lockwood has observed:

> Except in a few model mills, conditions of life and work generally exhibited the poverty, the crowding, and the lack of worker protection which characterized the introduction of the industrial system in the West early in the nineteenth century.[12]

As conditions in the mills deteriorated the incidence of absenteeism, work-related illness and desertion increased while efficiency remained low. Female textile workers were normally employed under contracts ranging in duration from one to three years, but desertions among new workers are thought to have been as high as 50% during the first six months, and in extreme cases as high as 30% within the first month.[13] These high turnover rates, coupled with the continued expansion of the textile industry, led to increasing competition between employers for mill workers, and recruiters commonly resorted to questionable methods in their attempts to achieve recruitment quotas.[14] These unscrupulous and sometimes illegal practices contributed both to a worsening of the working and living conditions in the mills and to the growing resistance of all but the most destitute farm households to the inducements of recruiting agents. So serious did this problem eventually become that by the early 1920s entire districts were regarded as 'worked out' for recruitment purposes within seven years.[15]

In coal mining the recruitment of labour had, since Tokugawa times, proved extremely difficult for a number of reasons. First was the difficulty in obtaining labour in the inaccessible regions where many mines were located, and second was the low regard in which coal mining was traditionally held.[16] These factors, coupled with the dangers and risks to health commonly associated with coal mining[17], ensured that from a very early period mine workers were recruited from the lowest strata of society. In 1919 alone, for example, there were more than 200,000 mining accidents involving over 900 fatalities and approximately 6,000 serious injuries.

Because labour for the coal mines was drawn principally from among landless peasants and members of the *eta* outcaste group, minework gradually came to be identified as an outcaste occupation, an association which survived both the Meiji Restoration and subsequent attempts to abolish the outcaste group. Convict labour was also used in mining, but it was the labelling of minework as an outcaste occupation which isolated mine workers from the rest of society and was at least partly responsible for the often callous treatment of employees by mine operators.

Traditionally, the recruitment of mine workers had been the preserve of the *yakuza* but after the enactment of the Mining Regulations of 1872 this system was gradually replaced by reliance on contractors and later on labour bosses – who were referred to as *hambagashira* in northern Japan and *nayagashira* in western Honshū and Kyūshū.[18] Although regional and other variations existed, labour bosses and contractors functioned as middlemen between the company and employees, and were responsible for the payment of wages and the recruitment and supervision of miners, as well as the provision of housing, food, work clothes and medical care. The *hambagashira*'s principal source of income was derived from the various charges he levied on the wages of his subordinates, and at some mines wages were paid not in cash but in the form of coupons. Even where wages were paid in cash, payments were often so irregular as to ensure the permanent indebtedness of workers to their labour bosses.

Many of the abuses commonly found in the recruitment of labour for the textile industry were equally widespread in the coal mining industry. The practice of advancing sums of money, for example, which had to be worked off before a miner could voluntarily leave employment was very common, as was the misrepresentation of the conditions of work by recruiters – a practice which frequently led to allegations of kidnapping. The systematic exploitation of mine workers also bred high levels of desertion, and since the income of labour bosses was largely dependent upon the retention of his workers, a secondary role for him became the policing of mining camps and the prevention of escapes. In parts of Hokkaidō private police forces were employed to deter desertions, while at the Takashima mine in Kyūshū public beatings were administered to miners caught attempting to escape as an example to other would-be deserters.

Despite the introduction of protective legislation for mine workers in 1890, coal mining continued to be regarded as an extremely unattractive occupation well into the twentieth century. Turnover rates were higher in mining than in all other industries with the exception of textiles,[19] and in 1924 the only industry offering lower wages than mining was textiles.[20]

Both textiles and coal mining had thus historically experienced extreme difficulty in the recruitment and retention of labour. Under the unusual economic conditions which existed between 1915 and 1919 labour shortages in these two industries became even more acute, and the importation of Korean workers was regarded as a cheap answer to the problem.

Government Controls on the Immigration and Recruitment of Korean Workers

Until 1910 the Korean community in Japan was composed primarily of students, political exiles and consular officials.[21] Although there may have been a small number of Koreans who were employed illegally in the coal mining industry before this time, the evidence is by no means conclusive.[22] Moreover, contemporary immigration laws appear to have been designed with the express purpose of preventing the entry of foreign labourers.[23] By the act of annexation, however, these immigration laws ceased to apply to Koreans. Nevertheless, as is shown in Table 4, it was Chinese and not Korean residents who made up the largest part of the foreign population until as late as 1915.

Although Japanese civil law was, in most instances, not extended to Korea, Koreans were now regarded as Japanese Nationals and were guaranteed the right to move freely and take up employment anywhere within the Empire.[24] Initially the number of immigrants entering Japan was small, particularly in comparison with the large numbers of Koreans migrating to southern Manchuria, and they were regarded as temporary workers who were expected to remain only long enough to relieve wartime labour shortages.[25] Although the official estimates of the

TABLE 4

Foreign Residents in Japan: Selected Years (1895–1915)

Year	U.K.	U.S.A.	France	Germany	China	Korea	Total
1895	1,878	1,022	391	493	3,642	12	7,438
1900	2,044	1,462	458	540	6,890	193	11,587
1905	2,114	1,612	531	616	10,388	303	15,564
1910	2,430	1,633	534	782	8,420	N.A.	13,799
1911	2,633	1,762	530	815	8,145	N.A.	13,885
1913	2,787	1,700	540	924	11,867	3,952	21,770
1915	2,330	1,611	402	706	12,046	5,046	22,141

Source: *Nihon Teikoku Tōkei Nenkan*, various years.
N.A. Not available.

number of Koreans moving between Japan and Korea throughout the first two decades after the annexation suggest that these expectations were largely shared by the immigrants themselves (though for different reasons) the Korean community itself, however impermanent it might appear, was permanently present. Moreover, once under way, immigration to Japan appears to have been self-perpetuating – regardless of changes in economic conditions within the receiving society. Even during the early period (1915–1920) an important source of encouragement for potential immigrants was the exaggerated tales spread by those who had already experienced the good life in Japan. Although life in Japan posed numerous difficulties, not the least of which was coping with an unfamiliar language, it was inevitable that the outlook of the immigrant too would be changed. For some, who had returned to Korea after a brief period spent in Osaka or Tokyo, village life was unexciting and unrewarding, and many re-entered Japan with the intention of remaining there more or less permanently.

For the first few years after the annexation the movement of Korean workers between Japan and Korea was not regarded by the authorities in either area as a particularly sensitive issue. It is, however, significant that as early as 1913 while enthusiasm for *dōka* was at its height, the Police Bureau, concerned that successful assimilation would interfere with the identification and control of Koreans, authorized the compilation of a manual highlighting social, physical and linguistic differences between Japanese and Koreans. This manual was subsequently circulated among all Prefectural Police Departments.[26]

There are no records available which document the extent of labour recruiting in Korea before about 1917, but there is no reason to suggest that many of the evils associated with recruiting in Japan (such as misrepresenting working and living conditions) were not equally widespread in Korea.[27] Moreover, the fact that the Government-General felt compelled to issue an ordinance regulating recruitment in Korea fully six years before comparable legislation was introduced in Japan was, in itself, a clear indication that labour recruitment had already become a source of serious concern for the colonial administration. Guidelines for the recruitment of Korean workers were first introduced by the Government-General in January 1918. Under these regulations prospective employers or their representative(s) in Korea were obliged to submit an application to the police in the recruitment area which was to include a draft copy of the contract of employment, as well as the type of work in which recruits were to be used, and the age range of the workers to be recruited. Employers were also required to include in the draft contract details of employment and work-related benefits. This did not, however, imply any obligation on the part of the employer to provide sickness or injury benefits; it merely required that details concerning these matters be included in the contract.

TABLE 5
Movement of Koreans between Japan and Korea (1917–1923)

Year	Number Crossing to Japan	Number Returning to Korea	Number Residing in Japan	Annual Increase
1917	14,012	3,927	10,085	10,085
1918	17,910	9,305	18,690	8,605
1919	20,968	12,739	26,919	8,229
1920	27,497	20,947	33,469	6,550
1921	38,118	25,536	46,051	12,582
1922	70,462	46,326	70,187	24,136
1923	97,395	89,745	77,837	7,650

Source:
Fukuoka Chihō Shokugyō Shōkai Jimukyoku (Fukuoka Regional Employment Exchange Office), '*Kannai Zaijū Chōsenjin Rōdō Jijō*' ('The Working Conditions of Koreans Living under the Jurisdiction of this Office'), Fukuoka, 1929, p. 5. (Cited hereafter as Fukuoka Regional Employment Exchange, '*Chōsenjin Rōdō Jijō*'.)

Note: The principal causes for the accelerated movement of Koreans to Japan after 1921 were the deteriorating economic conditions of farmers in Korea and the abolition of the *Ryokō Shōmeisho* system at the end of 1922. The equally marked drop in the rate of increase in 1923 was due almost entirely to the anti-Korean 'riots' which followed the Kanto earthquake of September 1923 and the subsequent reimposition of the *Ryokō Shōmeisho* system.

Recruiting agents were required to obtain licences from the local chief of police, and were prohibited from misrepresenting the nature of the work to prospective candidates, recruiting persons under fourteen years of age, or those under the age of twenty without first obtaining the written consent of their parents or legal guardian. Recruiters were also obliged to compile a register of recruits which would then have to be submitted for approval to the police, both in the recruitment area and at the port of departure. Violation of these regulations could result in fines not exceeding 200 yen, though the police were also empowered to revoke individual licences.[28]

In the absence of data concerning its application, the extent to which this set of regulations succeeded in curbing recruitment abuses is largely a matter of speculation. The evidence which does exist, however, suggests that the recruitment of Koreans continued to be regulated more by the demands of the Japanese labour market and other external factors than by the rigorous application of this law.[29] Table 5 clearly illustrates that despite the existence of these and subsequent restrictions on the movement of Koreans, the annual rate of increase in the number of Koreans residing in Japan remained fairly constant until 1921 when it began to rise sharply.

This is also substantiated by the Home Ministry's decision to issue a second set of regulations in December 1918. This directive, which was sent to all Prefectural Governors, bore all the hallmarks of later police directives and clearly reflected official anxieties over social unrest following the Rice Riots of the previous summer. It read in part:

> From the point of view of public safety, the recent increases in the number of Koreans being recruited and brought over to work in Japanese factories, due to the shortage of labour here in Japan, is a source of concern. Paralleling the end of the war in Europe there has been an economic slow-down in Japan, and the possibility that this will result in large numbers of unemployed Koreans drifting around the country is a potential source of unrest.[30]

Prefectural Governors were therefore advised to investigate those companies operating under their jurisdiction which had been employing Koreans with a view to ascertaining the companies' financial soundness, the number of Koreans employed and the wages paid to them. They were also instructed to check what provisions, if any, had been made to ensure that the Koreans employed by these companies would be able to pay their fare back to Korea in the event of their being dismissed by the companies.[31] Whatever effects these measures may have had upon recruitment methods or the terms of employment under which Koreans were brought to Japan were completely overshadowed by the tumultuous events which occurred in Korea during the following year.

Triggered by the death of the ex-Emperor Kojong, and inspired by President Woodrow Wilson's support for the principle of 'self determination,' the independence demonstrations which began in Seoul on March 1, 1919 dispelled the illusion that ten years of 'Imperial Benevolence' had gained the confidence and loyalty of the Korean people.[32] As the Independence Movement gained momentum and spread throughout Korea, the ruthless suppression of the demonstrators by the Japanese police and army led to increased outbreaks of violence, and by the end of March some areas were regarded as being in open revolt.[33] Embarrassed by the scale of the demonstrations, and determined to contain the disturbances, the Government-General issued an ordinance in April 1919 which was designed to limit the movement of Koreans. Thereafter Koreans wishing to travel abroad were to be required to submit to the police a written declaration detailing the purpose and destination of their intended journey. If their application was approved, they would be issued with a *Ryokō Shōmeisho* (Certificate of Travel) to be presented to the police at their final port of departure. Similarly Koreans wishing to return to Korea were required to present a travel certificate issued by the authorities to the police at their port of entry.[34]

While this law may have relieved some of the anxieties felt by security-conscious police amd military officials, it encountered resistance from Japanese firms still eager to employ Korean workers. In addition, it was a source of considerable embarrassment to the Japanese Government which was then campaigning against the imposition of controls on Japanese immigration to the United States. The author of a later report compiled in Osaka argued that although the *Ryokō Shōmeisho* system had represented order 'The fact that the freedom of movement of Koreans, who were our own countrymen, was not guaranteed, became a national disgrace.'[35]

The extent to which the *Shōmei* system, as it was commonly known, effectively reduced the number of Koreans entering Japan is open to question. Like its predecessor, its results can only be judged against the background of considerable social unrest in both countries and fluctuations in the Japanese labour market, particularly after the postwar economic slump began. Nevertheless, until its abolition in December 1922, this ordinance was the principal means of regulating the volume of immigration.[36]

The Early Recruitment of Korean Workers

According to a report submitted to the Ministry of Commerce and Agriculture in November 1917 by Yoshisaka Shunzō, the Superintendent of the Mines Inspectorate, the first company in Japan to recruit workers from Korea after the annexation was the Settsu Cotton

Spinning Company in Osaka in 1911.³⁷ In this report Yoshisaka gives no indication of the wages paid to Korean workers or of the conditions under which they were recruited and employed. He does, however, acknowledge that, because Koreans were unfamiliar with conditions in Japan, companies experienced considerable difficulty in recruiting them. In the case of the Akashi factory belonging to the Settsu Cotton Spinning Company, its first attempt at recruitment in Korea in 1912 resulted in only sixteen workers actually being taken on by the company. During the following five years eleven similar attempts to recruit workers for this factory led to the employment of only 208 individuals.³⁸ In an interview published by the *Fukuoka Nichi Nichi Shimbun* in November 1917, Yoshisaka commented briefly on the use of Korean labourers in Osaka and Wakayama Prefectures. He observed that due to the *dekasegi* nature of Japanese labour, 'The use of Koreans in certain types of factories is an attempt to counter high turnover rates among Japanese workers.'³⁹

As is shown in Table 6, the employment of Korean factory workers did not begin to accelerate until about 1917. Koreans were recruited for work in a variety of industries, but textile and mining companies were among the most active. Commenting on the paramount position occupied by textile firms as recruiters of Korean workers, the *Ōsaka Mainichi Shimbun* noted:

> In work which requires comparatively little skill like cotton spinning, as long as there is no difference in the level of ability between Japanese and Korean workers, the recruitment of Korean workers will continue in the future.⁴⁰

The presence in Korea of Japanese recruitment agents was also confirmed by a series of articles in the *Ōsaka Mainichi Shimbun* during August 1917 which reproduced the results of a survey conducted by the Shimonoseki Police Department. According to the police, the number of Koreans entering Japan each month by way of Shimonoseki had recently surpassed 500. Among the new arrivals:

> The great majority of the women are destined for factory work while all the men are to be used in work like coal mining, stevedoring, general labouring and construction work, requiring a minimum of skills.⁴¹

In common with other contemporary observers this writer concluded that:

> Even though these Koreans have various faults, in relation to their low wages their efficiency is not all that inferior. Moreover, it appears as if other companies are beginning to do the same, and until the present shortage of factory labour disappears we can

expect to see a rapid increase in the number of Korean workers being brought over.[42]

TABLE 6
Companies Employing Koreans Before 1918

Prefecture	Name of Company	Location of Factory or Mill	Date of First Known Employment of Koreans
Osaka	Settsu Cotton Spinning	Kizugawa	1911
Osaka	Tōyō Cotton Spinning	Sangenya	1914
Osaka	Sumitomo Steel Foundry	–	1916
Osaka	Amagasaki Cotton Spinning	Tsumori	1917
Osaka	Nitta Shipyards	–	1917
Osaka	Settsu Cotton Spinning	Hirano	1917
Osaka	Fujinagata Shipyards	–	1917
Osaka	Kibi Shipyards	–	1917
Hyōgo	Settsu Cotton Spinning	Akashi	1912
Hyōgo	Kawasaki Shipyards	–	1914
Hyōgo	Kōbe Steelworks	–	1916
Hyōgo	Fukushima Cotton Spinning	Shikama	1917
Hyōgo	Kawasaki Shipyards	Tokorowake	1917
Hyōgo	Mitsubishi Kōbe Shipyards	–	1917
Hyōgo	Kishimoto Nail Co.	–	1917
Hyōgo	Harima Shipyards	–	1917
Wakayama	Asahi Chemicals	–	1916
Wakayama	Naikai Cotton Spinning	–	1916
Wakayama	Wakayama Cotton Spinning	–	1916
Wakayama	Kiyō Weaving	–	1916
Wakayama	Yura Dyeworks	–	1917
Wakayama	Hinode Cotton Spinning	–	1917
Mie	Mie Distillery	–	1916
Mie	Kitsu Cotton Manufacturing	–	1917
Mie	Tōyō Cotton Spinning	Tsu	1917
Mie	Hiramatsu Woollens	–	1917
Mie	Ōhashi Foundry	–	1917
Okayama	Tōyōkan Match Co.	Okayama	1913
Okayama	Kurashiki Cotton Spinning	Masu	1917
Okayama	Kibi Textiles	–	1917
Okayama	Kurashiki Cotton Spinning	Tamashima	1917
Okayama	Ishii Textiles	–	1917

Source: Takeda, 'Hantōjin Mondai', pp. 103–104.

A somewhat more detailed account of the wartime recruitment of Korean factory girls by a large textile firm is contained in a slightly later report compiled by the Government-General. Citing the Kishiwada Cotton Spinning Company as a typical example, this report reads in part:

> As a result of the sudden expansion of the industrial sector in Japan due to the Great War, by about 1918 . . . a shortage of female factory labour in the cotton spinning industry developed. The Kishiwada Cotton Spinning Company, viewing the recruitment of Koreans as an answer to this shortage, despatched a number of its own officials to Korea. They returned with fifty Korean girls who were then taken on by the company. Although their efficiency was far lower [than Japanese girls], as they did not expect particularly good housing or dining facilities and since their livelihood and wages were much lower when compared with Japanese factory girls, the company judged the results to be relatively good. Therefore in July of the same year an additional 100 Korean girls were recruited and taken on at four of the company's factories.[43]

The method of recruitment referred to in the above passage was commonly known as 'Direct Company Recruitment.' While there is no evidence to suggest that recruitment methods in Korea differed from those practiced in Japan, later commentators classified recruitment of Koreans into the following four categories.

1 – *Shigan – Boshū* — Recruitment by application made by the employee himself in response to advertisements placed by the company. This, according to most contemporary surveys, was the most common way in which Koreans found employment in Japan.

2 – *Enko – Boshū* — Recruitment through the introduction of a friend or relative already employed by the company. It was common for this type of recruitment to involve the payment of an introduction fee to the intermediary. Although this type of recruitment was not founded upon a contractual agreement between employer and intermediary, it was not always easy to distinguish *Enko Boshū* from the third category.

3 – *Ukeoi – Boshū* — In this instance recruitment was carried out by either independent or company-designated labour recruiters who were commonly referred to as *Boshū Jūjisha*. As practised in both Japan and Korea it was customary for the recruiting agent or one of his assistants to visit areas where 'connections' with local leaders ensured successful recruitment. After collecting the recruits, the agent

4 – *Gyōsha – Chokusetsu Boshu* — was normally expected to escort them to the factory or mine on whose behalf he was working. This method of recruitment appears to have been used extensively by both textile and mining enterprises during the First World War.

4 – *Gyōsha – Chokusetsu Boshu* – This method of direct recruitment involved the despatch of company officials to Korea for the express purposes of recruitment and establishing recruitment areas. It was commonly used by textile and coal mining concerns – in particular by the Hokkaidō Steamship and Colliery Company.[44]

Although these distinctions are clear enough conceptually, in practice recruitment patterns varied by industry and region, and it was not uncommon for the same company to employ two or even three of the above methods of recruitment. In the coal mining industry, for example, regional variations in the methods of recruitment and a diversity of attitude toward the employment of Koreans militated against the emergence of a common recruitment policy for the entire industry.[45] Nonetheless, the coal mining industry provides the most reliable and comprehensive information concerning the early recruitment of Korean workers and the conditions under which they worked and lived. An article in the *Kōgyō Shimpō* in July 1912 expressed the opinion that the Hokkaidō Steamship and Colliery Company (hereafter referred to as *Hokutan*) could be expected to begin taking on Korean miners in the very near future, adding that the company had already contracted for the construction of housing facilities for Korean miners.[46] This prediction proved to be somewhat premature, since according to *Hokutan*'s own records it was not until the autumn of 1916 that the company decided to employ six Korean miners 'on an experimental basis' at its Yūbari mine.[47] Subsequent large-scale recruitment in Korea by *Hokutan* attests to the acceptable results of this experiment, while the company's own draft history recorded that, 'if Korean miners received proper supervision it was observed that they would work hard and were not inferior to Japanese miners'.[48]

At the suggestion of one of its first Korean employees, the manager of the Yūbari mine was sent to Vladivostok to recruit among the Korean community there. He recruited a further sixteen miners in Vladivostok, and by the end of 1916 a total of thirty-five Koreans were employed at Yūbari.[49] By late 1917 *Hokutan* had shifted its recruitment activities from the Russian Maritime Provinces to the port cities of Wonsan and Pusan in Korea.[50] At Wonsan the processing of recruited workers was managed entirely by company officials while the day-to-day business of recruiting was carried out by Korean assistants whose responsibility it

TABLE 7
Korean Miners Employed by Hokutan (1916–1930)

Year	Yūbari	Shin Yūbari	Manji	Noborikawa	Mayacki	Sōrachi	Poronai	Wakanabe	Ikushumpetsu	Total
1916	35									35
1917	192	57	102					76		370
1918	447	86	90					53	12	659
1919	423	64	120					105	20	754
1920	309	44	262					64	4	703
1921	184	90	271					75	3	577
1922	315	84	307		3	2	23	161	6	907
1923	240	68	304		3	2	9	177		819
1924	406	48	309		2	17	33	181	12	1,028
1925	446	73	311		2	4	12	177	11	1,005
1926	564	163	334	22	4	2	11	207	11	1,206
1927	519	136	385	27	7	2	8	210	7	1,323
1928	742	70	360	30	4	2	10	224	7	1,505
1929	569	34	318	18	63	2	6	136	11	1,205
1930	340		105		28	2	4		9	540

Source: *Hokutan Fifty-Year History*, pp. 317–318.

was to put up recruiting notices in outlying villages and to co-operate with village leaders who might be of assistance. At its Pusan outstation, *Hokutan* was not directly involved in the recruitment of Koreans. Instead, it designated a Japanese firm of labour brokers as its exclusive agent in southern Korea and relied on them to carry out the preliminary screening of recruits. Once these formalities had been completed, newly-recruited miners were taken by sea to either Tsuruga or Fushiki in Fukui Prefecture, and from there by rail as far as Aomori where they were met by other company officials who escorted them to the mines.[51] As is shown in Table 7, by 1919 more than 750 Koreans were working under contract to *Hokutan* in some of its largest mines. Although the company's draft history is unclear about the length of contract under which Koreans were first employed, later evidence suggests that it was probably for periods of from one to two years.[52]

Encouraged by *Hokutan*'s success with Korean miners, other mining concerns, particularly those in northern Kyūshū, began importing considerable numbers of Korean workers. With the exception of the Mitsui-owned Miike mine, most of the major coal producers were using Korean labour by the mid-1920s.[53] It is also possible from about this time to identify both a demographic pattern in the immigration of Koreans and in the occupational categories in which they were concentrated (Tables 8 and 9).

With the exception of Tokyo, where a large student population distorts the pattern, it is clear from these figures that the overwhelming majority of Koreans were employed as unskilled labour, and were concentrated in the burgeoning industrial regions around Osaka and northwestern Kyūshū.[54] At the end of 1923, for example, it was estimated that eight of every nine immigrants were manual labourers, and that within that category the majority were employed as coolies or general construction workers.[55] Commenting on this, an editorial in the *Osaka Mainichi Shimbun* suggested that the employment of Koreans as unskilled labour was inevitable since they lacked the dexterity of Japanese workers, and were superior only in 'mere physical strength.'[56] A later report prepared by the Osaka municipal authorities assessed the situation in the following way:

> ... the fact that they will perform, without complaint, filthy degrading work ..., which Japanese workers avoid, should be regarded as something which, along with the low wages they will accept, can be taken advantage of as one of their principal assets. In fact, if we consider that there exists a real demand for Korean workers as coolies, navvies and coal miners, there ought to be future prospects for them in these areas.[57]

TABLE 8

Korean Population in Japan: Selected Years (1913–1923)

	1913		1915		1917		1919		1921		1923	
1	Tokyo	572	Tokyo	574	Fukuoka	2,386	Fukuoka	5,560	Fukuoka	6,092	Osaka	21,984
2	Fukuoka	549	Yamaguchi	514	Osaka	2,235	Osaka	3,671	Osaka	5,069	Fukuoka	12,276
3	Osaka	338	Fukuoka	457	Hokkaidō	1,706	Hyōgo	2,630	Nagasaki	2,409	Hyōgo	5,561
4	Oita	306	Nagasaki	394	Hyōgo	1,624	Hokkaidō	2,524	Tokyo	2,404	Yamaguchi	4,871
5	Nagasaki	283	Osaka	336	Hiroshima	928	Yamaguchi	1,416	Hyōgo	2,215	Nagano	3,985
6	Yamaguchi	267	Oita	171	Tokyo	918	Nagasaki	1,412	Yamaguchi	1,654	Tokyo	3,609
7	Hyōgo	123	Hyōgo	155	Yamaguchi	778	Tokyo	994	Hokkaidō	1,622	Gifu	3,495
8	Mie	113	Kanagawa	100	Nagasaki	583	Hiroshima	774	Hiroshima	1,549	Hiroshima	3,216
	Others	1,084	Others	1,236	Others	3,344	Others	7,624	Others	9,260	Others	29,265
	Total	3,635	Total	3,917	Total	14,502	Total	26,605	Total	32,274	Total	88,262

Sources: Figures for 1913–1919, Naimushō Keihokyoku Hoanka (Home Ministry, Police Affairs Bureau, Security Section), 'Chōsenjin Gaikyō Dai San' ('A General View of Koreans No. 3'), 1920, in Pak, Z.K.S.S., Vol. I, p. 120. (Cited hereafter as 'Chōsenjin Gaikyō 3'.)
Figures for 1921, Naimushō Keihokyoku (Home Ministry, Police Affairs Bureau), 'Chōsenjin Kinkyō Gaiyō' ('A General View of the Recent Condition of Koreans'), 1922, in Pak, Z.K.S.S., Vol. I, pp. 126–128. (Cited hereafter as Naimushō, 'Chōsenjin Kinkyō Gaiyō'.)
Figures for 1923, Osaka-shi, 'Chōsenjin Rōdōsha Mondai', pp. 21–24.

Note: With the exception of 1923 all figures represent year-end totals. The totals for 1923, however, are based on surveys conducted by the various prefectural authorities at different times during 1923. In the case of Tokyo, for example, the 1923 figure must be regarded as being artificially low since it represents the results of a survey conducted at the end of September within weeks of the 'Great Earthquake', and did not take into account the hundreds of Koreans who died as a result of the earthquake or of the even greater number of Koreans who died at the hands of the police, military, and vigilante groups, or fled the area as a result of these incidents.

TABLE 9
Korean Immigrant Occupations: By Prefecture (1923)

Prefecture	Students	White Collar Workers	Coolie Type	Labourers %	Factory	Operatives %	Others, including those without employment	Total
Fukuoka	31	14	9,872	(81.7)	620	(5.0)	1,739	12,276
Nagasaki	35	3	1,593	(91.0)	24	(1.3)	95	1,750
Oita	—	—	1,274	(94.0)	42	(3.1)	37	1,354
Yamaguchi	45	50	4,124	(84.6)	106	(2.1)	546	4,871
Hiroshima	35	6	2,491	(77.3)	357	(11.0)	330	3,219
Osaka	43	16	10,471	(47.6)	7,568	(34.4)	3,886	21,984
Kyōto	105	4	2,267	(55.1)	1,620	(39.3)	119	4,115
Hyōgo	38	13	2,754	(50)	1,947	(35)	749	5,501
Wakayama	—	2	483	(44.1)	597	(54.5)	113	1,095
Gifu	—	—	3,420	(97.8)	1	(0.0)	74	3,495
Shizuoka	1	—	1,179	(82.6)	277	(19.4)	69	1,426
Aichi	4	14	1,335	(46.3)	1,375	(47.7)	154	2,882
Nagano	—	—	3,817	(95.7)	64	(1.6)	104	3,985
Toyama	—	—	965	(96.4)	25	(2.5)	11	1,001
Niigata	1	1	2,689	(98.2)	45	(1.6)	1	2,737
Tokyo	689	139	2,183	(60.4)	335	(9.2)	263	3,609
Hokkaidō	13	6	2,990	(90.9)	33	(1.0)	244	3,286
Total	1,040	268	53,907	(68.9)	15,036	(19.2)	8,534	78,586
All Japan Total	1,101	291	61,528	(69.7)	16,452	(18.7)	8,890	88,262

Source: *Osaki-shi*, 'Chōsenjin Rōdōsha Mondai', pp. 21–23. Also cited (with the exception of Hyōgo Prefecture) in Matsumura, op.cit., p. 140.

Note: (1) Only those prefectures with Korean populations in excess of one thousand are shown in the above chart.

(2) The figures shown above were not the result of a national survey but were compiled from prefectural surveys taken at various times during 1923. Given the importance of the earthquake of September 1923 in substantially reducing the Korean population in certain areas, the figures for Tokyo, for example, (which were produced at the end of September) should be treated as extremely unreliable since they reflect neither pre-earthquake nor post-1923 trends.

Korean Dekasegi Workers

In common with the Japanese migrant workers of an earlier period, the overwhelming majority of Korean workers who entered Japan led extremely unsettled lives. According to the Home Ministry, the following were the principal reasons for Koreans wishing to cross to Japan – (a) extreme poverty and difficulty in making their livelihood in Korea, (b) encouraging reports spread by Koreans who had been to Japan, (c) wages in Japan were higher than those in Korea, (d) the introduction of a Japanese living in Korea, or response to the promise of employment, (e) the introduction of a friend or relative living in Japan, (f) recruitment.[58] Similar surveys were carried out over a five-year period by the Ministry of Justice, the Tokyo Regional Employment Exchange, and the Social Affairs Bureau of the Osaka city government. Although figures were not supplied in these reports they all confirmed that the determining factors in causing the immigration were rural impoverishment and the attraction of higher wages in Japan.[59]

One official source described the migration of Koreans in the following way:

> ... the great majority of them drift across to Japan without any knowledge of conditions here, and dreaming of filling their pockets with gold. Their first feelings on arriving in Japan are probably best expressed by the phrase 'it sounded like paradise but when I saw it, it was hell.'[60]

TABLE 10

Comparative Daily Wages for Korean Workers in Japan and Korea: Selected Industries (1922)

Occupation/Industry	Japan	Korea
Farm worker (male)	1.64	0.92
Farm worker (female)	0.87	0.56
Dyeing	1.90	1.25
Laundry worker	1.80	1.20
Navvy	2.30	1.30
Stevedore	2.50	1.60
Coal Mining	2.20	1.30

Source: Osaka-shi, 'Chōsenjin Rōdōsha Mondai', pp. 64–67.
Note: All wages are in Yen per day.

But, despite poor working and living conditions, Japan remained an attractive destination for impoverished Korean farmers, since:

> ... the experience and distress of their livelihood in the past, which was brutalized to a degree where for certain periods they had no choice but to subsist on roots and the bark of trees, enables them to bear with ease their present lives which to us appear worse than that of convicts.[61]

Moreover, as is shown in Table 10, the daily wage for Korean labourers in Japan was in most cases at least 50% higher than the comparable wage in Korea.

An important feature of the early immigrant community was the impermanent nature of the life led by its members. Table 11 gives a rough estimate of the total number of Koreans entering and leaving Japan between 1917 and 1923, while Table 12 provides a more detailed estimate of the movement of Koreans between 1922 and 1923. In addition to illustrating the magnitude of the traffic passing between Pusan and Shimonoseki, these figures reveal several other distinctive features of the migration. Table 12, for example, indicates that the ratio of men to women remained fairly constant after 1920, ranging from 5.85 to 1 in 1921 to 6.6 to 1 in 1923, though significant regional variations did exist. In 1923, Hyōgo and Osaka Prefectures, which supported the most established immigrant communities, had ratios of 2.96 to 1 and 4.93 to 1 respectively, whereas in Fukuoka and Hokkaidō, which had high proportions of unaccompanied male mine workers, the corresponding figures were 8.88 to 1 and 11.5 to 1. Tables 11 and 12 also illustrate that the migration of Koreans fluctuated markedly depending upon the time of year. During the Lunar New Year period, for instance, when it was customary for Koreans to visit their home town or village, the number of Koreans returning home was quite high, compared with the number of entries into Japan during the same period. This pattern was repeated during the months of the summer harvest (July and August) when shortages of agricultural labour were experienced in certain parts of southern Korea.[62] It was also during the months immediately preceding the summer harvest (March–June), when many families in Korea were reduced to near-starvation, that the greatest number of Koreans migrated to Japan.

A further indication of the unsettled nature of the immigrant community is the fact that the number of persons establishing households in Japan remained consistently low throughout the period before 1924. Once again an absence of reliable data makes it extremely difficult to assess overall housing patterns before about 1920, and even after that time contemporary researchers experienced considerable difficulty in obtaining accurate measurements due to the high degree of

TABLE 11
Movement of Koreans between Korea and Japan (1917–July 1923)

Year	Number Crossing to Japan		Number Returning to Korea		Annual Increase		Total Population
	Male	Female	Male	Female	Male	Female	
1917	11,216	2,796	3,428	499	7,788	2,297	10,085
1918	11,513	177	1,789	62	9,724	115	19,924
1919	19,110	1,858	11,688	1,051	7,422	807	28,153
1920	24,625	2,872	18,606	2,341	6,019	531	34,703
1921	32,301	5,817	22,853	2,683	9,448	3,134	47,285
1922	78,663	13,075	51,296	7,076	27,367	5,999	80,651
1923 January	9,328	545	5,417	413	3,911	132	
February	6,190	445	5,895	470	295	-25	
March	23,776	1,473	4,104	429	19,672	1,044	
April	9,348	1,033	4,853	444	4,495	589	
May	8,359	1,009	5,173	514	3,186	495	
June	7,217	909	5,313	483	1,904	426	
July	9,597	825	6,484	589	3,113	236	120,124
Total	251,243	32,834	146,899	17,054			

Source: Osaka-shi, "Chōsenjin Rōdōsha Mondai", p. 16.
Note: The figures above refer only to Koreans passing between the ports of Pusan and Shimonoseki.

TABLE 12
Movement of Koreans between Korea and Japan (January 1922–July 1923)

Year	Crossing to Japan			Returning to Korea		
	Male	Female	Total	Male	Female	Total
A. 1922						
January	2,635	467	3,102	3,285	701	3,986
February	4,699	1,202	5,901	1,282	571	1,853
March	7,791	1,349	9,140	4,047	950	4,997
April	7,584	1,783	9,367	4,303	875	5,178
May	8,490	2,182	10,632	7,027	744	7,771
June	8,477	1,651	10,128	5,922	698	6,620
July	6,710	1,080	7,790	5,482	482	5,964
August	7,897	1,101	8,998	4,628	353	4,981
September	7,989	993	8,982	3,541	540	4,081
October	4,192	392	4,584	3,538	355	3,893
November	3,270	394	3,664	3,872	410	4,282
December	8,969	481	9,450	4,369	397	4,766
B. 1923						
January	9,328	545	9,873	5,417	413	5,820
February	6,190	445	6,635	5,895	470	6,363
March	23,776	1,473	25,249	4,104	429	4,533
April	9,348	1,033	10,381	4,853	444	5,197
May	8,359	1,009	9,368	5,173	514	5,687
June	7,217	909	8,126	5,313	484	5,797
July	9,597	825	10,422	6,484	589	7,073

Source: *Osaka-shi, Chōsenjin Rōdōsha Mondai*, pp. 11–12.
Note: The figures above refer to Koreans passing between the ports of Pusan and Shimonoseki.

occupational mobility among Korean workers.⁶³ Nevertheless, with the reservation that the figures presented below provide only a rough guide, it is possible to identify certain features of immigrant residence patterns. In Osaka, for example, which received the largest number of immigrants, the number of Koreans establishing households began to increase after 1921, although as late as 1924 only one in every seven immigrants was considered to be a householder (Table 13). Comparative figures for all Prefectures before 1921 are unavailable, making regional comparisons impossible. After 1921, however, it is possible to identify national patterns, and Table 14 gives figures for residence in the seven Prefectures with the largest Korean populations for the years 1921 and 1923 respectively.

As Tables 13 and 14 show, the number of Koreans establishing households was, on the whole, higher in those areas receiving the greatest number of immigrants. Nevertheless, a survey carried out by the Osaka Prefectural Government in 1923 revealed that among general labourers, who made up approximately 50% of the total Korean population in that area, fully 64% had resided there for less than one year, while only 13% had resided continuously in Osaka for a period of two or more years. The vast majority, 75%, were found to be living either in boarding houses or in rented accommodation, and fewer than 1% were accompanied by their families. The remainder were either unmarried or had left their families in Korea.⁶⁴

Immigrant Provinces of Origin

When the Province of origin of the Korean immigrant is considered, it is clearly evident, as is illustrated in Tables 15 and 16, that the majority were drawn from the southern third of Korea. In a survey conducted by the Osaka Prefectural Government in 1923, 1,000 immigrant workers living in those areas with the highest Korean populations were interviewed. The results revealed that approximately 80% had come from South Chŏlla Province, and that among those, just over 60% had come originally from Cheju Island. Over 77% of those interviewed listed as their previous occupation either farmer or agricultural worker, while only ten persons were found to have possessed factory skills before their arrival in Japan.⁶⁵

Contemporary observers were unanimous in citing the proximity between southern Korea and western Japan as the reason for the predominance of Koreans from that part of the peninsula among the immigrant community. Others were equally convinced that the immigration of Korean labourers to Japan was a natural movement since:

> ... migrations from underdeveloped to advanced nations are an extension of the same principle which encourages the migration of

TABLE 13
Korean Population of Osaka Prefecture by Length of Residence (1912-1924)

Year	Number of persons establishing households	Number of persons remaining in the same town or village for a minimum of ninety days	Other	Total	Ratio of those establishing households to total population
1912	50	104	94	246	1–5:
1914	14	161	41	216	1–15:
1916	106	428	228	762	1–7:
1918	115	2,104	1,078	3,297	1–28:
1920	313	3,171	1,010	4,494	1–14:
1921	548	5,544	1,329	7,421	1–14:
1922	1,925	7,595	3,717	13,337	1–7:
1923	3,298	11,320	9,017	23,635	1–7:
1924	3,748	12,664	10,456	26,848	1–7:

Source: General Affairs Department, *'Hanshin-Keihin'*, in Pak, Z.K.S.S, Vol. 1, pp. 398-399.

TABLE 14

Period of Residence of Koreans: Selected Prefectures (1921, 1923)

Prefecture	Number of persons establishing households		Number of persons remaining in the same town or village for a minimum of ninety days		Other		Total	
	1921	1923	1921	1923	1921	1923	1921	1923
Osaka	481	2,947	3,176	10,660	1,412	8,377	5,069 (1–11)	21,984 (1–7)
Hyōgo	660	1,267	917	2,781	638	1,454	2,215 (1–3.5)	5,502 (1–4.4)
Fukuoka	1,120	2,850	2,365	4,731	2,607	4,685	6,092 (1–5.4)	12,276 (1–4.4)
Tokyo	417	1,105	1,514	2,398	473	1,996	2,404 (1–5.7)	5,499 (1–5)
Yamaguchi	492	N.A.	785	N.A.	377	N.A.	1,654 (1–3.4)	N.A.
Hiroshima	401	1,365	596	1,300	552	554	1,549 (1–3.8)	3,219 (1–2.4)
Hokkaidō	341	N.A.	745	N.A.	536	N.A.	1,622 (1–4.8)	N.A.

Source: Figures for 1921 are taken from *Naimushō*, "Chōsenjin Kinkyō Gaiyō", in Pak, Z.K.S.S., Vol. 1, pp. 126–128. Figures for 1923 are taken from *Osaka-shi*, "Chōsenjin Rōdōsha Mondai", pp. 18–20.

Notes: (1) N.A. Not available.
(2) Figures in brackets represent the ratio of those setting up households to the total population.
(3) The national estimates for those setting up households were 1:5 and 1:9 for 1921 and 1923 respectively.

TABLE 15
Province of Origin of Koreans in Japan: Selected Prefectures (1923)

Province in Korea	Fukuoka	Hyōgo	Osaka	Aichi	Karafuto (Sakhalin) & Hokkaidō	Tokyo	Total For All Prefectures
South Chŏlla	2,374	500	2,352	382	235	452	18,050
North Chŏlla	1,697	171	546	53	112	158	3,332
South Kyŏngsang	3,032	3,806	6,425	1,362	1,134	1,077	28,628
North Kyŏngsang	1,766	624	2,013	581	444	526	11,404
South Ch'ungch'ŏng	692	76	439	168	133	151	2,220
North Ch'ungch'ŏng	288	36	132	45	72	152	1,108
Kyŏnggi	166	130	530	198	303	325	2,395
Kangwŏn	364	41	217	40	397	103	1,532
Hwanghae	266	18	67	17	131	128	726
South P'yŏngan	180	29	55	15	286	159	913
North P'yŏngan	168	6	29	10	246	120	672
South Hamgyŏng	35	64	144	9	706	157	1,261
North Hamgyŏng	21	1	35	2	354	101	574
Total	11,049	5,502	21,984	2,882	4,554	3,609	78,815

Source: *Osaka-shi*, "*Chōsenjin Rōdōsha Mondai*", pp. 69–71.

Note: The figure of 72,815 for the total population is significantly lower than the actual number for two reasons. First, a number of prefectures supporting significant Korean immigrant populations, notably Gifu, Nagano, Gumma and Kanagawa, were unable to submit the results of their surveys in time for them to be published in this report. This was in all likelihood due to the disruption of public services in many areas following the earthquake of September 1923. In addition, this chart does not take into account the large numbers of Koreans who died during the earthquake or fled the area soon after. Nevertheless, for the purpose of identifying the province of origin of the Korean immigrants during this period, the chart is the most reliable one available.

TABLE 16
Places of Origin of Koreans Residing in Japan: May 1924

Province	Students			Wage Labourers			Others			Total
	Male	Female	Total	Male	Female	Total	Male	Female	Total	
Kyŏnggi	211	37	248	1,895	349	2,244	334	122	456	2,948
S. Ch'ungch'ŏng	77	9	86	1,791	198	1,989	154	79	233	2,308
N. Ch'ungch'ŏng	60	7	67	975	98	1,073	82	41	123	1,263
S. Hamgyŏng	104	10	114	1,144	105	1,249	183	47	230	1,593
N. Hamgyŏng	40	14	54	306	32	338	29	19	48	440
S. Chŏlla	372	103	475	16,721	2,297	19,018	3,120	864	3,984	23,567
N. Chŏlla	88	8	96	2,079	244	2,323	307	141	448	2,867
S. Kyŏngsang	625	201	826	14,998	3,943	18,941	2,563	2,665	5,228	24,995
N. Kyŏngsang	232	47	279	12,984	965	13,949	761	673	1,434	15,662
S. P'yŏngan	36	18	54	650	24	674	107	106	213	941
N. P'yŏngan	75	9	84	403	73	476	42	31	73	633
Hwanghae	54	20	74	471	81	552	82	67	149	775
Kwangwŏn	35	8	43	1,158	45	1,203	120	49	169	1,415
Keijō (Seoul)	0	0	0	2	1	3	4	1	5	8
Unknown	0	0	0	6	0	6	9,707	4	9,711	9,717
Total	2,009	491	2,500	55,575	8,455	64,030	17,595	4,909	22,504	89,132

Source: *Naimushō, Shakai Kyoku Dai-ichi bu* (Home Ministry, Social Affairs Bureau, First Section) '*Chōsenjin Rōdōsha ni Kansuru Jōkyō*' ('The Condition of Korean Workers'), 1924, in Pak, Z.K.S.S., Vol. 1, pp. 455-456. (Cited hereafter as *Naimushō, Shakai Kyoku* – 1924.)

agricultural workers to cities and towns. Therefore, in our country, which has the highest wages and standard of living in Asia, the coming of Korean and Chinese migrant workers is in no way surprising.[66]

While geographical proximity and an ease of communication undoubtedly accelerated the migration to Japan, in themselves these factors do not provide an adequate answer to why such a massive movement off the land took place in southern Korea. If geography was the determining factor there still remains the question of why, for example, nearly 20% of all Korean immigrants living in the Chientao region of Manchuria in 1922 had come from the southern extremity of the Korean peninsula.[67] The second explanation is accurate enough, but does not adequately explain the interaction of the conditions in Korea which acted as the 'push factor' and the fluctuations of an extremely unstable labour market in Japan (the 'pull factor'). As we have already seen, the principal causes for the Korean migration to Japan were twofold: (a) colonial policies which led to the rapid growth of a large impoverished and landless peasant class in southern Korea, and a failure to develop an industrial base which could have absorbed a considerable proportion of the excess rural labour created by those policies; and (b) the instability of an essentially *dekasegi* type of labour market in Japan which could not meet the demands of industry during the war, and compelled entrepreneurs to compensate for labour shortages by recruiting relatively cheap labour from Korea. Of these two factors, the former, or 'push factor,' was the more constant of the two, and neither deteriorating employment opportunities brought on by the postwar depression, nor attempts by the Government to regulate the volume of immigration significantly curbed the movement of Korean workers to Japan.

Educational and other Welfare Facilities for Koreans in Japan

The sense of isolation experienced by Korean immigrants was compounded by extremely high rates of illiteracy and by the fact that very few Koreans had even a basic understanding of the Japanese language. According to a survey conducted in Osaka Prefecture in 1923, more than half the resident Korean population was illiterate. Of just over 18,000 persons interviewed (of whom 16,000 were manual workers) more than 15,000 were either illiterate or had received no more than the equivalent of three years' education at a lower elementary level. Moreover, more than 50% of the men and 80% of the women surveyed had not even a basic understanding of the Japanese language.[68]

Government reports frequently cited the language problem both as an obstacle to assimilation and as further evidence of cultural backwardness among Koreans.[69] The language barrier was also regarded as a major source of friction between Japanese and Korean workers, particularly in hazardous work such as coal mining, where an inability to communicate readily with one's workmates could increase the risk of accident or injury.[70] The management at *Hokutan*, for example, found it preferable to employ Koreans in groups composed entirely of Koreans and to give them a 'relatively safe place to work' since Japanese miners did not like working alongside them. By a 'relatively safe place to work' the management in this case meant 'restricting their tasks to tunnelling or coal-cutting'.[71] The situation in other industries was essentially the same, and according to a report produced by the Central Employment Exchange:

> Although there are numerous occasions when co-operative work is necessary in cotton spinning, Korean girls work with their friends and not with Japanese female workers. Even though they are superficially no different from Japanese girls, generally speaking their workplaces are separate.[72]

A survey in Osaka found that, 'in general Japanese workers treat Korean workers almost always as if they have no value whatsoever as workers', and concluded that:

> While they do not go out of their way to antagonize Japanese workers, when they work alongside Japanese workers, they do not perform efficiently. It is therefore better for them to be set work with others of their own kind.[73]

Given the concern voiced by Government officials and employers over the difficulties posed by the language barrier for both labour management and assimilation, remarkably little in the way of special educational facilities for Korean workers was provided. Undoubtedly the impermanence of the Korean community hindered such developments, but even in Osaka, where the immigrant community was somewhat more stable, the Government was forced to concede that educational facilities were entirely inadequate.[74] This failure to provide even basic training reinforces the impression that employers did not consider the Korean worker as other than a temporary substitute for proper Japanese workers.

As of 1924, despite evident interest on the part of many Korean workers, no provisions had been made at either Prefectural or national level to establish educational facilities for immigrant workers.[75] According to a report compiled by the Government-General in 1924 there were an estimated fifty-six night school programmes being operated in the Osaka area on a volunteer basis by Japanese teachers and other interested parties. The first local government authority to establish educational facilities for Koreans was the city of Kōbe where, late in 1922, under a grant furnished by the city government, two schools added Korean sections to their night school programmes. Funds were made available to employ two teachers (one Japanese and one Korean), and instruction was offered in Japanese, mathematics, morals, history, geography, and Chinese writing. The majority of the students were between fifteen and thirty years of age, and were working chiefly as day labourers or factory operatives.[76] Although the Government-General was not directly involved in the creation or operation of these night schools, its attitude toward the education of Koreans in Japan reflected its own policies in Korea and was expressed in the following way by the compiler of the 1924 report:

> When, with the sympathetic co-operation of Japanese educators, educational programmes to aid Koreans who are concentrated in various parts of our country are introduced under proper supervision, we believe that their efficacy should not be judged only on the basis of purely educational benefits but by whether they lend themselves to the achievement of the greater goal of *Naisen Yūwa* (Conciliation of Japan and Korea).[77]

With the exception of labour clubs, trade unions, and mutual aid associations organized by Korean students and workers themselves, very few welfare or employment exchange facilities for Koreans existed before 1925. Those which did were quasi-governmental agencies operating under and sometimes funded directly by the Home Ministry. A prototype of this sort of organization was the *Tōyō Kyōkai* (Oriental Institute), which was established in 1897 as a semi-official research centre. Its initial objectives were the promotion of mutual welfare and the spread of 'civilization' in Asia through the careful study of conditions in Taiwan, Manchuria and Korea. Following the annexation of Korea this organization shifted its emphasis to the advancement of *dōka* and *yūwa* among the peoples of Japan and Korea, and the promotion of a 'fuller appreciation of the annexation among the Korean people'.[78] As of 1920, the *Tōyō Kyōkai* had a dues-paying membership of approximately 3,500 and was operating with capital in excess of 500,000 yen. Its President was Gotō Shimpei while the Vice-President was Mizuno Rentarō – the Civil Governor of Korea. According to the Home Ministry, however, this organization exercised very little influence over Koreans in Japan, since it failed to provide any welfare facilities or other types of assistance to either labourers or students.[79]

The most important of the *yūwa* organizations was the *Sōaikai* (Mutual Love Association), the Tokyo headquarters of which was established in December 1921. Although the stated intention of the *Sōaikai* was the improvement of relations between Japanese and Koreans through the promotion of *dōka*, official support for this organization was motivated by the need to counter the appeal of radical ideologies among

Korean workers and students.[80] Financial assistance was provided from a variety of official sources, and by 1924 the *Sōaikai* had opened branches in six Prefectures as well as at Pusan in Korea. Prominent among its Japanese advisers were Maruyama Tsurukichi and Akaike Atsushi, both of whom had served as Directors-General of the Police Bureau in Korea and would later hold the post of Superintendent of the Metropolitan Police Bureau in Tokyo.[81]

The *Sōaikai* provided a variety of facilities for Korean workers including temporary hostel accommodation, subsidized medical care, language classes, and an employment exchange for day labourers. The *Sōaikai* also mediated in housing or labour disputes involving Koreans, and operated an information service which advised Koreans of conditions in Japan and disseminated information about Korean life to the general public in Japan.[82] There is very little reliable information concerning the effectiveness of these *Sōaikai*-sponsored welfare programmes, but by the latter half of the 1920s the entire organization had lost much of its social character and was regarded as an instrument of police control. During the final year of its existence the *Sōaikai* assisted the police in the disruption of Korean trade union activities, and co-operated with the Government-General in processing immigrants at its Pusan offices.[83]

A number of privately-operated welfare agencies were also established during the early 1920s. These tended to work along the same lines as the *Sōaikai* and were usually funded in part by the Home Ministry which regarded them as a useful instrument for the promotion of *yūwa* and *dōka*. Commenting on the shortage of such agencies, the Central Employment Exchange advised that this area required further investigation, but cautioned that the effectiveness of welfare programmes for Koreans was tempered by a tendency among those who received assistance to become excessively dependent on them.[84]

Although there were no legal restraints on the use of employment exchanges by Korean workers, the number applying for work through these facilities was not very large. In 1923, for example, the number of Koreans using public employment exchanges was only about 10,000, or fewer than 2% of the total number of persons using these facilities. Regional statistics are not available, but it is likely that the figures for Tokyo and Osaka-Kōbe were somewhat higher than the national average.[85] According to the Central Employment Exchange (referring here only to the situation in Tokyo), with the exception of day labourer exchanges, Korean workers failed to take advantage of this service due to: (a) language difficulties, (b) a lack of requisite skills, and, (c) the low regard in which Korean workers were held by employers. The same report found that Koreans also failed to find employment through private employment exchanges, and that the vast majority of immigrant workers continued to rely on the 'good offices' of labour contractors and labour bosses, particularly in the construction industry.[86]

The Korean Immigrant in Japan, 1920–1923

The abolition of restrictions on the entry of Koreans into Japan in December 1922 ushered in a period during which the size of the Korean community steadily expanded. As can be seen in Table 17, the number of Koreans in Japan increased from just under 35,000 at the end of 1920 to over 80,000 at the end of 1922 and rose a further 50% during the first seven months of 1923.

This coincides roughly with the period during which the Japanese economy suffered from a brief slump. The postwar recession affected different industries to varying degrees, but the decade after 1920 was nevertheless one of substantial overall growth. Even coal production, which suffered a proportionally greater decline in demand than many other industries, increased slightly between 1919 and 1929.[87] At the same time, there is ample evidence to suggest that wartime expansion in virtually all industries had accelerated the development of a more permanent class of urban industrial workers, whose ties with their villages were weaker than had previously been the case, and who found it more difficult to return to agriculture during periods of economic hardship.[88] As a result, the failure of many small and medium-sized factories after the war led to growing unemployment in the cities.[89] Commenting on the effects of the recession on Korean labourers, who were concentrated at the bottom end of the labour market, a Justice Ministry official noted:

> Due to the fluctuations which affected Japan's economy from the spring of 1920 in the Osaka-Kōbe area there were numerous instances of Koreans being dismissed from their jobs. After that there was a rise in unemployment among Koreans, and year by year it has become increasingly difficult for them to find work.[90]

A second feature of immigrant employment in the postwar period was the almost complete exclusion of Korean workers from large and medium-sized enterprises. The only exceptions to this were textiles, mining and glass manufacturing where it was believed that Koreans were well suited to the 'nature of the work' involved.[91] A report compiled by the Osaka city office regarded the failure of Koreans to find employment in large factories as a consequence of the introduction of more sophisticated production techniques for which Koreans were unsuited, and added that:

> . . . even if it were a period of severe labour shortage, there would be little scope for the employment of Korean workers because their basic quality is so poor.[92]

The same report noted that, despite the low wages they were prepared to accept, Koreans were also finding it difficult to secure steady employ-

TABLE 17
Koreans Residing in Japan (1917–July 1923)

Year	Number Crossing to Japan		Number Returning to Korea		Annual Increase		Total Population
	Male	Female	Male	Female	Male	Female	
1917	11,216	2,796	3,428	499	7,788	2,287	10,085
1918	11,513	177	1,789	62	9,724	115	19,924
1919	19,110	1,858	11,688	1,051	7,422	807	28,153
1920	24,625	2,872	18,606	2,341	6,019	531	34,703
1921	32,301	5,817	22,853	2,863	8,448	3,134	47,285
1922	78,663	13,075	51,296	7,076	27,367	5,999	80,651
					Monthly Increase		
1923 January	9,328	545	5,417	413	3,911	132	
February	6,190	445	5,895	470	295	−25	
March	23,776	1,473	4,104	429	19,672	1,044	
April	9,348	1,033	4,853	444	4,495	589	
May	8,359	1,009	5,173	514	3,186	495	
June	7,217	909	5,313	483	1,904	426	
July	9,597	825	6,484	589	3,113	236	
7 month Total	73,815	6,329	37,239	3,342			
Total	251,243	32,834	146,899	17,054			120,124

Source: Osaka-shi, "Chōsenjin Rōdōsha Mondai", p. 16.

ment in small factories, and concluded that the low position occupied by immigrant workers in the labour market was due primarily to their high mobility, a lack of skills, and a preference for dull monotonous labour. As a result, Korean labour did not undermine the position of Japanese workers, who tended to avoid low-status occupations like construction work and coolie-type labouring in which large numbers of Koreans could be found.[93]

While the author of this report conceded that competition between Japanese and Korean workers at the lower end of the labour market could become a potential source of friction, he dismissed this threat as largely an imaginary one since 'Korean workers are generally employed as unskilled labour while their Japanese counterparts are employed as skilled workers.' Moreover, he argued that, even where the two are used together, competition was limited since 'Korean workers are employed under the direction of the lowest grade of Japanese workers and coolies.'[94]

Whereas the overall importance of Korean workers in small and medium-sized manufacturing firms was not great (Table 18), in specific factories the percentage of Koreans was quite high. This was most likely to occur in textiles, where the practice of employing a large number of factory girls recruited from the same locale in Korea by a single factory or firm had been common since the First World War.[95] Beyond the Kansai area, however, with the possible exceptions of Wakayama and Aichi Prefectures where the use of Korean girls in textile mills was also quite common, it was unusual to find manufacturing firms employing significant numbers of Koreans.

Wages and Efficiency

Wages and income levels for Korean workers fluctuated markedly depending upon the type of work, the time of year, and even the region, making it impossible to produce absolutely reliable figures which would reflect national trends. This task is made all the more difficult by the fact that for the period before 1924 there exists only one set of national figures comparing wage levels between Japanese and immigrant workers. The figures presented in Table 19 are therefore useful only as an approximation of the actual situation. As they illustrate, the wages paid to Korean workers were significantly lower than those paid to their Japanese counterparts. Depending upon the industry, wage differentials ranged from 11% for laundry workers to over 70% for dye workers and knitwear workers, while the average for all occupations listed was approximately 33%.

Contemporary observers were agreed that the principal assets offered by Korean workers were their willingness to accept substantially lower

TABLE 18

Japanese and Korean Factory Workers: Manufacturing Industries, Osaka (1924)

Industry	Japanese			Korean		
	Male	Female	Total	Male	Female	Total
Dyeing	31,306	85,089	116,395	1,768	1,931	3,699
Chemicals	24,368	9,108	33,476	3,585	70	3,655
Engineering	50,493	4,376	54,869	2,883	105	2,988
Electrical	2,220	58	2,278	88	—	88
Food Stuffs	4,110	1,126	5,236	47	—	47
Timber, Leather Printing	22,624	5,370	27,994	853	27	880
Total	135,121	105,127	240,248	9,224	2,133	11,357

Source: *Osaka-shi – Shakai-bu Chōsa Ka* (Osaka City Social Affairs Department Survey Section), *Osaka Rōdō Nenpō* (Osaka Labour Bulletin), 1924, Vol. 2, pp. 17–21. Cited in Iwamura, op.cit., p. 34.

Note: The survey upon which the above figures were based was restricted to those factories employing a minimum of fifteen persons and therefore did not include the hundreds of smaller firms which accounted for a considerable proportion of the Japanese (and Korean) workforce.

TABLE 19

Comparative Daily Wages for Korean and Japanese Workers: Selected Industries (1923)

Occupation	Korean			Japanese			Differential B–A as proportion of A
	Maximum	Minimum	Average (A)	Maximum	Minimum	Average (B)	
Agricultural Worker (Male)	1.70	1.20	1.60	2.20	2.00	2.00	25%
Agricultural Worker (Female)	.90	.85	.85	1.20	1.20	1.20	41.1%
Laundry Worker	1.90	1.00	1.80	2.70	1.00	2.00	11%
Dye Worker	1.90	.80	1.20	2.80	.90	2.10	75%
Knitwear Worker	1.90	1.00	1.30	3.00	1.50	2.20	70%
Cotton Spinning	2.00	.90	1.20	2.80	1.00	1.70	41.65%
Glass Worker	3.00	.90	1.20	3.50	1.10	1.60	33.3%
Stevedore	2.50	1.70	2.00	3.00	2.00	2.50	25%
Coolie	1.70	1.00	1.70	2.00	1.80	1.90	12%
Navvy	2.50	1.70	2.00	2.80	2.00	2.50	25%
Miner	2.30	1.60	2.10	3.00	1.80	2.50	19%
Average	2.02	1.15	1.50	2.63	1.75	2.01	33.4%

Source: *Osaka-shi, 'Chōsenjin Rōdōsha Mondai'*, pp. 78–79.
Note: All figures in Yen.

wages and working conditions than their Japanese counterparts. This was viewed by some employers as an inevitable consequence of the poor quality of Korean workers since:

> Compared with Japanese workers they are inferior in terms of physical constitution and vigour. Moreover, because they lack the self-discipline to take the initiative and better themselves, their efficiency does not improve. Their manner of working is exceedingly slow . . . They blatantly idle about during working hours and, unlike Japanese navvies, have no sense of duty or gratitude toward the foreman. Even if, in order to make them work, they are hounded, scolded . . ., they are always looking for a chance to waste time.[96]

Among the complaints most frequently voiced by Japanese officials and journalists alike were that Korean workers were generally inefficient, indolent, and irresponsible toward both their work and their workmates. Koreans were also believed to be lacking in a sense of loyalty toward their friends, completely unreliable when it came to remaining at a specific job for an extended period of time, apt to squander their wages on drink and gambling, prone to 'indulging in violent behaviour', and willing to resort to illegal means in a scramble 'for their own petty gains'.[97] These were frequently presented as inherent character deficiencies common to all Koreans, and contributed greatly to the development of negative stereotypes.[98] An editorial in the *Osaka Asahi Shimbun*, for example, commenting on the friction which sometimes arose between Japanese and Korean workers, had the following to say:

> It appears that differences in language and customs as well as their easily-angered natures are a frequent cause of incidents. Moreover, they have a strong sense of revenge and will quickly band together over even trivial matters and attempt to retaliate. It therefore comes about that petty incidents sometimes develop into major confrontations.[99]

Similar sentiments were expressed in a report compiled by the Police Affairs Bureau in 1922 which concluded:

> Korean workers lack a sense of saving their money and spend the greater part of their wages on drinking and amusing themselves. Although they sometimes indulge in either boasting or fighting, unlike Korean students there are very few who go so far as to avoid associating with Japanese . . . Because by nature they are very emotional, Koreans occasionally indulge in violent actions.[100]

The fact that Korean workers were regularly exploited and subjected to brutal treatment by labour bosses and foremen, however, was rarely considered in either official reports or newspaper articles. The management at *Hokutan* conceded that supervisors and foremen were occasionally 'unkind' to Koreans due to a lack of sympathy,[101] while an article in the *Otaru Shimbun* gave as one reason for the high turnover rate among Korean miners the fact that foremen and supervisors 'do not fully understand Koreans and fail to treat them with kindness'.[102] Most official reports, however, attributed high rates of turnover and low levels of efficiency among Korean workers to the decay of Korean culture and the basic idleness and 'aimless nature' of the Korean people.[103] Newspapers frequently suggested that there was only limited scope for the employment of Koreans in areas requiring intelligence:

> There are some who say that Koreans are not suited for stevedoring, which requires some intelligence, but should continue to be used in types of work which require only physical strength.[104]

Nevertheless, there is evidence to suggest that Korean workers were as efficient as their Japanese counterparts in most types of work, and in some cases superior to them. A report on Korean (female) textile workers compiled by the Central Employment Exchange in Tokyo concluded that, in the factories surveyed, Korean operatives had better overall attendance records, and that when given proper training they were equal in skill to Japanese female workers.[105] Similar conclusions were reached by researchers in Osaka,[106] while *Hokutan*, which was a principal employer of Koreans throughout this period, recorded in its official history:

> Their efficiency at work depends largely on the quality of the supervision and leadership exercised over them. And it is not possible, as many Japanese believe, to ascribe their work record to laziness . . . Even though there are those whose working efficiency comes nowhere near that of an experienced Japanese miner, if properly led there are many Koreans who work more regularly and more diligently than do Japanese.[107]

A somewhat later report produced by the Fukuoka Regional Employment Exchange went even further, saying that 'Unattached Korean miners are preferable to their Japanese counterparts because they are more obedient and have higher rates of efficiency,' and 'Koreans are generally possessed of great strength, and, regardless of weather conditions, are extremely tenacious in their work.'[108] Turnover rates for Korean factory workers, however, appear to have been significantly higher than those for Japanese. One factor which almost certainly contributed to inefficiency and comparatively higher turnover rates among Korean workers was that, in addition to lower wages and poorer working conditions than those offered to Japanese, Koreans appear to have been customarily assigned the most onerous and dangerous tasks. Because this aspect of immigrant life was largely ignored by contemporary investigations, there are no statistics available concerning this issue before 1924. There is, however, evidence from a slightly later date that, particularly in mining, Koreans were disproportionately represented in the most unhealthy and hazardous types of work. In 1925, for example, at the Mitsubishi Shinnyū mine in north Kyūshū, Koreans comprised more than 30% of a total work force of just under 5,000 miners. Of the approximately 1,600 Korean miners employed, more than 90% were used as underground workers. Compared with a ratio of 1 to 2.3 for surface and underground workers among Japanese miners at the Shinnyū mine, the corresponding figure for Koreans was 1 to 14.[109] According to the I.L.O., compared with surface workers, underground workers were three times as likely to be injured or killed in mining accidents.[110] This was largely confirmed by the records of the Shinnyū mine which revealed that in 1927 the injury rate among Korean miners was 50% higher than that for Japanese miners.[111]

Immigrant Living and Working Conditions

Among contemporary observers the most commonly used adjectives to describe the livelihood of the Korean worker were 'squalid' and 'unstable'. As the following extract from a Home Ministry report illustrates, there was also a marked tendency to discount both individual differences within the immigrant community as well as the importance of the immediate social and physical environment in shaping social behaviour. Instead, observers relied on generalizations which emphasized the peculiar cultural attributes of the Korean, and set him apart from mainstream society in Japan:

> In customs, Koreans are basically different from Japanese, and, because their everyday lives are extremely unclean and disorganized, it is only natural that they are rejected by people living nearby. Koreans are generally narrow-minded, extremely suspicious and jealous, and are apt to misunderstand things. Moreover, there is a tendency among Japanese people to treat them as members of an inferior race.[112]

Although sporadic outbreaks of violence against Koreans (usually committed by labour contractors or company guards) were recorded by the police, less dramatic but more frequent incidents of discrimination were also evident in, for example, the unwillingness of Japanese landlords to rent property to Koreans. Koreans had different living habits, cooked different foods, were only rarely able to speak or understand Japanese, tended to be regarded as unreliable tenants and as both a source of crime and disease.[113] As a result, Koreans who did manage to find rented accommodation were commonly shunned by their neighbours or found themselves embroiled in housing disputes with either their neighbours or their landlords. Others, unsuccessful in finding any type of accommodation, were reduced to sleeping rough, or lived in abandoned tenements, river barges, or in flimsy huts – all of which failed to satisfy even minimum standards of housing or sanitation.[114] A report on the living conditions of Korean workers in the Osaka area summarized the situation in the following way:

> Korean workers experience great difficulty in finding accommodation. Both in terms of status and economics they inevitably end up at the bottom end of the scale when it comes to housing. Primarily they stay in cheap boarding houses run by Japanese, and very few succeed in renting houses. When they do, other Koreans tend to congregate there. The houses they succeed in renting, even in the remotest areas, tend to be in the most inconvenient locations where there is little normal demand. Others without housing construct shacks of wood and corrugated iron and live there.[115]

Japanese landlords commonly complained that Koreans were unreliable tenants, were often in arrears with their rent, failed to maintain the houses they rented, were generally noisy and would sublet houses to as many as thirty other persons thus generating considerable ill feeling among their Japanese neighbours. They also accused Koreans of carrying disease and vermin, and commonly refused to rent houses to them.[116] The contravention of established norms for housing, personal hygiene, and social behaviour also attracted the attention of journalists. This resulted in the publication of numerous articles and exposes such as the following which appeared in the Ōsaka Asahi Shimbun. Commenting on the appearance of a Korean settlement in the city of Moji, the writer concluded:

> In the conduct of the daily lives of these extremely backward and dirty Koreans, it is not surprising to find that it creates among the Japanese who live nearby a kind of discomfort and feelings of abhorrence. We are talking about groups of people lacking in any sense of hygiene, and there are many among them who will perpetually wear one set of Korean-style clothes until they literally shine with grime. Because ten or more of them live crowded together in a single eight-mat room using their cooking utensils and bedding even after they have become dirty, there is ample cause to fear the outbreak of epidemics during hot weather.[117]

As we have seen, most of these immigrants were unaccompanied young men, many of whom were illiterate in both Japanese and Korean, possessed no marketable skills and may never have seen a factory or tramcar before their arrival in Japan. Consequently employment opportunities for immigrants were confined to the very bottom stratum of the labour market, and Koreans took on the dirty, degrading and most physically taxing jobs – usually working for less pay and under poorer conditions than all but the most destitute Japanese would accept. Most led a precarious existence on the fringes of industry as poorly paid day labourers, and this affected not only their income, but also the areas in which they lived, the types of accommodation they lived in, their relations with the Japanese community and, of course, their status and function in society.

The erratic nature of their work offered no assurance that they would have work from one day to the next. Normally under contract by the day, the day labourer's income was dependent entirely upon the vagaries of the weather and the whims of labour contractors. Wages were often paid irregularly, and wage systems could be changed arbitrarily by employers or labour contractors.[118] Ignored for all practical purposes by existing labour laws, the Korean day labourer was completely reliant on the good will of his labour boss. There was no legal restraint on what labour bosses could charge for their services, nor on the methods which they adopted to control their subordinates. Consequently, some were paternalistic while others employed physical coercion to manage their workers, and brutality was far from uncommon.[119] Day labourers seldom knew where or for how long they would be working, when or how much they would be paid, and had no alternative but to accept these conditions or not to work at all. Under such conditions it was inevitable that there would be little continuity or regularity in the lives of most Korean workers. Lacking an established routine, such workers were unable to establish permanent relationships with either their workmates or with the members of the community in which they worked. The living conditions of these workers were therefore determined almost entirely by the *dekasegi* labour system, a system which isolated them from the host society not only in the work they did but also in the way they lived.

In Osaka, where by 1923 the largest immigrant community was located, the majority of Korean workers lived in tenements, cheap boarding houses, or in the homes of labour bosses. As in other major cities like Tokyo, Kōbe, and Yokohama, Koreans tended to live in the outlying towns and villages on the periphery of Osaka, and in those areas within the city where small and medium-sized factories were located.[120] A survey carried out in mid-1923 revealed the existence of more than 300 Korean-operated boarding houses which catered exclusively to Koreans.[121] This early survey sheds very little light on conditions within these boarding houses though many were in fact operated by Korean labour bosses or their wives as secondary sources of income.[122]

According to the same report, labour boss/boarding house operators were, as a group, the most prosperous within the immigrant community.[123] Standards of sanitation, food and accommodation were unregulated and generally inadequate, and in a survey of twenty Korean boarding houses in Osaka carried out in 1923, 579 individuals were found to be sharing a total of 267 mats – an average of just over two persons to a six foot by three foot mat. In some of those investigated, the overcrowding was so severe that people were found to be sleeping in clothes cupboards and kitchens.[124]

The conditions under which immigrant workers lived in Tokyo were entirely comparable with those in Osaka and other cities throughout Japan. The number of Koreans who were employed as regular workers in factories was quite small, the overwhelming majority being casual labourers who worked predominantly in the construction trades.[125] Koreans were most commonly found to be living in *hamba* operated by labour bosses in areas along the periphery of the city, or in cheap boarding houses within the city. Similarly, many of the boarding houses which catered to Korean day and casual labourers were operated by Korean labour contractors and labour bosses. According to a 1924 survey carried out by the Central Employment Exchange, most of the 358 Korean households in the Tokyo area were in fact lodging houses run by labour contractors.[126] In the case of construction workers employed on sites outside the city, normal practice was either to rent houses locally or to build temporary camps under the supervision of a labour boss. The size of such work crews varied considerably, but most existed only for the duration of a specific job. As a result, there was little continuity in membership from job to job, and many work crews were organized in the morning only to be dissolved the same night.[127]

Although the high mobility of most Koreans militated against the formation of ghettos, there was concern that the 'Korean tendency to live crowded together' might lead to the creation of *buraku* (settlements) similar to those in which the former outcastes lived.[128] One of the earliest of these settlements was established in Nishi-Nari County near Osaka in 1922 when a number of Koreans moved into an abandoned housing project. By mid-1924 thirteen households had been established in the area, and most of the adults were employed at local construction sites or small factories. The compilers of a Government-General report on immigrant living conditions regarded anti-social behaviour as endemic in this community and concluded that:

> . . . Korean vagrants are a frequent sight, while gambling and quarrelling are quite common. As far as hygiene is concerned, from the viewpoint of public morals, there are not a few regrettable items. Consequently, they are shunned by the Japanese in the area and live in isolation.[129]

Assessing the living conditions of Korean workers in company dormitories is difficult in two respects. First, no national figures relating to this issue are available, and considerable variations may well have existed both between industries and by region. Second, very few large firms employed Koreans as *shokkō* (factory operatives), preferring to use them as temporary workers for whom company housing was not normally provided.[130] Moreover, in the small and medium-sized factories where Koreans were used more extensively, dormitories or other forms of subsidized housing were seldom provided. Consequently, as in the case of general labourers, construction workers, coolies, and stevedores, Korean factory workers generally lived in boarding houses or in tenements operated by labour contractors and bosses.[131] With few exceptions, a similar situation existed in the mining industry. In north Kyūshū, for example, a later (1929) report compiled by the Fukuoka Regional Employment Exchange confirmed that the great majority of Korean miners lived in work camps operated by labour bosses.[132] Since a principal function as well as an important source of income for labour bosses had traditionally been the allocation of housing and other services, profiteering at the expense of Korean miners would have been at least as widespread as it was among Japanese miners. The principal exception to this was in the mines operated by *Hokutan*. There Koreans were '. . . housed in dormitories under the direct supervision of a full-time official who was responsible for supervising every aspect of their daily lives'.[133] Unlike other companies, *Hokutan* also maintained that there existed no differentials in either the basic wage rate paid to Korean and Japanese employees, or in the provision of work-related benefits. The company history did, however, make clear that it was the low living and cultural standards of Koreans which enabled them to live well within their means, and added that:

> . . . because a common characteristic of Korean miners is that they are lacking in a sense of safety and hygiene, accidents and disease arising both at and away from work are common among them.[134]

It is clear that the erratic nature of their work coupled with the equally insecure conditions under which the immigrant workers lived tended to isolate them from the host community. Those working in contract labour crews often had little idea of where they were located, and this unfamiliarity with the physical environment was paralleled by a distinct sense of social isolation. Many Japanese perceived the immigrant as socially and culturally separate and inferior. Such attitudes tended to focus on different issues at different times, but, in general, an acceptance of dirty degrading work which most Japanese found distasteful, and a lifestyle which ignored many social norms served to foster or reinforce more generalized anti-Korean stereotypes which had arisen during the period immediately before the annexation.

In general, hostility toward Koreans tended to spring from two different sources, both of which created the impression that Koreans were an alien and basically unassimilable element in society. The first concentrated upon the indolence, low moral character and lack of a sense of hygiene among the immigrants, and the second, restricted to the period after 1919, tended to associate Koreans with foreign ideologies which threatened the welfare of the state. This was clearly expressed by researchers in Osaka who concluded that:

> Although more than ten years have now elapsed since the annexation, manners, customs, and language remain different, and the fact cannot be avoided that throughout society – day and night – old engrained prejudices on both sides are difficult to reconcile. In particular, at times like the present, when the *Suihei Undō* (Levellers Movement) has arisen and is attracting widespread attention, when a large number of lower class Korean workers who possess few abilities, and whose assimilation is even more difficult, arrive in Japan and become even more anti-social, it is inevitable that they will create a new and dangerous problem. They will inevitably feel a sense of isolation, and become a breeding ground for unhealthy thoughts.[135]

While it is impossible to ascertain how widespread these official anxieties were, there can be little doubt that officially sanctioned beliefs which characterized Koreans as racially and culturally inferior played a vital role in shaping popular attitudes. As is illustrated in the following extract, it was incidents and events which tended to conform to official views that created the greatest impact on the public.

> It should not be doubted that there exist among many Japanese feelings of genuine friendship for Koreans. Although a tendency to shun Koreans can be found in the attitude of many Japanese at the present time, we cannot make the mistake of applying this to all Japanese. Nevertheless, it is very easy to collect opinions which exaggerate feelings of hostility toward Koreans because data which tends toward antipathy makes a greater impression on the general public than those which suggest friendship.[136]

Notes:
1. International Labour Office, *Industrial Labour in Japan*, Geneva, 1933, pp. 21–24. (Cited hereafter as *I.L.O. report, 1933*.)
2. William W. Lockwood, op.cit., pp. 37–40. Also see Hideo Aoyama and Toru Nishikawa, 'Business Fluctuations In The Japanese Economy During The Inter-War Period', *Kyoto University Economic Review*, Vol. 28, No. 1, 1958, pp. 20–21.
3. R. M. V. Collick, *Labour and Trades Unionism in the Japanese Coal Mining Industry, 1850–1935*, Unpublished Doctoral Dissertation, Oxford University, 1970, pp. 27(a), 31.
4. William W. Lockwood, op.cit., pp. 226, 470, 492–497. Also see Iwao Ayusawa, *A History of Labor in Modern Japan*, East-West Center Press, Honolulu, 1966, pp. 195–196.
5. Koji Taira, 'The Characteristics of Japanese Labor Markets', *Economic Development and Social Change*, Vol. 10, No. 2, 1962, p. 153. Also see Takejiro Shindo, *Labor In The Japanese Cotton Industry*, Pan-Pacific Press, Tokyo, 1961, pp. 3–5.
6. Taira, op.cit., p. 153. In Japan, industrial workers whose ties with their native agricultural villages have not been severed, and who migrate, either seasonally or for longer periods of time, to towns and cities in search of work are usually referred to as *dekasegi rōdōsha* (migrant workers).
7. Ibid. Also see Shunzō Yoshisaka, 'Labour Recruiting in Japan and its Control', *International Labour Review*, Vol. 12, No. 4, Geneva, 1925, p. 486.
8. William W. Lockwood, op.cit., p. 30.
9. *I.L.O. report, 1933*, p. 159. Also see Takejiro Shindo, op.cit., pp. 42–46, and Shunzō Yoshisaka, op.cit., p. 485.
10. Shunzō Yoshisaka, op.cit., pp. 488–489.
11. Ibid., p. 489. Also see Koji Taira, op.cit., p. 154.
12. William W. Lockwood, op.cit., p. 30.
13. Ibid., p. 556. Also see Shunzō Yoshisaka, op.cit., p. 488.
14. *I.L.O. report, 1933*, p. 161. Also see Shunzō Yoshisaka, op.cit., pp. 487–489.
15. Shunzō Yoshisaka, op.cit., pp. 488–489. Legislation at a national level to control the activities of recruiting agents and labour brokers was not introduced until 1925. Before that time, each Prefecture had been responsible for regulation recruitment activities in its own area. See *I.L.O. report, 1933*, pp. 146, 162–164.
16. Collick, op.cit., p.11. Unless otherwise stated all information concerning the recruitment of Japanese mine workers has been taken from this source.
17. *I.L.O. report, 1933*, p. 277.
18. Hereafter referred to as *hambagashira*.
19. In 1923 it was estimated that the turnover rate in the mining industry was over 100% as compared with a rate of between 40 and 60% among factory workers. See *Rōdō Undō Shiryō Iinkai* (Committee for Materials on the Labour Movement), *Nihon Rōdō Undō Shiryō* (*Materials on the Japanese Labour Movement*), Vol. X, Tokyo, 1959, pp. 208–209. The turnover rate for coal mining was probably much higher since the figure presented here includes workers in metal mining where labour turnover was considerably

lower than in coal mining alone. For a more detailed discussion of labour turnover in the mining industry see Collick, op.cit., pp. 184–191. This is also discussed in William W. Lockwood, op.cit., p. 486.
20. Collick, op.cit., pp. 40–41.
21. *Gendai Nihon: Chōsen Kankei-shi Shiryō Dai Sanshū* (Modern Japan: Historical Materials Relating to Korea, No. 3), *Zainichi Chōsenjin Taigū no Suii to Genjō (Changes in and the Present Treatment of Korean Residents in Japan)*, Kobokusha, Tokyo, 1975, p. 6. Published originally in 1955 as *Homū Kenkyū Hōkokusho* (Ministry of Justice Research Report, Vol. 43, No. 3). (Cited hereafter as *Gendai Nihon, Chōsenjin Suii to Genjō*.) Also see *Shihōshō* (Ministry of Justice), *Shihō Kenkyū* (Judicial Studies), Vol. 5, 'Naichi ni okeru Chōsenjin to Sono Hanzai ni tsuite' ('Concerning Koreans in Japan and Crimes Committed by Them'), (cited hereafter as *Shihōshō*, 'Chōsenjin to Hanzai'), Tokyo, 1927, in Pak Kyŏng-sik, comp., *Zainichi Chōsenjin Kankei Shiryō Shūsei (Collected Materials Concerning Koreans Residing in Japan)*, San-ichi Shobō, Tokyo, 1975, Vol. 1, p. 257. This set of materials is used extensively throughout the remainder of this study, and will be cited hereafter as Pak, Z.K.S.S., followed by the appropriate volume and page numbers.
22. Pak Jae-il, *Zainichi Chōsenjin ni Kansuru Sōgō Chōsa Kenkyū (A Comprehensive Investigation of Korean Residents in Japan)*, Shin-Kigensha, Tokyo, 1979, p. 22. Also see Pak Kyŏng-sik, *Zainichi Chōsenjin Undōshi: 8.15 Kaihōmae (A History of the Korean Peoples Movement in Japan Before the Liberation of August 15, 1945)*, San-ichi Shobō, Tokyo, 1979, p. 54. (Cited hereafter as Pak Kyŏng-sik, *Undōshi*.) This issue is also discussed briefly in *Shihōshō*, 'Chōsenjin to Hanzai', in Pak, Z.K.S.S., Vol. 1, p. 257.
23. Imperial Ordinance No. 352 issued in July 1899 was designed to control the residence of foreigners in areas outside the old concession areas. This ordinance is cited in Maeda Hajime, *Tokushu Rōmusha no Rōmu Kanri (The Labour Management of Special Workers)*, Sankaidō, Tokyo, 1943, p. 13. At the time this study was made, Maeda was Labour Section-Chief of the Hokkaidō Colliery and Steamship Company. As such he had considerable first-hand experience in the recruitment, deployment and management of Korean workers. A supplementary ordinance issued by the Home Ministry made it clear that the original ordinance was intended to limit the entry of Chinese coolie-labourers, who, it was believed, would disturb public morals, compete with Japanese workers and cause 'disorder in both industry and society.' Cited in Totsuka Hideo, '*Nihon ni okeru Gaikokujin Rōdōsha Mondai ni tsuite*' ('The Problem of Foreign Workers in Japan'), *Shakai Kagaku Kenkyū*, Tokyo University Press, 1974, p. 121.
24. *Gendai Nihon, Chōsenjin Suii to Genjō*, p. 31.
25. See, for example, Kushida Tamizō, '*Chōsen Rōdōsha no Inyū*' ('The Importation of Korean Workers'), *Kokkai Gakkai Zasshi*, No. 366, 1917, p. 138. Korean immigration to southern Manchuria is discussed at length in Setsure Tsurushima, 'Korean Immigrants in Kando in 1920s', *The Kansai University Review of Economics and Business*, Vol. 17, No. 1 and 2, pp. 48–52. (Kando is the Japanese rendering of Chientao.)
26. *Naimushō Keihokyoku* (Home Ministry Police Affairs Bureau), '*Chōsenjin Shikibetsu Shiryō ni Kansuru Ken*' ('Materials for the Identification of Koreans'), Internal Directive No. 1542, Tokyo, 1913, cited in Pak, Z.K.S.S., Vol. 1, pp. 27–29. Examples taken from this manual appear as Appendix B1. Three years later the Home Ministry issued the *Yōshisatsu*

Chōsenjin Shisatsu Naiki (Internal Instructions for the Observation of Koreans Requiring Surveillance), which were concerned primarily with Korean students and other dissidents. This directive is cited in Pak, Z.K.S.S., Vol. 1, pp. 23–24.
27. Pak Kyŏng-sik, *Undōshi*, p. 34.
28. Issued by administrative ordinance no. 6 under the title *Rōdōsha Boshū Torishimari Kisoku* (Regulations For the Control of the Recruitment of Workers), cited in Pak, Z.K.S.S., Vol. 1, pp. 30–31.
29. *Hokkaidō Tankō Kisen Kabushiki Kaisha Gojūnen-shi* (*Fifty-Year History of the Hokkaidō Steamship and Colliery Company*), Draft Manuscript, p. 317. (Cited hereafter as *Hokutan Fifty-Year History*.) Also see Pak Jae-il, op.cit., p. 24, and Matsumara Takao, op.cit., p. 112.
30. *Keihokyokuchō* (Police Affairs Bureau Chief), *Chōsenjin Rōdōsha no Boshū ni Kansuru Ken*, issued December 12, 1918. Cited in Pak, Z.K.S.S., Vol. 1, p. 34.
31. Ibid.
32. This is in reference to a proclamation made by Governor-General Hasegawa on March 5, 1919 in which he said 'During the ten years since annexation, the Imperial Benevolence has gradually reached all parts of the country, and it is now recognized throughout the world that the country has made a marked advancement in the securing of safety to life, and property, and the development of education and industry.' Cited in Frank Prentiss Baldwin, Jr., op.cit., p. 170.
33. Ibid., pp. 172–174.
34. This ordinance was issued under the title of *Chōsenjin no Ryokō Torishimari ni Kansuru Ken* (Concerning the Control of Travel by Koreans), in April 1919. It is cited in its entirety in Pak, Z.K.S.S., Vol. 1, p. 36. Also see Maeda Hajime, op.cit., p. 14.
35. *Osaka-shi Shakai-bu Chōsa-Ka* (Osaka City Social Affairs Department Survey Section), '*Chōsenjin Rōdōsha Mondai*' ('The Problem of Korean Workers'), 1924, p. 8. (Cited hereafter as *Osaka-shi, 'Chōsenjin Rōdōsha Mondai'*.) Also see K. K. Kawakami, 'Japan's Policy Toward Alien Immigration', *Current History*, Vol. 20, No. 3, 1924, pp. 472–474, and Robert McElroy, 'New Immigration Law Over Japan's Protest', *Current History*, Vol. 20, No. 4, 1924, pp. 648–652.
36. The *Ryokō Shōmei* system was abolished by administrative ordinance in December 1922. This ordinance is cited in Pak, Z.K.S.S., Vol. 1, p. 36.
37. Takeda Yukio, '*Naichi Zaijū Hantōjin Mondai*' ('The Problem of Peninsulars Living in Japan'), *Shakai Seisaku Jihō*, No. 213, 1938, p. 103. (Cited hereafter as Takeda, '*Hantōjin Mondai*'.)
38. Ibid.
39. *Fukuoka Nichi Nichi Shimbun*, November 24, 1917, quoted in Iwamura Toshio, *Zainichi Chōsenjin to Nihon Rōdōsha Kaikyū* (*Koreans in Japan and the Japanese Working Class*), Azekura Shobō, Tokyo, 1972, p. 12.
40. *Osaka Mainichi Shimbun*, December 26, 1917, in *Shimbun Kiji Shiryō Shūsei* (*Collected Materials from Newspaper Articles*), *Rōdō Hen* (Labour Series), Vol. 1, pp. 325–326. (Cited hereafter as *S.K.S.S.*)
41. *Osaka Mainichi Shimbun*, August 14, 1917, in *S.K.S.S., Rōdō Henō*, Vol. 1, p. 321.
42. Ibid., p. 322.
43. *Chōsen Sōtokufu Shomubu Chōsa-Ka* (Government-General of Korea, General Affairs Department, Survey Section), '*Hanshin Keihin Chihō no*

Chōsenjin Rōdōsha ('Korean Workers in the Osaka-Kobe and Tokyo-Yokohama Regions'), 1924, in Pak, Z.K.S.S., Vol. 1, p. 412. (Cited hereafter as *General Affairs Department*, '*Hanshin-Keihin*'.)

44. Maeda Hajime, op.cit., pp. 28–31.
45. According to a report compiled in Fukuoka, Korean miners were first recruited between 1917 and 1918 as a replacement for female workers. Many of the major coal producers employed Koreans, while others like Mitsui used none at all. See *Fukuoka Chihō Shokugyō Shōkai Jimukyoku* (Fukuoka Regional Employment Exchange Office), '*Shōkugyō Shōkai Jigyō yori Mitaru Tanzan Rōdō Jijō*' ('The Circumstances of Mining Labour from the View of Employment Exchange Enterprises'), Fukuoka, March 1934. As cited in *Rōdō Undō Shiryō Iinkai* (Committee for Materials on the Labour Movement), *Nihon Rōdō Undō Shiryō* (*Materials on the Japanese Labour Movement*), Vol. 7, Tokyo, 1964, p. 94.
46. *Kōgyō Shimpō*, July 20, 1912. As cited in *Hokutan Fifty-Year History*, p. 319.
47. *Hokutan Fifty-Year History*, p. 318.
48. Ibid., p. 320.
49. Ibid. Also see Nishida Minoru, '*Hokkaidō Kōgyō no Shimpō*' ('Progress of the Hokkaidō Mining Industry'), *Shokumin Kōhō*, No. 97, July 1917, p. 32.
50. Maeda Hajime, op.cit., p. 31. Also see *Chōsenjin Kyōsei Renkō Shinsō Chōsadan* (Group for the Disclosure of the True Facts Concerning the Forced Migration of Koreans), *Chōsenjin Kyōsei Renkō Kyōsei Rōdō no Kiroku - Hokkaidō, Chishima, Karafuto Hen* (*Record of the Forced Migration and Labour of Koreans: Hokkaidō, Kuriles, and Sakhalien Series*), Gendaishi Shuppankai, Tokyo, 1976, p. 34. (Cited hereafter as *Chōsenjin Kyōsei Renkō: Kyōsei Rōdō*).
51. Maeda Hajime, op.cit., pp. 31–33.
52. Ibid. Also see Hokutan *Fifty-Year History*, p.325.
53. Fukuoka Regional Employment Exchange, '*Chōsenjin Rōdō Jijō*', p. 129.
54. For example, see *Naimushō*, '*Chōsenjin Kinkyō Gaiyō*', in Pak, Z.K.S.S., Vol. 1, p. 123. Also see *Naimushō Keihokyoku Hoanka* (Home Ministry Police Affairs Bureau Security Section), '*Taishō Juyon-nen chū ni okeru Zairyū Chōsenjin no Jōkyō*' ('The Condition of Koreans in Japan During 1925'), Tokyo, 1925, in Pak, Z.K.S.S., Vol. 1, p. 152. (Cited hereafter as *Keihokyoku*, '*Zairyū Chōsenjin – 1925*'.)
55. *Osaka-shi*, '*Chōsenjin Rōdōsha Mondai*', p. 21.
56. *Osaka Mainichi Shimbun*, December 27, 1917, in S.K.S.S., *Rōdō Hen*, Vol. 1, p. 326.
57. *Osaka-shi*, '*Chōsenjin Rōdōsha Mondai*', p. 81.
58. *Keihokyoku*, '*Zairyū Chōsenjin – 1925*', in Pak, Z.K.S.S., Vol. 1, p. 156.
59. For example, see *Shihōshō*, '*Chōsenjin to Hanzai*', in Pak, Z.K.S.S., Vol. 1, p. 258. Also see *Osaka-shi*, '*Chōsenjin Rōdōsha Mondai*', pp. 64–68, 121, and *Chūō Shokugyō Shōkai Jimukyoku* (Central Employment Exchange Office), '*Tōkyō-fuka Zairyū Chōsenjin Rōdōsha ni Kansuru Chōsa*' ('A Survey Concerning Korean Workers in Tokyo Metropolitan Prefecture'). (Cited hereafter as *Central Employment Exchange – 1924*.)
60. *Keihokyoku*, '*Zairyū Chōsenjin – 1925*', in Pak, Z.K.S.S., Vol.1, p. 156.
61. *Osaka-shi*, '*Chōsenjin Rōdōsha Mondai*', p. 84.
62. *Osaka-shi*, '*Chōsenjin Rōdōsha Mondai*', pp. 10–11.
63. Ibid., p. 85.
64. *Osaka-fu Shokugyō Hodōkai* (Osaka Prefectural Employment Guidance

Association), 'Osaka-fu Zaijū Chōsenjin Seikatsu Chōsa' ('An Investigation into the Livelihood of Koreans Living in Osaka Prefecture'), Osaka, 1924, pp. 4–5. (Cited hereafter as Osaka-fu, 'Chōsenjin Seikatsu Chōsa'.)
65. Ibid., pp. 3, 8. The importance of Cheju Island as a jumping-off point for immigrants was reflected in the opening of a direct ferry service in February 1923 linking Cheju and Osaka. See Osaka-shi, 'Chōsenjin Rōdōsha Mondai', pp. 15–16.
66. Osaka-shi, 'Chōsenjin Rōdōsha Mondai', p. 6. A similar view is expressed in Kushida Tamizō, op.cit., p. 139.
67. Osaka-shi, 'Chōsenjin Rōdōsha Mondai', p. 71.
68. Ibid., p. 97. The results of this survey are summarized in Appendix B2. In the absence of national statistics on this subject, contemporary data compiled by the Osaka Prefectural and Municipal authorities have been used as principal sources since they provide the fullest treatment of this aspect of immigration. It should be noted, however, that all other official sources support the findings of the more extensive investigations carried out in Osaka.
69. Ibid., p. 102. Also see *Central Employment Exchange – 1924*, in Pak, Z.K.S.S., Vol. 1, p. 438, and *Naimushō*, 'Chōsenjin Kinkyō Gaiyō' in Pak, Z.K.S.S., Vol. 1, p. 123.
70. *Hokutan Fifty-Year History*, p. 329. Also see *General Affairs Department*, 'Hanshin-Keihin', in Pak, Z.K.S.S., Vol. 1, p. 415. This source indicates that disputes between Japanese and Koreans began occurring with some frequency from about 1922. In the first nine months of that year seventy-five such incidents were reported. In the first ten months of 1923 the figure rose to more than 200 though this was probably due to the anti-Korean rioting after the earthquake. During the same ten month period in 1924 the total number of recorded disputes dropped to forty-eight. Other sources, however, indicate that Koreans also co-operated with Japanese workers during labour disputes on numerous occasions, and were also involved in the Rice Riots of 1918. See *Keihokyoku*, 'Zairyū Chōsenjin – 1925', in Pak, Z.K.S.S., Vol. 1, pp. 179–180, and Inoue Kiyoshi and Watanabe Tōru, *Kome Sōdō no Kenkyū (A Study of the Rice Riots)*, Vol. 3, Yūhikaku, Tokyo, 1960, pp. 47–48, 103, 105.
71. *Hokutan Fifty-Year History*, p. 329. Also see Nishida Minoru, op.cit., p. 32.
72. *Central Employment Exchange – 1924*, in Pak, Z.K.S.S., Vol. 1, p. 437.
73. Osaka-shi, 'Chōsenjin Rōdōsha Mondai', p. 83.
74. *General Affairs Department*, 'Hanshin-Keihin', in Pak, Z.K.S.S., Vol. 1, p. 416.
75. Ibid., p. 424.
76. Ibid. Also see Ozawa Yūsaku, *Zainichi Chōsenjin Kyōiku-ron (A Study of Education for Korean Residents in Japan)*, Aki Shobō, Tokyo, 1977, p. 82.
77. *General Affairs Department*, 'Hanshin-Keihin', in Pak, Z.K.S.S., Vol. 1, p. 424.
78. 'Chōsenjin Gaikyō /3/', in Pak, Z.K.S.S., Vol. 1, p. 115.
79. Ibid., pp. 115–116.
80. *Central Employment Exchange – 1924*, in Pak, Z.K.S.S., Vol. 1, p. 440–441. Also see Pak Kyŏng-sik, *Undōshi*, p. 103, and Wagner, op.cit., p. 22.
81. *Central Employment Exchange – 1924*, in Pak, Z.K.S.S., Vol. 1, pp. 440–442.
82. Ibid. Also see *Naimushō, Shakai Kyoku – 1924*, in Pak, Z.K.S.S., Vol. 1, p. 530.

83. Wagner, op.cit., p. 22.
84. *Central Employment Exchange – 1924*, in Pak, Z.K.S.S., Vol. 1, p. 442.
85. Ibid., p. 438.
86. Ibid., pp. 434–435, 438. Also see *General Affairs Department, 'Hanshin-Keihin'*, in Pak, Z.K.S.S., Vol. 1, p. 427.
87. William W. Lockwood, op.cit., pp. 47, 115. Also see G. C. Allen, *A Short Economic History of Modern Japan*, George Allen & Unwin Ltd., London, 1972, p. 118.
88. Seishi Idei, 'The Unemployment Problem in Japan', *International Labour Review*, Vol. 22, No. 4, 1930, pp. 503–504.
89. *I.L.O. report, 1933*, pp. 289–291. Also see Takeda, '*Hantōjin Mondai*', p. 105.
90. *Shihōshō, 'Chōsenjin to Hanzai'*, in Pak, Z.K.S.S., Vol. 1, p. 258. Also see *Osaka-shi, 'Chōsenjin Rōdōsha Mondai'*, p. 76.
91. *Osaka-shi, 'Chōsenjin Rōdōsha Mondai'*, p. 26.
92. Ibid., p. 24.
93. Ibid., pp. 28–29.
94. Ibid., p. 29.
95. Iwamura, op.cit., pp. 31–32.
96. *Osaka-shi, 'Chōsenjin Rōdōsha Mondai'*, p. 80.
97. Ibid., pp. 26, 80. Also see *Keihokyoku, 'Zairyū Chōsenjin – 1925'*, in Pak, Z.K.S.S., Vol. 1, p. 157, *Central Employment Exchange – 1924*, in Pak, Z.K.S.S., Vol. 1, p. 437, *General Affairs Department, 'Hanshin-Keihin'*, in Pak, Z.K.S.S., Vol. 1, pp. 410–411, *Hokutan Fifty-Year History*, p. 326, and *Naimushō, 'Chōsenjin Kinkyō Gaiyō'*, in Pak, Z.K.S.S., Vol. 1, p. 123.
98. *Osaka-shi, Shakai bu Hōkoku Dai 177 gō* (Osaka City Social Affairs Department, Report No. 177), '*Chōsenjin Rōdōsha no Kinkyō*, (The Recent Condition of Korean Workers'), (cited hereafter as Sakai, '*Chōsenjin Rōdōsha no Kinkyō*'), Sakai Susumu comp., Osaka, 1933, p. 32.
99. *Osaka Asahi Shimbun*, July 26, 1918, in *S.K.S.S., Rōdō Hen*, Vol 1, p. 332. Also cited in Iwamura, op.cit., p. 21, and, Pak Kyŏng-sik, *Undōshi*, pp. 61–62.
100. *Naimushō, 'Chōsenjin Kinkyō Gaiyō'*, in Pak, Z.K.S.S., Vol. 1, p. 123. Also see Sakai, '*Chōsenjin Rōdōsha no Kinkyō*', p. 34.
101. *Hokutan Fifty-Year History*, p. 326.
102. *Otaru Shimbun*, July 28, 1919. Quoted in Iwamura, op.cit., p. 20.
103. One official commentator suggested, 'As has been pointed out by scholars, the general level of livelihood of Koreans at the present time corresponds to that which existed in Japan during the Nara Period.' Sakai, '*Chōsenjin Rōdōsha no Kinkyō*', op. cit., p. 1. For views similar to this expressed in other official reports see *Osaka-shi, 'Chōsenjin Rōdōsha Mondai'*, pp. 81–82, and *Keihokyoku, 'Zairyū Chōsenjin – 1925'*, in Pak, Z.K.S.S., Vol. 1, p. 157.
104. *Osaka Mainichi Shimbun*, December 26, 1917.
105. *Central Employment Exchange – 1924*, in Pak, Z.K.S.S., Vol. 1, p. 437.
106. *Osaka-shi, 'Chōsenjin Rōdōsha Mondai'*, p. 25.
107. *Hokutan Fifty-Year History*, p. 328.
108. Fukuoka Regional Employment Exchange, '*Chōsenjin Rōdō Jijō*', pp. 129–130.
109. *Osaka Chihō Shokugyō Shōkai Jimukyoku* (Osaka Regional Employment Exchange Office), *Keizaigakubu Kenkyūshitsu* (Department of Economic Studies Research Office), '*Chikuhō Tanzan Rōdō Jijō*' ('Working Conditions in the Chikuhō Coal Mines'), Osaka, 1926, p. 80.

THE IMMIGRATION OF KOREAN WORKERS TO JAPAN, 1910–1923   97

110. *I.L.O. report, 1933*, p. 228.
111. Fukuoka Regional Employment Exchange, '*Chōsenjin Rōdō Jijō*', p. 126. Also see Matsumura, op.cit., p. 148.
112. *Keihokyoku*, '*Zairyū Chōsenjin – 1925*', in Pak, Z.K.S.S., Vol. 1, p. 179.
113. *Osaka-fu Gakumubu Shakai Ka* (Osaka Prefecture Educational Affairs Department Social Affairs Section), '*Zaihan Chōsenjin no Seikatsu Jōtai*' ('The Livelihood of Koreans Living in Osaka'), Osaka, 1934, p. 97.
114. *Osaka-shi 'Chōsenjin Rōdōsha Mondai*', pp. 85–90.
115. Ibid., p. 89.
116. Ibid., pp. 88–89. Also see *Keihokyoku*, '*Zairyū Chōsenjin –1925*', in Pak, Z.K.S.S., Vol. 1, pp. 180–181.
117. *Osaka Asahi Shimbun*, March 24, 1919. Also cited in Pak Kyŏng-sik, *Undōshi*, p. 60.
118. Sakai, '*Chōsenjin Rōdōsha no Kinkyō*', p. 34. Also see *Osaka-shi*, '*Chōsenjin Rōdōsha Mondai*', pp. 77–78.
119. Sakai, '*Chōsenjin Rōdōsha no Kinkyō*', p. 34.
120. Iwamura, op.cit., p. 30.
121. *Osaka-shi*, '*Chōsenjin Rōdōsha Mondai*', p. 86. According to a second source, in 1923 approximately two-thirds of all cheap boarding houses and other types of lodgings catering to day labourers in Osaka were used exclusively by Koreans. Fifty-three of these boarding houses were located in the Tsuruhashi area alone. *Osaka Hyakunen-shi (Hundred Year History of Osaka)*, Osaka Prefectural Government, Osaka, 1968, p. 858.
122. *Osaka-shi*, '*Chōsenjin Rōdōsha Mondai*', p. 93.
123. Ibid., pp. 87–89.
124. Ibid., p. 89.
125. *Central Employment Exchange – 1924*, in Pak, Z.K.S.S., Vol. 1, pp. 433–437.
126. Ibid., p. 440. The same report noted that although a small number of Koreans had established more or less permanent residence in Shinagawa and Osaki, there was no indication of the formation of a Korean ghetto in Tokyo. Also see *General Affairs Department*, '*Hanshin-Keihin*', in Pak, Z.K.S.S., Vol. 1, p. 400, and '*Zaitōkyō Chōsenjin no Gaikyō*' ('A General View of Koreans Residing in Tokyo'), *Chōsen*, No. 88, July 1922, pp. 110–111.
127. *Central Employment Exchange – 1924*, in Pak, Z.K.S.S., Vol. 1, p. 440. Also see *Osaka Mainichi Shimbun*, December 26, 1917, in *S.K.S.S., Rōdō Hen*, Vol. 1, pp. 325–326, and *Osaka-shi*, '*Chōsenjin Rōdōsha Mondai*', p. 77.
128. *Osaka-shi*, '*Chōsenjin Rōdōsha Mondai*', p. 89. Also see *General Affairs Department*, '*Hanshin-Keihin*', in Pak, Z.K.S.S., Vol. 1, pp. 400, 411–412, and *Osaka-fu*, '*Chōsenjin Seikatsu Chōsa*', pp. 1–2. In the Osaka area Koreans were particularly visible in the following areas: Higashi-Nari County – the towns of Tsuruhashi, Nakamoto, Namazue; Nishi-Nari County – the towns of Imamiya, Toyozaki and Washijima; within the city of Osaka in Izumio and Ishioka, both of which were located in Nishi-ku (West Ward). In Tokyo Koreans were concentrated in the Counties of Kita-Toshima, Ebara, and Toyotama – and within the city in Fukugawa, Honjō, Kanda, Senjū and Asakusa Wards.
129. *General Affairs Department*, '*Hanshin-Keihin*', in Pak, Z.K.S.S., Vol. 1, p. 412.
130. *Central Employment Exchange – 1924*, in Pak, Z.K.S.S., Vol. 1, p. 437. When Koreans were provided with company housing they were housed

separately in what were sometimes referred to as *Senjin Shataku* (Korean company houses). There is little in the way of precise details concerning living conditions in these factory houses, but, given the extremely low standards of hygiene and sanitation which prevailed in company dormitories generally, overcrowding and disease must have been endemic. See Yoshisaka Shunzō, op.cit., pp. 488–489, and *I.L.O. report, 1933*, pp. 243–244.

131. *Central Employment Exchange – 1924*, in Pak, Z.K.S.S., Vol. 1, p. 437. Also see *General Affairs Department, 'Hanshin-Keihin'*, in Pak, Z.K.S.S., Vol. 1, pp. 411–412. Keihokyoku, '*Zairyū Chōsenjin – 1925*', in Pak, Z.K.S.S., Vol. 1, p. 157, and Sakai, 'Chōsenjin Rōdōsha no Kinkyō', pp. 43–44.
132. Fukuoka Regional Employment Exchange, '*Chōsenjin Rōdō Jijō*', p. 137.
133. *Hokutan Fifty-Year History*, p. 330.
134. Ibid., p. 329.
135. Osaka-shi, '*Chōsenjin Rōdōsha Mondai*', p. 5.
136. Ibid., p. 3.

Chapter 4

Korean Workers and the Formation of Labour Organizations in Japan

The trade union movement in Japan, which first arose in the mid-1890s, did not begin to have an appreciable impact on either Japanese industry or labour-management relations until after the First World War. With few exceptions, labour disputes before the turn of the century had been spontaneous expressions of worker discontent with what were often unbearable conditions, and were devoid of organization or ideological commitment.[1] Despite the non-revolutionary character of early trade unions, which were dominated in most cases by moderate Christian Socialists like Katayama Sen, the government responded with a series of repressive measures the most effective of which were the *Chian Keisatsu Hō* (Public Peace Police Law) and the *Gyōsei Shikkō Hō* (Administrative Action Law).[2] Although these laws reflected official antagonism toward the trade union movement in particular, they need to be considered in the wider context of consistent government attempts to suppress the growth of organizations and ideologies which were regarded as threats to the foundations of the state.[3] The unease generated by radical or even reformist ideologies dominated much of bureaucratic thinking after 1900, and culminated in the passage of the *Chian Iji Hō* (Peace Preservation Law) in 1925, which, along with the *Chian Keisatsu Hō*, was the principal instrument for the suppression of left-wing organizations and ideologies until 1945.[4]

The immediate effect of the *Chian Keisatsu Hō* was the stifling of trade unionism, but the failure of the Government to allow for a forum where the legitimate grievances of workers could be voiced tended to exacerbate the anger and frustration of workers.[5] A detailed analysis of labour disputes and strikes which occurred during the ten-year period following the introduction of the *Chian Keisatsu Hō* is made virtually impossible by the lack of reliable statistics, but among those which were recorded were strikes at the Ashio and Besshi Copper Mines in 1907. These involved considerable violence and were ended by military intervention.[6]

A less direct result of Government suppression was to turn a number of moderate reformers, who had been active in the formation of early trade unions, toward more radical ideologies. Katayama Sen, who had been a trade unionist in the Christian Socialist mould, turned toward communism during this period, while Kōtoku Denjirō, who had been one of the dominant figures in both the *Shakai Minshutō* (Social Democrat Party) and the *Shakaishugi Kyōkai* (Institute of Socialism), became an anarcho-syndicalist.[7]

The trade union movement re-emerged in 1912 with the organization of the *Yūaikai* (Fraternal Society) in Tokyo by Suzuki Bunji.[8] The manifesto issued by the *Yūaikai* contained no references to 'the working classes' or any other socialist concepts which could be construed as violations of the *Chian Keisatsu Hō,* and offered assurance that the new organization would be founded on moderation and conciliation.[9] By 1918 the *Yūaikai* had become a national organization with more than 100 branches representing approximately 30,000 members.[10]

Much of this expansion had been due to the economic effects of the First World War on the livelihood of industrial workers. Although money wages had risen during the war, it has been estimated that real wages actually declined as a result of a steady increase in prices. In the first eight months of 1918, for example, rice prices nearly doubled, thus increasing the hardship of the lowest-paid industrial workers.[11] The social and economic discontent which resulted from these conditions was given its fullest expression in the Rice Riots of 1918 as well as in the growing number of strikes and lockouts which occurred during the period immediately after the war. Despite the fact that ideology continued to play a secondary role in labour disputes (in 1919 demands for increased wages accounted for more than 80% of all recorded labour disputes), confrontations with management began to be conducted more systematically, displayed a higher degree of organization and involved far greater numbers of workers.[12]

Between 1903 and 1910 only 141 strikes had been recorded in Japan, but in 1919 alone approximately 500 strikes involving more than 60,000 workers occurred.[13] This period was also characterized by the diffusion of proletarian ideologies, principally Marxist or anarchist, and a leftward tilt became apparent even in such moderate organizations as the *Yūaikai*. In 1919 its name was altered to the *Dai Nippon Rōdō Sōdōmei Yūaikai* (Greater Japan Confederation of Labour-Fraternal Society), while in 1921 the term 'Fraternal' was discarded and the name changed to the *Nihon Rōdō Sōdōmei* (Japan Confederation of Labour).[14] One year earlier, occasioned by the first May Day demonstration held in Japan, a brief united front had been created between the *Yūaikai* and the more militant *Shinyūkai* (Faithful Friends Society) resulting in the establishment of the *Rōdō Kumiai Dōmeikai* (League of Labour Unions).[15] Although the League existed for only a very short period it reflected a more radical attitude on the part of trade union leaders toward their relations with management and a new determination to safeguard the interests of workers.[16] Influenced by younger and more militant trade unionists like Tanahashi Kotora and Asō Hisashi, the *Yūaikai*, as early as

1919, began to place much greater emphasis on such issues as the recognition of the worker's right to engage in collective bargaining, as well as the prohibition of child labour and nightwork, the introduction of a minimum wage and a system of workers' compensation.[17]

Following in the wake of the Russian Revolution came the Rice Riots of 1918 which spread to more than thirty prefectures, involved more than 500,000 people, and contributed to the collapse of the Terauchi Cabinet.[18] Domestic criticism of the Government's policies was fuelled by opposition to Japan's intervention in Siberia, while the Korean Independence Movement of 1919 threatened the security of Japan's richest colonial possession and provoked heated debates concerning the policy of assimilation. Moreover, as the postwar recession deepened, labour disputes grew in both size and organization and in the case of the Kawasaki Dockyard strike of 1921 violent confrontations between management and workers again resulted in military intervention.[19] In the Government's view all of these events underlined the threat of left-wing movements and ideologies, while for its opponents they provided a basis upon which those very ideas could be disseminated. The organization of the Japanese Communist Party (JCP) in 1922 and growing urban and rural discontent, both of which conformed to Marxist predictions, probably suggested to many, at both ends of the political spectrum, that Japan was indeed at a pre-revolutionary stage of development.[20]

Korean Workers and Organized Labour

A detailed treatment of efforts to organize Korean workers or of Korean involvement in the Japanese trade union movement before about 1920 is rendered virtually impossible by the absence of reliable data. The evidence which does exist, however, suggests that there was very little union activity among immigrant workers between 1910 and 1920, and that Koreans were largely indifferent to the trade union movement.[21] Not only were attempts by Korean workers and students to organize subject to the same types of official harassment as those of Japanese trade unionists, but the impermanent nature of the immigrant community itself, coupled with the language barrier, militated against both the formation of associations representing the interests of Korean workers, and co-operation with Japanese workers. As is illustrated in the following extract from a report compiled in Osaka in 1923, Korean workers were regarded as ideologically naive, lacking in a sense of solidarity, and possessing no understanding of the labour or socialist movement.[22]

> The unity of Korean workers, taken as a whole . . . is extremely weak. For example, workers in the same factory, or those working at the same construction site may unite among themselves, but this

> solidarity does not extend to workers in other factories or at other work sites. Not only that, but within the same factory, if the work place is different, there is generally little co-operation between workers . . . As yet they have not organized anything which could be regarded as a trade union. Moreover, they are quite lacking in a sense of mutual aid.[23]

It was commonly agreed (by official observers) that the principal barriers to the development of co-operation between Japanese and Korean workers were language and what were perceived as fundamental and unresolvable cultural differences. This view was expressed in both official and semi-official publications,[24] typical of which is the following:

> There are differences in character, customs, and manners between Japanese and Koreans. Not only do they not understand the Japanese language, but due to their general way of life being crude and unhygienic, they have not assimilated easily with Japanese ways of living. Consequently, there is a lack of intimate contact, and this also contributes to friction between Japanese and Koreans.[25]

Unlike Korean students, immigrant workers showed little interest in proletarian ideologies or in the labour movement,[26] and early worker organizations were characterized by low levels of organization, extremely small memberships, and the dominant role played in them by students and other intellectuals.[27] In this respect the difficulties encountered by Korean student-unionists in organizing workers were not dissimilar to those which confronted Japanese trade unionists during this period. With few exceptions early Japanese trade union organizers were also intellectuals (many of them the products of the elite Imperial Universities), whose ideological motivations were not necessarily either shared, or even understood, by the majority of Japanese workers.[28] This is at least in part borne out by the fact that even at its pre-Second World War height trade union membership represented less than 8% of the industrial labour force.[29] While Korean workers may have been less easily organized, for the reasons stated above, than their Japanese counterparts, they should not be regarded as different in kind but as being at one end of a continuum which included Japanese workers as well.

Those worker organizations which were established during this period were principally relief organizations, and were designed to promote the encouragement of mutual friendship among members, thrift, and the development of a spirit of mutual aid and assistance. In some, where the influence of radical students was more pronounced, the above objectives were often extended to include the promotion of friendship between students and workers, the development of class or national consciousness, and the investigation of labour problems affecting the condition of

Korean workers.[30] A comprehensive list of worker organizations established between 1910 and 1920 is not available since many were extremely short-lived and no account of their activities has survived.[31]

Of those early worker associations whose names are recorded, only the *Chōsenjin Chokinkai* (Korean Savings Society) actually established a mutual savings fund which was used to aid members who were unemployed or otherwise suffering from economic hardship.[32] Most of these organizations were dominated by Korean students and were a source of considerable concern to Home Ministry officials who viewed any attempts to unite students and workers (particularly after 1919) as potentially subversive. No fewer than six of the worker groups listed by the Home Ministry were placed under vigorous surveillance by the Police Affairs Bureau,[33] and, as of 1920, the entire executive committee of the *Kyōto Chōsenjin Rōdō Kyōsaikai* (Kyoto Mutual Aid Society of Korean Labour), for example, had been listed as A Class *Yōshisatsu Chōsenjin* (Koreans requiring surveillance).[34] Of particular concern to Government officials was the threat that student radicals might 'infect' Korean workers with what were euphemistically termed *fuon shisō* (unwholesome thoughts).[35] A later report produced by the Justice Ministry referred to these early attempts by students to 'radicalize' workers in the following way:

> ... Korean students had forged close links with Japanese socialist ideologues who had themselves recently come into prominence, and newly arrived students were met with ideological propaganda. On the other hand, they were also instigating the development of class consciousness among Korean workers, organizing unions and attempting to make use of them.[36]

Nevertheless, the vast majority of immigrant workers were unresponsive to these attempts by students and other intellectuals to organize them into trade unions. As late as 1923 officials in Osaka felt confident in reporting that:

> Unions have been organized, professing to offer a wide variety of benefits such as mutual aid and relief. At first there were more than seventy such groups, while at present there are twenty-three, but they generally dissolve by the second or third meeting. Moreover ... their character is very strongly that of relief organizations; there is not a single real labour union among them.[37]

By about 1920 Japanese trade unionists as well as moderate and left-wing intellectuals, stimulated by events both at home and abroad, had begun to promote closer co-operation between themselves and Korean workers and students. In 1919 the *Yūaikai* had resolved to secure 'equal treatment for Japanese and foreign workers,'[38] while the *Shinjinkai* (New

Man Society), inspired by the internationalism of Yoshino Sakuzō and others, included Korean and Chinese students among its members, and was outspoken in its opposition to the suppression of the independence movement in Korea.[39]

The first recorded instance of Korean participation in the Japanese labour movement occurred in August 1920 when the newly established Yūbari Federation of the National Union of Miners set up a Korean section.[40] This was precipitated by two principal factors. First, it will be recalled that *Hokutan* was at that time the single biggest employer of Koreans, employing more than 300 at the Yūbari mine alone. Moreover, *Hokutan*'s policy of providing separate housing facilities for Koreans and of using Korean miners in separate work crews appears to have stimulated solidarity among Korean miners and generated hostility towards what was essentially discriminatory treatment. Second was the presence at the headquarters of the National Union of Miners of *Shinjinkai* members who encouraged co-operation and worker solidarity between Japanese and Korean miners.[41] The most prominent of these individuals were Kawai Eizō – the newly elected president of the union – Yoshino Sakuzō, Sano Manabu, and Akamatsu Katsumaro, all of whom were registered as union advisers.[42] The formal opening of the Korean Section was held on August 1, 1920, and was presided over by Yasuda Tametarō, chairman of the Yūbari Federation.[43]

This event was reported in the August 20 issue of *Rōdō Shimpō*, the official publication of the National Union of Miners. In an article entitled 'The Joining of Hands of Japanese and Korean Workers', published in the same issue, Kawai Eizō welcomed the participation of Korean miners and urged that, regardless of national origin:

> . . . the oppressed ought to join hands with the oppressed. Real conciliation between Japan and Korea can be achieved only when the enlightened people of Japan and Korea join hands . . . Only through this sort of peaceful joining of hands will there be created a true 'producers' culture and a true people's culture.[44]

Although Kawai's use of terms like *Nissen Yūgō* (The Union of Japan and Korea) and references to the *Nissen Dōsoron* (Common Origin of Japan and Korea Theory), both of which were associated with Japanese colonial policy, was later criticized, his encouragement of solidarity between Japanese and Korean workers was the first voiced by a Japanese trade union leader.[45]

It was events which occurred in the summer of 1922, however, that cemented the relationship between Korean students and Japanese left-wing intellectuals and trade unionists, and ultimately resulted in the creation of the first Korean trade union in Japan. On July 29 the *Yomiuri Shimbun* published an article exposing the conditions verging on slave-labour under which approximately 600 Koreans were working at a hydroelectric plant construction site in Niigata Prefecture.[46] According to this article, Korean labourers, who comprised one half of a total work force of 1,200 at a construction site along the Shinano River, were being forced to work as many as sixteen hours a day under extremely poor conditions and were subject to regular brutality and mistreatment by their Japanese supervisors. Eye-witness accounts spoke of an unknown number of Koreans who had already died from exposure or malnutrition, and claims were made that attempted escapes were punished by severe beatings.[47]

Two days later a further account of the Shinano River Incident, as it was later to be known, appeared in the *Tonga Ilbo*, published in Seoul. This article also alleged that the corpses of Korean workers had been sighted floating in the river by local farmers, and claimed that the total number of Koreans who had been killed while attempting to escape or had died as a result of camp conditions may have been as high as 100.[48] Despite assurances by police officials in both Niigata and Tokyo that there was absolutely no truth in the allegations and 'rumours' printed by the *Yomiuri Shimbun*,[49] Korean organizations made preparations to conduct their own investigation of the incident.[50] On August 6 a reporter was sent by the *Tonga Ilbo* to Japan, while, on the same day, the Christian Youth Federation in Seoul organized its own investigatory group and sent a representative to Japan.[51] Throughout August preparations were made by Korean activists in Tokyo to hold a public meeting to discuss the incident, and on September 7 a 'Mass Debate Concerning the Massacre at the Shinano River' was held at the YMCA in Kanda and attended by approximately 1,000 people.[52] The meeting was chaired by Kim Yak-su, one of the most radical student activists, and speeches were made vigorously condemning the exploitation of Korean workers. Among those present were people such as Paek Mu, Chong Un-hae and Pak Yŏl, who were actively involved in the promotion of trade unionism among Korean workers.[53]

As a result of this mass meeting, a committee for the investigation of the condition of Korean workers in Japan was set up and a brief inspection tour of selected mines and factories employing Koreans was undertaken.[54] The September issue of *Zen'ei* (Vanguard), the official journal of the newly established Japan Communist Party, contained an article entitled 'The Solidarity of Japanese and Korean Workers' which condemned the Shinanogawa incident and urged greater co-operation between Japanese and Korean workers:

> The Japanese labour movement should join hands with Korean workers and form a united front against the exploitation . . . The Japanese labour movement must take up as one of its objectives co-operation with Korean leaders and make efforts to organize Korean workers into unions. At the same time, based on the ideal of equal

pay for equal work, the movement must also demand the abolition of 'special treatment' for Korean workers.[55]

Further encouragement of Korean participation in the labour movement was provided by a series of articles written by Suzuki Bunji following a tour of Korea in the summer of 1922. In these articles, published in the *Kokumin Shimbun* during the first week of September, Suzuki, the president of *Sōdōmei*, attacked the exploitation of workers in Korea and urged Korean workers to protect themselves by organizing trade unions.[56] Official anxieties were exacerbated by these developments, and a slightly later report compiled by the Social Affairs Bureau assessed the situation in 1922 in the following way:

> Among the 85,000 Korean workers in Japan, including miners, coolies, self supporting students and the like, very few have participated in Japanese labour organizations . . . Since 1922 a faction within the *Kugakusei Dōyūkai*, carried away by a kind of curiosity and a sense of racial inequality, has tended to align itself with Japanese left-wing groups. Moreover, in July 1922, Suzuki Bunji, the president of *Sōdōmei*, visited all parts of Korea, and after his return to Japan, severely criticized the exploitation of Korean workers in the mines of Korea. A faction within the *Dōyūkai* was particularly stirred by this and attempted to agitate Korean workers in Japan, turn them toward the 'class struggle', and form a mass-movement of Korean workers in Japan.[57]

Subsequently, in November 1922, the *Tōkyō Chōsen Rōdō Dōmeikai* (Tokyo League of Korean Labour) was established. Numbered among the members of its executive committee were well known labour activists like Paek Mu and Kim Chong-bŏm, while Fuse Tatsuji and Kuroda Hisao were appointed as legal advisers to the new union.[58] The *Tōkyō Dōmeikai* took as its principal objectives 'assistance to workers and the improvement of character',[59] and made clear in its manifesto that it would:

> advance the cause of Korean workers internationally, and with the final objective of absolute victory for the proletarian classes of the world, . . . to work for the furtherance of the class consciousness of Korean workers in Japan and for their security of employment.[60]

Although the *Tōkyō Dōmeikai* was later credited with having an active membership of 250,[61] it was dominated from its inception by a small group of students who had at various times co-operated with and been strongly influenced by prominent Japanese communists and anarchists. Korean students were known to have participated in public meetings and other activities sponsored by radical groups such as the Cosmos Club and the *Gyōminkai* (Dawn People's Society), and some, like Pak Yŏl, had become committed to anarchism under the influence of Ōsugi Sakae and Iwasa Sakutarō.[62]

It was against this background that the *Kokutōkai* (Black Wave Association), was organized in November 1921. Bringing together both communist and anarchist elements, this group was dominated by Kim Yak-su, Pak Yŏl, Kim Chong-bŏm and Paek Mu.[63] As was the case in most Japanese left-wing groups, the *Kokutōkai* was plagued by factionalism and ideological conflict which culminated in its dissolution early in 1922.[64] The anarchist faction split off and formed the *Kokuyūkai* (Black Friends Society) under the leadership of Pak Yŏl,[65] while the predominantly communist faction, which included Kim Yak-su, Paek Mu and Kim Chong-bŏm established the *Hokuseikai* (North Star Society).[66] It was from the communist faction that the nucleus of the *Tōkyō Chōsen Rōdō Dōmeikai* now emerged.

Encouraged by these developments in Tokyo, both the *Nihon Rōdō Sōdōmei Ōsaka Rengōkai* (Japan Confederation of Labour – Osaka Federation) and the *Nihon RōdōSōdōmei Kansai Rōdō Dōmeikai* (Japan Confederation of Labour – Kansai Labour League) adopted resolutions supporting the establishment of an Osaka-based Korean labour union. Kim Yak-su and Kim Chong-bŏm were sent to Osaka as representatives of the *Hokuseikai*, and with the assistance of Nishio Suehiro and Ōya Shōzō, representing the *Kansai Rōdō Dōmeikai*, a mass meeting to establish the *Ōsaka Chosen Rōdō Dōmeikai* (Osaka League of Korean Labour) was held on December 1, 1922. It is unclear what actually occurred at this meeting, which was under close police surveillance, but most sources agree that the leaders were unable to reach agreement over the exact nature of the relationship which would exist between the *Ōsaka Dōmeikai* and its counterpart in Tokyo. The debate degenerated into scuffling, and in the confusion which followed the police ordered the meeting to disperse and in the process arrested Ōya, Nishio and a number of Koreans.[67] A second meeting was held on December 3 where it was decided that the new union would concentrate on organizing Korean workers in the Osaka area and would also seek to form a united front with *Sōdōmei*.[68] Song Chang-bŏk was elected chairman, and a nine-member executive committee appointed. The manifesto of the *Ōsaka Dōmeikai*, the publication and distribution of which was immediately prohibited by the Governor of Osaka Prefecture, read:

1. We pledge to secure victory in the class struggle and the confirmation of the right to exist through the strength of our solidarity.
2. We pledge ourselves to the overthrow of the capitalist system, which squeezes the sweat and blood from our bodies, and to the establishment of a new society based upon 'production and labour'.[69]

Kim Yak-su, in an article published in the *Rōdō Shimbun*, praised the establishment of the *Ōsaka Chōsen Rōdō Dōmeikai* because until that time 'the Korean movement in Japan had been firmly in the grip of certain student groups. But hereafter, the movement will be led by the vanguard of the true proletarian classes.'[70] Other Korean trade unionists published articles calling for international solidarity and an end to colonial oppression,[71] while an article which appeared in the January 1923 issue of *Zen'ei* stressed the ideological importance of co-operation between Japanese and Korean workers and concluded:

> The Korean working class, without the co-operation of the Japanese working class, will never be able to realize its objective of liberation. Moreover the movement of the Japanese working class will never be able to form an effective battle-line against capitalist domination if it fails to co-operate actively with Korean workers. Our cry of 'Japanese and Korean Working Classes Unite', is the most urgent necessity for today's movement. In reality, the trade union movement based on class consciousness and the ideology of class struggle through class unity with Korean workers must be one of the most important aspects of our policy.[72]

Rhetoric aside, however, neither the Japan Communist Party nor the unions affiliated with *Sōdōmei* were powerful enough to effect this sort of unity between Japanese and Korean workers. Moreover, neither the *Ōsaka Chōsen Rōdō Dōmeikai* nor its counterpart in Tokyo as successful in mobilizing or politicizing large numbers of Korean workers. Although the Osaka League claimed to have organized 300 workers at its inaugural meeting, according to official sources its membership was extremely small – numbering only fifty in 1925. In fact, as of 1925 (figures for the period before this are unavailable), out of a total Korean labour force of slightly more than 100,000 fewer than 2,000 Korean workers had been organized into trade unions (under 2%).[73] The significance of the limited co-operation which developed during 1922 and 1923 between Korean and Japanese workers lies not so much in the actual numbers involved as in the alignment of Korean activists with the extreme left of the Japanese trade union and social movement that it signalled. That these developments did not escape the attention of the Government is well illustrated in the following extract from a report compiled by the Criminal Affairs Bureau of the Justice Ministry in 1929:

> On the Bolshevik side, the North Star Society, predecessor to the *Ichigatsukai* (January Society), was born. After the dissolution of the *Kokutōkai*, this divided into two groups of this type. Nevertheless, at that time, they as yet had no well-defined ideology, and if anything were organizations in which nationalistic ideas were paramount. I believe that at that time, the 'thought' of Koreans in

Tokyo was divided into two currents, nationalism and anarchism. After that, however, with the rapid dissemination of Soviet-type propaganda, a Japanese *shakaishugi* (socialist) association was organized . . . and then from about 1922 people like Yamakawa Hitoshi began to propagandize . . . a change of direction for the proletarian movement. It was from this that the 'thought' of Koreans was swept along and changed.[74]

Throughout the early part of 1923 Korean activists became increasingly visible in left-wing trade union activities. Koreans were particularly conspicuous in the movement to oppose the passage of the Law For The Control of Radical Social Movements, the Trade Union Law and the Law For The Mediation of Tenancy Disputes, which were collectively referred to as the *San-Aku Hōan* (Three Evil Bills).[75] The January 20 issue of the *Rōdō Shimbun*, for example, reported that at a meeting held in Tokyo Kim Chong-bŏm, of the Osaka League, had been selected as one of the managers of the forthcoming campaign to be sponsored by trade unions in the Osaka area.[76] At the climax of one such demonstration in Osaka on February 11, a clash involving approximately 300 Koreans and 100 police resulted in the arrest of a number of demonstrators. In reporting these events, the *Rōdōsha Shimbun* carried a large photograph of the fracas that had erupted in front of Tennōji Park,[77] while the February 5 edition of the *Rōdō Shimbun* listed among the organizations participating in the campaign against the 'Three Evil Bills' the Tokyo League, The North Star Society and the *Futei Senjinsha* (Company of Korean Malcontents), all of which were Korean organizations.[78]

In April the Central Committee of *Sōdōmei* adopted a resolution pledging its support for national liberation movements in all colonial areas,[79] and, in the May 1 edition of its official publication *Rōdō*, called for the establishment of a united front between the 'proletarian class movement in the home country and national liberation movements in colonial areas'.[80] The *Ōsaka Asahi Shimbun* reported that at the May Day demonstration in Osaka, the presence of 600 Korean workers among the approximately 4,000 participants was 'particularly noticeable', and that the principal theme of the demonstration had been the encouragement of solidarity between Japanese and Korean workers.[81] The same newspaper also reported that at the Tokyo May Day rally held in Shiba Park, Koreans and Japanese leftists had been singled out for harassment by the police. The writer of this article went on to say:

> When a Korean went up to the speaker's platform, the police who were waiting underneath immediately attempted to pull him down and hustle him away. While five or six people, shouting 'what is wrong with Koreans!', tried to protect him, the police mounted a sudden charge. A fistfight followed, and for a while everything was thrown into confusion.[82]

Despite the relatively small number of Koreans participating in these and other mass-meetings and demonstrations endorsed by the Japanese 'left', the activities of Japanese and Korean radicals during 1923 heightened the sense of unease felt by Government officials. These anxieties were reflected in the mass arrests in June of suspected communists and their sympathizers in both Japan and Korea.[83] As regards Koreans, these same fears resulted in a notification to all Prefectural Governors requesting them to co-operate with the Government-General in preventing further immigration to Japan. The reasons for this request were stated in the following way:

> Recently the number of Koreans crossing over to Japan has been increasing. This increase has been particularly noticeable since the abolition of the *Ryokō Shōmei* system by the Government-General in December of last year. Not only has this led to large numbers of Koreans wandering about the country owing to difficulties in finding employment during the present economic depression, but we are also concerned over the recent trend in which a marked increase has become apparent in the number of Koreans participating in the Social and Labour Movements, and involving themselves in organized activities. We are also concerned lest the numerous clashes between Japanese and Koreans breed a variety of future problems.[84]

Sentiments similar to these were expressed by Hiraga Makoto, the Chief of the Home Affairs Section of the Osaka Prefectural Government in July.[85] In his speech, Hiraga expressed grave concern over the way in which Korean workers and students, who had been exposed to radical ideologies in Japan, might come to participate in the independence movement. He warned his audience that it was only military and police power that maintained public order in Korea, and added that although the situation there might appear calm on the surface, 'there were extremely dangerous elements in the background.'[86] Adding that:

> ... The people must consciously create a popular movement, which will promote the welfare of the people, as well as work together with Koreans to accelerate their assimilation. If this is not done, then it will be difficult to avoid the above results among Koreans.[87]

The anxieties expressed by officials like Hiraga were directed principally at Korean students, and all contemporary government reports emphasized that it was only a small minority of Koreans who were actively participating in trade unions and other radical organizations. In common with similar ideological groups established by Japanese radicals, the effectiveness of these groups was undermined by the fact that their leaders frequently exhibited more interest in arguing about a theory by which their aims could be achieved than in the aims themselves. This, coupled with the apathy of most Korean workers and the continual harassment of activists by the police, drastically limited the appeal of such groups. Nevertheless, given the tone of contemporary newspaper and magazine articles concerning the immigration issue, by 1923 it had become extremely difficult to differentiate 'good' Koreans from *Futei Senjin* (Korean Malcontents), which was the official term for those who opposed Japanese policies.

Because relatively few workers (both Japanese and Korean) in Japan at this time were unionized it is extremely difficult to assess both the participation of Korean workers in the labour movement and the influence which trade union policies had on shaping popular attitudes toward Korean immigrant workers. Trade union publications such as the *Rōdō Shimbun* and *Rōdōsha Shimbun* frequently encouraged class solidarity among Japanese and Korean workers, but given the relatively small circulation of such publications it is quite likely that the views expressed in these publications exercised little appreciable influence on the great mass of workers who remained unpoliticized and were outside the trade union movement. Moreover, even leading leftists and trade union officials, who came increasingly to perceive an identity of interests in colonial liberation and social revolution at home, referred to Koreans as *Senjin*, an abbreviated and usually derogatory form of the word *Chōsenjin*, which was created by the government as part of its official policy of control and assimilation.[88]

During the period before 1925, however, hostility toward Koreans tended to spring from areas which were not purely economic. Although some later commentators argued that the immigration of impoverished Koreans resulted in the displacement of native workers, and that this acted as a continual source of tension between Japanese and Korean workers, the evidence, though scanty, does not appear to support this.[89] There is, for example, no evidence that Korean workers were used as strike breakers, while the maintenance of discriminatory wage differentials in all industries ensured that Japanese and Korean workers were only rarely in direct competition for jobs. Of far greater importance in shaping popular attitudes was a colonial ideology which regarded the Korean people as socially, culturally and politically inferior to the Japanese. It was this, coupled with the association of Koreans with radical organizations and other forms of undesirable political activity, which effectively isolated the immigrant and fostered hostility toward him.

Notes:
1. George O. Totten, 'Labor and Agrarian Disputes In Japan Following World War I', *Economic Development And Cultural Change*, Vol. IX, No. 1, Part 2, 1960, pp. 189–190. (Cited hereafter as Totten, 'Labor and Agrarian Disputes'.)
2. Both of these laws were introduced in 1900. The most controversial provisions of the *Chian Keisatsu Hō* were those dealing with political associations and the formation of labour organizations which advocated collective action on behalf of workers. Article XVII prohibited individuals from establishing organizations which aimed at or encouraged collective action against employers through strikes or lockouts. Articles IV, VIII, and XVIII empowered police officials to prohibit or dissolve outdoor meetings, or the distribution of printed materials regarded as posing a threat to public order. This law widened the scope of the pre-existing *Shūkai Oyobi Kessha Hō* (Meetings and Associations Law) of 1890, which had been designed to suppress political opposition to the Government, with the wide discretionary powers it awarded to the police, the *Chian Keisatsu Hō* became an immediate and effective tool by which trade union activities could be suppressed. The *Gyōsei Shikkō Hō* empowered the police to take immediate measures to prevent any person from disturbing public order. See Iwao Ayusawa, op.cit., pp. 70–72.
3. Collick, op.cit., pp. 198–199. Also see Iwao Ayusawa, op.cit., pp. 70–73.
4. For a detailed discussion of the passage and effectiveness of the Peace Preservation Law in suppressing political dissent see Richard H. Mitchell, *Thought Control in Prewar Japan*, Cornell University Press, Ithaca and London, 1976, pp. 56–182, and Elise Kurashige Tipton, *The Civil Police In The Suppression Of The Prewar Japanese Left*, Unpublished Doctoral Dissertation, Indiana University, 1977, pp. 41–60.
5. Iwao Ayusawa, op.cit., pp. 93–94.
6. Collick, op.cit., pp. 199–200. The total number of recorded strikes (57) for 1907 was the highest during the Meiji period. Also see *I.L.O. report, 1933*, op.cit., pp. 48–49.
7. Iwao Ayusawa, op.cit., pp. 73–74. Also see George O. Totten, III, *The Social Democratic Movement in Prewar Japan*, Yale University Press, New Haven, 1966, pp. 23–30, and F. G. Notehelfer, op.cit., pp. 55–132.
8. *I.L.O. report, 1933*, pp. 91–92.
9. Iwao Ayusawa, op.cit., pp. 98–99.
10. R. M. V. Collick, op.cit., p. 200. Also see Totten, 'Labor and Agrarian Disputes', p. 191.
11. Kozo Yamamura, 'The Japanese Economy, 1911–1930: Concentration, Conflicts and Crises', in Silberman and Harootunian, *Japan in Crisis*, pp. 306–309. Also see G. C. Allen, op.cit., p. 100.
12. Collick, op.cit., pp. 48–50.
13. *Nihon Rōdō Undō Shiryō*, Vol. 10, pp. 442–443. Also see Collick, op.cit., pp. 232–233.
14. Totten, 'Labor and Agrarian Disputes', p. 191. Also see Eitaro Kishimoto, 'The Characteristics of Labour-Management Relations in Japan and their Historical Formation (1)', *Kyoto University Economic Review*, Vol. 35, No. 2, 1965, pp. 48–52. (Cited hereafter as Kishimoto, 'Labor-Management Relations in Japan (1)'.)

15. *I.L.O. report, 1933*, p. 94. Also see Iwao Ayusawa, op.cit., pp. 136–138.
16. Iwao Ayusawa, op.cit., pp. 133–135. Also see *I.L.O. report, 1933*, pp. 99–100.
17. Kishimoto, 'Labour-Management Relations in Japan (1)', p. 52. Also see Eitaro Kishimoto, 'The Characteristics of Labour-Management Relations In Japan And Their Historical Formation (2)', *Kyoto University Economic Review*, Vol. 36, No. 1, 1966, pp. 19–24.
18. Totten, 'Labor and Agrarian Disputes', p. 183. Also see Kozo Yamamura, op.cit., p. 309.
19. See Totten, 'Labor and Agrarian Disputes', p. 211.
20. These anxieties were well expressed in a speech made by Tanaka Giichi in 1924, in which he said: 'Today there are Japanese who think that mankind should know no national boundaries. They plead for so-called internationalism and a world without national distinctions . . . But while they talk of worldwide international co-operation, these Japanese also incite labor conflict and class struggles at home . . . If we want to protect the national welfare, public order, and honor, we must destroy all of these "isms".' Quoted in Richard J. Smethurst, *A Social Basis for Prewar Japanese Militarism*, University of California Press, Berkeley, Los Angeles, London, 1974, p. 24.
21. Shihōshō, '*Chōsenjin to Hanzai*', in Pak, Z.K.S.S., Vol. 1, p. 274.
22. See *Central Employment Exchange – 1924*, in Pak, Z.K.S.S., Vol. 1, p. 438. Also see *Chōsen Sōtōkufu Keimukyoku Tōkyō Shuchōin* (Government-General Police Affairs Bureau, Tokyo Office), '*Zaikyō Chōsenjin Jōkyō*' ('The Condition of Koreans Residing in Tokyo'), Tokyo, 1924, in Pak, Z.K.S.S., Vol. 1, p. 137. (Cited hereafter as *Chōsen Sōtōkufu*, '*Zaikyō Chōsenjin Jōkyō*'.)
23. Osaka-shi, '*Chōsenjin Rōdōsha Mondai*', p. 82.
24. See, for example, *Kōjō Kenkyū*, June, 1921, pp. 21–22.
25. *Naimushō, Shakai Kyoku – 1924*, in Pak, Z.K.S.S., Vol. 1, p. 449.
26. According to official sources this was also true as regards the independence movement. See *Osaka-shi, 'Chōsenjin Rōdōsha Mondai'*, p. 120.
37. General Affairs Department, 'Hanshin-Keihin', in Pak, Z.K.S.S., Vol. 1, p. 411. Also see *Naimushō, Shakai Kyoku – 1924*, in Pak, Z.K.S.S., Vol. 1, pp. 446–447.
28. George M. Beckmann, 'The Radical Left and the Failure of Communism', James William Morley, ed., *Dilemmas of Growth in Prewar Japan*, Princeton University Press, Princeton, 1971, pp. 150–151. Also see Collick, op.cit., pp. 240–241.
29. Collick, op.cit., pp. 202–203.
30. '*Chōsenjin Gaikyō [3]*', in Pak, Z.K.S.S., Vol, 1. pp. 92–94.
31. A list of Korean worker organizations appears as Appendix C1.
32. '*Chōsenjin Gaikyō [3]*', in Pak, Z.K.S.S., Vol. 1, p. 92.
33. These groups were the *Zaihan Chōsenjin Shimbokkai, Tōkyō Rōdō Dōshikai, Chōsenjin Kugakusei Dōyūkai, Kyōto Chōsenjin Rōdō Kyōsaikai, Chōsenjin Rōdō Saishinkai*, and the *Senjin Rōdō Minyūkai*.
34. '*Chōsenjin Gaikyō [3]*', in Pak, Z.K.S.S., Vol. 1, pp. 92–93. Also see *Naimushō Keihokyoku Hoanka* (Home Ministry Police Affairs Bureau Security Section), '*Chōsenjin Gaikyō*' ('A General View of Koreans'), Tokyo, 1916, in Pak, Z.K.S.S., Vol. 1, p. 49. (Cited hereafter as '*Chōsenjin Gaikyō [1]*'.)
35. *Naimushō*, '*Chōsenjin Gaikyō [3]*', in Pak, Z.K.S.S., Vol. 1, pp. 90–91.

Also see *Keihokyoku*, '*Zairyu Chōsenjin – 1925*', in Pak, Z.K.S.S., Vol. 1, pp. 155–156.
36. *Shihōshō*, '*Chōsenjin to Hanzai*', in Pak, Z.K.S.S., Vol. 1, p. 298.
37. *Osaka-shi*, '*Chōsenjin Rōdōsha Mondai*', p. 82.
38. Iwao Ayusawa, op.cit., pp. 134–135.
39. Henry DeWitt Smith, II, *Japan's First Student Radicals*, Harvard University Press, Cambridge, 1972, p. 54.
40. Pak Kyŏng-sik, *Undōshi*, op.cit., p. 146.
41. Nimura Kazuo, '*Zenkoku Kōfu Kumiai no Soshiki to Katsudō [3]*' ('The Establishment and Activities of the National Union of Miners, part 3'), *Shiryō Shipō*, No. 85, Ohara Shakai Mondai Kenkyūjō, Tokyo, August, 1972, p. 12. (Cited hereafter as Nimura, '*Zenkoku Kōfu Kumiai [3]*'.)
42. Nimura Kazuo, '*Zenkoku Kōfu Kumiai no Soshiki to Katsudō [1]*' ('The Establishment and Activities of the National Union of Miners, part 1'), *Shiryō Shipō*, No. 159, Ohara Shakai Mondai Kenkyūjō, Tokyo, February, 1970, p.6.
43. *Otaru Shimbun*, August 6, 1920.
44. Kawai Eizō, '*Nissen Rōdōsha no Akushu*', *Rōdō Shimpō*, No. 47, August 20, 1920, quoted in Nimura, '*Zenkoku Kōfu Kumiai [3]*', p. 13.
45. Ibid., p. 13. Also see Pak Kyŏng-sik, *Undōshi*, op.cit., p. 146.
46. *Yomiuri Shimbun*, July 29, 1922. Quoted in Iwamura, op.cit., pp. 67–68, and, Pak Kyŏng-sik, *Chōsenjin Kyōsei Renkō no Kiroku* (A Record of the Force Migration of Koreans), Miraisha,Tokyo, 1973, pp. 218–220. (Cited hereafter as Pak Kyŏng-sik, *Kyōsei Renkō no Kiroku*.) A brief account of the *Shinanogawa Jiken* is also given in Imai Seiichi, *Nihon no Rekishi (The History of Japan)* No. 23, Chūō Kōronsha, Tokyo, 1978, p. 374.
47. *Yomiuri Shimbun*, July 29, 1922. Quoted in Iwamura, op.cit., p. 68, and Pak Kyŏng-sik, *Kyōsei Renkō* no Kiroku, pp. 218–220.
48. *Tonga Ilbo*, August 1, 1922. Quoted in Pak Kyŏng-sik, *Kyōsei Renkō no Kiroku*, p. 221.
49. *Niigata Mainichi Shimbun*, August 8, 12, 1922. Quoted in Kim Ch'an-jong, *Ame no Dōkoku (Lamentation of the Rain)*, Tahata Shoten, Tokyo, 1979, pp. 105–106.
50. Ibid., p. 103. Also see Pak Kyŏng-sik, *Undōshi*, p. 147, and Iwamura, op.cit., p. 68.
51. Kim Ch'an-jong, op.cit., pp. 103–107.
52. Iwamura, op.cit., p. 68. Also see Imai Seiichi, op.cit., p. 375.
53. Pak Kyŏng-sik, *Undōshi*, p. 147. Paek Mu, for example, was one of thirty members of the *Chōsen Kugakusei Dōyūkai* who had attended the 1922 May Day Rally in Tokyo. During the demonstrations he attempted to address the rally on the subject of Korean independence, but was prevented from doing so by the police. See *Naimushō, Shakai Kyoku – 1924*, in Pak, Z.K.S.S., Vol. 1, p. 446. Paek was also a founder member of the *Kokutokai* (Black Wave Association). See *Keihokyoku*, '*Zairyū Chōsenjin – 1925*', in Pak, Z.K.S.S., Vol. 1, p. 169.
54. Pak Kyŏng-sik, *Undōshi*, p. 147.
55. '*Nissen Rōdōsha no Danketsu*', *Zen'ei*, September 1922.
56. In particular see Suzuki Bunji, '*Rōdō Dantai*', ('Labour Associations'), September 21, 1922, and, '*Chōsen no Shōrai*' ('The Future of Korea"), September 23, 1922. Both are cited in S.K.S.S., *Rōdō Hen*, Vol. 1, pp. 374–375.
57. *Naimushō, Shakai Kyoku – 1924*, op.cit., in Pak, Z.K.S.S., Vol. 1, p. 446.

58. *Shihōshō*, 'Chosenjin to Hanzai', in Pak, Z.K.S.S., Vol. 1, p. 274. Also see *Chōsen Sōtokufu*, 'Zaikyō Chōsenjin Tōkyō', in Pak, Z.K.S.S., Vol. 1, p. 139, Iwamura, op.cit., p. 70, and Pak Kyŏng-sik, *Undōshi*, pp. 120–121.
59. *Chōsen Sōtokufu*, 'Zaikyō Chōsenjin Tōkyō' in Pak, Z.K.S.S., Vol. 1, p. 139.
60. Quoted in Pak Kyŏng-sik, *Undōshi*, p.120.
61. *Keihokyoku*, 'Zairyū Chōsenjin – 1925', in Pak, Z.K.S.S., Vol. 1, p. 161.
62. *Naimushō Keihokyoku Hoanka* (Home Ministry Police Affairs Bureau Security Section), 'Taishō Jūgonen chūni Okaru Zairyū Chōsenjin no Tōkyō' ('The Condition of Koreans in Japan During 1926'), Tokyo, 1926, in Pak, Z.K.S.S., Vol.1, p. 209. (Cited hereafter as *Keihokyoku*, 'Zairyū Chōsenjin – 1926'.)
63. Ibid.
64. Ibid. The effects of factionalism on the activities of Korean radicals in Korea and China is discussed at length in Robert A. Scalapino and Chong-Sik Lee, *Communism in Korea, Part I: The Movement*, University of California Press, Berkeley, Los Angeles, London, 1972, pp. 20–28, 67–69. (Cited hereafter as Scalapino and Lee, *Communism in Korea, Part I*.).
65. *Keihokyoku*, 'Zairyū Chōsenjin – 1925', in Pak, Z.K.S.S., Vol. 1, p. 162. Also see *Chōsen Sōtokufu*, 'Zaikyō Chōsenjin Tōkyō', in Pak, Z.K.S.S., Vol. 1, p. 139.
66. *Shihōshō*, 'Chōsenjin to Hanzai', in Pak, Z.K.S.S., Vol.1, p. 274. Also see 'Chōsenjin Tōkyō', in Pak, Z.K.S.S., Vol. 1, p. 139, and Pak Kyŏng-sik, *Undōshi*, p. 106.
67. Iwamura, op.cit., pp. 70–71. Also see Pak Kyong-sik, Undōshi, p. 122, and *Rōdōsha Shimbun*, December 15, 1922.
68. Pak Kyŏng-sik, *Undōshi*, pp. 122–123, 147.
69. Cited in ibid., pp. 122–123.
70. Kim Yak-su, 'Chōsen Rōdō Kaikyū no Shinkō Undō' ('The Newly Awakened Movement of the Korean Working Classes'), *Rōdō Shimbun*, December 5, 1922, cited in Iwamura, op.cit., p. 70.
71. See, for example, Kim Chong-bŏm., 'Osaka Chōsen Rōdō Dōmeikai ni taisuru Kansō', ('Thoughts Concerning the Osaka League of Korean Labour'), *Rōdōsha Shimbun*, December 15, 1922.
72. *Zen'ei*, January 1923. Cited in Iwamura, op.cit., pp. 71–72.
73. *Keihokyoku*, 'Zairyū Chōsenjin – 1925', in Pak, Z.K.S.S., Vol. 1, pp. 156, 162–163, 188.
74. *Shihōshō Keiji Kyoku* (Ministry of Justice Criminal Affairs Bureau), *Nihon Shakai Undō no Tōkyō* (The Present State of the Social Movement in Japan), 'Chōsenjin Mondai', ('The Korean Problem'), Tokyo, 1928, in Pak, Z.K.S.S., Vol. 1, p. 248. (Cited hereafter as *Shihōshō*, 'Chosenjin Mondai'.)
75. *Naimushō, Shakai Kyoku – 1924*, in Pak, Z.K.S.S., Vol. 1, p. 447.
76. *Rōdō Shimbun*, January 20, 1923.
77. *Rōdōsha Shimbun*, February 15, 1923.
78. *Rōdō Shimbun*, February 5, 1923.
79. Iwamura, op.cit., p. 78.
80. Cited in ibid.
81. *Osaka Asahi Shimbun*, May 2, 1923. Cited in Iwamura, op.cit., p. 78.
82. Cited in ibid.
83. Robert A. Scalapino, *Democracy And the Party Movement In Prewar Japan*, University of California Press, Berkeley, Los Angeles, London, 1975, p. 326.
84. *Naimushō Keihokyokuchō* (Home Ministry Director Police Affairs

Bureau), *Naimushō Kakukei Dai San Gō* (Home Ministry Police Notification No. 3), *Chōsenjin Rōdōsha Boshū ni Kansuru Ken* ('The Recruitment of Korean Workers'), Tokyo, May 14, 1923, cited in Pak, Z.K.S.S., Vol. 1, pp. 38–39.

85. This speech was given at the *Hōmeniin Rengōkai* (Standing Committee of District Commissioners). The *Hōmeniin* (District Commissioner) system was established in Osaka in 1918. *Hōmeniin* were responsible for the investigation of socially and economically deprived people living in the Osaka area. Its principal function, however, was not 'welfare' in the normal sense but social control over those elements regarded as the least stable and therefore the most likely to become a breeding ground for social unrest. This system developed out of a belief which gained wide support among prefectural officials following the Rice Riots that direct controls needed to be applied at the lowest administrative levels in areas where social disturbances were most likely to occur. For a more detailed treatment of the *Hōmeniin* system see Toyori Tatara, *1400 Years of Japanese Social Work From Its Origins Through The Allied Occupation, 552–1952*, Vol. 1, Unpublished Doctoral Dissertation, Bryn Mawr College, 1975, pp. 145–168. Also see Masayoshi Chūbachi and Koji Taira, 'Poverty in Modern Japan: Perceptions and Realities', in Hugh Patrick, ed., *Japanese Industrialization and Its Social Consequences*, University of California Press, Berkeley and Los Angeles, 1976, pp. 424–426.

86. Hiraga Makoto, '*Senjin Mondai ni tsuite*' ('Concerning the Korean Problem'), *Shakai Jigyō Kenkyū, Osaka Shakai Jigyō Kenkyūkai*, Vol. 11, No. 8, part 2, August 25, 1923, pp. 667–668.

87. Ibid., p. 670.

88. The Korean section of the National Union of Miners, for example, was referred to as the *Senjin-bu*. Also see Iwamura, op.cit., pp. 77–78.

89. See, for example, Miriam S. Farley, 'Korean Labour In Japan Depresses Wage Level', *Far Eastern Survey*, June 23, 1937, p. 151.

Chapter 5

The Korean Student Movement in Japan: From Nationalism to Socialism

Korean students first appeared in Japan nearly thirty years before the annexation of Korea. In common with Japanese students of an earlier generation, who studied abroad during the first years of Meiji, the first Korean students to be sent abroad were regarded, and regarded themselves, as a political and technical elite who would lay the foundations of a modern Korean state. This attitude was reinforced by their experiences in Japan where the new nationalism articulated in the slogan *Fukoku Kyōhei* (Enrich the Nation, Strengthen the Army) was encouraging the development of new political institutions and industries. Out of this exposure to Japanese modernization were born several attempts to carry out a 'Korean Restoration', first in 1884 and again in 1895. In both instances Korean students, who had previously studied in Japan, or had been directly influenced by Japanese liberals such as Fukuzawa Yukichi, were the dominant figures within the reform movement. To a certain extent therefore, Korean students in Japan were the inheritors of a tradition of student involvement in Korean politics, and must be discussed within that context.

For their own part, the Japanese authorities actively encouraged an often reluctant Korean Government to send its most promising young men to Japanese schools. Motivated by what Hilary Conroy has described as 'enlightened self interest', many prominent Japanese saw in these Korean students not only the foundation of a strong Korea which would stand alongside Japan as a bulwark against Western encroachment, but also an ideal opportunity to shape the attitudes of Korea's future leaders.[1]

The Japanese Government first raised the possibility of a student mission in 1877, but it was not until 1881 that the Korean court agreed to the despatch of students to Japan.[2] In the interim, Yi Tong-in, a shadowy figure, who was connected with both the Pusan mission of a Japanese Buddhist sect and a small circle of young reform-minded Koreans grouped around Kim Ok-kyun, Pak Yŏng-hyo and Sŏ Kwang-bŏm, had secretly crossed to Japan in 1879. After a brief stay in Kyoto, Yi made his way to Tokyo where he met Terada Motoyoshi, who was a student at *Keiō Gijuku*[3] and a temporary house guest of Fukuzawa

Yukichi. It was through Terada that Yi was introduced to Fukuzawa, thereby initiating a relationship between Fukuzawa and two generations of Korean students.[4]

It appears to have been on the strength of recommendations made by Yi and passed on by Kim Hong-jip, the leader of the second Korean diplomatic mission to Japan, that King Kojong agreed to send an observation mission to Japan.[5] Two of the members of the *sinsa yuramdan* (Gentleman's Touring Corps), as it was known, were enrolled at Keiō, while a third member of the party entered a school operated by Nakamura Masanao – an associate of Fukuzawa's and frequent contributor to the magazine *Meiroku Zasshi* (Civilization and Enlightenment).[6] In a letter written soon after the arrival of the mission, Fukuzawa remarked that the situation in Korea resembled that which had existed in Japan thirty years earlier, and concluded 'Hereafter we must endeavour to look after these students and enable them to develop their own country.'[7]

Fukuzawa's involvement with Korean students received further encouragement from the first of several visits to Japan by Kim Ok-kyun. Kim arrived in Tokyo in March 1882 and spent much of the following five months as Fukuzawa's house guest. In the years that followed Fukuzawa was Kim's most important source of information about the West, and it was under Fukuzawa's tutelage that Kim translated his beliefs into a concrete programme for the modernization of Korea.[8]

Kim returned to Japan in October 1882 and spent a further six months conferring with Fukuzawa concerning the future of the progressive movement. Divisions within the movement between those who favoured a gradual approach to modernization, and those like himself who advocated more fundamental reforms had convinced Kim of the need to send many more students to Japan.[9] Consequently, in 1883 a group of forty Korean students arrived in Japan and were enrolled at Keiō. Although Fukuzawa agreed to accept overall responsibility for this project, Iida Sanji, a protege of Fukuzawa, was made responsible for the day-to-day supervision of the students. Preparations were made to house the entire group in a disused barracks, and it was decided that, after receiving a thorough grounding in the Japanese language at Keiō, each student, upon the recommendation of Fukuzawa and Iida, would receive further specialized training at a variety of schools and government-operated institutions.[10]

Fukuzawa's hand was also evident in the subsequent activities of some of his proteges who returned to Korea in 1883. Yu Kil-chun, one of Fukuzawa's first Korean students, later translated Fukuzawa's *Moji no Oshie* (Elementary Reader For Children) into Korean, while he and Inoue Kakugorō founded Korea's first newspaper.[11] Fukuzawa's commitment to the progressive movement at this time was well summarized by his friend and pupil Inoue. According to Inoue, Fukuzawa's farewell to him on the eve of his departure to Korea contained the following reminder:

> Unless the Koreans acquire the knowledge of civilization and enjoy a secure life, there can be no genuine co-operation between them and Japan. Therefore, we should help them unreservedly through cultural inspiration. I take it as my mission to advocate this civilizing power among the Koreans so that they may progress toward civilization and enlightenment.[12]

Although the progressives succeeded in implementing a number of reforms between 1883 and 1884, their efforts were constantly thwarted by the entrenched power of the consevative Min family at the Korean court. Unable to overcome this resistance and disillusioned by the Japanese Government's failure to fully support the progressives, Kim, accompanied by many of his student adherents, returned to Korea in mid- 1884.[13] Their attempt to seize power later in the year, however, lacked popular support and the attempted coup was crushed within days, leaving the pro-Chinese faction in even firmer control of the government. Many Korean students had lost their lives during the insurrection, while others were imprisoned or forced into exile, and with Chinese influence in Korea now at its zenith no further student missions were sent to Japan until 1895.[14]

Following Japan's victory in the Sino-Japanese War of 1894–1895 and the installation of a pro-Japanese government in Seoul preparations were again made to send students to Japan for technical training. In view of the longstanding friendship which existed between prominent Korean officials and Fukuzawa Yukichi, it is not surprising that the Korean authorities sought Fukuzawa's assistance in creating a special programme for Korean students.[15] To avoid a repetition of past instances of student involvement in political affairs, a contract dealing with a broad range of student related matters was agreed upon by Kamata Eikichi, representing Keiō, and the Korean Minister of Education. As in the past, Keiō accepted responsibility for devising a special curriculum for Korean students and for ensuring their further training upon completion of this programme, at other schools or government institutions. For its own part, the Korean Government agreed to finance the programme, though Keiō would be responsible for supervising all aspects of the students' conduct and behaviour. It was also agreed that failure to maintain academic standards or involvement in political activities would result in immediate dismissal from the programme and repatriation to Korea.[16]

Within two months, however, these negotiations were superseded by events in Korea. Japanese involvement in the assassination of Queen Min in October 1895 led to the immediate return of many students to Korea, while others left Japan and continued their studies abroad, principally in the United States. Fewer than half of the original contingent of students managed to complete the programme at Keiō, and early in 1896 the Korean Government withdrew its support entirely and ordered all remaining students to return home.[17]

With the exception of an unsuccessful attempt to reactivate the student programme in 1899, the sending of further missions was suspended until 1904 when Japanese influence in Korea was once again on the rise. From about this time the Japanese Government began to assume a much more direct role in the education of Korean students in Japan, and the importance of private institutions, such as Keiō, which had figured strongly in the past, diminished rapidly.[18] Japan's newly acquired status as an Imperial power also had a profound effect upon the Korean students who came to Japan during the five year period before the annexation. The previously-held image of Japan as a supporter of the reform movement and a defender of Korean independence was gradually displaced by one which reflected her increasing ambitions in Korea. Student disillusionment with Japanese policies grew rapidly and as the prospect of annexation increased so too did the anti-Japanese activities of Korean students. They established numerous associations and societies, whose objectives were generally defined in terms of opposition to Japanese policies in Korea, and held many rallies and demonstrations at which Korean independence was passionately defended. Although such protests can hardly be considered to have been ideologically motivated, the response of the Japanese authorities to student strikes and other types of organized protest was indicative not only of a shift in official attitudes towards Korea, but of less tolerant attitudes towards student involvement in politics generally.

The first group of Korean students to study in Japan during this period arrived in Tokyo in November 1904. At the request of the Ministry of Education the majority were enrolled in a special preparatory course at Tokyo First Middle School, one of the most prestigious schools of its kind in Japan. The principal of this school, Katsura Tomokazu, was assigned complete control over all matters dealing with education and housing, and a special curriculum for Korean students was quickly devised. The vigorous atmosphere which prevailed at Tokyo First Middle School was reminiscent of that which was common in schools for military cadets. Extreme emphasis was placed upon physical, moral and social discipline, and misconduct was punishable by expulsion from the programme. Consequently, during the course's first year of operation nearly 50% of the original entrants were withdrawn from the programme and only half of them replaced.[19]

The first and most serious incident involving Korean students at Tokyo First Middle School was a student strike which occurred in

December 1905. The immediate cause for this strike was remarks made by Katsura Tomokazu concerning Korean students in an interview published by the *Hōchi Shimbun* early in December, though in the background was student opposition to and unease over the Treaty of Protection which had been concluded one month earlier. In articles published on consecutive days Katsura criticized the Korean students for lacking the proper discipline and application and suggested that higher education might not be necessary for Koreans.[20] The response of the students was immediate and, given the prevailing mood among them, entirely predictable. The next morning none of the Korean students appeared for their classes and they announced their intention to boycott all lessons until Katsura's statements were retracted.[21] The Japanese authorities responded by enlisting the aid of a number of Korean officials and attempted to persuade the students to end the strike. After repeated overtures had been rejected by the strikers, all thirty-seven were expelled from the programme. Seventeen of the students were later readmitted though the leaders were ordered to return to Korea.[22]

Until this time there had existed no national regulations governing the operation of study programmes for foreign students in Japan. As in the case of Korean students at Tokyo First Middle School and earlier at Keiō, overall responsibility for supervising the activities of foreign students, both at school and in their everyday lives, had been entrusted to the officials of the schools where these students were enrolled. In the view of Japanese officials in Korea and Japan it was this lack of centralized administrative control over foreign students which had lent itself to increasing political activism on the part of Korean students and encouraged the outbreak of incidents such as the one described above at Tokyo First Middle School. Consequently on January 1, 1906, the office of Korean Student Supervisor was created. Under regulations issued by the Government the Student Supervisor was made responsible for all aspects of the students' lives, and was required to submit tri-monthly reports on the attendance and behaviour of each student to the Ministry of Education.[23]

Despite these efforts by the Japanese Government to control the activities of Korean students there was an upsurge of what were perceived by officials as 'anti-Japanese' activities and a proliferation of Korean student organizations between 1906 and 1910. Most drew their membership on the basis of regional affiliation, or whether members were government-sponsored or privately financed. These organizations rarely overcame their regionalism and tended to disappear after a brief existence due to factional disputes.[24] 1906, however, witnessed the establishment of two organizations which were to play important roles in shaping the future course of the Korean student movement in Japan.

The first of these was the Korean Young Men's Christian Association in Tokyo, which was established in November 1906. Although its stated objectives were to encourage Christian ideals and engage in missionary work among Koreans living in Tokyo, its offices in the Kanda district quickly emerged as a principal meeting place for students and, in the view of the authorities, a centre of 'seditious activities'.[25] Later in the same month a number of students who had been involved in the Tokyo First Middle School strike organized the Japan Greater Korea Association of Students in Tokyo. This association sponsored meetings and demonstrations in support of anti-Japanese forces in Korea, and in March 1907 mobilized student opposition to a motion made at the *Mogi Kokka* (Imitation Diet – the name given to the Waseda University Debating Society) suggesting that the King of Korea be ranked among the Japanese nobility. Members of this group also participated in a demonstration, later referred to as the *Kikka Jiken* (Chrysanthemum Incident), which took place in November 1907. Several hundred Korean students, angered by a display at the Chrysanthemum Festival in the Hongō district of Tokyo, which depicted the King of Korea prostrating himself before *Shōgun* Tokugawa Ienobu, attacked the offending exhibit and in the ensuing melee a number of arrests were made.[26]

It was also during this period of growing opposition to Japanese policies that the number of Koreans enrolled in Japanese schools increased rapidly.[27] By 1910, the year in which the annexation was carried out, there were more than 500 Korean students in Japan. As Table 20 clearly shows, more than 90% of these students were self-financed, and it was they who were to be the most politically active group in Japan after the annexation.

TABLE 20

Number of Korean Students and Courses Enrolled in (May 1910)

Type of School	Curriculum Studies	Number of Students
Professional	Politics, Law, Economics	90 (11)
Schools	Technical (Jitsugyō)	72 (24)
	Literature (education)	10 (8)
	Medicine	20 (2)
Regular	Middle School	70 (2)
Schools	Primary School	8
Miscellaneous (including language schools)		137
Unidentified		97
Total		504 (47)

Source: Abe, 'Korean Students in Japan before 1945', p. 32.
Note: Figures in brackets refer to government-sponsored students.

Although most Koreans who entered Japan after 1910 were contract-workers and other types of labourers, it was students who were the most vocal opponents of Japanese colonial policies. Like their counterparts from other colonial areas receiving their education in the 'mother country', many Korean students rejected the very basis of Japanese colonialism and became passionate advocates of Korean independence. While student-sponsored resistance to Japanese policies had been a source of concern before 1910, police surveillance of student leaders and other dissidents was greatly intensified after the annexation.[28] The fact that virtually all official reports concerning Korean students were compiled by the Police Affairs Bureau is in itself indicative of government preoccupations. Their anxieties were confirmed when, in 1919, students were found to have been among the principal architects of both the Independence Movement and the Korean Provisional Government. Moreover, by the early 1920s Korean students were organizing groups for the investigation of Marxism and other proletarian ideologies, often with the clear intention of overthrowing the state and of completely transforming society along socialist lines.

Educational Opportunities in Japan

Official attitudes toward study in Japan were expressed in a series of regulations issued by the Government-General in 1911 and subsequently forwarded to all local authorities in Japan. These incorporated and strengthened many of the features of the 1905 regulations, and stipulated that the schools entered by sponsored students, the courses undertaken and the permitted period of study in Japan would all be designated by the Government-General. These were augmented by further regulations, redefining the responsibilities of the Korean Student Supervisor, which had first been laid down in 1906.[29]

An annual grant of 500 yen per student was allocated for government-sponsored students, with additional funds made available to cover travel and other miscellaneous expenses. On the other hand, students receiving government aid were required to inform the student supervisor of any change of address and to seek his approval if they intended to leave their place of study during holiday periods. Moreover, under the new regulations, the student supervisor was empowered to suspend the payment of government grants if a recipient was judged to have 'sullied his honour as a student in Japan through bad behaviour,' failed to obey the orders of the supervisor, violated school regulations, or was not expected to complete his course of study due to ill health or poor academic results.[30] The supervisor was also required to submit regular reports concerning both sponsored students and all schools which admitted Korean students.

The number of government-sponsored schools in Japan between 1910 and 1919 never exceeded fifty in a single year. And in keeping with the aims of the Government-General to select courses on the basis of their suitability for getting on in life after graduation, the vast majority (82.1%) of these students were sent to receive training in agriculture, medicine, forestry or irrigation. In marked contrast, only six individuals during this period were selected to study law, politics or economics.[31]

While it was not possible to impose such extensive restrictions on self-financed students, the 1911 regulations clearly expressed the Government-General's intention to limit their numbers also. Students wishing to finance their own education in Japan were first required to submit to the Government-General a formal application which was to include a *curriculum vitae*, the school and proposed course of study and their anticipated length of stay in Japan. The provincial authorities, to whom the application was first submitted, then conducted a thorough investigation of the applicant's background and the ability of his family to support his studies. After their arrival in Japan, these students were required to submit a second *curriculum vitae* to the student supervisor in Tokyo, appended to which would be their address in Japan, the name of the school and course to be attended, and a statement of guarantee signed by two guarantors who undertook responsibility for the payment of school fees. Only after these conditions were satisfied was the applicant permitted to enrol in school.[32]

Despite these controls, self-financed students constituted nearly 90% of the total number of students in Japan between 1912 and 1919. Unlike those with state sponsorship, self-financed students tended to enrol in programmes specializing in the social sciences, reflecting both a rejection of colonial education policies and a growing interest in politics, law and economics.[33]

As is shown in table 21, approximately 40% of all Korean students were enrolled in schools above the Middle School level, while a further 45% were enrolled in various types of preparatory school.

The high proportion of Korean students in preparatory schools was regarded by the orities as further evidence of the fecklessness of Koreans and of their inability to satisfy the rigorous educational standards set by most schools in Japan.[34] But, given the abbreviated and relatively inferior educational standards in Korea, it was inevitable that Korean students would be at a considerable disadvantage in the highly competitive educational system in Japan. Despite these handicaps, a significant number of Korean students were able to complete Professional School or University programmes in Japan.[35] Although Korean students attended schools throughout Japan, Table 22 clearly illustrates that the great majority were concentrated in Tokyo, and it is to these that the following discussion will mainly refer.[36]

TABLE 21

Types of Schools Attended by Korean Students (1920)

Type of School	Number of Students	Percent of Total
University	29	2.5
Professional School/University Preparatory Course	424	37.2
Technical School	72	6.3
Middle School (including Girls' Schools)	99	8.7
Preparatory Schools and Others	517	45.3
Total	1,141	100

Source: *Chōsen Sōtokufu Gakumu Kyoku* (Government-General of Korea Education Bureau), '*Zainaichi Chōsen Gakusei Jōkyō*' ('The Condition of Korean Students in Japan'), 1920, in Pak, Z.K.S.S., Vol. 1, p. 304. (Cited hereafter as '*Zainaichi Chōsen Gakusei Jōkyō*'.)

Note: Others include Language Schools which enrolled high numbers of Korean students throughout this period.

TABLE 22

Korean Students in Japan by Prefecture: Selected Years

Year	Tokyo	Kyoto	Osaka	Hyōgo	Others	Total
1915	362	28	8	13	70	481
1917	436	39	10	17	87	589
1920	682	47	10	12	77	828
1921	1,141	58	14	20	97	1,303

Sources: For 1915, '*Chōsenjin Gaikyō [1]*', in Pak, Z.K.S.S., Vol. 1, pp. 58–59.
For 1917, '*Chōsenjin Gaikyō [2]*', in Pak, Z.K.S.S., Vol. 1, pp. 62–63.
For 1920, '*Chōsenjin Gaikyō [3]*', in Pak, Z.K.S.S., Vol. 1, pp. 117–118.
For 1921, Naimushō, '*Chōsenjin Kinkyō Gaiyō*', in Pak, Z.K.S.S., Vol. 1, pp. 128–130.

Note: Only those Prefectures which figure consistently in the above update reports have been included in this Table.

The Korean Student Movement 1910–1918

It is not possible to dissociate the Korean student movement in Japan from the social and ideological environment into which it was born and developed. The body of ideas which provided the impetus of the so-called 'Taishō Democracy' movement also encouraged the crystallization of student opposition to Japanese colonial policies into a recognizable movement. The greatest single source of encouragement came from a small but highly influential group of Japanese University professors, like Yoshino Sakuzō and Fukuda Tokuzō, whose consistent criticism of the colonial administration in Korea held an obvious appeal for Korean students. A second important factor which influenced the activities of Korean students, particularly during the final year of the First World War, was the speeches made by Woodrow Wilson in support of the principle of national self-determination. For many young Korean intellectuals, in both Japan and Korea, Wilson's apparent commitment to the cause of colonial liberation reinforced their own opposition to Japanese rule and offered a political foundation upon which an independence movement could be built. The third major influence on both the social and political life of the Taishō period and the Korean student movement was the impact of the proletarian ideologies emphasizing the fundamental and irreconcilable differences between capital and labour, and between 'Imperial' nation and 'Colonial' possesion. The influence which anarcho-syndicalism and later Marxist-Leninist thought exercised over Korean intellectuals, particularly after the fragmentation of the nationalist movement in the 1920s, should not be underestimated, but during the first decade of colonial rule it was the struggle to preserve and strengthen a Korean sense of identity which mainly occupied the minds of students in Japan.[37]

Underpinning all student activism between 1910 and 1919 was the sense of anger and frustration expressed by Yi Kwang-su, Korea's first modern novelist,[38] early in 1916. He claimed that every 'people' had a right to life, but that the Koreans exercise of this right was being denied by Japanese colonial rule, and concluded that:

> At the present time the Japanese are coming to our country, oppressing our people and monopolizing all profitable activities, while our people can but gulp back the tears, abandon the homeland in which they have spent their lives and wander far across mountains and seas to foreign parts. What greater tragedy could there be than this? The authorities, moreover, far from feeling remorse, continue to deprive us of all liberty and power, and consider that their policies have proved successful. Can this be borne in silence?[39]

As is illustrated in Table 23, most student groups were formed during the First World War. Many other associations and fraternal societies were also established during this period, but most existed for only a very short time and exercised little or no influence on the student movement as a whole. Inevitably, therefore, the following discussion will concentrate on the activities of more stable groups like the Korean YMCA. Not only were the leaders of the student movement drawn from among these associations, but a number of these same student leaders later held positions of importance within the Korean Provisional Government, while others such as Yi Kwang-su and Chang Tŏk-su made significant contributions to the nationalist movement through journalism and literature.[40] These organizations and the activities they sponsored were also subjected to intensive surveillance and harassment by the police. The reasons for this are expressed quite clearly in the following extract from a police report compiled in 1916.

> On the surface these groups advocate such things as mutual friendship, physical and spiritual self-discipline and the study of arts and science. But at their meetings, under the guise of Sunday Prayer Meetings or academic debates, the conversation usually turns to politics or current affairs, and in many instances they use implicitly extreme phrases like 'the destruction of the present situation' and 'the overthrow of tyranny', and by doing so encourage or advocate anti-Japanese views.[41]

There is very little reliable information available concerning the activities of Korean students in Japan before about 1915. But encouraged by the outbreak of the war in Europe and the deterioration of relations between Japan and China, Korean students then became much more vocal in their criticism of Japanese policies. In November 1914 three students at Meiji University were arrested for writing articles on such topics as 'The Present Situation in Korea', 'The Spirit of Korean Students in Japan', and 'The Future of Our Nation'. One year later another group of students at Meiji University were found to have smuggled several hundred copies of Pak Un-sik's *Hanguk T'ongsa* ('The Tragic History of Korea') into Japan and distributed them among Korean students in Tokyo.[42]

Although there is no substantive evidence to indicate that Korean students in Tokyo were actively co-operating with anti-Japanese groups abroad, news of the conflict in Europe and the prospect of a war between China and Japan appears to have elicited similar responses among Koreans in Tokyo and elsewhere.[43] Pak Un-sik and Yi Tong-hwi, the leaders of the Korean Revolutionary Corps in China, for example, reasoned that Japan's support of the Entente Powers and her issuance of the Twenty-One Demands to China had aroused the hostility of both

TABLE 23
Principal Korean Student Organizations in Japan (1905–1918)

Name of Organization	Location	Date of Establishment	Date of Dissolution
ZaiTōkyō Chōsen Kirisutokyō Seinenkai (Korean Young Men's Christian Association in Tokyo) Hereafter referred to as the 'Korean YMCA'.	Tokyo	November 5, 1906	
ZaiNihon Tōkyō Taikan Ryūgakuseikai (Greater Korea Tokyo Association of Korean Students)	Tokyo	November 1906	
Taikan Gakuseikai (Greater Korea Student Association)	Tokyo	1908	
Taikan Kyōgakkai (Greater Korea Association for the Promotion of Education)	Tokyo	March 1909	August 1909
Chōsen Ryūgakusei Shimbokkai (Fraternal Association of Korean Students in Japan)	Tokyo	May 1911	March 1912
Zai Tōkyō Chōsen Ryūgakusei Gakuyūkai (Fraternal Association of Korean Students in Tokyo) Hereafter referred to as the Gakuyūkai	Tokyo	October 27, 1912	
Zaihan Chōsen Shimbokkai (Korean Friendship Society of Osaka)	Osaka	January 15, 1914	
Hantō Chūgakkai (Peninsular Association of Middle School Students	Tokyo	March 1914	
Kyōtō Chōsen Ryūgakusei Shimbokkai (Friendship Association of Korean Students in Kyoto)	Kyoto	January 24, 1915	
Tōa Dōmeikai (Far Eastern Alliance)	Tokyo	October 1915	
Chōsen Gakkai (Korean Learned Society)	Tokyo	November 10, 1915	
Chōsen Joshi Ryūgakusei Shimbokkai (Friendship Association of Korean Women Students in Japan)	Tokyo	1915	

Sources: '*Chōsenjin Gaikyō [2]*', in Pak, Z.K.S.S., Vol. 1, pp. 65–67.
'*Chōsenjin Gaikyō [3]*', in Pak, Z.K.S.S., Vol. 1, pp. 90–91.

Germany and China. Therefore, assuming an eventual German victory in Europe, they believed it likely that Germany and China would then attack Japan, and that Japan's inevitable defeat in such a conflict might well favour the restoration of Korean independence.[44] Similar views were expressed at a meeting in Tokyo during January 1915. The speaker believed that, were a war to break out between Japan and China, the United States would almost inevitably be drawn in on the side of China. 'Moreover,' he argued, 'if we were to declare the revival of Korea before the world, both China and the United States would in some way intervene. We should therefore hope for the earliest possible disruption of diplomatic relations between Japan and China.'[45]

In general, however, the speeches of Korean students at this time tended to reflect a deeper concern with identifying their own role as representatives and future leaders of the Korean people than with specific issues. Typical of this was a speech made by Song Chin-u in which he urged his audience to prepare for the future, saying:

> I believe that in the near future . . . there will also arise an opportunity for us the youth to realize our pure and noble spirit. Therefore, from this day forward, we must prepare ourselves to carry out our responsibilities.[46]

Such speeches were often made before large audiences, but they do not appear to have been regarded as particularly important by either the police or the Home Ministry.[47] By 1916, however, student speeches began to assume a more openly anti-Japanese tone, and there were frequent calls for students to employ 'direct action' against external aggressors.[48] The Government's response to this new militancy was an intensification of surveillance on all student activities. In July 1916 the Home Ministry issued a set of instructions to all Prefectural Governors, designed to systematize the surveillance of suspected dissidents and agitators throughout Japan. Under the *Yōshisatsu Chōsenjin Shisatsu Naiki* (Internal Regulations for the Observation of Koreans Requiring Surveillance), as they were known, every prefectural government was required to compile a register of known or suspected dissidents. Each entry was to contain the suspect's date of birth, occupation, address, special identifying features and other relevant materials such as any organizations of which he was a member, meetings attended, writings and other publications, photographs and handwriting specimens, associations with foreigners and, of course, a record of his movements within Japan and between Japan and Korea. The prefectural authorities were also requested to furnish copies of all dossiers to both the Police Affairs Bureau in Tokyo and, 'where relevant,' to the Government-General.[49] As is clearly evident from Table 24, the overwhelming majority of the suspected dissidents appearing on these lists were students living in Tokyo.

TABLE 24
Yōshisatsu Chōsenjin by Prefecture and Class: Selected Years (1916–1922)

Year	Tokyo A	Tokyo B	Tokyo Total	Kyoto A	Kyoto B	Kyoto Total	Osaka A	Osaka B	Osaka Total	Hyōgo A	Hyōgo B	Hyōgo Total	Others A	Others B	Others Total	Total A	Total B	Total
1916	71	100	171	1	27	28	4	96	100	0	77	77	11	141	148	83	441	524
1917	74	101	175	1	3	4	1	17	18	0	4	4	7	28	35	83	153	236
1918	43	76	119	2	3	5	2	20	22	1	3	4	7	26	33	55	131	186
1920	92	63	155	3	3	6	0	2	2	1	4	5	11	35	46	107	105	212
			(141)			(3)			(0)			(2)			(5)			(151)
1922	109	58	167	5	5	10	5	14	19	6	2	8	6	26	32	131	105	236

Sources: 'Chōsenjin Gaikyō [1]', in Pak, Z.K.S.S., Vol. 1, p. 59.
'Chōsenjin Gaikyō [2]', in Pak, Z.K.S.S., Vol. 1, pp. 63–64.
'Chōsenjin Gaikyō [3]', in Pak, Z.K.S.S., Vol. 1, pp. 83–84.
Naimushō, 'Chōsenjin Kinkyō Gaijō', in Pak, Z.K.S.S., Vol. 1, p. 125.

Note: Suspected dissidents were categorized as either A or B Class Yōshisatsu Chōsenjin. A Class referred to those who advocated strongly anti-Japanese views, or were believed capable of committing acts of terrorism against the state. B Class included all individuals who were suspected of holding anti-Japanese views.
(Figures in brackets refer to the number of students.)

Despite stepped-up surveillance and other forms of police harassment, students in Tokyo continued to publish provocative articles in their magazines and to sponsor meetings and debates at which there was outspoken criticism of the Government.[50] Given the presence of police officers and informers at all student gatherings, speakers tended to refer only indirectly to the issue of Korean independence. Frequent use of phrases like 'the responsibility of youth' or 'our destiny is none other than to fulfil our destiny as Koreans' conveyed student opposition to the assimilation policy pursued by the Government-General.[51] A more direct appeal for Korean independence can be found in an address given by Song Kye-baek at a mass meeting sponsored by the *Gakuyūkai* late in 1917. In it Song urged his fellow students, whom he referred to as 'the vanguard in the struggle for Korean independence', not to be enticed by the 'doctrines of Mammon' into betraying their fellow countrymen. Instead, he called upon them to reject any form of co-operation with the Japanese Government, and to sacrifice all in the struggle to achieve independence.[52]

One of the most militant student publications during this period was the *Reform News* edited by Yi Tal, the leader of the *Tōyō Seinen Dōshikai* (Comradely Association of Eastern Youth).[53] Typical of the articles published in this journal was one entitled 'Tell Us Of Your Real Intentions, Japan!' which appeared in the October 1918 issue. In it the author, who chose to remain anonymous, accused the Japanese Government of having imposed the annexation on the people of Korea through a mixture of deception and physical coercion, adding that:

> . . . rather than shedding unnecessary tears or accepting the sort of cruel treatment which is usually meted out to slaves or animals, I believe that, as far as possible, and with all our might we should seek revenge and become the vengeful spirits of patriotism.[54]

Within months of this article's publication, Korean students in Tokyo, as well as other nationalist groups operating independently in China and Korea, managed to crystallize their opposition to Japanese colonial rule into an 'Independence Movement'.

Korean Students in Tokyo and the Independence Movement of 1919

1 – Domestic and International Influences

Between 1910 and 1919 domestic criticism of the policies pursued by the Government-General was almost non-existent. Two prominent exceptions to this were Professor Yoshino Sakuzō and Kashiwagi Gien, both of whom were influential members of the Japan Congregational Church.[55] Writing in the April 1914 issue of the *Jōmō Church Monthly*, Kashiwagi challenged the view held by other church leaders that it was the obligation of Japanese Christians to help foster an awareness of being Japanese among the Korean people. He also doubted whether the objectives of missionary work and those of the colonial administration were even compatible and added:

> If there is anyone who uses the teachings of the Gospel as a tool for the promotion of imperialism, we have no choice but to condemn this practice. Whether we should make imperialism our national policy is, in any event, open to question.[56]

Kashiwagi also expressed sympathy for those Koreans who sought to regain their country's independence. While stopping short of recommending immediate independence for Korea, he reminded his readers that the basis for Japan's initial involvement in Korean affairs had been to preserve that nation's independence.[57]

This article by Kashiwagi is important in two respects. First, his criticism of 'assimilation' as pursued in Korea and his recognition of the right of the Korean people to seek their independence were the first such opinions to appear in the Japanese press after 1910. Second, although the readership of this journal was extremely limited in comparison with the national dailies, or even with magazines such as *Chūō Kōron* (Central Review), it seems likely that this article would have been read by Korean students.[58]

Yoshino Sakuzō's position as a member of the prestigious Law Faculty at Tokyo Imperial University, his sponsorship of student groups like the *Shinjinkai* and the *Reimeikai* (Dawn Society), and his consistent criticism of Japan's colonial policies all brought him into direct contact with Korean students. In June 1916, following a three-week tour of Korea and Manchuria, Yoshino presented his impressions of the colonial administration in an article published in *Chūō Kōron*.[59] In this article Yoshino was extremely critical of both the militaristic nature of the colonial administration and the activities of the Japan Congregational Church. He, like Kashiwagi, also challenged the commonly-held assumption that the Korean people could and should be assimilated, and urged that the policy of *dōka* be abandoned entirely. Though vague in his support for Korean independence, Yoshino recommended that the authorities adopt 'as the ideal policy for Korea' one which would, 'respect the independence of the Korean people as a race, and through the perfecting of this independence eventually grant political and economic self-government.'[60]

It was not, however, until 1919 that Yoshino's opposition to Japan's colonial ambitions resulted in much closer ties with Korean students in Tokyo. Immediately before the outbreak of the Korean independence demonstrations in that year a number of Korean students are thought to have regularly attended meetings of the *Reimeikai*, and at least one

Korean student, Kim Chun-yŏn, is known to have been a member of the *Shinjinkai*.[61]

As we have already seen, Korean students in Tokyo and elsewhere were keenly interested in international developments which might favour the restoration of Korean independence. Of particular importance in this respect were the wartime speeches made by Woodrow Wilson and, to a lesser extent, Russia's repudiation of imperialism after the 1917 revolution. While the example set by the Russian Revolution undoubtedly encouraged anti-Japanese groups operating close to or inside the Soviet Union, there is no evidence to suggest that events in Russia had any appreciable influence on the activities of Koreans in Tokyo or Korea. Wilson's repeated references to national self-determination as a principle which should be extended to all people, however, had an immediate impact on Korean nationalists around the world.[62]

In China and Japan, where Wilson's speeches had received widespread exposure in the press, news of the Armistice was greeted exuberantly by Koreans opposed to Japanese rule. In Shanghai one such group made plans to place the issue of Korean independence before the participants of the Paris Peace conference, and actively sought Wilson's assistance. They eventually sent their own representative to Paris, while other members were sent to Tokyo and Korea to assess the depth of nationalist support.[63] A similar though independent course of action was taken by the Korean National Association in the United States. Chŏng Han-gyŏng (Henry Chung) was selected to represent Korean interests at the peace conference, and Yi Sŭng-man (Syngman Rhee) and others were delegated to attend the League of Small Nations in New York.[64]

2 – The February Declaration of Independence

By mid-December news of these activities had reached the student community in Tokyo, and the possibility of organizing an independence movement within Japan appears to have been first discussed at a year-end party sponsored by the *Gakuyūkai* on December 29. The issue was again raised at a meeting held on the following day at the Korean YMCA which several hundred students are thought to have attended.[65] At both these meetings emotional speeches were made on the subject of Korean independence, and the assembled students were urged to 'sacrifice even their lives, if need be, in order to attain the ultimate objective'.[66] This was followed by a third meeting held on January 6, 1919, at the Korean YMCA, at which the students were told:

> Present trends are ideal for the launching of a Korean People's Independence Movement. Moreover, since our comrades abroad have already taken the initiative in this direction, we too must begin a concrete movement.[67]

In order to translate the enthusiasm of the participants into a coherent organization, an executive committee of eleven members was selected and after a lengthy meeting a plan was finally agreed upon. It was decided that a Declaration of Independence and a petition would be drawn up and presented to the Japanese cabinet, to members of both houses of the Diet and to all foreign embassies in Tokyo. This plan was submitted to a meeting of several hundred students held on the following day at the Korean YMCA and was enthusiastically approved. Since, in the view of the police, the speeches which followed this announcement constituted a 'threat to public peace and safety', a number of arrests were made and the meeting dispersed.[68] This was repeated on January 8, when several hundred students again gathered at the Korean YMCA to discuss the issue of Korean independence. The police quickly rushed in and arrested several speakers including two members of the executive committee.[69]

Realizing that further mass meetings of this type would be futile in the face of police harassment, the executive committee decided to continue their activities in secret. Chŏn Yŏng-t'aek, one of the original members of the committee, was forced to resign due to illness, and his place was taken by Yi Kwang-su, recently returned from a trip to China, and Kim Ch'ŏl-su, another well-known student activist. The students received further encouragement from Yi Kwang-su, who reported on the activities of the Shanghai group, and from similar reports published in the *Japan Advertiser*.[70] In rapid succession, the committee reorganized itself as the Korean Youth Independence Corps, entrusted Yi Kwang-su with the responsibility for drafting the Declaration of Independence, and sent its own representatives to Korea.[71]

The Police files are curiously silent concerning the activities of Korean students between mid-January and the first week in February. Apparently convinced that their earlier intervention had stifled the students, police investigations were not resumed until early February when rumours of renewed activity surfaced. In the interim, Yi Kwang-su, having successfully drafted the Declaration, was once again sent back to Shanghai to inform nationalist leaders there of the students' intentions, and to ensure that the student demonstrations now planned for February 8 would receive the attention of the foreign press.[72] Determined that the demonstrations should be carried out while the Diet was in session, students, including a number from Aoyama Gakuin as well as members of the *Joshi Shimbokkai*, began collecting money to cover printing and other expenses. It was apparently rumours concerning these fund-raising activities which led to renewed police surveillance and arrests on February 6.

The death of the former Emperor of Korea on January 22 led to further activity in Korea as both the Government-General and anti-Japanese groups made plans to mark his funeral, which was due to be held early in

March.[73] Student leaders in Tokyo were almost certainly aware of these developments, but made no effort to reschedule their own demonstrations. Copies of both the Declaration of Independence and a Petition for the Calling of a National Congress were printed, and by the evening of February 7 their preparations were complete.

Early the following morning copies of both documents were posted to Japanese Cabinet Ministers, all Diet members, the Government-General offices in Tokyo, all major Japanese newspapers, prominent journalists and intellectuals, and to all foreign embassies in Tokyo. The same afternoon, at approximately 3 p.m., a mass meeting, ostensibly to hold *Gakuyūkai* elections, was held at the Korean YMCA. The actual purpose of this meeting was made clear when members of the executive committee unfurled a banner on which the Declaration of Independence was written. The committee's intention to proclaim Korea's independence was then announced and the Declaration read aloud.[74] After enumerating their grievances against Japan, the students issued the following warning:

> Therefore, we the People of Korea demand that Japan and all the other nations of the world grant us the opportunity of National Self Determination. If this is not forthcoming, then we declare that we shall take whatever action is necessary to preserve our existence and shall obtain our independence.[75]

This was followed by the reading of an Independence Resolution which (a) criticized the annexation of Korea as something which threatened 'the very existence and development' of the Korean people, (b) urged that the principle of national self-determination be applied to the Korean people, and requested that students be permitted to send two delegates to the Paris Peace Conference, and (c) demanded that the Japanese Government call a Korean National Congress which would 'decide the fate of the Korean people'. This announcement too ended with a warning to the Japanese Government:

> If the above demands are rejected we shall declare eternal war against Japan and disavow all responsibility for the tragic consequences of such an action.[76]

The Petition calling for a National Congress, which was then read aloud, simply restated the students' earlier grievances and demands, and assured the nations of the world that:

> ... if the Korean people, who have possesed the experience of self-government since time immemorial, build a new nation built on new beliefs, then we believe it will be a nation which will contribute positively to the peace and civilization of both the Far

East and the world. If Japan agrees to this and assists us, we will feel no enmity towards her and will never forget our debt of gratitude to her as a leader striving for friendly relations in the truest sense . . .[77]

These announcements were greeted enthusiastically by the assembled students and, in the words of a police official writing one year later, 'the meeting became extremely agitated'. Consequently, just before 4 p.m. police from the West Kanda Police Station were rushed to the Korean YMCA and the students were ordered to disperse. When this was ignored, the police moved in and began making arrests. In all a total of twenty-seven Koreans, including all the members of the executive committee, were taken into custody.[78]

Most of those arrested were released by the police on February 9, but the remainder were charged with violation of the Publications Law and brought to trial before the Tokyo District Court. All were found guilty of offences arising from their involvement in drafting the Declaration of Independence, and received prison sentences ranging from seven to nine months.

Undeterred by the arrest and subsequent imprisonment of their leaders, a group of approximately 100 students gathered at Hibiya Park on February 12 to elect a new executive committee. A number of speakers attempted to address the rally but the police intervened and ordered the students to disperse. When this order was ignored, Yi Tal, who had been suggested to head the new committee, and a further thirteen students were taken into police custody. Further demonstrations occurred on February 15 when Korean students, in opposition to an expulsion order issued by the Student Supervisor to several students who had participated in the February 8 demonstrations, staged a boycott of the dormitory operated by the Government-General. Later in the same month another group of students drew up a manifesto, under the title of the Korea Youth Independence Corps, calling for the creation of a National Congress. When attempts were made to distribute copies of the manifesto among students who had gathered in Hibiya Park, the police, who were by then alert to such activities, immediately ordered the students to disperse and made a number of arrests.[79]

With so many of their leaders under detention and harassed by the now fully-mobilized police, student activities in Tokyo were temporarily suspended. But their enthusiasm was rekindled when news of the independence demonstrations in Seoul reached them. Students were urged by their leaders to return to Korea and lend assistance to the rapidly spreading independence movement, and it is estimated that between February and May more than 300 did so.[80]

The Response in Japan to the Independence Movement

The immediate response of the Japanese authorities in Korea to the demonstrations which began on March 1, was to ignore them, while at the same time imposing rigid controls on what could be reported in the press.[81] Until the end of the first week in March, the *Maeil Sinbo*, the most influential Korean-language newspaper in Seoul, limited its coverage to reporting the events surrounding the state funeral of Emperor Kojong. When censorship was lifted on March 7th, it and other leading newspapers in Korea adopted an uncompromising attitude toward the demonstrators. The Korean people were urged to support the Government-General and not to be misled by rumours that continued demonstrations would result in favourable consideration of Korean claims at the Paris Peace Conference.[82]

The major newspapers in Japan adopted an even harsher attitude. Most limited themselves to parroting official announcements, condemned the demonstrators as 'malcontents' and assigned responsibility for the disturbances to a small minority of agitators who had been manipulated by foreign elements.[83] Typical of this was an editorial entitled 'The Fusion Of Japan and Korea' which appeared in the March 4 edition of the *Ōsaka Mainichi Shimbun*. The author of this article argued in favour of the existence of historical and cultural precedents which justified the annexation and assimilation of Korea. Noting that the union of Japan and Korea was therefore a legitimate expression of national self-determination, the same writer then attacked the 'anti-Japanese plotters' in Korea not only for opposing the principle of self-determination but for also allowing themselves to be used as the 'tools of foreign interests'.[84] An identical view was taken by the *Tōkyo Nichi Nichi Shimbun* which advised the people 'not to misunderstand the principle of self-determination of races in applying it to their own country', and reminded its readers that:

> Between Korea and Japan there have been very friendly relations from olden times. The people living in both countries have been of the same stock. The amalgamation of the two nations was only a reversion to the original status from which the two have been separated . . . that this was a demonstration of the principle of self-determination of races . . . is more appropriate than that the Czechoslovaks should regard the Serbians as such.[85]

Except for a few sporadic outbreaks of violence confined to the area around Seoul, the initial demonstrations in Korea had been peaceful, and had flared into rioting only after the brutal response of the Japanese army and gendarmerie.[86] Nevertheless, the Japanese press consistently ignored well-documented incidents involving Japanese police, and characterized the demonstrators as 'armed mobs' which were terrorizing Japanese residents.[87] The *Ōsaka Mainichi Shimbun* published an interview with Yamagata Isaburō, the Civil Governor of Korea, who confirmed that:

> There is no doubt that the present rising in Korea owes its origin to an erroneous interpretation of the doctrine of self-determination, and the authorities are now engaged in appeasing the excited feeling among the Koreans, but it will be some time before a policy of reconciliation will be undertaken . . . Treatment of Koreans on an exactly equal footing as Japanese is beset with considerable difficulties . . . [88]

In the same interview Yamagata did, however, acknowledge that there was a need to reform the colonial administration, since 'flaws in the present system had been discovered'.[89] This theme was followed up by Kawasaki Katsumi, a *Kenseikai* member of the Lower House, who criticized the Government-General in a series of questions submitted to the Cabinet. In his view the riots in Korea had been caused both by foreign agitators and the Government's failure either to treat the 'natives' fairly or to recruit them as officials.[90] Both the *Jiji Shimpō* and the *Tōkyō Nichi Nichi Shimbun* also urged reforms but maintained that the immediate question was one of pacification.[91] The *Yorozu Chōhō*, however, in an editorial published on April 5, argued that Japan had made many sacrifices to ensure the 'future welfare' of the Korean people, and that Korean demands for independence showed a lack of understanding of all that Japan had done.[92]

Throughout April and May opposition in the Japanese press to Korean independence or self-rule was almost unanimous.[93] Those journals which did publish articles calling for a comprehensive review of colonial policy found the issue carrying the article quickly banned by the authorities. The *Hantō Jiron* (Peninsula Review), for example, published an article by a Japanese resident in Korea who criticized the colonial administration since it had:

> . . . applied to a people truly civilized in thoughts, history, literature, customs, habits, and social system, a colonial policy such as had been applied to inferior races . . . [94]

He then argued that the Government-General, by regarding the freedom of expression as an 'injurious influence', had created an environment in which the present disturbances were inevitable. The author of this article was forced to flee Korea even before its publication, while the assistant editor, a Korean, was imprisoned, and the journal itself ordered to suspend publication.[95]

A second attempt to present the 'Korean view' came as a result of a meeting of the *Reimeikai* in March. At the request of Yoshino Sakuzō and other *Reimeikai* members, Korean students were invited to attend and express their views concerning the Independence Movement.[96] Three days later at a *Reimeikai*-sponsored lecture meeting, Yoshino referred to the 'March 1 Movement' as a struggle for national liberation, and in the April issue of *Demokurashii*, the *Shinjinkai* expressed its support for the Korean people.[97] The same issue contained an article by a Korean student in which he criticized the Government-General's policy of assimilation, and likened the Independence Movement to the Rice Riots which had occurred in Japan in 1918. In his view both were expressions of the people's demands for 'life and security'. The author also suggested that Japan could not truly be considered to be the leader of Asia so long as it advocated prejudice toward the coloured races, and urged the Japanese people to cleanse themselves of 'class and racial' prejudices.[98] This article was, however, regarded by the government censors as extremely offensive, and the April issue of *Demokurashii* was consequently banned.[99]

In the same month, the results of an investigation into the causes of the disturbances in Korea carried out by members of the *Kenseikai* were published. Moriya Konosuke, a member of the investigation committee, cited the following as the principal causes of unrest in Korea: discrimination against the 'natives', 'red tapism', failure to give Koreans the right to present their grievances in a lawful manner, compulsory methods of assimilation and the 'propagation of the idea of racial self-determination among the natives'.[100] Yamamichi Jōkichi, another member of the *Kenseikai* mission, however, challenged the views expressed by Moriya and advised the Government to accelerate its assimilation policy. He further criticized the authorities for being lax in their responsibilities, adding that:

> If the Koreans are handled gently they immediately rise up in revolt; if you give them one thing, they demand two; if you give them two, they ask for four.[101]

During May and June, with the exception of a small group of liberals, the tone of newspaper and magazine articles continued to reflect such attitudes. In the July 1 issue of *Demokurashii* the superficial nationalism advocated by the bureaucrats and the military was criticized.[102] In the same month's issue of *Taiyō* ('The Sun'), Suehiro Shigeo, of Kyoto Imperial University, in an article entitled 'The Issue of Korean Autonomy', challenged the principle of *dōka* as fundamental to Japan's governing of Korea. Citing numerous attempts by European nations to assimilate their colonial subjects, Suehiro considered that:

> . . . The failure of the assimilation policy pursued by the Japanese Government in Korea does not cast any reflection on the ability of the authorities. The fault lies with the thing itself. This is especially the case now that the spirit of democracy and the idea of self-determination of peoples is in such great vogue throughout the world . . .[103]

Suehiro then went on to suggest, as an alternative to assimilation or immediate independence, a form of limited self-government with a view to preparing the Korean people for eventual independence.

Given the limited readership of liberal journals such as *Taiyō*, *Demokurashii* and *Chūō Kōrun*, however, it could be argued that Suehiro, like Yoshino, was merely preaching to the converted. The impression fostered in Japan was one which characterized the Korean people as ignorant, indolent, easily manipulated and prone to violence. Opponents of the colonial regime were referred to as 'malcontents', and Korean students in particular were regarded with ever-increasing anxiety. This concern was well summarized in a report produced by the military authorities in Korea in July 1919:

> It is normal for those who study abroad to have understanding and sympathy for the country in which they are studying. But students who come to Japan do not fit this pattern. Even leaving aside those who arrive as committed anti-Japanists, Chinese and Korean students in Japan, in proportion to the length of their studies, become increasingly anti-Japanese in their attitudes . . . This is largely to do with the attitude held by the Japanese toward these students. The attitude of most Japanese is one of contempt, and faced with this cold reception how can they come to regard Japan with respect? It is therefore necessary that these students be treated sympathetically as true brothers, so that they will come to love and respect the true Japanese spirit, and consider themselves as true Japanese as well.[104]

Revised Government Regulations Concerning Koreans in Japan (1920–1923)

In the immediate aftermath of the disturbances in Korea, the Government-General adopted measures designed to contain the riots and to minimize contacts between Koreans in Japan and those in Korea. The most important of these were contained in an ordinance issued in April 1919 by the Director of Police Affairs.[105] Until its abolition in December 1922 these regulations were the principle means by which the entry of Koreans into Japan was controlled. Even before this time, however, the Home Ministry issued a series of notifications which were intended to increase surveillance and controls over the activities of Korean students in Japan. The most important of these requested all local police authorities to complete (within forty days) a survey and register of the names of all Korean students living under their jurisdiction.[106] The information sought by the Police Affairs Bureau was identical to that contained in the *Yōshisatsu Chōsenjin Shisatsu Naiki* of 1916. By implication, therefore, all Korean students, regardless of their political sympathies, were to be placed under surveillance.

Similar attempts to control the activities of Korean students were made by official bodies other than the police. Late in 1919, for example, the Government-General announced its intention of placing the Korean YMCA in Tokyo under the direction of the Japan Congregational Church, and of transferring all Korean students presently living in the YMCA-operated dormitory to one under the direct supervision of the Government-General.[107] This decision was criticized by Yoshino Sakuzō in an article in the February-March, 1920 issue of *Shinjin* ('New Man'). Yoshino argued that the Koreans should not immediately be labelled as 'rebels' if in fact their protests were morally justified. He added:

> From a legal viewpoint, Koreans are no different from Japanese. But in reality Koreans are not of the Yamato race. Moreover, within the Japanese Empire, which is the creation of the Yamato race, there is no hiding the fact that the status of Koreans is like that of a step-child . . . were it a case of some Japanese planning rebellion then they would indeed be unforgivable malcontents. But that the Koreans, who are not of the Yamato race, and moreover have been annexed in the way they have and are being governed under the conditions which exist in Korea, should not look upon Japan in the same way that I do – though regrettable can only be regarded as natural and inevitable.[108]

Maruyama Tsurukichi, the Director of Police Affairs in Korea, replied to this by accusing Yoshino of stirring up trouble.[109] The result was an angry debate which was carried over into the next month's issue of *Shinjin*. In his response to Maruyama's accusation, Yoshino argued that the Korean student issue should not be discussed in isolation since it touched upon the much broader issue of Japanese colonialism, and concluded that 'to attempt to regain one's independence is a moral cause which ought to be acknowledged whether the people involved be Japanese, Korean or Chinese . . . '[110]

With the arrival of the new Saitō administration in September 1919 steps were also taken to revise the regulations governing Korean students in Japan. In November of the following year, the 1911 regulations were rescinded only to be replaced by the *Zainaichi Kampi Chōsen Gakusei Kitei* (Regulations Governing Government-Sponsored Korean Students in Japan).[111] Under the new code the Government would continue to exercise discretionary control over the schools and courses such students would enter, but no mention was made concerning the supervision of sponsored students 'in their daily lives'.[112] Moreover, as is suggested in the title of the new regulations, Korean students in Japan would henceforth be referred to as *Zainaichi Chōsen Gakusei* (Korean Students in Japan Proper) as opposed to *Chōsen Ryūgakusei* (Koreans Studying Abroad). This is a subtle difference, of course, but implied that at least in official jargon Korean students would no longer be regarded as 'foreign'. These more relaxed regulations did not, however, signal a significant rise in the number of sponsored students in Japan.[113]

At about the same time, the office of Student Supervisor was abolished and the responsibility for supervising Korean students was transferred to the semi-official *Tōyō Kyōkai*, the president of which was Mizuno Rentarō.[114] This was followed two years later by a further revision of the 1920 regulations which was intended to increase the number of sponsored students in Japan. But, to a great extent, this was accomplished by reducing the size of student grants by nearly 50%, and by extending the selection process to include students already studying in Japan at their own expense.[115]

TABLE 25

Korean Students in Japan (1918–1925)

Year	Number of Students		Total
	Government-Sponsored	Self-Financed	
1919	34	644	678
1920	35	1,195	1,230
1921	40	2,195	2,235
1922	54	3,168	3,222
1923	56	936 (2)	992
1924 (1)	63	1,467	1,530
1925	70	1,624	1,694

Source: *Chōsen Sōtokufu Gakumu Kyoku* (Government-General of Korean Education Bureau), '*Chōsen Kyōiku Yōran*' ('A General View of Education in Korea'), 1926 edition, p. 218. (Cited hereafter as '*Kyōiku Yōran*, 1926'.)

Note: (1) Figures for 1924 and 1925 respectively refer to totals compiled in September of each year. All other figures represent year-end totals.

(2) The sudden decrease in the number of privately-financed students in 1923 was the result of the anti-Korean disturbances following the earthquake of 1923.

The Korean Student Movement 1920–1923

An important feature of Korean student activities in Japan after the suppression of the independence movement of 1919, was the rapid spread of proletarian ideologies and the emergence of left-wing organizations supported in a few cases by Japanese ideologues. This trend was encouraged by several factors. First, the departure or imprisonment of many student leaders during 1919 and 1920 left a vacuum which was gradually filled by younger students whose attitudes had been shaped almost entirely during the period when Korea was under Japanese rule. Although nationalism remained a dominant theme, these younger and often more militant students were extremely receptive to anarcho-syndicalist and Marxist-Leninist ideology. In the words of a Home Ministry report:

> Since these students have been unable to achieve their long-cherished hopes for Korean independence through normal channels, some of them entertain hopes that by co-operating with Japanese ideologues in the creation of a revolutionary movement which will transform Japan into a 'red' state their own interests will be served. As a result, these two groups have grown closer together.[116]

Second, disillusionment with the Western democracies, particularly after the Washington Conference of 1921, encouraged many Korean students in Japan as well as elsewhere to seek an ideological alternative to Wilsonian idealism. Nevertheless, these young politically-motivated students had only a tenuous grasp of Marxism or anarcho-syndicalism and were largely drawn to these ideologies because of their emphasis on 'transformation' and 'liberation'.[117]

The radicalization of Korean students, in both Japan and Korea, was also encouraged by the inability of the nationalists to produce a coherent strategy after 1919 and the failure of the Korean Provisional Government in Shanghai to establish itself as an effective basis for sustained and organized political activity. The nationalist cause was weakened not only by the fact that its leadership was too widely dispersed, but, more importantly, by deep divisions between the 'extremists' who advocated armed struggle against the Japanese and the 'moderates' who believed that the cause of Korean independence would best be served through some form of limited co-operation with the colonial administration. The failure of the nationalists to resolve these issues was, of course, seized upon by the authorities in Japan and Korea and turned to their own advantage, thus weakening the appeal of the nationalists even further. As Bruce Cumings, in his study of the Korean War, has observed:

> . . . the existence of moderate Korean nationalists, willing to make accommodations to Japanese rule, painted the less moderate groups in extreme colors; the colonial authorities could repress the 'extremists', who naturally were a much greater threat, while nurturing the moderates and giving them the impression that, through their activities, one day an independent Korea would emerge.[118]

Leftist ideology, initially in the form of anarcho-syndicalism, however, offered students a more radical alternative; one which eschewed any co-operation with the colonial oppressor and called for immediate and violent armed struggle to end Japanese rule.[119]

The fourth and most important source of encouragement for student radicalism was the postwar social and political environment in Japan. Contacts between Korean students and Japanese radicals are thought to have occurred as early as 1914,[120] but it was not until about 1920 that Japanese leftists, particularly anarcho-syndicalists such as Iwasa Sakutarō and Ōsugi Sakae, became actively involved in Korean student affairs. Korean students are also known to have attended meetings of Sakai Toshihiko's Cosmos Club, and of the *Gyōminkai* led by Takatsu Seidō, while the first agents sent by the Comintern to establish a dialogue with the Japanese left were Koreans who had studied at universities in Tokyo.[121] The influence of the Japanese 'liberal left' was also reflected in many of the activities sponsored by Korean student groups during this period. Early student attempts to organize Korean workers bear a close resemblance to the efforts of Japanese students to establish links between themselves and workers through the *Rōgakkai* (Worker Student Society), while the inspiration for student lecture tours to Korea was almost certainly provided by the provincial speaking tours sponsored by the *Shinjinkai* during the early 1920s.[122]

As was the case before the independence movement of 1919, Korean student activities between 1920 and 1923 were dominated by a small group of militants. According to a report compiled by the police in 1920, the four most influential and therefore 'dangerous' student organizations were controlled by fewer than thirty individuals.[123]

Although most student organizations had temporarily suspended all activities after the events of February-March 1919, by the end of the year many had re-surfaced. The Korean YMCA, for example, resumed its activities in October 1919 and within weeks was once again sponsoring lecture and debate meetings at which student leaders re-affirmed their determination to achieve Korean independence. At one such meeting held in February 1920 disillusionment with the Western democracies was clearly evident in the speeches made by student activists. Some called upon their audience to emulate the success of revolutionaries in

TABLE 26

Principal Korean Student Groups Active in Japan between 1912 and 1923

Name of Organization	Political Affiliation	Location	Date of Establishment	Date of Dissolution	1924 Membership
Joshi Gakuyūkai (Fraternal Association of Women Students)	Successor to the Joshi Shimbokkai	Tokyo	January 1920		30
Tōkyō Chōsen Kugakusei Dōyūkai (Comradely Association of Self-Supporting Korean Students in Tokyo)		Tokyo	November 1920		50
Kokutōkai (Black Wave Association)	Anarcho-syndicalist/Communist	Tokyo	November 1921	November 1922	—
Kugakusei Keisetsukai (Self-supporting Student Association for Diligent Study)		Tokyo	December 1921		100
Kokuyūkai (Black Friends Society)	Anarchist	Tokyo	November 1922		30
Hokuseikai (North Star Society)	Communist	Tokyo	November 1922		50
Zainihon Chōsen Musan Seinenkai (Korean Proletarian Youth Association in Japan)	Communist	Tokyo	June 1923		—

Sources: 'Chōsenjin Gakyō [3]', in Pak, Z.K.S.S., Vol. 1, pp. 89–93; Chōsen Sōtokufu, 'Zaikyō Chōsenjin Jōkyō', in Pak, Z.K.S.S., Vol. 1, pp. 138–141.

Russia,[124] while others urged the formation of a mass-based organization since:

> The so-called politicians of all countries continue to advocate militarism and self interest and have turned the war of peace to their own advantage. The Peace Treaty signed in Paris produced only inconclusive results and the League of Nations will hereafter abandon the peoples of the world to suffering . . . [125]

Later in the same month a meeting was held in Tokyo to discuss methods of re-activating the independence movement. This resulted in the printing of a pamphlet reaffirming student commitment to the ideal of independence; preparations were also made for a demonstration to mark the anniversary of the March 1 Independence Movement. Despite police surveillance approximately fifty students gathered at the Korean YMCA on March 1, 1920. They were immediately ordered to disperse and, when this order was ignored, the police entered the hall and made a number of arrests. Undeterred, the remaining students proceeded to Hibiya Park where amidst shouts of *'Manse!'* ('10,000 Years!', the Korean equivalent of the Japanese *'Banzai!'*) several speakers attempted to address the rally. The police again intervened and arrested nearly all the participants.[126] While this incident is, in itself, not of great significance, it does indicate a new determination on the part of the police to prevent a repetition of the previous year's events. It also marks the first of many subsequent demonstrations by Koreans in Japan to commemorate the independence movement of 1919.

It was also during 1920 that the first documented contacts between Korean students and Japanese radicals occurred. Of particular concern to the police was the increasing participation of Korean students in activities sponsored by groups like the Cosmos Club, *Gyōminkai* and the *Jiyū Remmei* (Freedom League).[127] While the exact nature of the role played by Korean students in these and other radical organizations is unclear, police records indicate that on at least one occasion Korean students attending a Cosmos Club meeting gave speeches openly advocating social revolution.[128]

The views of Korean student militants during the early 1920s can be classified roughly as being either communist or anarcho-syndicalist, although whether they can be regarded as ideologically committed in the same sense as Yamakawa Hitoshi or Ōsugi Sakae is rather more doubtful.[129] Student links with the radical left were reinforced by the arrival in the summer of 1920 of Yi Ch'un-suk, a Comintern agent and graduate of Chūō University in Tokyo. Yi's mission appears to have been the creation of a dialogue with Japanese leftists and the establishment of a socialist movement involving Korean students and workers in Tokyo. Yi was unsuccessful in his dealings with Yamakawa and Sakai, but, with the assistance of Yi Chŭng-nim, a student at Meiji University, was able to persuade Ōsugi to attend a Comintern-sponsored conference of Far Eastern Revolutionaries scheduled for the following autumn in Shanghai. Police records indicate that prior to Ōsugi's departure in October, Yi Chŭng-nim secretly sailed to Shanghai and returned with funds probably supplied by the Comintern. He then returned to Shanghai soon after Ōsugi's arrival and was rewarded for his efforts with further financial assistance, this time supplied by Yi Ch'un-suk himself. By this time Yi Chung-nim was on familiar terms with not only Ōsugi but also with Yamakawa, Sakai, Kondō Eizō, Takatsu Seidō and Arahata Kanson, and it was Yi who, acting as the Comintern's agent in 1921, was instrumental in arranging co-operative links between Japanese communists and the Comintern.[130]

Later in the same year the *Tōkyō Chōsen Kugakusei Dōyūkai* (Comradely Association of Self-Supporting Korean Students in Tokyo) was formed to forge an alliance between anarchists and bolsheviks. But despite early enthusiasm for socialism, there was only sporadic support for ideologically committed Korean student groups. This, coupled with police harassment and factional disputes within groups like the *Dōyūkai* quickly reduced their influence among students.[131] Until 1923 the dominant themes in student politics remained nationalistic, and it was the issue of Korean independence which continued to evoke the greatest response among students in Tokyo.[132]

In September 1921 a number of students met to discuss methods of focusing the attention of the forthcoming Washington Conference on the issue of Korean independence. It was decided at this meeting to draft a declaration of independence, and in a repetition of the events of February 1919, to send this document accompanied by a manifesto to the Government-General, the Japanese Cabinet and Diet, newspapers in Korea and Japan, prominent intellectuals, foreign embassies in Tokyo and to the participants of the Washington Conference. It was also decided to complement these activities with a school strike and demonstrations set to begin on November 5, one week before the conference was due to open.[133]

Consequently, on the morning of November 5 approximately 300 students gathered at the Korean YMCA ostensibly to hold a meeting of the *Gakuyūkai*. Several speakers urged the formation of a General Association of Korean Students, while others were reported to have called upon the nations participating at the Washington Conference to consider the issue of Korean independence. As at all such large student gatherings there was a sizeable police presence and following these speeches, they quickly ordered the meeting to disperse. Ignoring this order, the organizers of the demonstration, all of whom were subsequently prosecuted for violation of the Publications Law, managed to distribute several hundred copies of the Declaration of Independence.[134]

Declaration of Independence

> A longing for and a love of peace are emotions natural to all men. The numerous movements which emerged after the Great War and were carried out for the sake of international, national and social justice and humanity bear witness to this fact. The Washington Conference is an attempt to deal with these issues in a concrete way, and this organization, affirming the peaceful path of justice and humanity and realizing the fundamental relationship between the Korean question and world peace, gives its blessing to the complete fulfilment of the objectives of the conference. What must be understood is that world peace lies in the final resolution of the problems of the Far East and that the establishment of peace in that area depends upon a just solution to the question of Korean independence. To an even greater extent the central issues confronting the present conference are those concerning the coastal nations of the Far East and the Pacific. Therefore, we, placing our absolute faith, hopes, and expectations in this, and in order to achieve these principles, announce the following to the Washington Conference and the governments and people of the Great Powers through the attached manifesto.

> Manifesto

> 1. The independence of Korea underpins not only the peace of the Far East, but World peace as well.
> 2. Present conditions in Korea provide clear evidence of the falsehoods that lie at the root of the so-called merger of Japan and Korea.
> 3. We affirm that the Korean people under continued domination by Japan will never attain their true development.
> 4. We affirm that if Japan, for whatever reason, continues with its present policies then it will become impossible to preserve world peace.
> 5. On the basis of the reasons stated above, we affirm that it is the legitimate duty of the Washington Conference to debate and arrive at a decision concerning the independence of Korea.
> 6. We affirm that it is right for the governments and people of the Great Powers to assist Korean independence.
> 7. Our organization endorses the entire case presented before the Washington Conference by the representatives of the Korean Provisional Government.[135]

Further demonstrations took place on November 11 and 14 though on each occasion the meetings were interrupted by the police and a number of arrests were made. This series of demonstrations was the high-water mark of the nationalist-inspired student movement.

The failure of the Washington Conference to act upon these demands, coupled with the collapse of the Korean Provisional Government in 1921 and the prevailing ideological mood in Japan, all contributed to the emergence of more radical student organizations.[136] This transition was outlined by a Home Ministry official in the following way:

> ... this period (1918–1921) was the highpoint of the Korean independence movement, and although desperate attempts were made to achieve independence it resulted in failure. The speeches of President Wilson, in particular those concerning justice, humanity and national self-determination, were revered as heavenly gospel. Korean students hoped that once the Declaration of Independence was drafted, American assistance would be forthcoming . . . But the expected aid never materialized, . . . the voice of the Koreans was ignored and their hopes and expectations dashed, and they became disillusioned. With the Washington Conference the second turning point in the ideology of the Koreans occurred . . . Changes in ideological trends among Korean students should be seen as reflecting shifts in popular attitudes in Korea and the birth of the 'social movement' in Japan – and particularly in Tokyo . . . these trends, and the environment in which Koreans in Tokyo lived, quite naturally exerted considerable influence upon them.[137]

This shift was visibly demonstrated by the formation in November 1921 of the Black Wave Association, which Robert Scalapino has referred to as 'the first truly radical group'.[138] The executive of this group was comprised entirely of members of the *Kugakusei Dōyūkai*, with Pak Yŏl and Kim Yak-su as its principal leaders.[139] Both Ōsugi Sakae and Iwasa Sakutarō acted as advisers to this group, though, as the following citation makes clear, relations between Korean radicals and their Japanese supporters were not always satisfactory.

> ... there are aspects of socialism which are incompatible with the principle of 'for the fatherland' which is advocated by the Koreans. Generally the Japanese hold the Koreans in contempt and there is a tendency for them either to regard the Korean movement as mere child's play or to attempt to make use of the Koreans. The Koreans are aware of this and realize that many Japanese ideologues are so-called professionals, and do not like them for this reason. Due to mutual dissatisfaction, communications were not normally main-

tained on a permanent basis, and, in particular, contacts between Koreans and people like Ōsugi, Takatsu, Iwasa and Yamakawa became almost impossible.[140]

During its brief existence, the Black Wave Association sponsored lecture tours in Korea and attempted to instill a sense of class-consciousness among its worker-members. In February 1922 Pak Yŏl, accompanied by other members of the association, crossed to Korea, and on February 4 the *Chosŏn Ilbo* ('Korea Daily News') published a declaration signed by him urging Korean students and workers to co-operate with left-wing organizations in Japan. Pak and the other authors of this declaration also announced their intention to establish an organization in Korea which would train workers for the 'class struggle'.[141]

From its inception, however, the Black Wave Association suffered from severe ideological divisions among its members, similar to those which plagued the fragile anarchist-bolshevik alliance of Japanese radicals at this period. A final rupture between the communist faction led by Kim Yak-su and the anarchist faction dominated by Pak Yŏl resulted in the splitting of the association in November 1922 into the anarchist *Kokuyūkai* (Black Friends Society) and the communist *Hokuseikai* (North Star Society).[142]

The leaders of the *Hokuseikai* moved quickly to forge links with the newly-formed Japan Communist Party, and Katayama Sen, writing in 1924, described this organization as 'a strongly communist-type group operating under the guidance of the Japan Communist Party'.[143] Through its journal *Ch'okhudae* (Scouting Party – published in Korean) the *Hokuseikai* stated its intention to: (a) make it clear they regarded the Japanese ruling classes, and not the proletariat, as the enemies of the Korean people, (b) strengthen the solidarity and joint ideology of the Japanese and Korean masses, and, (c) establish a single labour organization which would represent all Korean workers in Japan.[144] Both it and the *Kokuyūkai* were regarded by the police as extremely dangerous organizations whose activities would have to be carefully monitored.[145]

During the first half of 1923 Korean militants, representing both the anarchist and communist factions, became increasingly visible in activities sponsored by Japanese left-wing organizations. Koreans participated in May Day demonstrations in both Tokyo and Osaka, and in July Kim Yak-su and Ch'oe Kap-ch'un representing the Tokyo League of Korean Labour attended a mass meeting of the *Kantō Rōdō Dōmei* (Kantō Labour League) held in Chiba prefecture.[146] In common with other Korean organizations the *Hokuseikai* also sponsored lecture tours in Korea. During one such tour in August 1923 Kim Yak-su and

Kim Kwang-bŏm, accompanied by Takatsu Seidō, Kitahara Tatsuo and Fuse Tatsuji, toured parts of Korea urging the workers to co-operate with their counterparts in Japan.[147]

Although the Korean student movement never advocated violence, the impression fostered by both official and unofficial commentators in Japan was that Korean students were recalcitrant and entirely capable of committing seditious acts.[148] But, with the exception of the assassination in February 1921 of the pro-Japanese president of the *Kukmin Hyophoe* (National Association) by a former student, student activities in Japan appear to have been for the most part non-violent.[149] The only organization known to have advocated the violent overthrow of the state was the *Futeisha* (Company of Malcontents), a secret anarchist society organized by Pak Yŏl in the spring of 1923.[150] Through its journal *Futei Senjin* ('The Stalwart Korean') the *Futeisha* published articles attacking restrictions on the entry of Koreans into Japan and the assimilation policies of the Government-General and advocated 'direct action' as a legitimate means of ending Japanese domination of Korea.[151] It was this reference to direct action which was of particular concern to the authorities and throughout its existence this group was subjected to the most vigorous surveillance.[152] Pak's establishment of the *Futeisha* as a secret society appears to have been an attempt to counteract police harassment although he seems to have been less than successful in this respect. All meetings of the *Futeisha* were placed under police surveillance and most of the activities planned by Pak and his 'shock troops' were interrupted by the police. The first of the 'direct action' enterprises carried out by the *Futeisha* was an attack on Chang Tŏk-su, an early leader of the student independence movement and editor of the independent-nationalist newspaper *Tonga Ilbo*, during a visit to Tokyo at the end of April.[153] Subsequent activities included an attempt to smuggle explosives into Japan with the assistance of a Korean terrorist organization in Shanghai known as the *Ŭiyŏldan* (Righteous Fighters Corps).[154] Although the smuggling attempt failed and it is uncertain whether the *Futeisha* had the capability or intention of actually engaging in terrorist activities, the rumoured bomb plot was regarded as a very real threat by the police and resulted in the arrest of Pak and his wife Kaneko Ayako. Both were later indicted for high treason and sentenced to death though this was subsequently commuted to life imprisonment.[155]

Despite the relatively small number of students involved in 'extremist' groups like the *Hokuseikai* and the *Kokuyūkai*, or participating in activities sponsored by the Japanese left, these developments greatly heightened the unease felt by the authorities in Japan and Korea. There can also be little doubt that the alignment of student organizations with Japanese radicals, coupled with the stereotyped image of Korean workers as alien and inferior, reinforced hostility and prejudice toward the immigrant community. This is confirmed by a slightly later report compiled by the Government-General which attempted to account for the fact that rumours of a Korean insurrection at the time of the Great Earthquake had been accepted so readily by both the police and the public. The author of this report suggested that the Japanese people had been made uneasy by the presence of Korean workers who were generally regarded as uncivilized, violent and prone to gambling and fighting. The same report then goes on to say (with clear reference to the Pak Yŏl incident) that:

> ... many plots had been uncovered where Korean malcontents had formed groups under a variety of names in the factories where they were employed and had attempted to carry out acts of sabotage, smuggled explosives into the country and plotted to blow up buildings.[156]

Adding that:

> ... although they are in fact only a small minority and most Koreans are in complete ignorance, the Japanese people, who are unaware of this fact, misunderstand the situation and, thinking that there are many of these dangerous and violent types among the Koreans, believe that there is a vicious element in the character of the Korean people.[157]

The following chapter will discuss the way in which this hardening of attitudes resulted in the persecution of Koreans and other 'subversive elements' following the earthquake of 1923.

Notes:
1. Conroy, op. cit., pp. 124–168, 267–272.
2. See *Dai Nihon Gaikō Monjo (Documents Relating to the Foreign Affairs of Japan)*, 1936–1956, Vol. 10, pp. 307–308.
3. Which had, of course, been founded by Fukuzawa in 1868. *Keiō Gijuku* (now Keiō University) will be referred to hereafter simply as Keiō.
4. Nagai Michio, Tanaka Hiroshi, Hara Yoshio, *Ajia Ryūgakusei to Nihon (Asian Students in Japan)*, NHK Books, No.186, Tokyo, 1973, p. 51. (Cited hereafter as *Ajia Ryūgakusei.*) Also see Im Kwan Hwang, op. cit., pp. 129–133, and Abe, 'Korean Students in Japan Before 1945', p. 22.
5. *Ajia Ryūgakusei*, pp. 51–53. Also see Im Kwan Hwang, op. cit., pp. 109, 134, and Duechler, op. cit., pp.101–102. The first *sinsa yuramdan* was composed of twelve members, each of whom was accompanied by a minimum of two assistants, one interpreter, and one servant. In all, there were sixty-two people involved in the mission.
6. Im Kwan Hwang, op. cit., p. 134. This is also discussed briefly in *Ajia Ryūgakusei*, p. 53, and Abe, 'Korean Students in Japan Before 1945', pp. 21–22.
7. Ishikawa Kammei, *Fukuzawa Yukichi Den (Biography of Fukuzawa Yukichi)*, Iwanami Shoten, Tokyo, 1932, Vol. 3, p. 289.
8. Im Kwan Hwang, op. cit., pp. 135–138. Also see *Ajia Ryūgakusei*, pp. 54–55, and Duechler, op. cit., pp. 199–202.
9. Im Kwan Hwang, op. cit., p. 139. Also see Harold F. Cook, 'Kim Ok-kyun's Second Visit To Japan', pp. 31–37.
10. *Keiō Gijuku Gojūnen-shi (Fifty-Year History of Keiō Gijuku)*, Tokyo, 1907, p. 539. Also see Abe, 'Korean Students in Japan Before 1945', p. 23, and *Ajia Ryūgakusei*, pp. 56–58. Sŏ Chae-p'il (anglicized to Philip Jaisohn) was one of Korea's most prominent and articulate early nationalist leaders. His studies at the Toyama Army Academy in Japan were interrupted by the attempted coup d'etat of 1884 in Korea in which he was a participant. Following the failure of the coup, he fled first to Japan and then to America where he graduated from university and later took American citizenship. After his return to Korea in 1896 Sŏ published *The Independent*, a Korean language newspaper through which he introduced Western concepts of education, administration and economics. He, along with Yun Ch'i-ho and Yi Sŭng-man (Syngman Rhee), was instrumental in the establishment of the *Tongnip Hyop'hoe* (Independence Club) in 1896.
11. Im Kwan Hwang, op. cit., pp. 162–164. Also see Conroy, op. cit., p. 137.
12. Inoue Kakugorō, *Fukuzawa Sensei no Chōsen Gokeiei to Gendai no Bunka to ni tsuite (Professor Fukuzawa's Program For Korea and Modern Korean Culture)*, Meiji Printing Company, Tokyo, 1934, pp. 7–9. As cited in Im Kwan Hwang, op. cit., p. 166.
13. *Ajia Ryūgakusei*, pp.59–60. Also see Im Kwan Hwang, op. cit., pp. 182–192, and Kang Chae-on, *Chōsen no Jōi to Kaika (Korea's Policy of Exclusionism and the Opening of the Country)*, Heibonsha, Tokyo, 1977, pp. 182–183.
14. *Ajia Ryūgakusei*, pp. 60–61.
15. Among those who returned from exile to assume positions in the Korean Government were Pak Yŏng-hyo, Sŏ Kwang-bŏm and Yu Kil-chun. See

Chong-sil Lee, op. cit., pp. 41–42, 59.
16. Abe, 'Korean Students in Japan Before 1945', pp. 25–26. This contract was deeply resented by Korean students in Tokyo as something which 'forfeited the human rights of Korean students', and, 'displayed a lack of trust in the Korean Government'. See the *Shimbokkaihō*, No. 6, 1895. As cited in *Ajia Ryūgakusei*, p. 71. The arrival of the first group of more than 100 students is discussed in the *Jijō Shimpō*, May 2, 1895.
17. Abe, 'Korean Students in Japan Before 1945', pp. 26–27.
18. Ibid., p. 28.
19. Ibid., pp. 28–29.
20. *Hōchi Shimbun*, December 2 and 3, 1905. Both articles were entitled 'Comments made by Mr. Katsura the Principal of Tokyo First Middle School'.
21. Abe, 'Korean Students in Japan Before 1945', p. 29. Also see Abe Hiroshi, '*Kyū Kan Matsu no Nihon Ryūgaku (III) – Shiryōteki Kōsatsu*' ('On the Documents Relating to Korean Students in Japan During the Late Yi Period (III)'), *Kan*, Vol. 3, No. 7, 1975, pp. 104–114. (Cited hereafter as Abe, 'Korean Students During the Late Yi Period'.) The leader of the strike was Ch'oe Rin (In), who first arrived in Japan as a scholarship student in 1904. After his graduation from Meiji University in 1909, Ch'oe returned to Korea and became active in *Ch'ŏndogyo* (Teaching of the Heavenly Way), an important religious sect which is often regarded as the successor to the *Tonghaks*. Ch'oe was later to become one of the principal leaders of the March 1 Movement in Korea, though his subsequent collaboration with the Japanese during the 1930s has led some commentators to minimize his role in the early nationalist movement. See Frank Prentiss Baldwin, Jr., op. cit., pp. 41, 52–78.
22. Abe, 'Korean Students in Japan Before 1945', p. 30. This order appears to have been disregarded by the strike leaders, many of whom simply transferred to private schools. Ch'oe Rin, for example, entered Meiji University.
23. Ibid., pp. 32–33. These regulations reflected the views of Shidehara Hiroshi who, in his capacity as *Gakubu San'yo Kan* (Educational Councillor) to the Korean Government, was the most influential Japanese official in the Ministry of Education. Also see E. Patricia Tsurumi, op. cit., p. 164.
24. The first Korean student organization was the *Dai Chōsenjin Nihon Ryūgakusei Shimbokkai* (Greater Fraternal Association of Korean Students in Japan) founded in 1895 by students at Keiō. Between February 1896 and the association's dissolution in 1898 it also published a journal entitled the *Shimbokkai Kaihō* (Fraternal Report) in which current events in Korea were discussed. See *Ajia Ryūgakusei*, pp. 69–70, and Abe, 'Korean Students in Japan Before 1945', p. 31. Hereafter, except where otherwise noted, all Korean groups established in Japan will be given with their Japanese readings while those in Korea and elsewhere will be given in their romanized Korean form.
25. '*Chōsenjin Gaikyō [3]*', in Pak, Z.K.S.S., Vol. 1, p. 87.
26. Abe, 'Korean Students in Japan Before 1945', p. 31. Other important student groups established during this period include the Greater Korea Student Association (1908), and the Greater Korea Association for the Promotion of Education (1909), both of which were regarded as centres of anti-Japanese activity. See *Naimushō Keihokyoku Hoanka* (Home Minis-

try Police Affairs Bureau Security Section), '*Chōsenjin Gaikyō*' ('The General Condition of Koreans'), 1916, in Pak, Z.K.S.S., Vol. 1, p. 49. (Cited hereafter as '*Chōsenjin Gaikyō [1]*'), and Pak Kyŏng-sik, *Undōshi*, p. 69.
27. There were, however, far more Chinese students in Japan at this time than there were Korean. One estimate puts the number of Chinese students in 1906 at more than 13,000. More important, however, was the fact that despite its emergence as an Imperial power, Japan, and in particular Tokyo, had become a Mecca for Asian students, political exiles and revolutionaries of various persuasions. It was in Tokyo, for example, that Sun Yat-sen established the *T'ung-meng-hui* (United League), the precursor to the *Kuomintang*. Although there is no evidence which suggests co-operative links between Chinese and Korean nationalists in Japan, it seems likely that the activities of Sun and his supporters were a source of encouragement for Korean students. See Marius B. Jiansen, *The Japanese and Sun Yat-sen*, pp. 112–114.
28. For example, see *Naimushō, Chōsenjin Kinkyō Gaiyō*, in Pak, Z.K.S.S., Vol. 1, p. 112. Also see *Naimushō Keihokyoku* (Home Ministry Police Affairs Bureau), '*Chōsenjin Gaikyō [Dai ni]*' ('The General Condition of Koreans *[2]*'), 1918, in Pak, Z.K.S.S., Vol. 1, p. 62. (Cited hereafter as '*Chōsenjin Gaikyō [2]*'.) And, Keihokyoku, '*Zairyū Chōsenjin – 1925*', in Pak, Z.K.S.S., Vol. 1, p. 152.
29. These regulations are cited in Abe, 'Korean Students in Japan Before 1945', pp. 35–37. Also see *Chōsen Sōtokufu Gakumu Kyoku* (Government-General Education Bureau), '*Chōsen Kyōiku Yōran*' ('A General View of Education in Korea'), 1919, p. 105.
30. Abe, 'Korean Students in Japan Before 1945', p. 37.
31. Figures for this period 1910–1919 appear as Appendix C2. In a notification issued by the Government-General on June 30, 1911, the authorities made clear their intention to limit the number of sponsored-students in Japan. Paragraph one read: 'Since study abroad requires more in the way of expenses than does study in Korea, apart from those skills and techniques which cannot be acquired in Korea, we consider it better for them to complete their studies in Korea as far as is possible.' As cited in Abe, 'Korean Students in Japan Before 1945', p. 35.
32. Abe, 'Korean Students in Japan Before 1945', p. 37.
33. See Appendix C3, and *Naimushō Keihokyoku* (Home Ministry Police Affairs Bureau), '*Zaikyō Chōsen Ryūgakusei Gaikyō*' ('The General Condition of Korean Students in Tokyo'), 1925, in Pak, Z.K.S.S., Vol. 1, pp. 327–328. (Cited hereafter as '*Zaikyō Chōsen Ryūgakusei Gaikyō*'.)
34. '*Zainaichi Chōsen Gakusei Jōkyō*', in Pak, Z.K.S.S., Vol. 1, p. 300. It is also significant that most Korean students attended schools in the less prestigious private sector. See Nanba Nariakira, *Chōsen Gakusei no Gyōshō (The Dawn Bell For Korean Students)*, Reitakukai, Tokyo, 1923, pp. 60–125.
35. Figures for Korean students graduating from schools in Japan (1912–1919) appear as Appendix C4.
36. Although the Japanese records are not entirely reliable, most of the Korean students who came to Japan during this period were the sons of landlords and other members of the pre-annexation elite. See Se Hee Yoo, *The Korean Communist Movement And The Peasantry Under Japanese Rule*, Unpublished Doctoral Dissertation, Columbia University, 1974,

p. 105. Figures indicating the province of origin of Korean students during this period appear as Appendix C5.

37. Some later commentators, in the main Japanese Marxist, have tended to over-emphasize the influence generated by the Russian Revolution. For example, see Yamaba Kentarō, '*San-ichi Undō ni tsuite 1–2*' (Concerning the March First Movement, 1–2), *Rekishigaku Kenkyū*, No. 184, 185, June–July, 1955. Also see Yoshiura Daizō, comp., *Shihōshō Keiji Kyoku* (Ministry of Justice Bureau of Criminal Affairs), *Shisō Kenkyū Shiryō* (Thought Study Materials), No. 71, '*Chōsenjin Kyōsanshugi Undō*' ('The Korean Communist Movement'), Tokyo, 1940, pp. 14–15, 21–23. (Cited hereafter as '*Kyōsanshugi Undō*'.)

38. Yi Kwang-su (1892–?) was a native of North P'yongan Province. After graduating from Meiji Gakuin in 1910 he returned to Korea and was employed as a teacher. In 1915 he returned to Japan and entered Waseda University. Yi is credited with having drafted the February 1919 Declaration of Independence. Yi later co-operated with the Japanese authorities and accepted a teaching post at the Manchurian National University where he urged students to co-operate in the Japanese war effort. See Kim Donguk, *History of Korean Literature*, Leon Hurvitz, trans., The Centre For East Asian Cultural Studies, Tokyo, 1980, pp. 240–241, and Peter Lee, *Korean Literature: Topics and Themes*, University of Arizona Press, Tucson, 1965.

39. As cited in '*Chōsenjin Gaikyō [1]*, in Pak, Z.K.S.S., Vol. 1, p. 52.

40. Chang Tŏk-su (1895–1947) was born in Hwanghae Province. After his graduation from Waseda University in 1916, he was active in nationalist activities in Shanghai. In 1920 Chang became the first editor of the *Tonga Ilbo* (East Asia Daily) newspaper in Seoul, and in 1925 he received his Master's degree from Columbia University in New York. Following the liberation of Korea in 1945, he was a prominent member of the *Hanguk* (Korean National) Democratic Party until his assassination in 1947.

41. '*Chōsenjin Gaikyō [1]*', in Pak, Z.K.S.S., Vol. 1, p. 48.

42. Ibid., pp. 50–51.

43. This fear was continually expressed in all official records concerning the activities of Korean students in Japan compiled between 1916–1923. A 1924 report compiled by the Government-General, however, acknowledged that contacts between Korean students in Tokyo and anti-Japanese emigre groups abroad were conducted almost entirely on a personal basis and not, as had previously been assumed, via a well established communications network between organizations. See *Chōsen Sōtokufu*, '*Zaikyō Chōsenjin Jōkyō*', in Pak, Z.K.S.S., Vol. 1, pp.144–145.

44. A more detailed account of Yi Tong-hwi's career can be found in Scalapino and Lee, *Communism In Korea, Part I*, pp.6–50. Also see Chong-sik Lee, op. cit., pp. 101–102.

45. '*Chōsenjin Gaikyō [1]*', in Pak, Z.K.S.S., Vol. 1, p. 51. This speech was attributed to Song Chin-u (1890–1945). Song studied law at Meiji University and was later imprisoned for his role in the independence demonstrations of 1919. He later became editor of the *Tonga Ilbo*. It is unclear whether Song, like many other early nationalists, later collaborated with the Japanese. Song was active in politics for a brief period after the Second World War until his assassination in December 1945.

46. As cited in ibid.

47. Ibid., pp. 51–54. Also see '*Chōsenjin Gaikyō [2]*', in Pak, Z.K.S.S., Vol. 1,

p. 65. The efficiency with which the Japanese police thwarted later attempts to establish a communist party in Korea was also evident in the harassment of Korean student groups in Tokyo from 1915 on. Conversations involving only two or three students were regularly recorded in full by the police indicating the presence of a network of police informers operating within student organizations.
48. 'Chōsenjin Gaikyō [1]', in Pak, Z.K.S.S., Vol. 1, p. 53. Taken from a speech attributed to Chang Tŏk-su. Similar sentiments were expressed in a speech given by another student at Waseda University. He said: 'There are times when I am filled with emotion at having come to this country, which is virtually an enemy country, and being in a position of being taught everything by enemies. You newly arrived students should keep your spirits high so that in the future you will become warriors capable of great deeds.'
49. This directive is cited in its entirety in Pak, Z.K.S.S., Vol. 1, pp. 23–25.
50. 'Chōsenjin Gaikyō [3]', in Pak, Z.K.S.S., Vol. 1, pp. 94–98. Also see 'Chōsenjin Gaikyō [2]', in Pak, Z.K.S.S., Vol. 1, p. 69.
51. 'Chōsenjin Gaikyō [2]', in Pak, Z.K.S.S., Vol. 1, pp. 73–74.
52. Ibid., pp. 72–73.
53. Of the three issues published during this journal's brief existence none escaped the police blacklist. This had little effect on circulation, however, since the *Reform News* was distributed on a subscription basis. See 'Chōsenjin Gaikyō [3]', in Pak, Z.K.S.S., Vol. 1, p. 95.
54. Cited in ibid.
55. Takayoshi Matsuo, 'The Japanese Protestants in Korea, Part One', pp. 422–423.
56. As cited in ibid., p. 425. This article was entitled '*Watase-shi no 'Chōsen Kyōka no Kyūmu' o Yomu*' ('On Reading Mr. Watase's 'The Urgent Task of Education Korea''). Watase Tsunekichi was a leading figure within the Japan Congregational Church and was also an enthusiastic supporter of Government-General policies. Also see Takayoshi Matsuo, 'The Japanese Protestants in Korea, Part Two', *Modern Asian Studies*, Vol. 13, Part 4, Oct. 1979, pp. 590–611. (Cited hereafter as Takayoshi Matsuo, 'The Japanese Protestants in Korea, Part Two'.)
57. Takayoshi Matsuo, 'The Japanese Protestants in Korea, Part One', p. 426.
58. This is because copies of the *Jōmō Kyōkai Geppō* would almost certainly have been available to members of other Christian organizations like the Korean YMCA.
59. This article was entitled '*Man-Kan o Shisatsu shite*' ('Observations of Manchuria and Korea'). This was the first of a number of articles dealing with Korea which appeared in *Chūō Kōron*. See Matsuo Takayoshi, *Yoshino Sakuzō – Chūgoku – Chōsen Ron (Yoshino Sakuzō: Essays on China and Korea)*, Heibonsha, Tokyo, 1970. (Cited hereafter as Yoshino, '*Chūgoku – Chōsen Ron*'.)
60. Cited in Iwamura, op. cit., p. 23.
61. Smith, *Japan's First Student Radicals*, p. 54.
62. See Frank Prentiss Baldwin, Jr., op. cit., pp. 14–32.
63. The leaders of this group, the New Korea Youth Association, were Yŏ Un-hyŏng, Chang Tŏk-su, Kim Ch'ŏl and Sŏ No-hyŏk. See ibid., pp. 32–37, and Chong-sik Lee, op. cit., pp. 103–104. Yŏ Un-hyŏng was born in 1885 in Kyonggi Province into an impoverished *Yangban* family. He was involved in both the early independence movement and the establishment

of the Korean Provisional Government. In 1921 Yŏ, along with Kim Kyu-sik and other Koreans, attended the First Congress of the Toilers of the Far East in Moscow. He was later arrested by Japanese police and imprisoned for three years. At the end of the war he, along with Song Chin-u and An Chae-hang, was chosen by the last Governor-General, Endō Ryūsaku, to help form a transitional government.

64. Frank Prentiss Baldwin, Jr., op. cit., p. 45. Also see Chong-sik Lee, op. cit., pp. 102–103. A more detailed account of early nationalist activities in the United States can be found in Jyung-chan Kim, 'Korean Community Organizations in America: Their Characteristics and Problems', Hyung-chan Kim, ed., *The Korean Diaspora*, Clio Press, Santa Barbara, 1977, pp. 65–72.
65. '*Chōsenjin Gaikyō [3]*', in Pak, Z.K.S.S., Vol. 1, p. 98. Students in Tokyo first learned of the activities of Korean nationalist groups abroad on about December 15. See the *Japan Advertiser*, Dec. 15, 1918, Jan. 7, 1919, and *Tōkyō Asahi Shimbun*, Dec. 15, 1918. Also referred to in Kang Tŏksang, '*Ni Hachi Sengen to Tokyo Ryūgakusei*' ('The February 8 Declaration and Korean Students in Tokyo'), *Sanzen Ri*, No. 10, Feb. 1979, p. 44.
66. '*Chōsenjin Gaikyō [3]*', in Pak, Z.K.S.S., Vol. 1, p. 98.
67. Cited in ibid., p. 99.
68. Ibid.
69. Ibid. Unless otherwise stated, the principal source for the following discussion of events in Tokyo has been '*Chōsenjin Gaikyō [3]*', in Pak, Z.K.S.S., Vol. 1, pp. 98–110.
70. Frank Prentiss Baldwin, Jr., op. cit., p. 40.
71. See Ko Chun-sok, *Minami Chōsen Gakusei Tosōshi (A History of the Struggles of the Students of South Korea)*, Shakai Hyōronsha, Tokyo, 1976, p. 22. Song Kye-baek, one of the student representatives, took with him a copy of the declaration which was passed on to Ch'ŏndogyo leaders in Seoul. See Frank Prentiss Baldwin, Jr., op. cit., p. 41. Also see Chong-Sik Lee, op. cit., pp. 108–109, and Pak Kyŏng-sik, *Undōshi*, p. 88.
72. Yi Kwang-su arrived in China on February 3 and *The China Press* and the *North China Daily* newspapers published the student declaration on February 9 and 10 respectively. See Pak Kyŏng-sik, *Undōshi*, pp. 87–88.
73. Frank Prentiss Baldwin, Jr., op. cit., pp. 160–168.
74. A translation of these documents appear as Appendix C9.
75. Cited in '*Chōsenjin Gaikyō [3]*', in Pak, Z.K.S.S., Vol. 1, p. 103.
76. Cited in ibid.
77. Cited in ibid., p. 104.
78. Ibid., p. 99. All except Yi Kwang-su who had left for China at the end of January.
79. Ibid., pp. 100–108. Students in the Osaka area also attempted to hold independence demonstrations in March 1919. The leader of this group was Yŏm Sang-sŏp, a former student at Keiō University.
80. Ibid., pp.101–108. Also see Frank Prentiss Baldwin, Jr., op. cit., p. 113. Others made their way to Shanghai and helped to establish the Korean Provisional Government there. See Appendix C7.
81. Frank Prentiss Baldwin, Jr., op. cit., p. 169.
82. Ibid., pp. 170–171. Also see the *Seoul Press*, March 21. As cited in Kondō, *Banzai Sōjō Jiken*, Vol. 3, p. 95.
83. The suggestion of foreign missionary involvement in the independence movement, which was subsequently proved to be untrue, first appeared in

the *Tōkyō Nichi Nichi Shimbun*, Jan. 15, 1919. Also see Kondō, *Banzai Sōjō Jiken*, Vol. 3, pp. 98–102 for further press coverage of this issue.
84. *Osaka Mainichi Shimbun*, March 4, 1919. As cited in Iwamura, op. cit., p. 26.
85. Cited in the *Japan Advertiser*, March 5, 1919.
86. See Frank Prentiss Baldwin, Jr., op. cit., pp. 84–96, and Newell Martin, 'Japan's Attempt to Exterminate Korean Christians', Milford Connecticut, 1919. Cited in Kondō, *Banzai Sōjō Jiken*, Vol. 3, pp. 127–155. A letter attached to this document was also submitted to the United States Senate, and appears in the Congressional Record, Oct. 14, 1919, Vol. 58, No. 120, p. 7322.
87. Iwamura, op. cit., p. 26.
88. As cited in the *Japan Advertiser*, March 16, 1919.
89. Ibid.
90. *Japan Times and Mail*, March 13, 1919.
91. *Japan Times and Mail*, April 11, 1919.
92. *Yorozu Chōhō*, April 5, 1919. As cited in Iwamura, op. cit., p. 27.
93. The most consistent criticism of the Government came from among Japanese Christians. See Takayoshi Matsuo, 'The Japanese Protestants in Korea, Part Two'. Surprisingly, criticism from the Japanese 'left' was almost non-existent during this period. In fact, references to the March 1 Movement in left-wing journals were notable only by their absence. See Pak Kyŏng-sik, *Chōsen San-ichi Dokuritsu Undō (The March 1 Independence Movement in Korea)*, Heibonsha, Tokyo, 1976, pp. 253–276.
94. Contained in Consular Despatch, No. 43, from U.S. Consul General in Seoul to the State Department, May 9, 1919.
95. Ibid.
96. This meeting took place on March 19. See '*Chōsenjin Gaikyō [3]*', in Pak, Z.K.S.S., Vol. 1, p. 101. Also see Iwamura, op. cit., p. 23.
97. Iwamura, op. cit., p. 23. Also see Smith, *Japan's First Student Radicals*, p. 54.
98. This article was written by Yŏm Sang-sŏp, and is cited in Iwamura, op. cit., pp. 23–24. This article must have been written just before Yŏm's attempt to organize an independence demonstration in Osaka.
99. Smith, *Japan's First Student Radicals*, p. 54.
100. *Japan Times and Mail*, April 19, 1919.
101. As cited in Frank Prentiss Baldwin, Jr., op. cit., p. 187.
102. Iwamura op. cit., p.24.
103. *Taiyō*, No. 25, July 1919, pp. 79–80. As cited in Wonmo Dong, *Japanese Policy and Practice In Korea*, p. 263.
104. *Chōsen Gun-Sambō-bu* (Headquarters, [Japanese] Army in Korea), '*Sōjō no Gen'in Oyobi Tōchi ni Chūi Subeki Ken Narabi Gunbi ni tsuite*' ('Concerning the Causes of the Disturbances, Military Preparedness and Other Issues Relating to the Administration of Korea which Requires Special Attention'), July, 1919. As cited in Kang Tŏk-sang, comp., *Gendai-shi Shiryō (26) (Materials in Contemporary History, Vol. 26), Chōsen (ni) (Korea, Part II)*, '*San-ichi Undō (ni)*', ('The March 1 Movement [2]), *Misuzu Shobō*, Tokyo, 1967, pp. 651–652. (Cited hereafter as Kang, *Chōsen II.*)
105. See Chapter 3.
106. This directive was entitled *Zairyū Chōsenjin Gakusei Meibo Chōsei ni Kansuru Tsūchō* (Notification Concerning the Preparation of a Register of

Names of Korean Students in Japan), and was issued in May 1919. Two earlier notifications were issued by the Home Ministry in July 1918. The first dealt with Koreans who attempted to sail to America via Japanese-controlled ports. The second concerned Koreans travelling between Japan and Korea, and made clear reference to the harmful effects which student publications might have if they were circulated in Korea. All are contained in Pak, Z.K.S.S., Vol. 1, pp. 32–37.

107. Takayoshi Matsuo, 'The Japanese Protestants in Korea, Part Two', p. 606.
108. Yoshino Sakuzō, *'Chōsen Seinenkai Mondai'* ('The Korean YMCA Problem'), *Shinjin* (New Man), Feb.–March 1920. As cited in Yoshino, *'Chūgoku-Chōsen Ron'*, pp. 265–266.
109. Takayoshi Matsuo, 'The Japanese Protestants in Korea, Part Two', p. 606.
110. *Shinjin*, April 1920. As cited in Yoshino, *'Chūgoku-Chōsen Ron'*, pp. 285–286.
111. *'Zainaichi Chōsen Ryūgakusei Jōkyō'*, in Pak, Z.K.S.S., Vol. 1, p. 300.
112. Abe, 'Korean Students in Japan Before 1945', p. 47.
113. This was at least partly due to the educational reforms instituted by Governor-General Saitō between 1919 and 1922, culminating in the establishment of Keijō Imperial University. See Abe, 'Higher Learning in Korea', pp. 181–189. Although the regulations on Professional Schools were also relaxed under Saitō, opportunities for higher education in Korea consistently lagged behind demand throughout the colonial period, leading to a steady increase in the number of Korean students in schools (above Middle School Level) in Japan. In 1935, for example, 47% of all Korean students enrolled in schools above the Middle School level were in Japan. Five years later this figure rose to over 60%. See Wonmo Dong, *Japanese Colonial Policy And Practice In Korea*, pp. 424–432.
114. *'Zainaichi Chōsen Gakusei Jōkyō'*, in Pak, Z.K.S.S., Vol. 1, pp. 299–300. For further information concerning the functions of the *Tōyō Kyōkai* see *'Chōsenjin Gaikyō [3]'*, in Pak, Z.K.S.S., Vol. 1, p. 115. Also see Abe, 'Korean Students in Japan Before 1945', p. 48.
115. *'Kyōiku Yōran, 1926'*, pp. 219–220.
116. Naimushō, *'Chōsenjin Kinkyō Gaiyō'*, in Pak, Z.K.S.S., Vol. 1, p. 124.
117. Shihōshō, *'Chōsenjin to Hanzai'*, in Pak, Z.K.S.S., Vol. 1, pp. 295–296.
118. Cumings, op. cit., p. 33.
119. From 1923, however, following the murder of Ōsugi Sakae and the imprisonment of Pak Yŏl (the principal Korean anarchist leader in Japan) the appeal of anarcho-syndicalism began to recede.
120. *'Chōsenjin Gaikyō [3]'*, in Pak, Z.K.S.S., Vol. 1, p. 115. The exposure of Korean students to radical ideologies was facilitated by their concentration in certain private universities which were as politically active as Tokyo Imperial University. The *Gyōminkai*, for example, which provided the basis for the first Japanese Communist Party, was established at Waseda University where, in 1923, more than 250 Korean students were enrolled. See Nanba Nariakira, op. cit., pp. 79–85.
121. Yi Ch'un-suk, a graduate of Meiji University and former Vice-Minister of Military Affairs in the Korean Provisional Government, was sent as the first Comintern agent to Japan by Yi Tong-hwi in mid-1920. He was assisted by Yi Chŭng-nim, a student at Meiji University, who later acted as the Comintern's Tokyo representative. See *Naimushō*, *'Chōsenjin*

Kinkyō Gaiyō', in Pak, Z.K.S.S., Vol. 1, pp. 124–125. and Scalapino and Lee, *Communism In Korea, Part I*, pp. 28–29. Also see George M. Beckman and Okubo Genji, *The Japanese Communist Party 1922–1925*, Stanford University Press, Stanford, 1969, pp. 30–32.

122. The *Rōgakkai* was established in December 1917 by a group of young intellectuals within the *Yūaikai*. For further information concerning this organization see Smith, *Japan's First Student Radicals*, pp. 38–40, 69–70.
123. '*Chōsenjin Gaikyō [3]*', in Pak, Z.K.S.S., Vol. 1, pp. 87–91. The four groups referred to were the Korean YMCA, *Chōsen Ryūgakusei Gakuyūkai*, *Chōsen Gakkai* and the *Chōsen Kugakusei Dōyūkai*.
124. Cited in '*Chōsenjin Gaikyō [3]*', in Pak, Z.K.S.S., Vol. 1, pp. 87–88.
125. Cited in ibid., p. 88.
126. Ibid., p. 105.
127. *Chōsen Sōtokufu*, '*Zaikyō Chōsenjin Tōkyō*', in Pak, Z.K.S.S., Vol. 1, p. 145. For a more detailed treatment of the *Gyōminkai* and other radical societies formed during this period see Robert A. Scalapino, *The Japanese Communist Movement, 1920–1966*, University of California Press, Berkeley and Los Angeles, 1967, pp. 10–18. Also see Smith, *Japan's First Student Radicals*, pp. 53, 90–100.
128. *Chōsen Sōtokufu*, '*Zaikyō Chōsenjin Tōkyō*', in Pak, Z.K.S.S., Vol. 1, p. 145. Also see *Naimushō*, '*Chōsenjin Kinkyō Gaiyō*', in Pak, Z.K.S.S., Vol. 1, p. 124. For an official interpretation of the spread of socialist ideology among Korean students see '*Zaikyō Chōsen Ryūgakusei Gaikyō*', in Pak, Z.K.S.S., Vol. 1, pp. 326–327.
129. There is very little reliable information available concerning the ideology of early Korean communists and other radicals. See Scalapino and Lee, *Communism In Korea, Part I*, pp. 3–4, 63–64. Also see Yoo Se Hee, op. cit., pp. 90–110.
130. *Naimushō*, '*Chōsenjin Kinkyō Gaiyō*', in Pak, Z.K.S.S., Vol. 1, pp. 124–125. Also see Scalapino and Lee, *Communism In Korea, Part I*, pp. 28–29, and Beckman and Okubo, op. cit., p. 30.
131. *Chōsen Sōtokufu*, '*Zaikyō Chōsenjin Tōkyō*', in Pak, Z.K.S.S., Vol. 1, pp. 140, 145. Among the leaders of this group were Kim Yak-su, Paek Mu, and Pak Yŏl. Kim Yak-su first arrived in Tokyo in 1916. He later studied at the Peking Military Academy and returned to Japan after the March 1 Movement, where he became active in left-wing student politics. Kim was a leading figure in the *Kugakusei Dōyūkai*, *Kokutōkai* and the *Hokuseikai*. He returned to Korea in August 1923 and was the driving force behind the establishment of the Construction Society (later renamed the North Wind Society – which played a key role in the creation of the Korean Communist Party in 1925) which was designed to liaise with the remaining members of the *Hokuseikai* in Tokyo. Paek Mu, whose real name was Paek Man-jo, was a native of North Kyŏngsang Province. He, along with Kim Yak-su, was instrumental in the establishment of the first Korean trade unions in Japan. Pak Yŏl (in Japanese Boku Retsu), whose real name was Pak Chun-sik, was also a native of North Kyŏngsang Province. He was the principal anarchist leader from 1922 until his arrest and subsequent imprisonment for high treason in 1923–1924.
132. *Keihokyoku*, '*Zairyū Chōsenjin – 1925*', in Pak, Z.K.S.S., Vol. 1, p. 153. The compiler of this report observed that, 'Those involved in the "socialist" movement have been influenced by foreign ideologies. Although there are those who appear to be dedicated to anarchism or

communism and advocate so-called "socialist" ideas, when confronted with nationalist ideology they immediately abandon the former in favour of the latter. The "socialist" movement therefore appears to be an appendage of the nationalist movement.' A similar view is expressed in both 'Kyōsanshugi Undō', pp. 13–14, and Shihōshō, 'Chōsenjin to Hanzai', in Pak, Z.K.S.S., Vol. 1, p. 295.

133. 'Zaikyō Chōsen Ryūgakusei Gaikyō', in Pak, Z.K.S.S., Vol. 1, p. 325.
134. Naimushō, 'Chōsenjin Kinkyō Gaiyō', in Pak, Z.K.S.S., Vol. 1, pp. 122–123. Also see 'Zaikyō Chōsen Ryūgakusei Gaikyō', in Pak, Z.K.S.S., Vol. 1, p. 325.
135. As cited in 'Zaikyō Chōsen Ryūgakusei Gaikyō', in Pak, Z.K.S.S., Vol. 1, pp. 325–326.
136. The Washington Conference decided that the 'Korean Problem' was an internal matter to be resolved by the Japanese Government alone. See ibid., p. 326, and 'Kyōsanshugi Undō', pp. 21–33. Although it maintained a nominal existence into the 1930s, after 1921 the Provisional Government failed to provide a meaningful and effective focus for nationalist activities. See Chong-Sik Lee, op. cit., pp. 129–179.
137. 'Zaikyō Chōsen Ryūgakusei Gaikyō', in Pak, Z.K.S.S., Vol. 1, pp. 326–327.
138. Scalapino and Lee, Communism In Korea, Part I, p. 57.
139. Chōsen Sōtokufu, 'Zaikyō Chōsenjin Tōkyō', in Pak, Z.K.S.S., Vol. 1, p. 140.
140. Chōsen Sōtokufu, 'Zaikyō Chōsenjin Tōkyō', in Pak, Z.K.S.S., Vol. 1, p. 145. Due to a lack of reliable information it is impossible to provide a general assessment of the attitudes of Japanese radicals toward Koreans. There are indications, however, that even while publicly encouraging solidarity between Japanese and Koreans, at least some Japanese leftists were infected by the same contemptuous attitudes which characterized pronouncements. The June 1 issue of the Rōdōsha Shimbun, for example, reported that two trade union officials, who had been under police surveillance, had felt slighted when the authorities treated them like Koreans and failed to recognize them as the famous revolutionaries they believed themselves to be. Cited in Iwamura, op. cit., p. 77.
141. Pak Kyŏng-sik, 'Nihon Teikokushugi Ka ni okeru Zainichi Chōsenjin Undō (1)', ('The Korean Peoples Movement in Japan under Japanese Imperialism [1]', Chōsen Geppō, Vol. 2, No. 4, Tokyo, March 1957, p. 8. (Cited hereafter as Pak, 'The Korean Peoples Movement, 1'.)
142. 'Kyōsanshugi Undō', pp. 31–32. Also see Keihokyoku, 'Zairyū Chōsenjin – 1925', in Pak, Z.K.S.S., Vol. 1, p. 162, and Pak Kyŏng-sik, Undōshi, p. 106.
143. Cited in Iwamura, op. cit., p. 74.
144. Ibid. Also see Chōsen Sōtokufu, 'Zaikyō Chōsenjin Tōkyō', in Pak, Z.K.S.S., Vol. 1, pp. 145–146, Keihokyoku, 'Zairyū Chōsenjin – 1925', in Pak, Z.K.S.S., Vol. 1, p. 163, and 'Zaikyō Chōsen Ryūgakusei Gaikyō', in Pak, Z.K.S.S., Vol. 1, pp. 328–332.
145. The North Star Society, for example, was listed as a 'thought research group' on police files, and was later regarded as the direct antecedent of the Korean Communist Movement in Japan. See 'Kyōsanshugi Undō', pp. 31–32. Also see Shihōshō, 'Chōsenjin to Hanzai', in Pak, Z.K.S.S., Vol. 1, p. 248.
146. Iwamura, op. cit., p. 78. Also see Chōsen Sōtokufu, 'Zaikyō Chōsenjin Tōkyō', in Pak, Z.K.S.S., Vol. 1, p. 145.

147. Pak, 'The Korean Peoples Movement, 1', p. 8. Also see Pak Kyŏng-sik, *Undōshi*, p. 107, and Yoo Se Hee, op. cit., p. 113.
148. See *Chōsen Sōtokufu Kanbō Gaijika* (Government-General of Korea Secretariat External Affairs Section), '*Kantō Chihō Shinsaiji ni okeru Chōsenjin Mondai*' ('The Korean Problem at the Time of the Kantō Earthquake'). (Cited hereafter as *Chōsen Sōtokufu*, '*Chōsenjin Mondai*'), 1924. Cited in Kang Tŏk-sang and Kŭm Byŏng-dong, comps., *Gendai Shi Shiryō (6) (Materials in Contemporary History, Vol. 6), 'Kantō Dai Shinsai to Chōsenjin*' ('The Great Kantō Earthquake and Koreans'), Misuzu Shobō, Tokyo, 1963, pp.454–455. (Cited hereafter as Kang, *Kantō Dai Shinsei to Chōsenjin*). Although this particular passage does not refer exclusively to Korean students, it is quite apparent, given the history of student activism in Japan, that the author of this report was referring to the extreme left of the student movement.
149. Min Wŏn-sik was the president of the *Kukmin Hyophoe*, the most effective of the pro-Japanese organizations which emerged in Korea after 1920. Early in 1920 Min arrived in Tokyo and presented a petition to the speaker of the Lower House calling for the extension of the political franchise to Korea. This petition argued that the recruitment of Koreans into government service and the right of Koreans to elect their own representatives to the Diet were a fundamental part of the principle of assimilation. This and other similar attempts by pro-Japanese groups, however, failed to convince the Government – and Koreans were not granted the franchise until 1945. Korean residents in Japan, however, were enfranchised under the Universal Suffrage Law of 1925 – provided they met Japanese voting requirements. See *Keihokyoku*, '*Zairyū Chōsenjin – 1925*', in Pak, Z.K.S.S., Vol. 1, pp. 182–183, and *Shihōshō*, '*Chōsenjin to Hanzai*', in Pak, Z.K.S.S., Vol. 1, p. 297. Also see Wonmo Dong, *Japanese Colonial Policy And Practice In Korea*, pp. 194–215, 270–274.
150. Kim Il-son, *Pak Yol*, Gōdō Shuppan, Tokyo, 1973, p. 8. Also see Iwamura, op. cit., pp. 73–74.
151. *Futei Senjin*, No. 2, December 1922, pp. 1–3. The title of this magazine is printed in the characters meaning 'Stalwart Korean' but are given a reading which, in the absence of the Chinese ideographs, is the common term for 'Korean Malcontent'. See Pak Kyŏng-sik, *Undōshi*, p. 106, and Kim Il-son, op. cit., pp. 80–83.
152. '*Kyōsanshugi Undō*', pp. 31–32. Also see '*Zaikyō Chōsen Ryūgakusei Gaikyō*', in Pak, Z.K.S.S., Vol. 1, pp. 328–334.
153. Kim Il-son, op. cit., p. 118.
154. Iwamura, op. cit., pp. 73–74.
155. Mitchell, op. cit., pp. 34–35.
156. *Chōsen Sōtokufu*, '*Chōsenjin Mondai*', in Kang, *Kantō Dai Shinsai to Chōsenjin*, p. 454.
157. Ibid.

Chapter 6

Myth and Reality: The Great Kantō Earthquake

The brief reign of the Taishō Emperor (1912–1926) encompassed a period of tremendous economic and social change in Japan, but an incident that affected the lives of the Japanese people far more immediately than this was the Great Kantō Earthquake of 1923. At approximately two minutes before noon on September 1, a series of violent earth tremors convulsed much of the eastern part of the densely populated and heavily industrialized Kantō region. In the epicentral area stretching from Shizuoka Prefecture in the south to Chiba Prefecture in the north, a number of coastal towns were levelled; a village in Kanagawa Prefecture was swept into the sea by an enormous mud flow, and within minutes the town of Odawara virtually ceased to exist.[1]

In all, seven Prefectures were affected by the earthquake, but it was in Kanagawa Prefecture and Tokyo Metropolitan Prefecture that the loss of life and property was greatest. Although the tremors alone severely disrupted all public services and destroyed many buildings both public and private, it was the ensuing firestorm which caused the most widespread destruction in both Tokyo and Yokohama. Coming as they did when most people were preparing the mid-day meal, the shock waves overturned thousands of stoves and braziers, and few of the terrified people had time to extinguish the flames before rushing out of doors. Fed by unusually high winds, firestorms quickly developed and engulfed areas of both cities. The fire brigades, handicapped by inadequate supplies of water, were unable to cope with the situation.[2]

In Tokyo, by the evening of September 2, the entire district extending from Minami Senjū in the north to Kanasugi in the south had been reduced to ashes. The fires continued to burn in some parts of the stricken city until the following day, leaving in their wake tens of thousands of dead and more than one million refugees. By nightfall, nearly half a million people were huddled in front of the Imperial Palace, and another 400,000 had sought temporary shelter in Ueno Park.[3]

According to a report compiled by the Social Affairs Bureau of the Home Ministry in 1926, the number of fatalities in Tokyo and Yokohama was estimated at close to 80,000, and the number of people listed missing or injured at nearly 50,000. In Tokyo alone more than 350,000 private homes were either destroyed or damaged, and in Yokohama approximately 90% of all homes were damaged or destroyed. Numerous foreign legations, universities and museums were gutted by the fires, as were the buildings housing the Ministries of Home Affairs, Finance, Education, Agriculture, Commerce and Railways.[4] So complete was the isolation of the Tokyo-Yokohama area that it was several hours before the Chief of the Yokohama Police Department was able to transmit the following message from a ship anchored in Yokohama harbour:

> Today, at noon, a great earthquake occurred and was immediately followed by a conflagration, which has turned the whole city into a sea of fire, causing countless casualties. All facilities of traffic have been destroyed and communications cut off. We have neither water nor food. For God's sake, send relief at once.[5]

By mid-afternoon on September 1, rumours of an impending uprising by groups of disaffected Koreans had begun to circulate in the Kawasaki and Yokohama areas. The source of these rumours, which were later proved to be unfounded, appears to have been one Yamaguchi Seiken, a well-known labour agitator in the Yokohama area.[6] Although later denied by Yamaguchi and his followers, an investigation by officials from the Justice Ministry confirmed that at approximately 3 p.m. on September 1, Yamaguchi had organized a *Yokohama Shinsai Hogodan* (Yokohama Earthquake Protection Association) in Nakamura-chō, Yokohama. After arming this volunteer force with weapons taken from a nearby Middle School, Yamaguchi is reported to have warned his followers that several hundred armed Koreans were marching on Kuboyama. It was also alleged that at this meeting Yamaguchi had advised his listeners to wear red armbands, since it was thought that anyone not doing so would be murdered by the approaching Koreans.[7]

Although the rumoured attack by Koreans failed to materialize, serious looting was reported to have taken place in Nakamura-chō, as well as in the neighbouring wards of Negishi-chō and Yamamoto-chō; most of this was committed by members of the *Hogodan*.[8] More important, however, is the fact that it was from police substations in these same areas that further (unconfirmed) reports concerning Koreans were submitted to police headquarters at Yamanote-Honmachi at about 7 p.m. There can be little doubt that these later reports alleging that the citizens of these areas had armed themselves in order to repulse an attack by a group of approximately 200 Koreans who were 'setting fires,' 'poisoning wells' and 'raping and looting,'[9] substantially added to confusion in downtown Yokohama. By the following morning rumours of seditious acts being committed by Korean malcontents had enveloped the entire city.

Map of Tokyo and surrounding districts showing the areas where the rumoured Korean uprising received the most attention.

According to surveys conducted before and after the earthquake, the following areas within Tokyo Prefecture supported the largest number of Koreans: Honjō, Kanda, Ushigome, Koish*i*kawa, Hongo, Fukagawa, Otsuka, Senju, Asakusa, Kita Toshima, Toyotama, Ebara and Minami Adachi.

Similar reports were submitted to the Metropolitan Police Department (M.P.D.) in Tokyo from police substations in Ōji and Shiba Atago, though the rumoured attack by Koreans was at first confined chiefly to the Kōtō and Yamanote areas. But, by the morning of September 2, rumours of a Korean uprising began moving north from Yokohama, and by noon, the panic had reached Shinagawa, Ōmori, Chōfu, Tamagawa and Setagaya, and by late afternoon had spread throughout the western part of Tokyo.[10]

Reports had reached M.P.D. Headquarters from police stations as far afield as Nakano, Yodobashi and Terashima of Koreans having been arrested for well-poisoning and attempting to detonate bombs. These reports were investigated and proved to be unfounded. Nevertheless, the trickle of reports concerning violence by Koreans which had begun early in the morning had, by late afternoon, become a torrent.[11]

At 3.00 p.m., the police chief of the Tomizaka substation reported the arrest of a number of Koreans who had been rioting and committing acts of arson. This report was immediately investigated and proved to be untrue. At approximately the same time, a report was filed by the police in Kagurazaka concerning the arrest of Korean arsonists by members of the public, and within an hour an urgent appeal for reinforcements was received from the police in Ōtsuka due to an anticipated attack by a group of Koreans on the nearby arsenal.[12]

Reports were received from the police in Shibuya of the approach of nearly 200 heavily armed Koreans who had crossed the Tama river and were advancing on the city. Similar reports were received from the police in Setagaya and Nakano, and even wilder rumours of an armed clash between units of the army and an estimated force of 2,000 Korean insurgents at Sangenjaya were widely circulated at police headquarters. It was even believed that yet another group of Koreans nearly a thousand strong had attacked the residence of Imperial Prince Kuni.[13]

Refugees streaming out of the stricken city of Yokohama brought with them further tales of outbreaks of organized violence by Koreans, many of which were accepted by the police in Tokyo though never substantiated. In Setagaya, the chief of police, after receiving unconfirmed reports of the approach from the Kawasaki area of hundreds of Koreans who had set fires, poisoned wells and brutally murdered women and children, hastily mobilized the local youth association and fire brigade for the defence of the area under his jurisdiction.[14]

The content of every rumour was essentially the same, and by September 3, rumours of reported Korean uprisings had permeated not only the Kantō area but the entire country. As far north as Hokkaidō widespread panic occurred due to fears of well-poisoning by Koreans, and rumours of impending attacks by bands of Korean extremists continued to erupt across the whole of Japan for nearly a fortnight after the earthquake.[15]

In Gumma Prefecture, for example, a report that the cities of Maebashi and Kiryū had been set afire by attacking Koreans was widely believed, and by September 3 vigilance committees had been organized in all the towns and villages along the border with Saitama Prefecture.[16] The September 5 edition of the *Sanyō Shimpō* reported a series of serious clashes between 'Korean Malcontents' and local army reservists in Gifu Prefecture,[17] and on the following day the same newspaper reported that the police in Okayama Prefecture had been issued with orders to prevent the further movement of Koreans toward Tokyo.[18] Although the authorities later conceded that fears concerning the activities of Koreans had been exaggerated, considerable attention continued to be focussed on those incidents in which Koreans were thought to have been involved. The *Ōsaka Mainichi Shimbun*, for example, published a list of crimes committed by Koreans which had been released by the police in Tokyo. These included: the apprehension of a Korean on the evening of September 1 who had attempted to steal clothing from a shop in Honjō-ward; an attempted assault on a Japanese woman by a Korean named Kim Son-jun on the same evening and in the same area; an attempt by a group of thirty Koreans led by one Kang Kum-san to steal cloth from a shop in Honjō-ward on the same evening; the shooting of an unidentified Korean on September 2 who was attempting to destroy the Edogawa bridge in Tokyo; and (perhaps the most damning) an incident involving the apprehension and death of a Korean identified as Li O-gen on September 3. This was reported in the following way:

> A Chosenese named Li O-gen was seen near a well with some white powder, and when questioned by a Japanese stated it was salt. The Japanese then made him taste it to see if he was telling the truth. The Chosenese died immediately.[19]

Curiously, however, the suspects in all of these cases either managed to escape from custody or died while being apprehended. None was ever brought to trial.

The Japanese Government not only made strenuous efforts at the time to minimize its own responsibility for the outrages committed against Koreans in the days that followed, but later fostered the impression both at home and abroad that there had in fact been a conspiracy between an unidentified group of dissident Koreans and Japanese radicals. For example, the Kantō Martial Law Headquarters issued a statement on September 9 to the effect that although the number of Koreans involved in seditious activities had been 'extremely small':

> Koreans and Bolsheviks did their best to incite riots by disquieting speeches, but the prevalence of such outrages has been kept down

by the presence of soldiers, police, army reservists, and members of Young Men's Associations.[20]

The authorities also restricted press coverage of the anti-Korean riots and later attempted to dismiss the murders of Koreans as being only a series of unrelated incidents perpetuated by hysterical mobs and overzealous vigilance groups. Nevertheless, a careful investigation of the events and of the decisions taken by highly placed officials in various Ministries as well as in the M.P.D. not only casts doubt upon the official interpretation of events, but clearly indicates that the Government itself was responsible for the dissemination of unsubstantiated rumours, and therefore indirectly for the actions taken by these very groups.

A week earlier, Prime Minister Kato Tomasaburō had died, and the elder statesman Yamamoto Gombei had been designated as his successor. At the time of the earthquake, however, Yamamoto had not yet succeeded in forming a new cabinet, and an interim Government led by Uchida Kōsai was managing the affairs of state. Mizuno Rentarō, a career bureaucrat who was then Minister of Home Affairs in this interim cabinet, played a critical role in the formulation of relief and police measures during the first uneasy hours after the earthquake.[21]

Immediately after the earthquake, an emergency cabinet meeting was held to discuss the implementation of measures which would ensure the smooth and rapid movement of relief supplies and the maintenance of public order in the devastated areas. As a result, Imperial Ordinance No. 397 establishing a *Rinji Shinsai Kyūgo Jimukyoku* (Emergency Earthquake Relief Bureau) was issued. Simultaneously, Prime Minister Uchida and Home Minister Mizuno were appointed its chairman and vice-chairman respectively.[22] Also present at this meeting was Akaike Atsushi, Inspector-General of the Tokyo M.P.D. The imminent danger of a food shortage and the public unrest such a shortage might cause were perceived as the most pressing issues. Since the Government Rice Warehouse in Fukugawa had already been destroyed, and the Army Provisions Depot at Etchūjima was also threatened by fire it was decided that certain extraordinary measures would have to be adopted. Akaike, the official chiefly responsible for the maintenance of public peace and safety within the capital, was also the member most anxious lest the panic result in mass disturbances. What most concerned him at the time was the possibility that the shortage of food might lead to rioting in the city. If the hundreds of thousands of terrified refugees did not receive food and water, he felt, 'there was no predicting what might occur'. In his words, 'Everything hinged upon the measures that we might adopt . . . I believed that we had no choice but to accept this enormous responsibility and take decisive action.'[23]

Consequently, under the provisions of the Administrative Enforcement Law of 1890 an Emergency Requisition Ordinance was promulgated, taking effect from the morning of September 2. Akaike later wrote about his role in the implementation of this decree:

> I ordered that all food shops be temporarily placed under police control in order to prevent outbreaks of violence and looting . . . Since time immemorial violence in every country has begun with food riots, and therefore nothing is more important than the prevention of famine.[24]

Prior to the cabinet meeting mentioned above, Ishimitsu Maomi, deputy commander of the First Division of the Tokyo garrison, ordered the partial mobilization of the troops under his command. Moreover, at about 4.30 p.m. on September 1, Inspector-General Akaike, fearful that the police alone were not equipped to cope with the type of unrest he feared, formally applied for the full mobilization of the Tokyo garrison.[25] Units of the army and *Kempeitai* (Gendarmerie) were quickly despatched to guard the Imperial Palace, banks, public buildings, railway terminals and collecting depots for relief goods.[26]

Clearly then, the Japanese authorities were exceedingly concerned about the possibility of civil disorder in the capital. Akaike later wrote in this context: 'When I returned to my office at about 9 p.m. on the evening of the 2nd, I received reports . . . of 2,000 Koreans, who had crossed at [the River Tama], rioting in various parts of Tokyo.' Akaike appears to have been convinced by these reports that Korean extremists were capable of mounting such an attack, but felt that the great majority of Koreans were in no way involved. He therefore ordered the suppression of the rioters while making it clear that the majority of Koreans were to be protected.[27]

Home Minister Mizuno, too, was greeted with similar reports on the morning of the 2nd, and consulted with a number of officials as to the most effective measures to be taken in light of the tide of rumours concerning Koreans. One of the men with whom he discussed the matter was Akaike, and according to the October 13 edition of the *Kahoku Shimpō* it was Akaike who emphatically pressed for the imposition of Martial Law in Tokyo.[28] Mizuno later recalled that:

> On the following morning [September 2], while the people were still in a confused state, there arose from somewhere or other unsubstantiated rumours concerning Koreans who were rioting. People like Railway Minister Ōgi reported that the people in the Tamagawa area had been thrown into turmoil by rumours of a Korean uprising. I immediately sent for the Inspector-General of the M.P.D. [Akaike], and when I asked him about it, he replied that there was no apparent source for the wild rumours which were then circulating. Since that was the situation . . . after giving the

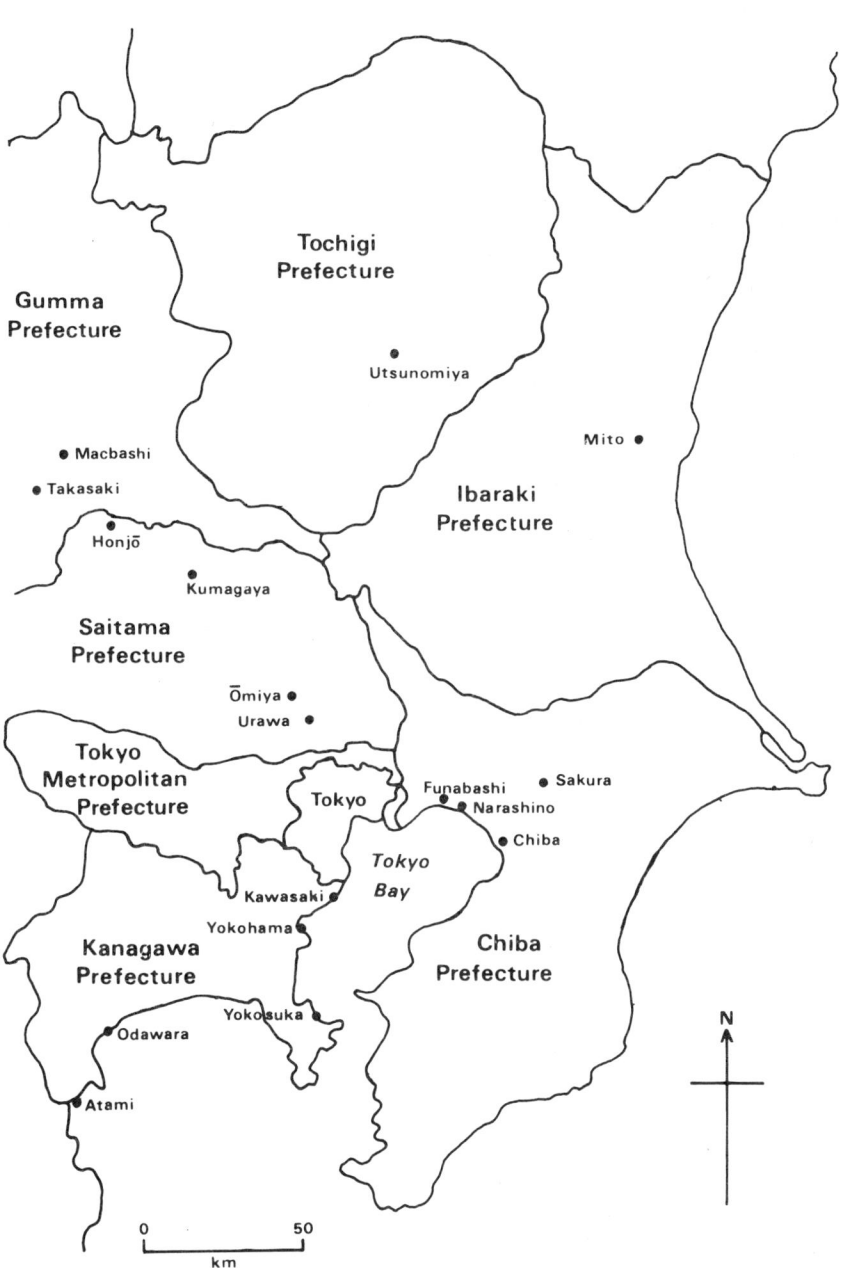

Sketch Map of Tokyo and Surrounding Prefectures

matter considerable thought . . . I came to the conclusion that the only course of action available was to impose Martial Law.[29]

Precedent demanded that the decision to impose Martial Law had to be approved by the Privy Council. Due to the disruption of public services, however, Mizuno was unable to convene the Council, and after receiving the approval of Councillor Itō Miyoji and Prime Minister Uchida, the decision was taken by the cabinet to seek Imperial sanction for this emergency measure. Consequently, later that afternoon Martial Law was imposed not only in Tokyo but in the five surrounding districts of Ebara, Toyotama, Kita Toshima, Minami Adachi and Minami Katsushika.[30]

But, even before the promulgation of partial Martial Law in the Tokyo area, both the M.P.D. and the Ministry of Home Affairs had taken steps which not only lent credence to the rumours but facilitated their dissemination throughout the entire country as well as overseas. On the afternoon of September 2, Gotō Fumio, Chief of the Bureau of Police Affairs within the Home Ministry sent a message by courier to the naval transmission station at Funabashi in Chiba Prefecture. The message was then relayed to every Prefectural Governor. It read in part:

> There are organized groups of Korean extremists taking advantage of the disaster in Tokyo and attempting to commit acts of sedition. Some have been seen carrying bombs, spreading oil and setting fires. Partial Martial Law has already been declared in Tokyo and we request that you increase secret surveillance in all areas and take firm measures in dealing with the activities of Koreans.[31]

Messages of this nature continued to be transmitted throughout the country, and on the following day the Governor of Yamaguchi Prefecture received a message from the Police Affairs Bureau advising him to 'increase surveillance on Koreans entering the country, and to take whatever steps are necessary to prevent the entry of suspicious individuals.'[32]

The Army Minister too, believing that the troops at his disposal in Tokyo would be insufficient to cope with the potential threat to the security of the capital ordered the Kōfu and Sakura Divisions to Tokyo early on the morning of September 2.[33]

Once Martial Law went into effect, both the Police and the Army took extreme measures which, if nothing else, stilled any remaining doubts that the public might have had about the truth of the rumours. The Police in both Tokyo and Yokohama began putting up posters and distributing leaflets, urging the still bewildered and credulous public to be particularly vigilant since there had been outbreaks of rioting and other types of violent behaviour by bands of Korean malcontents.[34]

Moriyama Saneyoshi, Commander of the Narashino Division attached to the Tokyo garrison issued the following instructions to the troops under his command on the afternoon of September 2:

> ... At this time of great unrest, you must prevent people from taking advantage of the situation and disturbing public order. If after receiving a warning they refuse to obey, you may use your weapons.[35]

At 5 p.m. on the same day he explicitly identified those elements when he issued a directive to the police under his jurisdiction saying that there were Koreans who were continuing to commit mischief, and that there had already been a number of arrests made in places like Ōtsuka and Yodobashi in Tokyo. 'Let me remind you,' he continued, 'not to relax your guard and to take firm action against these Koreans.'[36]

Perhaps the most damning evidence of official responsibility for the dissemination of rumours came not from the political left, as one might have expected, but from the reactionary right. Uchida Ryōhei, the doyen of Japanese ultra-nationalists and leader of the *Kokuryūkai* (Amur River Society), later confirmed police responsibility for the transmission of misinformation concerning Koreans. In his view, 'Taking into account all the facts, it appears that the rumours of a Korean uprising began with warnings given by the police in Yokohama.' He recollected that, 'People were advised to guard against the actions of Koreans and even to kill them if they seemed suspicious.'[37]

As limited communications were restored, the Home Ministry hastened to inform the authorities in surrounding districts of the situation in Tokyo, and to recommend measures to be applied in their areas. The Saitama Prefectural authorities, who were among the first to be notified by the Ministry, revealed through their actions the way in which officials at every level co-operated in the dissemination of false reports. According to statements later made in the Diet, the Chief Administrative Officer of the Saitama desk in the Home Ministry returned to his office at approximately 5 p.m. on the 2nd, after attending a meeting at the Ministry. He immediately reported the results of the meeting to the Vice-Governor of Saitama Prefecture, who in turn proceeded to relay the following advice to the *Gun* (County) officials under his jurisdiction:

> It may be that large numbers of Korean malcontents who are rioting and taking advantage of the disaster in Tokyo are crossing from the Kawaguchi side into Saitama Prefecture ... Because of the weakness of the police at the present time, I would like you to act in concert with local chapters of the Army Reserves, Youth Association, and Fire Brigades ... In the event of an emergency

you should immediately take suitable measures to discuss the proper course of action . . .[38]

This notification was then passed on by the County Offices to the towns and villages under their jurisdiction either by telephone or by messenger.

In this way, the *Jikeidan* (vigilance groups) began to emerge not only in Tokyo and Yokohama but throughout much of the Kantō region. The first such groups appeared in Yokohama on the evening of September 1, but the vast majority of the *Jikeidan* were not organized until after the Martial Law decree went into effect on the following day.[39] It can be seen from Table 27 that approximately 3,700 such groups were organized in seven separate prefectures, with the figure in Tokyo alone reaching nearly 1,600.

TABLE 27

Jikeidan Organised Following the Earthquake

Prefecture	Number of *Jikeidan*
Tokyo (Metropolitan Prefecture)	1,593
Kanagawa	603
Saitama	300
Chiba	366
Ibaraki	336
Gumma	469
Tochigi	19

Source: *Keihokyoku*, 'Policing Following the Earthquake', p. 28.

Note: Identical figures are also given in Matsuo, '*Dai Shinsai to Gyakusatsu, I*', p. 53. Matsuo notes that these figures were compiled towards the end of October, and also points out that by September 6 approximately 1,150 *Jikeidan* had been organized in Tokyo and the counties surrounding it. It is therefore likely that the number of *Jikeidan* active in the Kantō at the height of the 'Korean scare' (September 2–7) was considerably higher than at the end of October when civil order had been restored.

Writing two months later, Mizuno Rentarō vigorously defended the formation of the *Jikeidan* as 'a manifestation of the natural feeling of mutual caring for one's neighbourhood and mutual aid within neighbourhoods'.[40] In both Mizuno's article and the official interpretation of the activities of the *Jikeidan*, the emergence and spread of such organizations was vigorously defended as a natural and entirely spontaneous expression of mutual assistance among the people. Nevertheless, as we have seen in the case of Saitama Prefecture where some of the most extreme anti-Korean riots occurred, it was the rumours and misinformation disclosed by officials at the national, prefectural, county and even village level which not only encouraged the organization of the *Jikeidan*, but later transformed them from relief associations into armed mobs whose principal objective was the harassment of Koreans. The way in which the *Jikeidan* in one area deteriorated into an armed mob was clear from an editorial which appeared in the October 25 edition of the *Sanyō Shimpō*. It read in part:

> At first, the *Jikeidan* in the town of Honjō in Kodama County were very useful. Co-operating with local reservists, members of Youth Associations and the Fire Brigade, its members met the refugees coming from Tokyo and helped in the distribution of emergency . . . rations. But due to the rumours, the *Jikeidan* gradually lost all sense of discipline and began dragging coolies and pedlars from the trains . . .[41]

On the evening of September 2, the formation of the new Yamamoto cabinet was completed, and Gotō Shimpei was installed as Minister for Home Affairs. Although clearly concerned about the wave of violence being directed against Koreans, Gotō appears to have been unable to control the activities of the *Jikeidan*. On September 3, as more units from provincial garrisons began arriving in the Tokyo area, the zone under Martial Law was expanded to include all of Tokyo and Kanagawa Prefectures.[42] Moreover, under Imperial Ordinance 400 issued on the same day, General Fukuda Masatarō was appointed chief executive officer of the Kantō Martial Law Command.[43] The powers invested in this office gave him jurisdiction not only over matters of relief and public safety in the area under Martial Law, but also over administrative and judicial affairs as well. He was therefore empowered to prohibit public gatherings and the publication of public notices, newspapers and magazines, to censor letters and telegrams, order his troops to enter and search private homes, and to prohibit passage through the area by land and sea.[44] On September 4, Saitama and Chiba Prefectures were also placed under Martial Law,[45] and by September 10, the number of troops mobilized in the Kantō had reached nearly 50,000.[46]

The dissemination of exaggerated reports of an uprising by Korean extremists was further intensified throughout the following day. The Naval Transmission station at Funabashi continued to broadcast appeals for aid to all parts of the country,[47] and on September 4, the commandant of the station ordered the transmission of the following order to the *Jikeidan* in the village of Hōten in Chiba Prefecture, which had been organized previously at his behest by the village headman. 'In the spirit of the highest sense of patriotism, you are ordered to annihilate the said enemy.'[48] After nearly three days of warnings and rumours of an uprising by Koreans, the *Jikeidan* in Hōten presumably had little difficulty in identifying the 'said enemy' and duly annihilating them.

Not only did the Army, Police and Home Ministry encourage the *Jikeidan* to mistreat Koreans, but in a number of instances went so far as to arm them with weapons supplied by nearby arsenals or military garrisons.[49] The well-known left-wing novelist Eguchi Kiyoshi remembered seeing a large poster on a wall in Koishikawa in Tokyo. On it, alongside official announcements concerning the formation of the Yamamoto cabinet, the following notice was written:

> Among a section of Koreans and Socialists there are some who are plotting unrest and sedition. In order that they not be given the chance to take advantage, citizens are please urged to be particularly vigilant and to co-operate with the police. Even women and children are poisoning wells. Be careful of well water.[50]

Unable to produce or distribute ordinary newspapers, the *Tōkyō Nichi Nichi Shimbun* and others began printing abbreviated wall-poster newspapers as early as September 2 to relay official notices to the general public. One such paper appealed for the establishment of *Jikeidan* in the metropolitan area as a response to the seditious acts of Japanese socialists and Korean malcontents.[51]

Jikeidan throughout the Kantō began arming themselves with bamboo spears, swords, axes, clubs and other such weapons. Positioning themselves at major intersections and other strategic places they began to stop and interrogate anyone who attempted to pass them, and there were numerous incidents where Koreans, once discovered, were summarily executed.[52]

The actions of the army too were not above reproach as regards the mistreatment and even murder of innocent Koreans. As troops began arriving in Tokyo, along with being assigned to normal garrison duties and relief work, some units were detached to investigate those areas of the city where the anti-Korean rumours had been most widespread. In the Kōtō area, troops under the Martial Law Command murdered a number of Koreans, and Etchūya Riichi, author of 'Earthquake Diary of a Private Soldier' revealed how it was the actions taken by elements of the 13th regiment of the Narashino cavalry that ignited the infamous Kameido incident:

> It was about 2.00 p.m. [Sept. 2] when we arrived at Kameido, and the victims were like a flood overflowing. As the first action taken by the regiment, we searched the trains. An officer with drawn sword inspected both inside and out of every carriage. Every train

was crammed with people; they were packed like locusts even as far as the coal piled up in front of the locomotive, and Koreans who were among them were dragged off. Immediately after this, they were thrown in succession under our drawn swords and bayonets. Seething like a tempest from the midst of the Japanese came a chorus of cries of 'Banzai! Traitors! Kill all Koreans!' We soldiers whose blood offering had set this off, began hunting down and killing Koreans from evening until nightfall.[53]

The actions of the Narashino cavalry described by Etchūya undoubtedly helped to trigger the outbreak of police and *Jikeidan* violence against Koreans that occurred during the following days in Kameido. In a related incident on the evening of September 3, nine members of the Nankatsu Labour Association in Tokyo were seized by the police and taken to the Kameido police station where they were murdered either by members of the police or by soldiers assigned to maintain public order in the area. The report later filed by the officer in command stated simply that: 'they were stabbed to death in accordance with article 12 of the Garrison Regulations'. Their only crime, it would seem, had been that they were labour activists, and when interrogated at the police station, responded by singing the 'Labour Song'.[54] When the families of the victims inquired after them, they were informed that the nine men had already been released from custody, whereas in fact the bodies had previously been secretly disposed of. It was not until October 10 that the facts surfaced, though no action was ever taken against the officers or men involved.[55]

Although scattered reports alleging socialist participation in the acts of sedition committed by Koreans were received by the Tokyo M.P.D. as early as September 1, reports of this nature did not begin to circulate widely until the 3rd or 4th.[56] Nevertheless, during the first week of September the police – in an almost unprecedented demonstration of misapplied enthusiasm – arrested more than a thousand labour leaders and suspected radicals in the Tokyo area alone. The most infamous involved the arrest of the anarchist Ōsugi Sakae, his common-law wife and his nephew, and his murder by an army officer while in police custody. Criticized by the Home Ministry for this action, the Ministry of the Army issued an official apology, adding that:

> His motivation . . . was the fear lest Ōsugi and the others, capitalizing on the chaos, should commit unjust acts against the state. It seems that he wanted to eliminate poisonous elements from the state.[57]

As regards other atrocities committed by military units, both Matsuo Takayoshi and Imai Seiichi have referred to the experience of a certain

Shimizu Ikutarō. Shimizu, a middle school student at the time of the earthquake, had taken refuge in the military barracks at Ishikawa Kōfudai in Chiba city, and watched and listened as the soldiers cleaned the blood from their bayonets and swords, and joked about the Koreans they had just killed.[58]

According to Matsuo, on September 4, on two separate occasions, Koreans were murdered while in custody of the Chiba Garrison.[59] The official investigation of these incidents was later released and revealed the following:

> . . . Two Korean malcontents had been living with a labour contractor in the village of Shinozaki . . . It was concluded that there was nothing to be done but hand them over to Divisional Headquarters for disposition. While Sergeant Sakamoto and eight other soldiers were escorting them . . . the two Koreans without warning grabbed for Sakamoto's gun, began throwing small stones at the soldiers and attacked them with sticks. Because the situation became exceedingly dangerous, Sergeant Sakamoto ordered two of his men . . . to shoot the two Koreans.[60]

The official review of the second incident mirrored the first in every detail except that the number of Koreans involved was greater. In both cases, the evidence supplied by the soldiers was accepted without question and no action was ever taken against them. It is, however, rather difficult to believe that two unarmed and probably terrified Koreans would attack eight heavily armed troopers who were guarding them. Even if these incidents were accurately reported, provocation such as the throwing of 'small stones' would hardly seem to warrant such an extreme response unless the soldiers had in fact been issued with orders to kill suspected 'malcontents'.

By the evening of September 3, the situation in many areas was clearly beyond the control of the competent authorities. The rumoured uprising by Korean and Japanese extremists had failed to materialize, but the *Jikeidan* continued to methodically hunt down and kill Koreans. Another source of concern for the police was evidence that roadblocks erected by these groups had begun to interfere with the flow of relief goods into Tokyo.[61] Consequently, 30,000 leaflets were distributed throughout the Tokyo Metropolitan area, and police on patrol issued the following orders over loudspeakers:

> Although there has been reckless behaviour since yesterday on the part of a small minority of Koreans, due to vigorous vigilance all traces of this have now disappeared. Since the great majority of Koreans are well behaved and are not engaging in any sort of violent behaviour, care must be taken not to oppress them unlawfully, or to

inflict any violence upon them. Furthermore, should there be any incidents of unrest, the army or police are to be notified immediately.[62]

This was accompanied by a directive issued by the M.P.D. to all police chiefs prohibiting the possession of arms by members of the *Jikeidan*. Adding that, 'should anyone refuse to obey and continue to carry weapons, you should consider suitable measures such as taking them into custody. There should be no lapses in your vigilance.'[63] On the same day, the Police Affairs Bureau notified all newspapers that many of the previously reported incidents involving acts of sedition committed by Koreans had been no more than rumours. Moreover, since it was now felt that further rumours of this sort would only lead to increased social unrest, the publication of any articles concerning Koreans would result in a ban on the sale and distribution of the offending newspaper.[64] These police notifications were reinforced by a directive prohibiting the possession of weapons by members of the *Jikeidan* which was issued on September 4 by the Martial Law Command.[65]

Nevertheless, due in large measure to the Government's determination to maintain the fiction of an organized conspiracy by Koreans to subvert the state, these and other directives, instead of quelling public unease, only served to exacerbate an already grim situation. There were even indications by this time that armed vigilance groups had begun to attack police stations where Koreans were known to have taken refuge. The worst such incidents occurred on September 4 when Koreans under the protection of the police in the towns of Honjō and Jimbohara in Saitama Prefecture were attacked by armed mobs. It was later estimated that only two of the approximately 200 Koreans involved in these incidents survived.[66]

In the aftermath of the earthquake, and in later years, successive Japanese Governments made strenuous efforts to foster the impression that they had tried to safeguard the lives of Korean residents. Temporary 'reception centres' for Koreans were set up in many parts of Japan, and, as is illustrated in Table 28, approximately 24,000 Koreans were housed in these centres. It appears however, that in many instances 'protective custody' was confused with 'preventive detention.' Among the first to be interned were radical activists like Pyŏn Hŭi-yong, Yi Tong-ji and Chŏng T'ae-song, all of whom were associated with left-wing groups such as the *Hokuseikai*, the *Futeisha* or the *Kokutōkai*.[67]

On September 4, the Tokyo M.P.D., in a belated effort to end the violence, invited members of the Tokyo branch of the *Sōaikai* to a meeting at police headquarters. At this meeting it was decided that from September 10, beginning with a group of 120 'volunteers', Korean labourers would be employed by the Prefectural Government as

TABLE 28

Koreans Held in Protective Custody: September–October 1923*

Prefecture	Number of Koreans Voluntarily Seeking Protection	Number of Koreans previously taken into Custody by the Police	Number of Koreans taken into Custody by the Jikeidan	Others	Total
Tokyo	1,170	6,653	3,173	911	11,907
Kanagawa	180	871	160	1,055	2,266
Kyoto	53	273	–	–	326
Osaka	4	26	–	–	30
Hyōgo	11	–	–	407	418
Saitama	28	420	23	170	641
Gumma	21	113	39	438	611
Chiba	–	204	1	5	210
Ibaraki	4	102	–	–	106
Tochigi	23	99	4	421	547
Aichi	491	–	–	15	506
Shizuoka	1	368	–	–	369
Nagano	39	731	8	–	778
Okayama	1,334	–	–	–	1,334
Hiroshima	16	–	–	1,464	1,480
Yamaguchi	13	–	–	1,632	1,645
Others	208	120	4	209	541
Total	3,596	9,980	3,412	6,727	23,715**

Source: *Keihokyoku*, 'Policing Following the Earthquake', pp. 43–45.

Note: * The length of protective custody varied slightly from prefecture to prefecture, but with the exception of Tokyo, Kanagawa, Ibaraki, Tochigi, Aichi, Nagano, Aomori, Yamagata, Okayama, Hiroshima and Yamaguchi where Koreans were detained until the end of October or early November, most other detainees were released by the end of September.

** The total number of women detained was 2,023.

maintenance workers on the roads in the burnt-out areas of Tokyo. It was also decided that this would receive extensive coverage by the press, since it was hoped that the sight of Koreans performing *Shakai Hōshi* (Public Service) would help to bring an end to the violence being directed against them.[68] As a result, it is estimated that between September 1923 and March 1924 the *Sōaikai* supplied 300–400 Koreans per day for relief work in Tokyo.[69] Given the semi-official nature of the *Sōaikai*, however, this proposal now seems closer to enforced mobilization than to voluntary public service.

On September 5, Prime Minister Yamamoto made the following appeal to the nation:

> I am given to understand that something like animosity is entertained by the citizens toward the Koreans because of alleged reports about riotous acts contemplated by some malcontents among the Koreans, taking advantage of the disastrous earthquake and fires. Should the Koreans act in such a manner as to confirm the report, the public should immediately alert the Army or Police, who are charged with the preservation of peace and order, and place the matter in their hands. That the public themselves should take measures to persecute and threaten Koreans, is not only inconsistent with the principle of Japan-Korea assimilation but such practices, if reported overseas, will certainly produce undesirable effects . . . I sincerely hope that the nation will seriously reflect on the matter and maintain an attitude of self-respect.[70]

After the above statement by the Prime Minister, the anti-Korean riots began to recede, though as late as September 7 there were sporadic outbreaks of violence particularly in the Kōtō area of Tokyo. On September 20 the *Jikeidan* were officially placed under police supervision, and as the army began its withdrawal on about September 25, the *Jikeidan* were used extensively in relief work by the Metropolitan authorities. The last of these vigilance groups were not in fact dissolved until the end of October.[71]

The actual number of Koreans killed throughout the Kantō region during the first week of September 1923 remains the subject of considerable controversy.[72] Some sources cite figures as high as 6,000,[73] while the figures released by the Police Affairs Bureau limit the number to only 231 dead and forty-three injured, and do not include Koreans killed by members of the police or army.[74] The October 21 edition of the *Tōkyō Nichi Nichi Shimbun* carried the results of its own inquiry into the matter, and suggested that the number of Koreans killed was approximately 400.[75] According to a later report compiled by the Police Affairs Bureau, it was estimated that three Chinese and fifty-nine Japanese (who were apparently mistaken for Koreans) had also died as a result of mob violence.[76] But doubt was cast upon these estimates by the results of an investigation conducted by the Chinese Legation which revealed that more than 150 Chinese nationals were unaccounted for.[77] Official estimates were also challenged by Yoshino Sakuzō who carried out his own investigation. According to Yoshino, approximately 2,600 Koreans had been murdered in the Kantō, with the figure for Tokyo and Kanagawa Prefectures alone exceeding 1,800.[78] More recently Pak Kyŏng-sik has concluded that the number of Koreans murdered was at least twenty times the official estimate.[79] Moreover, while the figures produced by the Police Affairs Bureau cannot be rejected out of hand, further doubt is cast upon their reliability by the actions subsequently taken by the Government.

On September 5 a meeting was held at the Police Department of the Emergency Earthquake Relief Bureau. They discussed, first, the most appropriate method of limiting both international and domestic criticism of the Government's attitude toward the Korean issue during the preceding week, and, second, how they should prevent this very issue from inflaming anti-Japanese sentiment in Korea. Present at this meeting were representatives of the Army, Navy, Home Ministry, Tokyo M.P.D. and the Martial Law Command.[80] In a secret memorandum entitled *Chōsen Mondai ni Kansuru Kyōtei* (Policy Concerning the Korean Problem), they agreed:

(a) to put it about that although there had been sporadic outbreaks of violence by Koreans, the danger had now passed, and that most Koreans had remained peaceful, and that in any case many more Japanese than Koreans had been assaulted during the confusion.

(b) to investigate and confirm when possible those incidents in which Koreans committed or attempted to commit acts of violence and sedition.

(c) to discuss and implement suitable means of preventing Koreans from spreading unfavourable publicity in either Korea or Manchuria.

(d) to create the impression (particularly overseas) that both Korean and Japanese 'Reds' had in fact encouraged acts of violence.[81]

The results of this thorough investigation were announced in the national press on October 21, where it was revealed that the police were filing charges against a total of twenty-three Koreans. Of the twenty-three, the surnames of sixteen were unknown and for that reason they had never been caught, while of the remaining seven, one had committed suicide by swallowing poison, two had managed to escape from custody after firing pistols at the vigilantes who had arrested them, while a fourth was never apprehended.[82] In Yokohama where a similar investigation was carried out, criminal charges were filed against a total of about forty Koreans, most of whom were never identified or apprehended.[83] Moreover, in both Tokyo and Yokohama, despite the enormous publicity which had accompanied these announcements by the police, the charges against most of the remaining suspects were dropped for lack of evidence.[84]

In order to implement the other decisions taken at the meeting of the Emergency Earthquake Relief Bureau, an Imperial Ordinance for the Preservation of Public Order was issued on September 7. It read:

> Any person who, by whatever means, instigates others to acts of violence, disturbance, and other crimes endangering the lives, physical safety or property of the public, fabricates news of a disquieting character with a view to disturbing the public safety and order, or spreads wild rumours of threatening significance and thereby disturbs the public shall be punished by penal servitude or imprisonment for a period not exceeding 10 years or a fine not exceeding 3,000 yen.[85]

This measure was quite effective in stifling what protest there was among the 'Left', and imposed quite severe restrictions on the type of article which could thereafter legally be published by newspapers and magazines. This did not, however, appear to apply to inflammatory remarks made by Government officials in the press, as in the case of General Izome Rokurō who, on the same day the Ordinance was implemented, announced through the *Shimotsuke Shimbun* that 'there appeared to have been a conspiracy involving socialists and Russian radicals behind the recent seditious behaviour of Korean malcontents'.[86] General Izome's remarks were certainly in violation of at least the spirit of the above Ordinance; there is no record, however, of his having received even an official reprimand.

On September 9 the Emergency Earthquake Relief Bureau met to discuss methods of dealing with incidents involving members of the *Jikeidan*. They concluded that legally the incidents involving injuries could not be overlooked. However, due to the many extenuating circumstances at the time of the earthquake, the scope of arrests and prosecutions would be limited to only the most extreme cases. Furthermore, in light of the present social unease, those arrests should be delayed, and the public procurator should await the guidance of the Ministry of Justice before proceeding in the matter. In the interim all efforts should be made to ascertain the facts of any violent incidents involving the *Jikeidan*.[87]

Although estimates do vary, subsequent investigations led to the arrest of between 600 and 700 *Jikeidan* members throughout the Kantō region.[88] Not all the accused were actually indicted, and in the trials in Tokyo and Yokohama Prefectures, which lasted until March 1924, only 125 individuals were prosecuted. Of these, two were acquitted, 91 received suspended sentences, and in only thirty-two cases were the formal sentences actually carried out.[89] The maximum penalty imposed by either court was four years penal servitude, imposed in only two instances.[90] In almost all these cases however, general pardons were issued to commemorate the marriage of Crown Prince Hirohito in January of the following year.[91]

The trial of thirty-five former members of the *Jikeidan* in Saitama Prefecture, who were accused of murdering nearly 200 Koreans, began on October 22. According to reports published in both the *Tōkyō Nichi Nichi Shimbun* and the *Ōsaka Mainichi Shimbun* an almost carnival atmosphere surrounded the trial as 'witty statements' made by the defendants evoked laughter from the gallery.[92] In response to questions put to them by the presiding Judge, one of the defendants replied, 'Yes, I participated in the murder of three Chosenese. I know I did something very wrong. The next time, I am going to run away . . . ,'[93] while a second replied that he had merely tapped the head of a Korean with a club, and defended his action by stating that he had been intoxicated at the time.[94] In reporting the trial, the *Sanyō Shimpō* noted that most of the defendants had received only three to four years' education and that 'consequently their reasons for committing these crimes were also simplistic. All had believed the rumours concerning a Korean uprising, and some admitted that at the time they "felt it was rather an honour to kill wicked people". When asked by the Judge, "What do you think of your actions now?" they all replied abjectly "I think I did bad things".'[95] In Saitama Prefecture, a total of fifteen persons were found guilty and sentenced to terms of imprisonment ranging from 4 years (1) to six months (4), though most of them were also pardoned early in the following year.[96]

In order to prevent Korean refugees from returning to Korea and spreading rumours there about the situation in Tokyo and Yokohama, the Japanese authorities in both Japan and Korea took steps to prevent the flow of information between the two countries. On the morning of September 3, the Government-General received a telegram via the naval transmitter at Funabashi informing it of the seditious actions taken by Koreans in the Tokyo area, and announcing that partial Martial Law had already been imposed. It added: 'your co-operation is requested in strengthening controls over Koreans in Korea, and in preventing any Koreans attempting to cross over to Japan.'[97] The Government-General responded by immediately reimposing the travel certificate regulations which had been rescinded in December 1922. These regulations were not removed until May of the following year.[98] Among the other measures adopted by the authorities in Korea were: (a) the prohibition of newspaper articles concerning the alleged massacre of Koreans in Tokyo; (b) the confiscation of all newspapers imported from Japan; and (c) an agreement between the Government-General, the Osaka Prefectural Police Department and the Communications Ministry, under which all telegrams relating to the Korean issue were confiscated.[99] Although the *Keijō Nippō* reported on September 6 that 'good Koreans' would not be prevented from crossing to Japan, the same paper two days later reported that, in compliance with decisions reached by the Japanese Cabinet and Police Affairs Bureau, all travel to Japan had been prohibited in order to prevent discord between Japanese and Koreans.[100] Thereafter, until the end of September, the only people allowed to cross to Japan were students enrolled in schools in the Kansai region and officials on state business.[101]

On September 8, the Tokyo M.P.D. issued a bulletin to all police chiefs under its jurisdiction advising them that under the present circumstances the return of Koreans to Korea was unadvisable, adding that since there had been a relaxation of tension between Japanese and Koreans, there was no longer any obstacle to their continued residence in Tokyo. Therefore, any Korean wishing to return to Korea should be 'gently but firmly' dissuaded from doing so.[102] In a second, more strongly worded bulletin issued on the following day the M.P.D. advised that since unfavourable reports had already received limited circulation in Korea, Koreans were to be 'restrained' from returning to Korea.[103] Despite these precautions, between September 1 and the end of October, an estimated 28,443 Koreans returned to Korea, approximately 6,500 of whom were thought to have fled from the earthquake area.[104] Consequently, internment centres similar to those in Japan[105] were quickly set up in the Pusan area.[106] While medical treatment and other services, such as free transport to their places of origin, were provided for these refugees, surveillance of the activities of returnees was increased and 'loose tongues were punished'.[107] On September 10, the Imperial Ordinance for the Preservation of Public Order, which had been issued in Japan three days earlier, went into effect in Korea, and thereafter public meetings concerning the earthquake were strictly forbidden and surveillance of suspected troublemakers was increased.[108]

All the official sources cited in this chapter maintained that attempts had been made by an unidentified group of Korean and Japanese extremists to foment civil disorder amidst the confusion following the earthquake, although none of the allegations were ever substantiated.[109] Moreover, two disturbing questions were left unanswered by all these reports. What were the sources from which the rumours of a Korean uprising emanated, and who or what was responsible for their immediate and widespread circulation? In both cases, the evidence strongly suggests that the responsibility lay with the actions taken by the civilian and military leadership during the first critical hours following the earthquake. This, coupled with the subsequent attempt by the Government to publicize rumour as fact while minimizing its own role in the persecution of Koreans, has led later commentators to suggest that the 'Korean scare' was actually manufactured both as a pretext for the imposition of Martial Law and as a means of preventing a repetition of the civil disorder at the time of the 1918 Rice Riots.[110] However, given the immediacy of the crisis which confronted men like Home Minister Mizuno and the disruption of nearly all means of communication, this conspiracy theory must be regarded as merely speculative. Not only is it likely that Martial Law would have been imposed even in the absence of anti-Korean rumours, but, given the overall situation, the Government can hardly be criticized for expecting the presence of the army to have a calming effect. As was pointed out in the previous chapter, a more likely explanation for the initial response of the authorities to the rumoured uprising was the unease which characterized official and unofficial attitudes toward the 'Korean Problem'. Not only were Koreans regarded as being by nature prone to violence, but due to the involvement of Korean students in extremist societies, Koreans had gradually come to be associated with 'bolshevism' and 'revolution'. The way in which these attitudes determined the measures implemented by senior officials in both the Home Ministry and M.P.D. can best be illustrated by briefly summarizing the respective careers of Mizuno Rentarō and Akaike Atsushi, the two officials most directly responsible for matters of internal security during the period immediately after the earthquake.

Five years earlier, Mizuno, as Home Minister, had been instrumental in the formulation of measures adopted by the Government to suppress the Rice Riots. Mizuno was also a strong supporter of the *Hōmen-iin* (District Committeeman) system, which was used by the Government after the Rice Riots to contain social tension in urban areas. Perhaps because of these experiences, Mizuno came to be regarded as a specialist in dealing with civil disturbances, and when the Korean Independence Movement of 1919 threatened to erupt into civil war, he was appointed Civil Governor of Korea under Governor-General Saitō. Among the senior officials attached to the Home Ministry whom Mizuno persuaded to accompany him to Korea were the Inspector-General of the Tokyo M.P.D., the Governor of Saitama and Shizuoka Prefectures, the Chief of the Internal Affairs Bureau of the Osaka Prefectural Government and the Chief of the Urban Areas and Prefectures Section of the Home Ministry. Akaike Atsushi, who at that time was a member of the House of Peers, was appointed by Mizuno as the Director of the powerful Police Affairs Bureau in Korea.[111] Mizuno remained in Korea from September 1919 until June 1921, and as the highest-ranking civilian appointee in the colonial administration was the official with direct responsibility for the day-to-day functioning of the Government. It was therefore under Mizuno and Akaike that the Korean independence movement was ruthlessly suppressed.[112] It is also clear that, given their experience in Korea, both Mizuno and Akaike were likely to regard Koreans, be they in Korea or Japan, as entirely capable of organizing an armed insurrection – particularly at a time when the Government and all other social services were in confusion.[113] In view of this, their response to rumours about Koreans at the time of the earthquake becomes much more comprehensible.

While it is impossible to provide a precise measurement of public opinion, it is clear from the actions taken by the *Jikeidan* and the subsequent statements made by *Jikeidan* members at their trials that official attitudes toward the 'Korean Problem' had percolated throughout large parts of Japanese society. One explanation for this apparently easy transmission and acceptance of such attitudes probably lies in the fact that the *Jikeidan* were largely made up of members of the *Teikoku Zaigō Gunjinkai* (Imperial Army Reservist Association – I.A.R.A.) and the *Seinendan* (National Youth Association), both of which were officially sponsored organizations.[114]

Although established as a private organization, the I.A.R.A. had, from its inception, been under the control of the Army Minister. Responsibility for co-ordinating the activities of local reservist units was usually assigned to Regional Army Headquarters, and the organizational chain of command led directly to I.A.R.A. Headquarters in Tokyo. This headquarters was staffed almost exclusively by retired or active army officers of field rank or above.[115] It is also likely that many of these officers had either seen action in Korea or had served in the army of occupation and probably held views consistent with those expressed earlier by General Izome Rokurō. In the view of General Tanaka Giichi,[116] the founder of the I.A.R.A., it was the army (and by extension the army-dominated I.A.R.A.) which should serve as the principal means of frustrating those forces which he regarded as threatening the well-being of the state. In 1925 Tanaka observed that the victory of fascism over socialism in Italy had brought renewed faith and prosperity to that country and added that:

> We too must pay attention to this point . . . The main force in saving the Japanese people from this kind of national crisis is the army and reservist association.[117]

Members of the I.A.R.A. not only received rigorous physical training, but were also subjected to various forms of ideological indoctrination, all of which were designed to inculcate the values of *Nihonshugi* (Japanism) and militarism. Senior officials of the Army, Home and Education

Ministries were frequent contributors to the I.A.R.A. Journal, *Senyū* (Comrades in Arms).

The National Youth Association was also formed in 1915 under Government (Home and Education Ministry) auspices; its members were subjected to the same type of ideological education and paramilitary training as those of the I.A.R.A.[118] It is hardly surprising, therefore, that in the chaos and confusion which followed the earthquake they were able to mobilize quickly and to implement zealously the orders transmitted to them by the Home Ministry and Martial Law Command. Moreover, the subsequent actions taken by these groups and the later statements made by *Jikeidan* members provide the firmest evidence that officially-sanctioned attitudes toward Koreans and socialists had gained widespread acceptance throughout Japan.

Press and Public Reaction to the Treatment of Koreans

Between early September and October 20, the Martial Law Command exercised complete control over the publication of newspapers and magazine articles dealing with the Korean issue, and during that period even the liberal press could do no more than parrot official pronouncements. While there was condemnation of the Government's handling of the 'affair' after censorship had been lifted, coverage of incidents involving the persecution of Koreans was overshadowed by the attention given to the murder of Ōsugi Sakae. Moreover, even when criticism of the Government did appear, it was often accompanied by exaggerated accounts of crimes committed by recalcitrant Koreans or by the *Jikeidan*. The *Tōkyō Nichi Nichi Shimbun*, for example, devoted nearly a full page of its October 21 edition to a description of incidents involving *Jikeidan* and Koreans in Gumma and Saitama Prefectures.[119] But the same edition lent credence to the official interpretation of events by suggesting that Yamaguchi Seiken had been responsible for starting the rumours of a Korean uprising in Yokohama. Another article published on the same day described in detail a week-long battle between Japanese villagers and Korean labourers which was alleged to have taken place in Nagano Prefecture, and an article entitled '*Shinsai no Konran ni Jōji Senjin no Akunaki Bōkō*' ('Insatiable Acts of Violence Committed by Koreans Who Took Advantage of the Confusion During the Earthquake') reproduced the previously-mentioned allegations made by the police. Consequently, the spectre of Koreans 'poisoning wells', 'raping and murdering Japanese women' and committing acts of vandalism was once again raised.[120]

The effectiveness of official propaganda was also evident in an editorial entitled 'An Appeal to My Korean Friends' written by the editor of *The Japan Times and Mail*. Writing as one who had always 'mixed' with Koreans as a 'friend and equal', the author assured his readers that 'No feeling of antipathy has ever existed among the Japanese people against Koreans except in cases of those malcontents . . . who have continuously agitated the otherwise peaceful people of Korea . . .'. While conceding that frightful crimes had been committed against Koreans by 'frenzied mobs', he went on to say that the rumours which had caused this violence had been intended to 'add to the general confusion in order to permit anarchistic activities'. Since, in his view, these rumours were partially substantiated when 'some Koreans started to pilfer stores, rob people and assault women', it was to protect themselves and their families that members of the public had killed suspected malcontents.[121]

When the matter involved violence committed by the *Jikeidan* against Koreans, however, the Government was strongly criticized for even bringing the cases before the courts. The *Osaka Mainichi Shimbun*, for example, printed a resolution presented to the Home and Justice Ministers demanding a fuller explanation of the involvement of the authorities in the mobilization of the *Jikeidan*, and questioning the wisdom of prosecuting 'the members of vigilance committees only, while the numerous crimes committed by the police are left unnoticed'.[122] The same newspaper also printed the views of a 'well-known jurist', who argued that it would be wrong to regard the misconduct of the *Jikeidan* as ordinary crimes since their actions were not those of 'sane persons'. It would be best, he suggested, to treat those individuals as having suffered from 'temporary insanity'.[123]

The uneasiness over the 'Korean problem' which characterized official attitudes after the earthquake was also evident in the attitudes of the 'liberal left'. At a meeting of the editorial staff of the magazine *Kaizō* (Reconstruction) held on September 3, for example, many of those present are reported to have believed the rumours of a Korean uprising. One of the participants at this meeting later wrote:

> In the course of the meeting the rumour concerning the approach of a band of some 200 Koreans from the Kanagawa area was brought up, and the meeting broke up on that note. When at last we . . . made our way along the tracks as far as Shinjuku, we were told that there was fighting in the streets of Meguro, which we had just left, and that violence had also erupted in Ikebukuro! Of the people present at the meeting Yohena and myself were the only ones who, from the start, had not believed this foolishness. We had previously become friendly with some Koreans and could not believe them capable of such misdeeds, and, moreover, we were aware that it wasn't that easy to get hold of weapons.[124]

Even among labour activists who might otherwise have been expected to be at the vanguard of a protest movement, reasons were found to justify rather than to deny the rumoured uprising. Nakabashi Kisaburō, a member of the executive of the Osaka branch of *Sōdōmei* later wrote:

> At the time we only received inaccurate reports which said that Koreans were rioting in Tokyo under cover of the confusion following the earthquake. Because we were well aware of the harsh treatment usually meted out to Koreans we thought it possible that they could rise up.[125]

There were, of course, exceptions, and the *Tōkyō Asahi Shimbun* strongly criticized the Government's handling of the affair, arguing:

> We most certainly cannot believe as has been propagandized by the authorities hitherto that the responsibility for the rumours lies only with disaffected elements and the credulity of the general public . . . We have no evidence that the army and police immediately and rationally cut off the spread of these rumours and suppressed them. On the contrary, it was from these very sources that the rumours were transmitted, and we can also find numerous incidents where they took actions which gave even greater authority to the rumours.[126]

In a similar editorial published by the *Yorozu Chōhō* on the same day the writer questioned whether it was 'not the case that against the Koreans there were frightful crimes committed which have not yet been announced'.[127] Two days later, however, the same newspaper published an editorial suggesting that the Koreans had only reaped what they had sown, since the 'Koreanophobia' which now afflicted the Japanese people and had given rise to the riots of the previous month was in large measure due to the anti-Japanese activities of Korean extremists in recent years.[128]

In a special issue of the socialist magazine *Tanemaku Hito* (The Sower), the writer, in an article entitled '*Chōsenjin Gyakusatsu*' ('The Massacre of Koreans'), advised his readers to re-examine the distorted version of events publicized by the authorities. He asked:

> Is it really the case that the threat to the lives of those Koreans was produced by nothing more than rumours and idle gossip? Who were the authors of the rumours and gossip? . . . The major newspapers of the centre have referred only to the fine actions of the National Youth Association. Why is there no criticism of the excesses committed by them, and why do the major newspapers now attempt to maintain silence? . . . We . . . along with the great mass of people must penetrate to the real target of protest.[129]

With few exceptions, however, the most consistent criticism of the Government came from Japanese liberals. The leadership of the J.C.P. had been decimated by the wholesale arrests of the previous June, and after the earthquake was in no position to invite further repression by challenging the Government over the Korean affair. Moreover, as Matsuo Takayoshi has argued, neither the socialists nor the leaders of the labour movement appear to have recognized that the fate of their own movements was directly linked to the 'Korean Problem'.[130] Consequently, protests from the radical left were notable by their absence.

By contrast, there were several attempts by 'liberals' to discover what had precipitated the massacres and to expose the Government's responsibility for provoking the *Jikeidan* to harass Koreans.[131] In late September, Fuse Tatsuji, Katayama Sen, Yamazaki Kesaya and Tasaka Sadao, all of whom were associated with the *Jiyū Hōsōdan* (Civil Liberties Legal Association), announced that they would be conducting an investigation into the circumstances surrounding the murder of Koreans after the earthquake.[132] Their findings were published one year later in a brief report entitled *Senjin Sawagi no Chōsa* (An Investigation of the Korean Disturbance), which was written by Fuse Tatsuji. In the opening paragraph of this report, however, Fuse conceded that although it had been the association's intention to investigate the murder of Koreans and to discover who or what was responsible for these incidents, this had been made virtually impossible by the authorities who had not only failed to render any assistance but had actively obstructed their efforts.[133] Despite these serious limitations, Fuse, in a carefully constructed argument, criticized the Government's reports as being both incomplete and inaccurate. With regard to the number of Koreans killed, Fuse argued that the official estimate of approximately 300 was far too low, and concluded that the whereabouts of between 6 and 7,000 Koreans remained unaccounted for.[134] He also challenged the official view that some Koreans *had* been involved in seditious activities but that there were also, unfortunately, occasions when otherwise good Koreans had been mistakenly persecuted by members of the public. This Fuse regarded as 'no more than a fiction', and he argued that the Government had not only failed to fully investigate the source of the rumours which had led to the murders, but by referring to the crimes as being committed by 'Koreans' at the time of the earthquake, had indirectly encouraged the harassment of Koreans in general.[135] He also regarded the Government's argument that acts of violence against Koreans had been committed solely by members of the *Jikeidan* as completely unacceptable. According to Fuse, the official account was contradicted by the fact that the *Jikeidan* members presently on trial claimed that they had not simply taken it upon themselves to murder Koreans but had been instigated to do so, or even led, by members of the police.[136] In conclusion, he noted that the association's investigation would continue and expressed the hope that in the future the Government would be more co-operative.

In the November issue of *Chūō Kōron* Yoshino Sakuzō also criticized the Government's handling of the Korean affair, and called for the adoption of measures which would express the remorse felt by the Japanese people for the murder of innocent Koreans. This, he argued, should not be done in order to advance the 'conciliation' of Japan and Korea in a political sense, but because it was the 'proper moral obligation of the Japanese people as citizens of a great nation to do so'.[137] Yoshino also argued that the reason that the people had so readily accepted the rumours of acts of violence by Koreans was because the failure of Japanese rule in Korea had not only provoked widespread dissatisfaction among the Korean people, but had created latent animosity toward Koreans among the Japanese people.[138] It was Yoshino alone, therefore, who argued that the fundamental causes of the anti-Korean riots could be found in the nature of Japanese colonial rule. But, given the relatively limited audience reached by Yoshino or Fuse, it is quite likely that most Japanese shared the opinion of the *Yorozu Chōhō* article mentioned earlier, which suggested that the Koreans, by failing to acknowledge the beneficial results of colonial rule, were largely responsible for what had befallen them.

Notes:
1. Charles Davison, *The Japanese Earthquake of 1923*, Thomas Murphy and Co., 1931, p. 35.
2. Except where otherwise stated all information concerning physical damage caused by the earthquake has been taken from the official report compiled by the Japanese Home Ministry, Bureau of Social Affairs, entitled *The Great Earthquake of 1923 in Japan*, 1926 (in English). (Cited hereafter as *Home Ministry Report*.)
3. Imai Seiichi, *Nihon no Rekishi (The History of Japan), No. 23, Taishō Demokurashii (Taishō Democracy)*, Chūō Kōronsha, 1978, pp. 377–378.
4. *Home Ministry Report*, p. 129.
5. As cited in ibid., p. 129.
6. Yoshikawa Mitsusada, *Kantō Dai Shinsai no Chian Kaiko (Public Order at the Time of the Great Kantō Earthquake: My Recollections)*, p. 7. (Cited hereafter as Yoshikawa, *Recollections*.) Matsuo Takayoshi, '*Kantō Dai Shinsai Ka no Chōsenjin Gyakusatsu Jiken (Jō)*' ('Massacres of Koreans at the Time of the Great Kantō Earthquake, Part I'), *Shisō*, No. 471, 1963, p. 45. (Cited hereafter as Matsuo, '*Dai Shinsai to Gyakusatsu I*'.)
7. Ibid.
8. Ibid. The *Hogodan* is also reported to have requisitioned supplies from local shopkeepers. Also see *The Ōsaka Mainichi* (English Edition), October 21, 1923. This paper reported that the warnings issued by Yamaguchi had an immediate effect, and that 'even policemen wore red cloth around their arm.'
9. *Kanagawa-Ken Keisatsu-bu* (Kanagawa Prefecture Police Department), '*Taishō Dai Shinkasai-shi*' ('Record of the Great Taisho Earthquake Disaster'), 1926, p. 394. As cited in Matsuo, '*Dai Shinsai to Gyakusatsu, I*', p. 45.
10. Matsuo, '*Dai Shinsai to Gyakusatsu, I*', p. 46.
11. Ibid, p. 47.
12. Unattributed, '*Keimubu no Katsudō*' ('Actions taken by the Police Department'), *Jikei*, No. 51, Nov. 1923, p. 7. Also see Matsuo, '*Dai Shinsai to Gyakusatsu, I*', p. 47.
13. Matsuo, '*Dai Shinsai to Gyakusatsu, I*', p. 47.
14. Ibid.
15. Ibid. Matsuo mentions only Hokkaidō but similar reports were carried in both the national and local press. The *Kahoku Shimpō*, printed in Sendai, for example, reported on Sept. 4 that large groups of Korean malcontents had been causing serious disturbances in Tokyo, poisoning wells and setting fires. By the following day the same newspaper reported that Koreans were massing for an uprising in Tokyo, and that other groups of Korean malcontents were known to be operating in both Gumma and Fukushima Prefectures. Similar reports can also be found in the *Sanyō Shimpō* (published in Okayama) Sept. 4, 5, 6, and the *Fukuoka Nichi Nichi Shimbun* Sept. 4, as well as in the national press.
16. *The Ōsaka Mainichi* (English Edition), October 21, 1923.
17. *Sanyō Shimpō*, September 5, 1923.
18. *Sanyō Shimpō*, September 6, 1923.
19. *The Ōsaka Mainichi* (English Edition), October 21, 1923. Also see Matsuo, '*Dai Shinsai to Gyakusatsu, I*', p. 46.

20. *The Ōsaka Mainichi* (English Edition), September 11, 1923.
21. Imai, op.cit., p. 379.
22. Nakajima Yōichirō, *Kantō Daishinsai (The Great Kantō Earthquake)*, Yūzankaku Shuppan Kabushiki Kaisha, Tokyo, 1973, pp. 41–43. Also see Imai, op.cit., p. 380, and Kang, *Kantō Daishinsai to Chōsenjin*, pp. 69–72.
23. Akaike Atsushi, '*Dai Shinsai Tōji ni okeru Shokan*' ('My Thoughts on the Period of the Great Earthquake'), in *Jikei*, No. 51, Nov. 1923, p. 211.
24. Ibid., p. 210.
25. Matsuo, '*Dai Shinsai to Gyakusatsu, I*', pp. 47–48.
26. Imai, op.cit., p. 381.
27. Akaike Atsushi, op.cit., p. 216.
28. Cited in Iwamura, op.cit., p. 82, and Kang, *Kantō Dai Shinsai to Chōsenjin*, p. 17. Akaike's role in the decision to announce martial law was also reported in the *Ōsaka Asahi Shimbun*, October 9, 1923.
29. *Tōkyō Shisei Chōsakai* (Tokyo Municipal Survey Association), *Teito Fukkō Hiroku (Confidential Report on the Reconstruction of the Capital)*, '*Mizuno Rentarō Danwa*' ('A Conversation with Mizuno Rentarō'), Tokyo, 1930, as cited in Kang, *Kantō Dai Shinsai to Chōsenjin*, p. 11. Also cited in Matsuo, '*Dai Shinsai to Gyakusatsu, I*', p. 48.
30. *Home Ministry Report*, p. 561. Also see Imai, op.cit., p. 386.
31. As cited in Kang, *Kantō Dai Shinsai to Chōsenjin*, p. 18.
32. As cited in ibid.
33. Matsuo, '*Dai Shinsai to Gyakusatsu, I*', p. 48.
34. *Kokumin Shimbun*, October 14, 1923. This is taken from an article entitled '*Keisatsu Kanken no Meitō wo Motomu*' ('Requesting a Definite Response from Police Officials'), which was written by Uesugi Shinkichi, a right-wing ideologue and Professor of Law at Tokyo University. Although the word 'Koreans' has been censored in the original, it is clear that Uesugi was in fact referring to Koreans. Cited in Kang, *Kantō Dai Shinsai to Chōsenjin*, p. 148, and Takahashi Shin'ichi, et.al., *Rekishi no Shinjitsu: Kantō Dai Shinsai to Chōsenjin Gyakusatsu (History and Fact: The Great Kantō Earthquake and the Massacres of Koreans)*, Gendaishi Shuppankai, Tokyo, 1975, pp. 244–245. (Cited hereafter as Takahashi, *Rekishi no Shinjitsu*.) Also see Iwamura, op.cit., pp. 83–84, and Imai, op.cit., pp. 383–384.
35. As cited in Kang, *Kantō Dai Shinsai to Chōsenjin*, p. 100.
36. As cited in Matsuo, '*Dai Shinsai to Gyakusatsu, I*', p. 48.
37. Uchida Ryōhei, '*Shinsai Zengo no Keirin ni tsuite*' ('Concerning the Administration of Earthquake Relief Measures'). Cited in Kang, *Kantō Dai Shinsai to Chōsenjin*, p. 243.
38. This was reported in the October 19, 1923 edition of the *Fukuoka Nichi Nichi Shimbun*, as cited in Kang, *Kantō Dai Shinsai to Chōsenjin*, p. 145. The *Ōsaka Mainichi Shimbun* alleged that on September 4, the police 'realizing that this note was too strongly worded' had issued a second less inflammatory circular on September 4 (but dated it September 2) in order to avoid responsibility for crimes committed against Koreans by vigilance groups in Saitama. See *The Ōsaka Mainichi* (English Edition), October 21, 1923. For a summary of official notifications concerning the activities of Korean malcontents and other extremists issued by the authorities in Saitama Prefecture see *Kantō Dai Shinsai Gojū Shūnen Chōsenjin Giseisha Chōsa Tsuitō Jigyō Jikkō Iinkai* (The Standing Committee for Investigative and Memorial Enterprises, Fifty-year Memorial for Korean

Victims of the Great Kantō Earthquake), *Kakusareteita Rekishi – Kantō Dai Shinsai to Saitama no Chōsenjin Gyakusatsu Jiken (The Hidden History – The Great Kantō Earthquake and the Massacre of Koreans in Saitama*), Nitchō Kyōkai Saitama Rengōkai-nai, Ōmiya, 1974, pp. 242–255. (Cited hereafter as *Kakusareteita Rekishi*.)
39. *Naimushō Keihokyoku* (Home Ministry Police Affairs Bureau), '*Taishō Jūninen Kugatsu Tsuitachi Shinsaigo Keikai Keibi Ippan*' ('An Outline of Vigilance and Policing Following the Earthquake of September, 1923'), undated, pp. 28–29. (Cited hereafter as *Keihokyoku*, 'Policing Following the Earthquake').
40. Mizuno Rentarō, '*Jikeidan to Shimin no Jichi Kunren*' ('Vigilance Associations and Training in Self Government for Citizens'), in *Jikei*, No. 51, Nov. 1923, p. 205.
41. As cited in Iwamura, op.cit., p. 87.
42. Imperial Ordinance No. 401. Cited in Kang, *Kantō Dai Shinsai to Chōsenjin*, p. 100.
43. Cited in ibid., p. 96. Also see *Home Ministry Report*, pp. 13, 561–562.
44. Cited in Kang, *Kantō Dai Shinsai to Chōsenjin*, pp. 99–100. Also see Imai, op.cit., pp. 386–387.
45. Imperial Ordinance No. 402. Cited in Kang, *Kantō Dai Shinsai to Chōsenjin*, p. 105.
46. Imai, op.cit., p. 388.
47. See Kang, *Kantō Dai Shinsai to Chōsenjin*, pp. 19–30, 36–38.
48. As cited in Matsuo, '*Dai Shinsai to Gyakusatsu, I*', p. 50.
49. Iwamura, op.cit., pp. 87–88.
50. As cited in ibid., p. 88.
51. Ibid., p. 92.
52. Imai, op.cit., p. 388. Also see Matsuo, '*Dai Shinsai to Gyakusatsu, I*', p. 53. In Saitama Prefecture, where organized attacks on Koreans were particularly serious, it was estimated that between September 3 and 4 approximately 170 Koreans were murdered by *Jikeidan* members. See the *Tōkyō Nichi Nichi Shimbun*, October 21, 1923.
53. Etchūya Riichi, '*Kantō Dai Shinsai no Omoide*' ('My Recollections of the Great Kantō Earthquake'), *Nihon to Chōsen*, September 1961. As cited in Takahashi, *Rekishi no Shinjitsu*, p. 285. Also cited in Iwamura, op.cit., p. 85.
54. A. Morgan Young, *Japan in Recent Times: 1912–1926*, Greenwood Press, Westpoint, Connecticut, 1973, p. 300.
55. Ibid. Also see Imai, op.cit., p. 389, Takahashi, *Rekishi no Shinjitsu*, pp. 86–87, and *Rōdō Undōshi Kenkyū*, No. 37, July 1963. This is a special edition commemorating the 40th anniversary of the Great Kantō Earthquake and contains several articles concerning the Nankatsu Labour Association. In particular see Fujinuma Eishirō, '*Kameido Jiken no Giseisha*' ('The Victims of the Kameido Incident'), pp. 21–24.
56. Young, op.cit., pp. 299–300. Iwamura, op.cit., pp. 93–94 has noted that radicals and other left-wing sympathizers in the Osaka area were also taken into police custody from about September 3. Also see *Keihokyoku*, 'Policing Following the Earthquake', pp. 45–46. According to this report, *Tokubetsu Yōshisatsunin* (Person's Requiring Special Surveillance), labour activists and others who 'might attempt to take advantage of the chaotic conditions in Tokyo' were either prevented from reaching Tokyo, or, if already in the capital, were either arrested or placed under the most vigorous surveillance.

57. As cited in Arima Tatsuo, *The Failure of Freedom*, Harvard University Press, Cambridge, 1969, pp. 68–69.
58. See Matsuo, '*Dai Shinsai to Gyakusatsu, I* ', p. 52, and Imai, op.cit., pp. 388–389.
59. Matsuo, '*Dai Shinsai to Gyakusatsu, I* ', pp. 51–52.
60. *Shihōshō* (Ministry of Justice) *Shinsaigo ni Okeru Keiji Jihan Oyobi Kore ni Kanren Suru Jikō Chōsasho (Crimes Committed after the Earthquake and Investigations of the Facts concerning these Crimes)*, November 1923. As cited in Kang, *Kantō Dai Shinsai to Chōsenjin*, pp. 445–446. The second incident involving Sergeant Sakamoto is cited on p. 447. Both are also discussed in Matsuo, '*Dai Shinsai to Gyakusatsu, I*', p. 52. It seems quite likely that the Sergeant Sakamoto mentioned in this report was the same soldier identified as having shot and killed a Korean who was attempting to destroy the Edogawa bridge in Chiba. See *The Ōsaka Mainichi* (English Edition), October 21, 1923.
61. Imai, op.cit., pp. 389–390.
62. As cited in Matsuo, '*Dai Shinsai to Gyakusatsu, I*', p. 55.
63. As cited in ibid., p. 56.
64. Cited in ibid.
65. *Keihokyoku*, 'Policing Following the Earthquake', pp. 30–31.
66. See *Kakusareteita Rekishi*, pp. 38–44, 142–144, 146–147, and Imai, op.cit., p. 390. For examples of how these incidents were reported in the press see *The Ōsaka Mainichi* (English Edition), October 21, *Tōkyō Nichi Nichi Shimbun*, October 21, *Ōsaka Mainichi Shimbun*, October 20.
67. See Kang, *Kantō Dai Shinsai to Chōsenjin*, pp. 256, 264–265. The total number of Korean students interned during this period was relatively small. This was because approximately two-thirds of the estimated students in Tokyo had not yet returned from the summer holidays (in Korea) while others are thought to have fled before they could be arrested. The *Sanyō Shimpō* (September 30), for example, reported that 70% of all Korean and Chinese students had returned home.
68. Matsuo Takayoshi, '*Kantō Dai Shinsai ka no Chōsenjin Gyakusatsu Jiken*' *(Ge)* ('Massacres of Koreans at the Time of the Great Kantō Earthquake' Part II), *Shisō*, No. 476, 1964, p. 111. (Cited hereafter as Matsuo, '*Dai Shinsai to Gyakusatsu, II*'.)
69. Central Employment Exchange – 1924, in Pak, Z.K.S.S., Vol. 1, p. 441. If this figure is accurate, then it represents approximately 10% of the total number of Koreans remaining in Tokyo after the earthquake. See *Chōsen Sōtokufu*, '*Zaikyō Chōsenjin Jōkyō*', in Pak, Z.K.S.S., Vol. 1, p. 134.
70. As cited in *Home Ministry Report*, pp. 558–559.
71. Matsuo, '*Dai Shinsai to Gyakusatsu, I*', p. 57.
72. Ibid., pp. 53–54. Also see Imai, op.cit., pp. 390–391.
73. See Takahashi, *Rekishi no Shinjitsu*, pp. 205–213, Nakajima Yoichirō, op.cit., pp. 172–177, and Kang, *Kantō Dai Shinsai to Chōsenjin*, pp. 338–341.
74. *Keihokyoku*, 'Policing Following the Earthquake', pp. 53–55.
75. *Tōkyō Nichi Nichi Shimbun*, October 21, 1923. The following statistics were given by this newspaper, Tokyo (37), Kanagawa (150), Chiba (62), Saitama (166), Gumma (17). Total 432.
76. Matsuo, '*Dai Shinsai to Gyakusatsu, I*', p. 54. Also see *Keihokyoku*, 'Policing Following the Earthquake', pp. 46–47.
77. Imai, op.cit., p. 391. Also see *The Ōsaka Mainichi* (English Edition), October 25, 1923, and Matsuo, '*Dai Shinsai to Gyakusatsu, I*', p. 54.

78. Yoshino Sakuzō, 'Chōsenjin Gyakusatsu Jiken'. Cited in Kang, Kantō Dai Shinsai to Chōsenjin, pp. 357–362.
79. Pak Kyŏng-sik, Undōshi, p. 149.
80. Matsuo, 'Dai Shinsai to Gyakusatsu, I', p. 57.
81. Cited in Kang, Kantō Dai Shinsai to Chōsenjin, pp. 79–80. These decisions were, of course, taken well before official investigations were begun.
82. Matsuo, 'Dai Shinsai to Gyakusatsu,I', p. 58.
83. Kang, Kantō Dai Shinsai to Chōsenjin, pp. 425–426. Of the remaining 5 suspects, 2 were being sought for stealing a total of 4.92 Yen while a third was suspected of stealing about 98 Yen. In only one of the remaining cases was violence alleged to have occurred.
84. Matsuo, 'Dai Shinsai to Gyakusatsu, I', p. 58. Also see the Tōkyō Nichi Nichi Shimbun, October 21, Ōsaka Asahi Shimbun, October 21, and The Ōsaka Mainichi (English Edition), October 21, for examples of how the initial announcements made by the police were presented to the public.
85. Imperial Ordinance No. 403. As cited in Home Ministry Report, p. 562. Also cited in Kang, Kantō Dai Shinsai to Chōsenjin, p. 75.
86. Shimotsuke Shimbun, September 7, 1923. Cited in Kang, Kantō Dai Shinsai to Chōsenjin, p. 357. Also see Imai, op.cit., p. 392, and Matsuo, 'Dai Shinsai to Gyakusatsu, I', p. 59
87. Cited in Matsuo, 'Dai Shinsai to Gyakusatsu, I', pp. 59–60.
88. Ibid., p. 60.
89. Ibid., p. 61. Of the 91 persons receiving suspended sentences, the formal sentences were 2 years imprisonment (10), 1 year and 6 months imprisonment (31), 1 year (32), 6 months (13), 10 months (3), 8 months (2).
90. Ibid. Other sentences included, 3 years imprisonment (5), 2 years imprisonment (13), 1 year and 6 months imprisonment (11), 1 year imprisonment (1).
91. Ibid., p. 60. Also see the Ōsaka Asahi Shimbun, January 27, 1924.
92. The Ōsaka Mainichi (English Edition), October 23, 1923. Also see the Tōkyō Nichi Nichi Shimbun of the same date.
93. As cited in The Ōsaka Mainichi (English Edition), October 23, 1923.
94. Ibid.
95. Sanyō Shimpō, October 26, 1923.
96. Matsuo, 'Dai Shinsai to Gyakusatsu, I', p. 60.
97. As cited in Kang, Kantō Dai Shinsai to Chōsenjin, p. 18.
98. Central Employment Exchange – 1924, in Pak, Z.K.S.S., Vol. 1, p. 430.
99. Matsuo, 'Dai Shinsai to Gyakusatsu, II', pp. 111–112.
100. Keijō Nippō, September 6, 8, 1923. Cited in Matsuo, 'Dai Shinsai to Gyakusatsu, II', p. 110.
101. Keijō Nippō, September 21, 1923. Cited in Matsuo, 'Dai Shinsai to Gyakusatsu, II, p. 110.
102. Senjin Kikokusetsu ni Kansuru Ken (Concerning the Return of Koreans to Korea). As cited in Kang, Kantō Dai Shinsai to Chōsenjin, pp. 45-46.
103. Senjin Hogo ni Kansuru Ken (Concerning the Protection of Koreans). Cited in Kang, Kantō Dai Shinsai to Chōsenjin, p. 46.
104. Naimushō Shakai Kyoku (Home Ministry Social Affairs Bureau), Taishō Shinsai Shi (Record of the Taishō Earthquake), Tokyo, 1962, Vol. 1, p. 573. (Cited hereafter as Naimushō, Shinsai Shi.) A later Naimushō report gives an even higher figure of 40,000 for the number of Koreans who returned to Korea after the earthquake. This, according to the estimates provided by the same ministry, represented approximately one half the number of Koreans thought to have been living in Japan at the time of the earthquake.

See *Keihokyoku, 'Zairyū Chōsenjin – 1925'*, in Pak, Z.K.S.S., Vol. 1, p. 152.
105. The principal internment centres for Tokyo and Chiba Prefectures were established at the Meguro Race Track and the Narashino Parade Ground. Other Prefectures operated their own centres. See Matsuo, *'Dai Shinsai to Gyakusatsu, I'*, p. 50. Moreover, with regard to Koreans interned in Japan it had been decided that *Yōshisatsu Chōsenjin* and other Koreans under surveillance were to be housed separately from other Koreans, and that students were also to be housed separately. See Kang, *Kantō Dai Shinsai to Chōsenjin*, p. 84.
106. *Naimushō, Shinsai Shi*, Vol. 1, pp. 572–573. Also see *Chōsen Sōtokufu, 'Chōsenjin Mondai'*, in Kang, *Kantō Dai Shinsai to Chōsenjin*, pp. 461–462.
107. Maruyama Tsurukichi, *Gojūnen Tokoro Dokoro ([My Reminiscences] Fifty Years Here and There)*, Dai Nihon Yūben Kai Kodansha, Tokyo, 1934, p. 347. As cited in Matsuo, *'Dai Shinsai to Gyakusatsu, II'*, p. 112.
108. Ibid. Examples of newspaper articles published by the *Tonga Ilbo* and subsequently seized by the authorities in Korea, as well as a list of incidents where individuals attempted to spread rumours concerning the earthquake can be found in *Chōsen Sōtokufu* (Government-General of Korea), *Chian Jōkyō* (The Condition of Public Order), 1923. Cited in Kang, *Kantō Dai Shinsai to Chōsenjin*, pp. 499–516, 525.
109. It is worth noting here that Mitchell, op. cit., p. 39, n. 57, suggests that a later report compiled by the Police Affairs Bureau 'clearly stated that the rumours about the Koreans were false,' and 'that the public had learned a lesson from the rash acts against Koreans . . . and were now inclined to treat Koreans better.' (p. 41). This is somewhat misleading since the passage reads '. . . due to the circulation of rumours concerning Koreans at the time of the earthquake, the public mind was enraged and there developed a great sense of animosity toward Koreans causing the outbreak of violence between the two. In 1924 the public mind gradually calmed, and, as the real truth behind the disgraceful incidents involving Koreans at the time of the earthquake became known, sympathy was expressed *toward the average Korean*, and *both sides* felt remorse for their rash behaviour' [my emphasis]. See *Keihokyoku, 'Zairyū Chōsenjin – 1925'*, in Pak, Z.K.S.S., Vol. 1, p. 179.
110. For example, see Iwamura, op.cit., p. 90, and Imai, op.cit., pp. 384–385.
111. Frank Prentiss Baldwin, Jr., op.cit., p. 179.
112. Ibid, pp. 186–213.
113. On Mizuno's first day in Korea he witnessed an attempt to assassinate Governor-General Saitō following the official welcome ceremony in Seoul. See ibid., p. 191.
114. Government Reports compiled after the earthquake, however, tended to minimize the role of officials in the organization and mobilization of the *Jikeidan*. There was also an attempt by the authorities to shift the responsibility for crimes committed by these groups to the exaggerated rumours spread by refugees fleeing the Tokyo-Yokohama area. But, as was illustrated most clearly in Saitama Prefecture, it was the Government which was responsible not only for organizing the *Jikeidan*, but for transforming them into armed para-military groups. See *Keihokyoku*, 'Policing Following the Earthquake', pp. 26–27.
115. Smethurst, op.cit., pp. 16-20. The first president of this organization, which by 1918 claimed a membership of more than 2 million, was Governor-General Terauchi Masatake.

116. Tanaka, a protégé of Yamagata Aritomo, served as Army Minister in the Yamamoto cabinet, and later held the post of Prime Minister.
117. Kawatani Yorio, *Tanaka Giichi Den (The Biography of Tanaka Giichi)*, Tokyo, 1929, pp. 198–199, as cited in Smethurst, op.cit., pp. 22–23.
118. Smethurst, op.cit., pp. 26–27.
119. *Tōkyō Nichi Nichi Shimbun*, October 21, 1923.
120. Ibid.
121. *The Japan Times and Mail*, October 24, 1923.
122. *The Osaka Mainichi* (English Edition), October 25, 1923. The points raised in this resolution were similar to questions submitted by Nagai Ryutarō (*Kenseikai*) and Tabuchi Toyokichi (Independent) during an emergency session of the 47th Diet in December 1923. Although clearly disturbed by these and other questions concerning the 'Kameido Incident' and the murder of Korean and Chinese residents, Prime Minister Yamamoto replied that all incidents were under investigation by the Police and Ministry of Justice, and that he was at present unprepared to provide a more complete answer. There is no record of any of these questions being discussed in the Diet after this time. See Kang, *Kantō Dai Shinsai to Chōsenjin*, pp. 473–488, and Matsuo, '*Dai Shinsai to Gyakusatsu, II*', pp. 114–116.
123. *The Osaka Mainichi* (English Edition), October 25, 1923.
124. Higa Shunchō, *Okinawa no Saigetsu (My Years in Okinawa)*, 1969. As cited in Iwamura, op.cit., p. 86.
125. As cited in Iwamura, op.cit., p. 100.
126. *Tōkyō Asahi Shimbun*, October 22, 1923. As cited in Matsuo, '*Dai Shinsai to Gyakusatsu, II*', p. 116.
127. *Yorozu Chōhō*, October 22, 1923. As cited in Matsuo, '*Dai Shinsai to Gyakusatsu, II* ', p. 117.
128. *Yorozu Chōhō*, October 24, 1923. As cited in ibid.
129. *Tanemaku Hito*, October 1923. As cited in Kang, *Kantō Dai Shinsai to Chōsenjin*, p. 591.
130. Matsuo, '*Dai Shinsai to Gyakusatsu, II*', p. 118.
131. Ibid., p. 116. Also see Iwamura, op.cit., pp. 99–100. On September 23, Yamamoto Sanehiko, the president of the *Kaizōsha*, sponsored a conference at which it was hoped policies for the construction of a 'New Japan' would be investigated. The 23rd Day Association, as it was later known, brought together prominent liberal-left writers, intellectuals and politicians, as well as Yamakawa Hitoshi (of the extreme left) and Ōkawa Shūmei, an important figure in ultra-nationalist circles (see below). At the meeting it was decided that among the issues to be investigated would be the treatment of Koreans and Socialists after the earthquake. But the association never met again and also failed to publish the results of its inquiry. Matsuo notes that the failure of this group to effectively challenge the official interpretation of events may have been due to Government interference. In light of the difficulties later encountered by the *Jiyū Hōsōdan* in conducting its own investigation, it seems likely that this took the form of denying the investigators access to official materials. In 1921 Ōkawa and Kita Ikki had formed the *Yūzonsha* (Society for the Preservation of the National Essence), but in 1924 Ōkawa broke away to form the *Gyōchisha* (Society to Realize the Way of Heaven on Earth). During the early 1930's Ōkawa became an even more influential voice for the radical right and was deeply involved in the assassination of Prime Minister Inukai Tsuyoshi in 1932. He was also a frequent contributor to

Taishō Kōron (Taishō Review), a right-wing journal published by the I.A.R.A. See Smethurst, op.cit., pp. 166, 170. Another prominent right-wing critic of the Government's handling of the 'Korean Problem' was Uesugi Shinkichi, a professor of Law at Tokyo Imperial University who also served as the first president of the ultra-nationalist *Kenkokukai* (Society for National Construction). In an article published in the October 14 edition of the *Kokumin Shimbun*, Uesugi, 'expressing the doubts of millions', argued that (a) the police had broadcast the rumours, (b) the *Jikeidan* had been permitted to carry arms and had been led to believe that the killing of Koreans was also permissible, (c) no attempt had been made to suppress the violence, (d) the police themselves had unlawfully arrested and assaulted many people, and (e) many doubts remained concerning the murder of Ōsugi Sakae. Cited in Kang, *Kantō Dai Shinsai to Chōsenjin*, p. 148.

132. Iwamura, op.cit., p. 100. The *Jiyū Hōsōdan* still provides legal counsel for people involved in radical causes. See Smith, *Japan's First Student Radicals*, p. 243.
133. *Nihon Bengoshi Kyōkai Rokuji* (Record of the Japan Lawyers Association), September 1924. Cited in Kang, *Kantō Dai Shinsai to Chōsenjin*, p. 587.
134. Ibid.
135. Ibid., p. 588.
136. Ibid., pp. 588–589.
137. Yoshino Sakuzō, '*Chōsenjin Gyakusatsu Jiken ni tsuite*' ('The Korean Massacre Incidents'), *Chūō Kōron*, November 1923. Cited in Kang, *Kantō Dai Shinsai to Chōsenjin*, p. 364.
138. Ibid., p. 365.

Conclusion

Despite later attempts by government officials to portray the events of 1923 as no more than an 'unhappy' interlude, which had only temporarily interrupted the process of assimilation,[1] the gulf which separated the rhetoric of *dōka* from the realities of colonial control and exploitation had been tragically revealed. Moreover, while considerable changes in both the size and composition of the Korean community took place between 1923 and 1945, the attitudes and beliefs which had informed both official policy and public opinion in the past were now firmly in place.

Throughout the pre-1945 period the 'Korean Problem', as it was then referred to, was discussed categorically, with little regard for either regional variations or differences within local communities. Even during the 1930s, for example, when Korean communities in Osaka, Kobe and Tokyo were beginning to lose their transient character, social researchers and journalists alike continued to refer to the 'wandering nature and basic idleness' of the immigrant worker. This, it was commonly believed, coupled with an inherent insensitivity to dirt and discomfort, made Koreans immune to the threat of unemployment.[2] The racist ideology of which such beliefs were an integral part also justified the subordination and exploitation of colonial immigrants.

While Koreans were for the most part excluded from the skilled labour market, they were regarded as, *by nature*, ideally suited for dirty, taxing and often dangerous work in industries which were normally avoided by Japanese workers; in areas such as coal mining and construction work there was an almost continuous demand for their labour. On average, Korean workers received wages 50% lower than their Japanese counterparts, and this, as well as their willingness to accept inferior living and working conditions served as their principal attraction to Japanese employers. But, above all, it was their status as colonial workers which determined not only wage levels but also relations between Koreans and the Japanese majority society.

In so far as they complemented the needs of metropolitan Japan, modernization and development were the twin objectives of the Japanese colonial elite in Korea. The strategies employed were modelled upon those which had assisted in the creation of the Meiji state, and by employing the full coercive and extractive powers of the colonial regime Japanese planners were able to bring Korean agriculture into the twentieth century. The victims of this abrupt transformation were the Korean peasants and tenant farmers, whose land holding rights were largely ignored by the colonial administration. The flow of human resources from Korea to Japan which resulted was equally the product of labour market conditions in Japan, where there existed a steady demand for low-paid industrial labour.

Although Koreans initially entered Japan in response to the promises made by labour recruiters, conditions in Korea were such that attempts to restrict or prohibit Korean immigration were likened to 'attempting to stop water from running down hill'.[3] The daily ferry service linking Pusan and Shimonoseki was often crowded to capacity with 'white clad' Korean farmers for whom work in the Japanese coal mines was preferable to starvation in Korea.[4] The fact that the first waves of immigrants regarded themselves as temporary sojourners rather than as permanent residents had at least two important effects. First, both the formation of Korean trade unions and co-operation with Japanese trade unionists were inhibited, since they had no commitment to improving working conditions for future generations. Such disputes as did arise tended to be spontaneous outbursts over such issues as wage reductions, rather than an expression of an ideologically motivated class struggle. Second, the maintenance of ties with the Korean homeland increased the immigrant's attractiveness to Japanese employers, since social costs such as housing and health care could be either minimized or disregarded altogether.

While Korean ghettos did not begin to appear until the late 1920s, housing posed particular problems for Koreans and served as a source of considerable tension between them and the host society. Due to the extremely low wages they received and their virtual exclusion from the normal housing market, Koreans were commonly reduced to living in over-crowded boarding houses or in *Hamba* adjacent to construction sites or mining camps. Living conditions were reputed to be worst in the *barakku* shanty towns, which were a common sight in cities throughout the Kansai and Kantō regions. For the most part these shanty towns, which were described in one survey as providing 'the lowest level of human habitation',[5] were completely cut off from any contact with local Japanese who regarded such areas as a breeding ground for crime, disease and anti-social behaviour. Even when they did manage to find rented accommodation, Koreans were frequently exploited by unscrupulous landlords (both Japanese and Korean), and as the immigrant community grew there was a corresponding increase in the number of housing disputes. This in turn led to further stereotyping of the immigrant as churlish, aggressive and prone to violent behaviour. At the same time, the participation of Korean students and intellectuals in left-wing political movements, whose origins were also foreign, not only reconfirmed the basic alienage of the immigrant, but generated further animosity toward Koreans as political agitators and revolutionaries.

The persecution of Koreans in September 1923 should therefore be seen as a logical outcome of Japanese colonial policies and of the ideology which sanctioned them. Although government spokesmen and other unofficial commentators would continue to refer to the 'onerous task'[6] of bringing the two races together, assimilation became increasingly subordinate to political control, while the beliefs so dramatically exposed in 1923 continued to determine the pattern of immigrant-host relations until at least 1945.

Throughout the period after 1923 the issues raised here have received barely a mention in Japanese school textbooks, while for Korean residents September 1st is still commemorated as a watershed in the history of their community. At no time was this more clearly expressed than in August 1945 when, within days of the Japanese surrender, wall posters bearing the inscription '*Kantō Dai Shinsai wo Wasureruna*' ('Don't forget the Great Kantō Earthquake') appeared throughout the city of Seoul.[7]

Notes:

1. '*Naimushō Shakai Kyoku – 1924*', in Pak, Z.K.S.S., Vol. 1, p. 449. It was also assumed that the Independence Day Memorial Demonstrations would 'disappear entirely within a few years'. See Chōsen Sōtokufu, '*Zaikyō Chōsenjin Jōkyō*, in Pak, Z.K.S.S., Vol. 1, p. 149.
2. Sakai, '*Chōsenjin Rōdōsha no Kinkyō*', pp. 32–33. Even those officials responsible for the promotion of *dōka* commonly referred to the indolence and laziness of the Korean people as the greatest obstacle to assimilation. This was certainly the view expressed by Hiraga Makoto, who served in the dual capacity of Director of the *Naisen Kyōwakai* (Japan-Korea Harmonization Society) and head of the Osaka Prefectural Home Affairs Department. See Hiraga Makoto, '*Osaka ni okeru Senjin Hogo Shisetsu*' ('Protection Facilities for Koreans in Osaka'), *Chōsen*, No. 109, May, 1924, pp. 78–83. And General Affairs Department. '*Hanshin-Keihin*', in Pak, Z.K.S.S., Vol. 1, pp. 424–426.
3. Chōsen Sōtokufu Keimukyoku (Government-General of Korea Police Affairs Bureau), '*Chōsenjin Rōdōsha Naichi Tokō Hogo Torishimari Jōkyō*' ('The Management and Protection of Korean Workers Crossing to Japan'), 1933, in Pak, Z.K.S.S., Vol. 2, p. 895.
4. Zensei Eisuke, '*Chōsenjin no Naichi Tokō*' ('The Crossing of Koreans to Japan'), *Gaikō Jihō*, No. 607, March 1930, p. 175.
5. '*Chōsenjin Jūtaku Mondai – 1930*', in Pak, Z.K.S.S., Vol. 2, p. 1192. Also see Osaka-shi Shakai-bu Chōsa-ka (Osaka City Social Affairs Department Survey Section), '*Barakku Kyojū Chōsenjin no Rōdō to Seikatsu*' ('The Livelihood and Work of Koreans Living in the Barakku'), 1927, pp. 1–23.
6. Minami Jirō (Governor-General of Korea), 'Japanese-Korean 'Fusion' Said Vital to Creation of New Order in E. Asia', *China Weekly Review*, August 19, 1939, p. 378.
7. Hayashi Shigeru, et. al., *Nihon Shūsen-shi (A History of the End of the War in Japan)*, Vol. 2, Yomiuri Shimbun-sha, Tokyo, 1962, pp. 229–230.

Appendices

APPENDIX A1

Sketch Map of Korea

APPENDIX A2

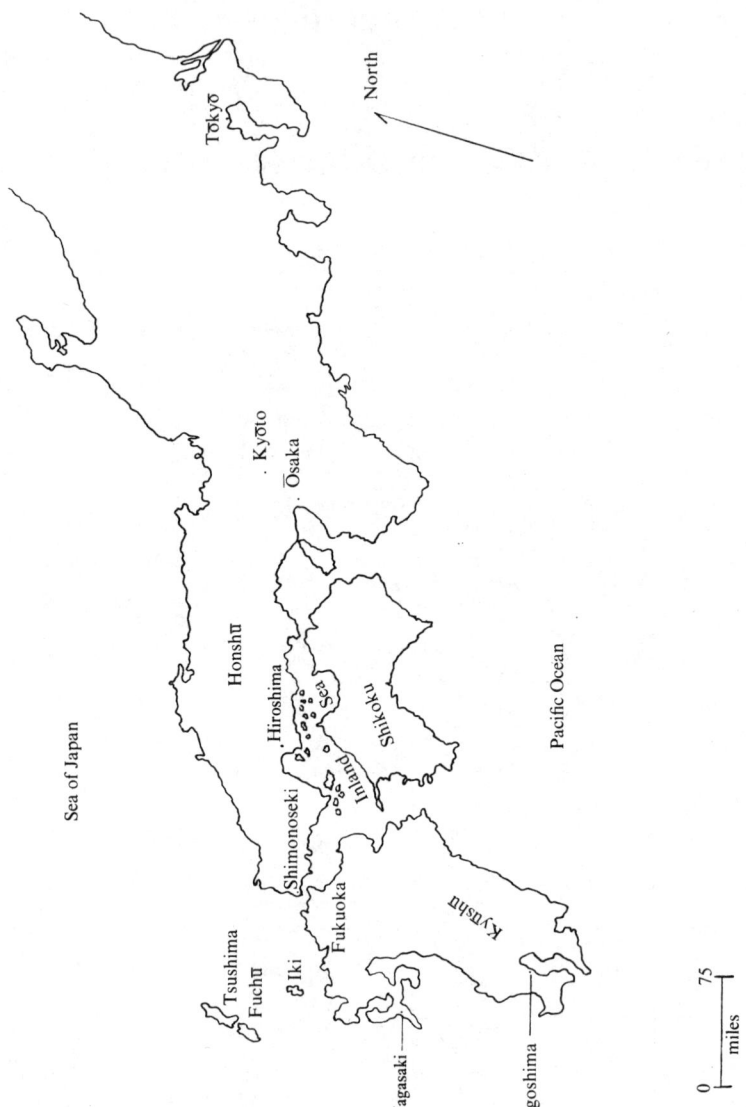

Sketch Map of Western and Central Japan

APPENDIX B1

Chōsenjin Shiki betsu Shiryō ni Kansuru Ken
(Materials for the Identification of Koreans): October 1913

The following are examples taken from a circular sent by the Home Ministry Police Affairs Bureau Chief to all prefectural authorities in Japan.

1. Although there is little difference in height between them and Japanese, Koreans are more erect in stance and there are few of them who are stooped or hunchbacked.
2. They find it difficult to pronounce voiced consonants like ga – gi – gu – ge – go.
3. They find it difficult to sit on their heels Japanese style, so they sit cross-legged.
4. It is their custom not to look directly at women but from the side.
5. When they retire, Koreans do not wear bed clothes.
6. When walking they put their heels down first and put little weight on their toes, therefore walking splay-footed and giving the impression of having a very bold attitude.

Source: Pak, Z.K.S.S., Vol. 1, pp. 27–29.

APPENDIX B2

Educational Background of Koreans in Osaka 1923

Education	Ability in Japanese	Male	Female	Sub Total	Total
Graduate of Technical School or Equivalent	A	6	0	6	6
	B	0	0	0	
	C	0	0	0	
Graduate of Middle School or Equivalent	A	26	1	27	33
	B	5	0	5	
	C	1	0	1	
Those with 2 or 3 years of Middle School or Equivalent	A	64	2	66	107
	B	18	0	18	
	C	23	0	23	
Graduate of Higher Elementary School or Equivalent	A	399	1	400	641
	B	161	2	163	
	C	78	0	78	
Those with an educational level equal to Lower Elementary School	A	779	51	830	2,157
	B	872	48	920	
	C	351	56	407	
Those with an educational level equal to 2–3 years Lower Elementary School	A	898	49	947	5,449
	B	1,977	167	2,144	
	C	2,164	194	2,358	
Illiterate	A	493	57	550	9,798
	B	1,976	296	2,272	
	C	4,931	2,045	6,976	
Total	A	2,665	161	2,826	18,191
	B	5,009	513	5,522	
	C	7,548	2,295	9,843	

Source: *Osaka-shi*, 'Chōsenjin Rōdōsha Mondai', pp. 97–98.
Note: A = Those fluent in Japanese.
     B = Those with a slight understanding of Japanese.
     C = Those completely unable to understand Japanese.

APPENDIX B3

Contemporary Interviews with Korean Labourers

I was born in . . . in South Kyŏngsang province. I have two older brothers and a younger sister . . . I am only a graduate of a normal primary school, but because I enjoy reading I have reached a stage where I have no difficulty with everyday reading and writing . . .

After graduating from school at the age of twelve, I went to Pusan and got a job in a sake shop called Hamamoto. Because they later went bankrupt, I found work in a candy shop called Yamato-ya in Taishō-chō. Both of these were Japanese-owned shops. I then left there and went to work for a Japanese rice merchant, and at the age of seventeen, without anything particular in mind, I left my motherland and came to Japan. Though I can't recall the name, my first job was in a steelworks in Kobe, and in the same year I came to Osaka and worked as a rivetter at the Osaka Forging Works. I remained there for two years and then moved on to the Ihama Steelworks where I did the same job. I then changed to the Azuma Engineering Co. in Nishi Nari County and worked in the engine repair section. In March of this year I quit that job . . . and temporarily went back to Korea. But, I, who had been living just like a Japanese, found my hometown rather dull, and in the middle of April I returned to Japan. Because there were no jobs which suited me, I found a job as a stevedore through the harbour construction employment office.

How do I feel toward the Japanese people? To put it briefly – I hate their guts. The Japanese police and other officials in Korea are very arrogant. Many Koreans hope to become policemen, but, no matter how hard they work, their monthly salaries seem to be 50% less. The gendarmerie also do wicked things, but because there aren't any gendarmes in my area, I can't really say for sure. In order to acquire land, the Japanese in Korea lend small amounts of money with large amounts of land as security, and it is forever happening that without any notice, on some pretext like 'the term has expired', they will grab the land before the situation can be sorted out. Moreover, Japanese regularly beat Koreans, and since being beaten is not pleasant, though in fact this hasn't happened to me, it is truly sad. For this reason, I have often gotten into fights with Japanese, and I have been stabbed on occasion, but though my body may die my spirit will never flag. It may be that the reason I have acquired this dislike of losing is because I was brought up in a Japanese household . . . and was especially fond of reading *Yakuza* stories. My feelings when I came to Japan were the same, and I couldn't help but hate the Japanese. Only the socialists don't make fun of us, and refer to us as Chōsenjin (Koreans). I like them . . .

I loathe the overbearing attitude of the Japanese toward Koreans, but when it comes to independence this is a different matter. The Korean way of doing things is too clumsy to be true. There are many fine people even among those born in Korea, and many people of world class have gone to Europe and America. I admire the courage of Yang Gun-hwan who assassinated Min Wŏn-sik, and I feel that I would like to personally take something to him in prison. I am in support of the labour movement and make no distinction between Japanese and Koreans. I have never been involved in a labour strike. And there is no one whom I particularly admire.

Source: *Osaka-shi Shakai bu Chōsaka* (Osaka City Social Affairs Dept. Survey Section), '*Rōdō Chōsa Hokoku Dai Jūichi*' ('Labour Survey Report No. 11'), 1921. As cited in Iwamura, pp. 66–67.

Note: This interview was conducted in 1921 with a twenty-one year old Korean immigrant worker living in Osaka.

My present monthly income is about 90 Yen. I brought my wife and child over from Korea a few days ago. We also have five of my fellow factory operatives lodging with us, and we talk together about how we must work hard. It was in 1919 that I came to Osaka. By that time a great many of my fellow Koreans were in Osaka. I had been a peasant farmer in Korea. I took a wife when I was twenty-three . . . In the following year I came to Japan along with seven other men from my village. On the way two broke off to become coolie labourers in the mines . . . Because one of our group had a friend in Osaka we went to his house, and since it was a lodging house we too lodged there. Four days later I was taken on at this factory, and my starting wage was 60 sen per day. But because my lodging expenses were 50 sen per day, I had 10 sen left over. Sake? Tobacco? I don't like either . . . I used to smoke tobacco in Korea but I gave it up when I came to Japan. Because I worked the night shift, I saved more than 5 Yen per month. My job was cleaning and carrying glass products. I never felt in any way hard pressed . . . During this period I became assistant to a Japanese factory operative, and gradually I became capable of holding the moulds. I became a finisher and could retouch pieces, cut off and separate them from the blower, and within three years got a fairly basic knowledge and experience of glass production, and manufacturing. That was in March of this year, and the company had just begun laying people off. I begged the boss to use me no matter how low the pay . . . Luckily I got him to keep me on . . . At present I work as a blower. I think that in the future I can make a living by this job. Japanese factory operatives? . . . They've always treated me with sincerity. As far as possible I have worked quietly without making a fuss at whatever job I have been given . . . though it's not as if there haven't been times when I've gotten angry or wanted to cry. Nevertheless, when I see my fellow Koreans complaining about one thing or another, or bragging, I don't like it very much . . . You want to know how much I send to my family each month? At first about 5 or 6 Yen . . . and after about a year I was able to send about 10 Yen . . . My wife, in only four years, has received savings of 270 Yen . . . My child is a girl and I will send her to a Japanese school to get a Japanese education. As yet she doesn't understand Japanese, nor does my wife. I want to quickly get them both to learn Japanese. I like Japan to the extent that I want to die here . . . The five I came with? They are all doing well. One is studying at night school, one became a navvy and is sending money home. All of them are serious, and are working hard at their jobs.

Source: *Osaka-shi, Chōsenjin Rōdōsha Mondai*, pp. 106–107.
Note: The interviewee was a twenty-nine year old factory operative in a glass factory in Osaka. The compilers of this report referred to him as a success story, and observed that his success had been determined both by the fact that he was a diligent worker and that he was used as a supervisor of Korean workers.

APPENDIX B4
A Note on Statistics

Just as industrial statistics in Japan before about 1920 cannot be relied upon for precise measurements of economic activity, early statistics concerning Korean immigrants are useful at best as only a rough approximation of the actual situation. Internal Government reports, usually prepared by the Social Affairs Section of various prefectural and municipal authorities, provide the fullest and most consistent data concerning Koreans, but the compilation of these materials did not begin until the mid-1920s leaving a far from complete picture of the period between 1910 and 1920. Before 1924, with the exception of a single report on the activities of Korean students in Japan produced by the *Chōsen Sōtōkufu Gakumu Kyoku* (Government-General of Korea Educational Affairs Bureau), all materials concerning Koreans were compiled by the *Naimushō Keihokyoku* (Home Ministry Police Affairs Bureau). These reports were prepared with a view to assessing the activities of students and other radicals, and give considerably less attention to the conditions under which immigrant workers lived and worked. Although the *Naimushō* reports provide valuable insights into early official perceptions of the immigrant community they are less reliable than later reports in describing the actual size, location, and employment patterns of the Korean community in Japan. Difficulties first arise when the annual immigration figures supplied by the Home Ministry are compared with those provided by the national census which was conducted at ten years intervals from 1920 on. As is shown below, the Home Ministry estimates produced during the census years vary from those provided by the census itself by as much as 40%.

APPENDIX B4 I
Comparison of Home Ministry and National Census Figures for the Korean Immigrant Population (1920–1940)

Year	National Census (A)	Home Ministry (B)	A–B
1920	40,755	30,175	10,580
1930	419,009	298,091	120,918
1940	1,241,315	1,190,444	50,871

Source: Pak Jae-il, op.cit., p. 20.

Although the police figures cannot be discounted altogether, most commentators agree that the methods used by police officials in conducting surveys of this type were neither as sophisticated nor as reliable as those employed during the compilation of national census statistics. Further doubt is cast upon the reliability of police estimates by the fact that the Government itself regarded these figures as only a very rough approximation.[1] A second set of annual police figures also exists for the period after 1920, which use the estimates provided by the ten year census as the basis for calculating annual rates of increase. But the reliability of these figures too is questionable, since they make no allowance for natural rates of population increase and refer only to those Koreans entering and leaving Japan by way of Shimonoseki, even though alternative routes were commonly used. Pak Jae-il, who has carried out a thorough investigation of this issue, offers a third method for measuring annual population increase among Koreans in Japan. He suggests that by accepting as accurate the national census figures at the beginning of each decade, an estimate of annual rates of increase can be obtained by dividing the discrepancy between the police figures and census figures for that decade by nine and adding the figures thus obtained to the police survey figures for each year in the decade. This method does of course assume that the population increase omitted from the police figures was constant during any particular decade. A comparison of Pak Jae-il's figures and those supplied by the Police Affairs Bureau is shown below.

APPENDIX B4 II

Estimates of Korean Population in Japan (1913–1919)

Year	Police Figures		Pak Jae-il Estimates	
	Annual Estimate	Increase over previous year	Annual Estimate	Increase over previous year
1913	3,635	–	3,952	–
1914	3,542	-93	4,176	224
1915	3,917	375	5,046	870
1916	5,624	1,707	7,225	2,179
1917	14,502	8,878	17,463	10,238
1918	22,411	7,909	27,340	9,877
1919	26,605	4,194	35,995	8,655

Sources: Police figures are taken from *Shihōshō*, 'Chōsenjin to Hanzai', in Pak, Z.K.S.S., Vol. 1, p. 258. Other figures are taken from Pak Jae-il, op.cit., p. 23.

APPENDIX B5

Comparative Daily Wages for Japanese and Korean Workers Selected: Industries (1924)

Occupation	Maximum	Japanese Minimum	Average (A)	Maximum	Korean Minimum	Average (B)	Differential: A–B as proportion of A
Engineering	2.6	1.20	1.66	1.97	1.01	1.26	24%
Day Labourer	2.68	1.5	2.04	2.22	1.14	1.62	20.5%
Construction Worker	3.11	1.77	2.27	2.28	1.51	1.94	14.5%
Cotton Spinning	2.20	0.98	1.47	1.85	0.83	1.33	9.5%
Dye Worker	1.94	1.32	1.50	1.52	0.94	1.13	24.6%
Stevedore	4.85	2.41	3.25	3.16	1.75	2.3	29.2%
Glass Worker	2.24	1.14	1.57	1.59	0.94	1.18	24.8%
Mining and Metallurgy	3.08	1.58	2.08	2.57	1.38	1.8	13.4%
Average	2.83	1.48	1.98	2.14	1.18	1.57	20.06%

Source: *Naimushō Shakai Kyoku*, 'Chōsenjin Rōdōsha ni Kansuru Jōkyō', 1924, in Pak, Z.K.S.S, Vol. 1, pp. 498–530.

Note: See next page.

Although Pak's figures offer a more accurate estimate of population increase, he also fails to consider Koreans entering Japan by routes other than via Pusan and Shimonoseki. Other routes, both legal and illegal, are known to have been used but I have been unable to obtain evidence of records being kept in the case of the former, while in the latter, for obvious reasons, no files were kept at all.

Notes:
(1) All figures in Yen.
(2) Figures for Metal Workers taken from prefectural surveys in Nara, Shimane, Kagawa, Hiroshima, Aichi, Fukuoka, Kumamoto, Hokkaidō.
Figures for Day Labourers taken from prefectural surveys in Osaka, Tokyo, Kanagawa, Hyōgo, Shiga.
Figures for Navvies taken from prefectural surveys in Osaka, Saitama, Yamagata, Kanagawa, Hyōgo, Gumma, Mie, Chiba, Shizuoka, Shiga.
Figures for Cotton Spinning taken from prefectural surveys in Osaka, Hyōgo, Mie, Wakayama, Ōita.
Figures for Dye Workers taken from prefectural surveys in Osaka, Hyōgo, Mie, Wakayama, Gifu.
Figures for Stevedores taken from prefectural surveys in Osaka, Kanagawa, Hyōgo, Mie, Gifu, Tottori.
Figures for Glass Workers taken from prefectural surveys in Osaka, Hyōgo, Kagawa, Nara, Fukuoka, Kumamoto, Saitama, Okayama, Hiroshima, Aichi, Shiga, Saga, Ishikawa.
Figures for Mining taken from prefectural surveys in Hokkaidō, Gifu, Fukuoka, Akita, Tottori, Okayama, Yamaguchi, Nagano, Saga.
(3) As with other reports compiled during this period, the figures presented above should be regarded as only a rough approximation of the wages being paid to Korean and Japanese workers in various industries. An accurate assessment of wage differentials is made all the more difficult by the fact that prefectural surveys tended to classify employment categories differently. In the Table above, therefore, the category construction worker refers to both *Dokō* and *Dogata* – both of which may be translated as 'coolie', 'navvy' or 'construction worker'. With regard to the category mining and metallurgy, those engaged in the excavation of coal as well as those involved in the refining of ore are included, while among dyeworkers, with the exception of Mie prefecture where the wage figures were for apprentices, the exact nature of the work is unclear.

APPENDIX C1
Korean Worker Organizations: 1910–1920

Name		Location	Year Established
Zaihan Chōsenjin Shimbokkai	(Osaka Korean Friendship Society)	Osaka	1914
Chōsenjin Shimbokkai	(Korean Friendship Society)	Wakayama	1916
Ketsumei Kyōdaikai	(Fraternal Pledge Society)	Kagoshima	1916
Dōmei Gōshikai	(Joint Fund Society)	Osaka	1916
Tōkyō Rōdō Dōshikai	(Tokyo Fraternal Society of Labour)	Tokyo	1917
Chōsenjin Chokinkai	(Korean Savings Society)	Osaka	1919
Chōsenjin Hyōgo Konshinkai	(Hyōgo Korean Fellowship Society)	Hyōgo	1919
Chōsenjin Kugakusei Dōyūkai	(Korean Self-Supporting Students Friendship Society)	Tokyo	1920
Senjin Yūwakai	(Korean Harmonious Friends Society)	Kōbe	1920
Kyōtō Chōsenjin Rōdō Kyōsaikai	(Kyoto Mutual Aid Society of Korean Labour)	Kyoto	1920
Chōsenjin Rōdō Saishinkai	(Society for the Relief and Advancement of Korean Workers)	Kobe	1920
Senjin Rōdō Minyūkai	(Korean Labour People's Society)	Nagoya	1920

Sources: 'Chōsenjin Gaikyō [1]', in Pak, Z.K.S.S., Vol. I, p. 49, 'Chōsenjin Gaikyō [3]', in Pak, Z.K.S.S., Vol. I, pp. 92–93, and Pak Kyong-sik, Undōshi, pp. 63, 120.

Note: (1) Although the Chōsenjin Kugakusei Dōyūkai was organized as a student society, the participation of its members in the first Korean trade unions warrants its inclusion in the above list.

(2) The list above contains only the major worker groups organized during this period and should be regarded as a representative sample.

APPENDIX C2

Courses of Study undertaken by Government-Sponsored Students 1910–1919

Course	Number of Students
Politics	6
Commerce	41
Agriculture, Forestry, Irrigation	102
Industry	72
Medicine	88
Education	34
Fine Arts	0
Other	26
Total	369

Source: *Chōsen Sōtokufu Tōkei Nenpō*, 1910–1919. As cited in Abe, 'Korean Students in Japan before 1945', p. 36.

APPENDIX C3

Courses undertaken by Korean Students (at Professional School level or higher) 1920

Course	Number of Students	Percent of Total
Law, Politics, Economics, Sociology	308	68.0
Commerce	31	6.8
Literature and Philosophy	39	8.6
Teacher Training	14	3.2
Fine Arts	6	1.3
Science and Industry	15	3.3
Agriculture and Forestry	7	1.5
Medicine	33	7.3
Total	453	100

Source: '*Zainaichi Chōsen Gakusei Tōkyō*', in Pak, Z.K.S.S., Vol. 1, p. 304.

Note: This survey included students enrolled in Professional Schools (384), University Preparatory programmes (40) and Universities (29). Although not indicated in the above figures 421 of the students were self-financing.

APPENDIX C4

Korean Students Graduating from Japanese Schools and those Failing to Complete Programmes (1912–1919)
(Includes Students Attending Preparatory and Middle Schools)

Year	Number of Students Graduating		Number of Students Failing to Complete Courses	
	Government-Sponsored	Self-Financed	Government-Sponsored	Self-Financed
1912	2	23	–	28
1913	6	30	1	17
1914	4	35	–	29
1915	4	35	–	31
1916	4	33	–	35
1917	10	46	–	35
1918	3	64	–	36
1919	10	50	–	58
Total	43	316	1	269

Source: Abe, 'Korean Students in Japan before 1945', p. 42.

APPENDIX C5
Korean Students in Tokyo by Province of Origin 1920–1923

Province of Origin	1920			1921			1922			1923		
	Male	Female	Total	Male	Female	Total	Male	Female	Total	Male	Female	Total
Kyŏnggi	197	16	213	252	29	281	257	33	290	70	18	88
N. Ch'ungch'ŏng	25	—	25	34	—	34	49	1	50	34	—	34
S. Ch'ungch'ŏng	30	6	36	69	2	71	81	3	84	34	—	34
N. Chŏlla	57	2	59	98	2	100	106	3	109	38	—	38
S. Chŏlla	131	3	134	188	—	188	242	2	244	75	4	79
N. Kyŏngsang	80	4	84	154	11	165	163	12	175	60	—	60
S. Kyŏngsang	215	6	221	259	13	272	242	14	256	84	6	90
Hwanghae	31	—	31	72	1	73	97	3	100	28	2	30
S. P'yŏngan	28	5	33	90	11	101	161	12	173	61	4	65
N. P'yŏngan	41	—	41	16	2	18	116	3	119	38	2	40
Kangwon	13	—	13	24	—	24	42	—	42	15	1	16
S. Hamyŏng	66	—	66	132	1	133	206	2	208	58	4	62
N. Hamyŏng	32	—	32	56	—	56	62	—	62	20	—	20
Total	946	42	988	1,444	72	1,516	1,824	88	1,912	615	41	656

Source: 'Zaikyō Chōsen Ryūgakusei Gaikyō', in Pak, Z.K.S.S., Vol. 1, p. 309.

Note: Although the figures above refer only to students in Tokyo, they can be considered to be representative since the vast majority of the Korean student population was concentrated in Tokyo.

APPENDIX C6

The Declaration of Independence

The *Zen Chōsen Seinen Dokuritsudan* (All Korea Youth Independence Corps), as representatives of the twenty million people of Korea, declare before the whole world our intention to realize the victory of righteousness and freedom, and to attain our independence.

Our people, who possess a history which has endured for four thousand three hundred years, are truly one of the oldest civilized peoples in the world. Although Korea has, since the Period of the Three Kingdoms, frequently served China, this was no more than a diplomatic formality agreed between the rulers of the two countries. Korea was the nation of the Korean people and at no time did she ever relinquish her status as a unified state or fall under the actual domination of a foreign state. Japan, claiming the existence of an interdependent relationship between herself and Korea, took the initiative, as a result of the Sino-Japanese War, and recognized Korea's independence. Not only did the other Great Powers, including England, the United States, France, Germany and Russia, also recognize Korea's independence but also promised to protect this. Korea responded to these gestures by initiating programmes to reform and strengthen the nation. Since Russia, then a rising power in Far Eastern affairs, was seen to be a threat to both peace in the Far East and to Korea's independence, Japan concluded a mutual-defence alliance with Korea and engaged in war with Russia. The objectives of Japan's alliance with Korea were the preservation of peace and the protection of Korea's independence. Korea was unable to provide military assistance but in grateful recognition of Japan's efforts on her behalf, fulfilled her obligations wherever possible, and even to the extent of surrendering certain of her sovereign rights pursued the objectives of maintaining peace and preserving her own independence. At the end of the war a peace conference was held between Japan and Russia through the good offices of President Roosevelt. Not only was Korea not permitted to participate in this peace conference, but Japan and Russia concluded that henceforth Japan would exercise undisputed sovereign rights over Korean affairs. Japan therefore, relying on its military superiority, violated its previous oath 'to preserve the independence of Korea', and deceived and coerced the weak-minded King of Korea and his ministers. Moreover, with the proviso that it would be 'until such time as national strength is achieved and real independence is possible' Japan deprived Korea of her right to conduct foreign relations and transferred this right to itself as the Protector Country. After this time Korea was no longer able to conduct direct negotiations with the Great Powers. Again under the proviso that 'until conditions are appropriate', Japan deprived Korea of all judicial and police powers, and under a third proviso which read 'until a conscription decree can be enforced', proceeded to disband the Korean army. All weapons were seized and Japanese military and gendarmerie forces appeared throughout Korea. Japanese police were even employed to guard the Imperial Palace. After this the unresisting Korean Emperor abdicated and the mentally incompetent Crown Prince, acting as a Japanese pawn, formed a so-called amalgamated cabinet, and behind a wall of secrecy and military might the treaty of annexation was signed. In this way we became the victims of our erstwhile ally who had promised to aid and guide our country which possessed a history of five thousand years. Japan's aggression against Korea was achieved through the use of deception and physical coercion, and we believe that disgraceful actions such as these are deserving of special mention in the history of the world.

When the Treaty of Protection was concluded, not only did the Emperor and a number of his ministers attempt to oppose Japan, but after its announcement the people rose up and resisted with their bare hands. When judicial and police powers were taken away and the army disbanded, the people again resisted. When the annexation was carried out, a resistance movement emerged though the people possessed not even hand-guns. Just how many Koreans have fallen before the superior weaponry of the Japanese is not known, but in the ten year period since the annexation hundreds of thousands have sacrificed themselves for the cause of Korean Independence. Nevertheless, though our hands and feet be bound and our tongues stilled under a cruel military government, the independence movement will never die. Seen in this way it is clear that the annexation of Korea by Japan was certainly not carried out with the consent of the people. The fact that our people have suffered a fate contrary to their wishes, and that this fate is the result of the deceit and coercion of an ambitious Imperial Japan is something which we have the right to demand the world to rectify. Today when the world is being rebuilt on the basis of justice, we believe that the United States and England, as the leaders of world reform, by reason of their having recognized the protectorate and annexation, now have the responsibility for rectifying these past crimes. Furthermore, when we consider the government policies implemented by Japan since the annexation, in contradiction to the declaration made at that time, the happiness and prosperity of our people have been disregarded and the Japanese have enforced the sort of policies a conqueror would inflict upon a subjugated people. Our people are not permitted the right of political participation, the freedom of assembly and association or the freedom of speech and the press. Even our rights of religious beliefs and the right to engage in business suffer numerous restrictions, while in government administration, law, and enforcement of the law, the human rights of the Korean people are violated. Both publicly and privately discrimination between

Koreans and Japanese on the basis of superior and inferior is built up. Since our people receive an education inferior to that offered to Japanese residents, the Korean people will be reduced to remaining the slaves of the Japanese forever. History is revised and our sacred historical and racial myths and prestige are being eradicated. With the exception of a small number of officials, the Japanese monopolize all organs of government, communications and transport, and the military. Consequently, our people are not permitted the opportunity of obtaining the expertise and experience necessary if we are to administer our own country in the future. Under this sort of militaristic, autocratic, unjust and unequal government our people will never be able to enjoy their lives and natural development. Moreover, unrestricted immigration to Korea is encouraged and assisted, and since Korea was already overpopulated, our own people have no alternative but to disperse to foreign parts. Not only state but also private enterprises are monopolized by the Japanese, thus depriving Koreans of occupations and employment, while, on the other hand, the wealth of Korea is being diverted to Japan. In both trade and industry the Japanese are given special incentives while Koreans are given no opportunity of participating in their country's industrial development. From whatever direction one looks the aspirations of the Korean people and the Japanese people are in direct conflict, and whenever there is a conflict it is the Korean people who suffer the disadvantages. In order that we may have the right to exist, we demand our independence. Finally, even when one considers this issue from the viewpoint of maintaining peace in the Far East, Russia, which in the past threatened peace, has now abandoned its imperialist ambitions and is attempting to establish a new nation on the basis of Justice, Freedom and Humanity. Similar changes are being wrought by the people of China. Added to this, when the League of Nations is fully functional, no strong nation will attempt to use force to further its imperialistic ambitions. Therefore, not only will the basic reasons for the annexation be nullified, but because the Korean people will create untold revolutionary upheavals, Korea, which was annexed by Japan, will sadly become the cause of disturbing the peace of Asia. Although we have attempted to achieve the freedom of the Korean people by legal means, if we fail to achieve our objectives we will take whatever action is necessary in order to gain the right to exist. To this end, we, one and all, are prepared to sacrifice our lives. How can this be the basis of peace in Asia? We possess not a single soldier, nor have we the military power to resist Japan, but should Japan fail to respond to our first demands we shall declare an eternal blood-feud against her.

Our people have, since time immemorial, possessed a high level of culture and the experience of five thousand years of national life. Although the misery resulting from the evil effects of many years of despotic rule have brought us to our present plight, if we construct a new state and join the ranks of the advanced nations on the basis of Democracy founded in Justice and Freedom, we, who have loved culture since the founding of our nation will, without fail, be able to contribute to world peace and human civilization.

Therefore, we, the People of Korea, demand that Japan and all the other nations of the world grant us the opportunity of National Self-Determination. If this is not forthcoming, then we declare that we shall take whatever action is necessary to preserve our existence and shall obtain our independence.

Signed by the Representatives of the *Chōsen Seinen Dokuritsu-dan*

Ch'oe P'al-yong
Kim To-yŏn
Yi Kwang-su
Kim Ch'ŏl-su
Paek Kwan-su

Yun Ch'ang-sŏk
Yi Chong-gŭn
Song Kye-baek
Ch'oe Kŭn-u
Kim Sang-dŏk
So Ch'un

The Independence Resolution

1. We, for the reasons that not only was the annexation of Korea not carried out through the free will of the Korean people, but that it threatens the very existence and development of our people, and will be the cause of endangering the peace of Asia, demand our independence.
2. We demand that the Japanese Diet and Government call a Korean National Congress and that its terms of reference include the opportunity for it to decide the fate of the Korean people.
3. We demand that the principle of National Self-Determination declared at the International Peace Conference be applied to the Korean people as well, and in order to achieve this objective, we request that the embassies of all countries represented in Japan transmit our intentions to their respective governments. At the same time, we should be permitted to send two delegates to the Peace Conference where they will act in concert with the Korean delegates already sent there.
4. If the above demands are rejected we shall declare eternal war against Japan and disavow all responsibility for the tragic consequences of such an action.

Petition For the Calling of a National Congress

We, the People of Korea, throughout the four thousand three hundred years since the founding of our nation, have managed our own affairs of state, and are truly one of the oldest civilized peoples in the world.

Although Korea has, since the time of the Three Kingdoms, frequently served China, this was no more than a diplomatic formality agreed between the rulers of the two countries. Since we have never in the past been under the actual rule of another people, we can under no circumstances permit ourselves to be ruled by an alien race at the cost of our long traditions and history and national self respect and dignity. Both the Treaty of Protection and the Treaty of Annexation were carried out entirely under the threat of military force. That these were not carried out in accordance with the wishes of the Korean people is borne out by the unremitting independence movement which has continued ever since. Moreover, it is clear that the Korean Emperor and his government, at the time these treaties were made, took various steps to oppose them, and, although it has been said that the Korean people have submitted willingly to Japanese rule, this is not the case.

Not only have we been denied every means of resistance, but also every opportunity of demonstrating our determination to exist. Nevertheless, even under these conditions, is it not the case that a variety of independence movements have emerged in Korea? However, the movements which have arisen in Korea have had their very existence denied or have been dismissed either as assassination plots or as the activities of criminals. The Korean people, in the decade since the annexation, have come to realize that under Japanese rule their existence and development are threatened. The freedom of association, the right of political participation, the freedom of speech and the press, as well as the freedom to respect the life of a civilized people have all been denied. Although these are rights which all people should hold, in Korea they are violated by the various agencies of the government, judiciary and police. Moreover, all appeals against these violations are suppressed. Furthermore, in Korea, the Japanese monopolize all, or the majority, of the private and official organs and Koreans are denied the opportunity of gaining even the expertise or experience necessary for self-government. Employment opportunities are denied, as is the opportunity to realize social or national ideals. Moreover, in all public and private affairs a wall of discrimination has been built between Japanese and Koreans. Korea is openly referred to as a colony of the Mother Country and the Korean people are treated like the subjugated natives of a colony. In education too, a discriminatory system has been established and Koreans receive an education inferior to that offered to Japanese residents. This is an attempt to reduce the Korean people to a state of perpetual enslavement to the Japanese, and, in the long run, the Korean people will be unable to preserve their natural existence or achieve their development as a people under such a government.

Although Korea is a country that has long suffered from overpopulation, the unrestricted immigration of Japanese into Korea, which is encouraged and subsidized by the government, has brought about a situation where our people become landless and have no choice but to wander to distant lands. All positions of authority are held exclusively by the Japanese, and in industry too the Japanese receive special incentives. In this way, the aspirations of Japan and Korea are in conflict, and, as a result, the wealth of the Korean people diminishes day by day.

Moreover, when considered in terms of peace in the Far East, which was the single most important reason for the annexation, Russia, which at one time threatened the peace, has repudiated imperialism and is engaged in building a new nation. Not only have similar changes occurred in China, but if the League of Nations is successful, no strong country will dare to aggress against a small and weak nation. Therefore, our nation, Korea, can live on under favourable conditions.

Unhappily, due to years of autocratic government and irregular conditions, the situation in Korea has decayed. But, if the Korean people, who have possessed the experience of self-government since time immemorial, build a new nation based on new beliefs, then we believe it will be a nation which will contribute positively to the peace and civilization of both the Far East and the world. If Japan agrees to this and assists us, we will feel no enmity toward her and will never forget our debt of gratitude to her as a leader striving for friendly relations in the truest sense. For the reasons presented above, we petition the Diet of Imperial Japan to call a Korean National Congress and give us the opportunity of National Self-Determination.

Feb. 1919.   *Chōsen Seinen Dokuritsu-dan*
    Ch'oe P'al-yong   Yun Ch'ang-sŏk
    Kim To-yŏn   Yi Chong-gŭn
    Yi Kwang-su   Song Kye-baek
    Kim Ch'ŏl-su   Ch'oe Kŭn-u
    Paek Kwan-su   Kim Sang-dŏk
                             So Ch'un

APPENDIX C7
Positions held by Former Students in the Shanghai Provisional Government (1920)

Name	School in Japan	Position in Provisional Government
Sin Ik-hŭi	Graduate of Waseda University	Vice-Minister of Judicial Affairs
Yun Ch'i-jun	Graduate of Meiji University	Vivce-Minister of Financial Affairs
Yi Ch'un-suk	Graduate of Chuo University	Vice-Minister of Military Affairs
Son Tu-hwan	Studied at Meiji University	Member of Police Committee
Chu Yo-han	Studied at Tokyo First Higher School	Reporter for *Tongnip Shinmun* (Independence News)
An Sŭng-man	Studied at Tokyo Higher Commercial School	Representative for Kyonggi Province
Sin Sok-u	Graduate of Waseda University	President of the *Shimbokkai*
Chang Tŏk-su	Graduate of Waseda University	Member of the New Korea Youth Association
Yu Kyŏng-hwan	Studied at Chūō University	Vice-President of the Youth Association
Hong Chinŭi	Graduated from Meiji University	Representative of Cholla Province
Na Yong-gyun	Graduated at Waseda University	Representative of Cholla Province
Yi Kyu-hong	Graduated at Meiji University	Chief of Publications of the Youth Association
Yun Ch'ang-man	Studied at Waseda University	Member of Youth Association

Source: 'Chōsenjin Gaikyō /3/', in Pak, Z.K.S.S., Vol. 1, p. 110.
Note: This is not a complete list and refers only to the most important nationalist organizations in Shanghai.

Bibliography

A. *Unpublished Documents*

Hokkaidō Tankō Kisen Kabushiki Kaisha (Hokkaidō Steamship and Colliery Company Limited), *Hokkaidō Tankō Kisen Kabushiki Kaisha Gojūnen Shikō (Draft Fifty-Year History of the Hokkaidō Steamship and Colliery Company)*, about 1940.
Kajima-Gumi Rōdō-bu (Kajima Company Labour Section), "*Chōsenjin Rōdōsha no Kanri ni tsuite*' ('The Management of Korean Workers'), Tokyo, 1942.

B. *Contemporary Published Material*

1. *Official Surveys and Other Government Publications (in Japanese)*

Chōsen Sōtokufu (Government-General of Korea), *Chōsen Sōtokufu Tōkei Nenpō (Statistical Almanac of the Government-General of Korea)*, 1909–1919, Keijō, 1920.
——.*Shisei Nijū-Gonenshi (Twenty-five Year History of the Government-General)*, Keijō, 1935.
Chōsen Sōtokufu Gakumu Kyoku (Educational Affairs Bureau), '*Chōsen Kyōiku Yōran*' ('A General View of Education in Korea'), Keijō, 1919.
——.'*Zainaichi Chōsen Gakusei Jōkyō*' ('The Condition of Korean Students in Japan'), Keijō, 1920. (Pak, Vol 1)
——.'*Chōsen Kyōiku Yōran*' ('A General View of Education in Korea'), Keijō, 1926.
Chōsen Sōtokufu Keimukyoku (Police Affairs Bureau), '*Chōsenjin Rōdōsha Naichi Tokō Hogo Torishimari Jōkyō*' ('Control and Protection of Korean Workers Crossing to Japan'), Keijō, 1933. (Pak, Vol. 2)
——.'*Chōsenjin Rōdōsha Naichi Tokō Torishimari Jōkyō*', ('The Management of Korean Workers Crossing to Japan'), 1933. (Pak, Vol.2)
Chōsen Sōtokufu Keimukyoku Tōkyō Shutchōin (Police Affairs Bureau Tokyo Office), '*Zaikyō Chōsenjin Jōkyō*' ('The Condition of Koreans Residing in Tokyo'), Tokyo, 1924. (Pak, Vol. 1)
Chōsen Sōtokufu Shomubu Chōsaka (General Affairs Department Survey Section), '*Hanshin Keihin Chihō no Chōsenjin Rōdōsha*' ('Korean Workers in the Osaka-Kobe and Tokyo-Yokohama Regions'), Keijō, 1924. (Pak, Vol.1)
Chūō Shokugyō Shōkai Jimukyoku (Central Employment Exchange Office), '*Tōkyō-fuka Zairyū Chōsenjin Rōdōsha ni Kansuru Chōsa*' ('A Survey Concerning Korean Workers in Tokyo Metropolitan Prefecture'), Tokyo, 1924. (Pak, Vol.1)
Fukuoka Chihō Shokugyō Shōkai Jimukyoku (Fukuoka Regional Employment Exchange Office), '*Chikuhō Tankō Rōdōsha Shusshinchi Chōsa*' ('A Survey of the Birthplace of Mineworkers in the Chikuhō Coalfield'), Fukuoka, 1928.

——.'Nōgyō oyobi Saisekigyō Naisenjin Rōdō Jijō' ('The Working Conditions of Japanese and Koreans in Agriculture and Quarrying'), Fukuoka, 1928.
——.'Kannai Zaijū Chōsenjin Rōdō Jijō ('The Working Conditions of Koreans Living Under the Jurisdiction of This Office'), Fukuoka, 1929. (Pak, Vol. 2)
——.'Shokugyō Shōkai yori Mitaru Tanzan Rōdō Jijō ('The Circumstances of Mining Labour From the View of Employment Exchange Enterprises'), Fukuoka, 1934.
——.'Tankōfu no Shusshinchi Chōsa' ('A Survey of the Birthplace of Coal Miners'), Fukuoka, 1934.
Kōbe-shi Shakaika (Kōbe City Social Affairs Section), 'Kōbe-shi Zaijū Chōsenjin no Genjō' ('The Present Condition of Koreans in Kōbe'), Kōbe, 1930. (Pak, Vol. 2)
——.'Chōsenjin no Seikatsu Jōtai Chōsa' ('A Survey of the Livelihood Conditions of Koreans'), Kōbe, 1936. (Pak, Vol. 3)
Kōbe Shiyakusho Shakaika (Kōbe City Office Social Affairs Section), 'Zaishin Hantō Minzoku no Genjō' ('The Present Condition of People of the Peninsular Race [i.e. Koreans] in Kōbe'), Kōbe, 1927.
Nagoya Chihō Shokugyō Shōkai Jimukyoku (Nagoya Regional Employment Exchange Office), 'Chōsenjin Rōdōsha ni Kansuru Chōsa' ('A Survey Concerning Korean Workers'), Nagoya, 1928.
Naimushō Keihokyoku (Home Ministry Police Affairs Bureau), 'Chōsenjin Gaikyō [Dai ni]' ('A General View of Koreans [No. 2]'), Tokyo, 1918. (Pak, Vol. 1)
——.'Chōsenjin Kinkyō Gaiyō' ('A General View of the Present Condition of Koreans'), Tokyo, 1922. (Pak, Vol. 1.)
——.'Zaikyō Chōsen Ryūgakusei Gaikyō' ('The General Condition of Korean Students in Tokyo'), Tokyo, 1925. (Pak, Vol. 1)
——.'Taishō Jūni-nen Kugatsu Tsuitachi Shinsaigo Keikai Keibi Ippan' ('An Outline of Vigilance and Policing Following the Earthquake of September 1, 1923'), Tokyo, undated.
——.'Shakai Undō no Jōkyō' ('The Present Condition of the Social Movement'), Tokyo, published annually from 1929–1942. (Pak, Vols. 2–5)
Naimushō Keihokyoku Hoanka (Security Section), 'Chōsenjin Gaikyō' ('A General View of Koreans'), Tokyo, 1916. (Pak, Vol. 1)
——.'Chōsenjin Gaikyō [Dai san]' ('A General View of Koreans [No. 3]'), Tokyo, 1920. (Pak, Vol. 1)
——.'Taishō Jūyon-nen chū ni okeru Zairyū Chōsenjin no Jōkyō' ('The Condition of Koreans in Japan During 1925'), Tokyo, 1925. (Pak, Vol. 1)
——.'Taishō Jūgo-nen chū ni okeru Zairyū Chōsenjin no Jōkyō' ('The Condition of Koreans in Japan During 1926'), Tokyo, 1926. (Pak, Vol. 1)
Naimushō Shakai Kyoku (Home Ministry Social Affairs Bureau), 'Taishō Shinsai Shi' ('Record of the Taishō Earthquake'),Tokyo, 1926.
Naimushō Shakai Kyoku Dai-ichi bu (Home Ministry Social Affairs Bureau First Section), 'Chōsenjin Rōdōsha ni Kansuru Jōkyō' ('Conditions Relating to Korean Workers'), Tokyo, 1924. (Pak, Vol. 1)
Osaka Chihō Shokugyō Shōkai Kimukyoku (Osaka Regional Employment Exchange Office), Keizaigakubu Kenkyūshitsu (Department of Economic Studies Research Office), 'Chikuhō Tanzan Rōdō Jijō' ('Working Conditions in the Chikuhō Coal Mines'), Osaka, 1926.
——.'Chōsenjin Rōdōsha Chōsa' ('A Survey of Korean Workers'), Osaka, 1930. (Pak, Vol. 2)

Osaka-fu Gakumubu Shakaika (Osaka Prefectural Educational Affairs Department Social Affairs Section), '*Zaihan Chōsenjin no Seikatsu Jōtai*' ('The Livelihood of Koreans Living in Osaka'), Osaka, 1934

Osaka-fu Shokugyō Hodōkai (Osaka Prefectural Employment Guidance Association), '*Osaka-fu Zaijū Chōsenjin Seikatsu Chōsa*' ('An Investigation into the Livelihood of Koreans Living in Osaka Metropolitan Prefecture'), Osaka, 1924.

Osaka-shi Shakai bu Chōsa Ka (Osaka City Social Affairs Department Survey Section), '*Chōsenjin Rōdōsha Mondai*' ('The Problem of Korean Workers'), Osaka, 1924. (Pak, Vol. 1)

——. '*Barakku Kyojū Chōsenjin no Rōdō to Seikatsu*' ('The Livelihood and Work of Koreans Living in Workers' Hostels'), Osaka, 1927.

——.'*Hon-shi ni okeru Chōsenjin no Seikatsu Gaikyō*' ('A General View of the Livelihood of Koreans in Osaka'), Osaka, 1929. (Pak, Vol. 2)

——.*Shakai-bu Hōkoku Dai 120 gō* (Social Affairs Department Report No. 120), '*Hon-shi ni okeru Chōsenjin Jūtaku Mondai*' ('The Korean Housing Problem in Osaka'), Osaka, 1930. (Pak, Vol. 2)

——.*Shakai-bu Hōkoku Dai 123 gō* (Social Affairs Department Report No. 123), '*Naze Chōsenjin wa Tōrai Suru Ka*' ('Why Do Koreans Cross Over to Japan?'), Osaka, 1930.

——.*Shakai-bu Hōkoku Dai 131 gō* (Social Affairs Department Report No. 131), '*Hon-shi ni okeru Chōsenjin Kōjō Rōdōsha*' ('Korean Factory Workers in Osaka'), Osaka, 1931. (Pak, Vol. 2)

——.*Shakai-bu Hōkoku Dai 143 gō* (Social Affairs Department Report No. 143), '*Hon-shi ni okeru Chōsenjin no Seikei*' ('The Livelihood of Koreans in Osaka'), Osaka, 1931.

Osaka-shi Shakaibu Rōdōka (Osaka City Social Affairs Department Labour Section), *Shakaibu Hōkoku Dai 177 gō* (Social Affairs Department Report No. 177), '*Chōsenjin Rōdōsha no Kinkyō*' ('The Recent Condition of Korean Workers'), Osaka, 1933. (Sakai, Susumu, (comp.)).

Shihōshō (Ministry of Justice), *Shihō Kenkyū* (Judicial Studies), Vol. 5, '*Naichi ni okeru Chōsenjin to Sono Hanzai ni tsuite*' ('Concerning Koreans Residing in Japan and Crimes Committed by Them'), Tokyo, 1927. (Pak, Vol. 1)

Shihōshō Keiji Kyoku (Ministry of Justice Criminal Affairs Bureau), *Nihon Shakai Undō no Jōkyō* (The Present State of the Social Movement in Japan), '*Chōsenjin Mondai*' ('The Korean Problem'), Tokyo, 1928. (Pak, Vol. 1)

——.*Shisō Geppō* (Thought Monthly), No. 40, October, 1937. (Pak, Vol. 3)

——.*Shisō Kenkyū Shiryō* (Thought Study Materials), No. 71, '*Chōsenjin Kyōsanshugi Undō*', ('The Korean Communist Movement'), Tokyo, 1940. (Yoshiura Daizō, (comp.)).

Tōkyō Chihō Shokugyō Shōkai Jimukyoku (Tokyo Regional Employment Exchange Office), '*Shokugyō Shōkaijo to Chōsenjin Rōdōsha*' ('Employment Exchanges and Korean Workers'), Tokyo, 1924. (Pak, Vol. 1)

Tōkyō-fu Shakaika (Tokyo Prefecture Social Affairs Section), '*Zaikyō Chōsenjin Rōdōsha no Genjō*' ('The Present Condition of Korean Workers in Tokyo'), Tokyo, 1929. (Pak, Vol. 2)

——.'*Zaikyō Chōsenjin Rōdōsha no Genjō*' ('The Present Condition of Korean Workers in Tokyo'), 1936. (Pak, Vol. 3)

Tōkyō-fu Shokugyō Shōkaijo (Tokyo Prefectural Employment Exchange),

'*Saikin ni okeru Chōsenjin Kyūshoku Jōkyō*' ('The Recent Condition of Koreans Seeking Employment'), Tokyo, 1928.

Yamaguchi-Ken Keisatsu-bu Tokubetsu Kōtōka (Yamaguchi Prefectural Police Department Special Higher Police Section), '*Raiō Chōsenjin Tokubetsu Chōsa Jōkyō*' ('A Special Survey of the Entry and Departure of Koreans'), 1927. (Pak, Vol. 1)

2. *Official Publications (in English)*

Government-General of Korea, *Annual Report on Reform and Progress in Korea*, Keijō, 1909–1923.

——.*Annual Report on the Administration of Chosen*, 1923–1924, Keijō, 1925.

Japan, Home Ministry Bureau of Social Affairs, *The Great Earthquake of 1923 in Japan*, Tokyo, 1926.

O.S.S./State Department Intelligence and Research Reports, No. 1, *Japan and Its Occupied Territories During World War II*, University Publications of America, Inc., Washington, D.C., 1977:

    Reel 1–4 Strategic Survey of Japan, February 28, 1942

    Reel 1–8 Preliminary Survey of Japanese Social and Psychological Conditions, October 12, 1942

    Reel 2–23 Manpower in Japanese-Occupied Area, Part I: Japan, August 26, 1944

    Reel 4–9 Aliens in Japan

    Reel 5–3 Industrial Distribution of the Population of Japan, April, 1945

    Reel 16–9 Programs of Japan in Korea, February 10, 1945

Residency-General of Korea, *Annual Report on Reform and Progress in Korea*, 1908–1909, Tokyo, 1909.

The United States Strategic Bombing Survey, Manpower, Food and Civilian Supplies Division, *The Japanese Wartime Standard of Living And Utilization of Manpower*, Washington, D.C., 1947.

United States, National Archives and Records Service, General Services Administration, *Records of the Department of State Relating to the Internal Affairs of Korea: 1910–1929*, Washington, D.C., 1962.

3. *Socialist and Trades Union Publications*

Chōsen Jiron (La Revuo Korea – The Korea Review)
Futei Senjin (The Stalwart Korean)
Nihon Rōdō Shimbun (Japan Labour News)
Rōdō Dōmei (Labour Alliance)
Rōdō Shimbun (The Labour News)
Rōdō Undō (Laborista Movado – The Labour Movement)
Rōdōsha (The Worker)
Rōdōsha Shimbun (The Worker's News)
Senki (Battlefront)
Shinkō (New Light)
Shisō Undō (Thought Movement)
Shūkan Heimin Shimbun (Commoner's News-Weekly)
Susume (Advance)
Zen'ei (Vanguard)

4. *Newspapers (in Japanese)*

Fukuoka Nichi Nichi Shimbun
Jiji Shimpō

Kahoku Shimpō
Keijō Nippō
Kokumin Shimbun
Manshū Nichi Nichi Shimbun
Ōsaka Asahi Shimbun
Ōsaka Mainichi Shimbun
Otaru Shimbun
Yorozu Chōhō
Sanyō Shimpō
Shin Harima
Tōkyō Asahi Shimbun
Tōkyō Nichi Nichi Shimbun
Yomiuri Shimbun
Yūbin Hōchi Shimbun

5. *Newspapers (in English)*
Japan Chronicle
Japan Times and Weekly Mail
Seoul Press
Seoul Press, Administrative Reforms In Korea, Articles Reprinted from the Seoul Press, Keijō, 1919
People's Korea

C. Compilations of Contemporary Materials

1. *Newspapers*

Kōbe Daigaku Keizai Keiei Kenkyūjo (Kobe University Economics and Management Research Institute), (ed.), *Shimbun Kiji Shiryō Shūsei (Collection of Materials From Newspaper Articles)*, Tokyo, 1973.

Shimbun Shūsei Meiji Hennen Shi Hensankai (Editorial Committee for the History of Meiji in Collected Newspapers), (ed.), *Shimbun Shūsei Meiji Hennen Shi (The History of Meiji in Collected Newspapers)*, Tokyo, 1936.

2. *Other Materials*

Kim, Chong-myong, (comp.), *Nikkan Gaikō Shiryō Shūsei (Collected Materials on Japanese-Korean Relations)*, Tokyo, 1962–1965.

Pak, Kyŏng-sik, (comp.), *Zainichi Chōsenjin Kankei Shiryō Shūsei (Collected Materials Concerning Koreans in Japan)*, Tokyo, 1975–1976. This collection contains more than 5,000 pages of original materials compiled in Japan and Korea between 1910 and 1945. All reports and surveys, which have been cited and appear in this collection, are listed separately and are followed by (Pak, Vol.).

Rōdō Undō Shiryō Iinkai (Committee for Materials on the Labour Movement), (ed.), *Nihon Rōdō Undō Shiryō (Materials on the Japanese Labour Movement)*, Tokyo, 1959–1968.

Takeda, Yukio, '*Kyōwa Jigyō to wa nan na Mono ka*' ('What is the Harmonization Project?'), Chūō Kyōwakai Publication, Tokyo, 1940.

Unattributed, '*Kanagawa Ken Kyōwakai Yōran*' ('An Outline of the Kanagawa Prefecture Harmonization Society'), Kanagawa Prefecture Kyōwakai Publication, September, 1939.

D. *Secondary Sources*

1. *Books (in Japanese)*

Amagasaki Shiyakusho (Amagasaki City Office, *Amagasaki-shi Shi* (The History of Amagasaki City), Amagasaki, 1970.

Aoyanagi, Tsunatarō (Nammei), *Sōtoku Seiji (The Politics of the Government-General)*, Keijō, 1918.

——.*Chōsen Dokuritsu Sōjō Shiron (An Historical Interpretation of the Korean Independence Disturbances)*, Keijō, 1921.

——.*Chōsen Tōchi Ron (A Study of the Administration of Korea)*. Keijō, 1923.

Buraku Mondai Kenkyūjo (Buraku Problems Research Institute), *Buraku-shi, Shirizu 2 gō* (Buraku History, Series, No. 2), *Zainichi Chōsenjin Rōdōsha to Suihei Undō (Korean Workers in Japan and the Levellers Movement)*, Kyoto, 1974.

Chang, Tu-sik, *Aru Zainichi Chōsenjin no Kiroku (The Record of A Korean in Japan)*, Tokyo, 1966.

Chikuhō Sekitan Kōgyō-shi Nempyō Hensan Iinkai (Editorial Committee for a Chronology of the Coal Mining Industry in the Chikuhō Coalfield), *Chikuhō Sekitan Kōgyō-shi Nenpyō (Chronology of the Coal Mining Industry in the Chikuhō Coalfield)*, Fukuoka, 1973.

Chōsen Dai Gakkō (The Korean University [in Japan]). *Chōsen ni Kansuru Kenkyū Shiryō (Research Materials Concerning Korea)*, Vol. 9, *Kantō Dai Shinsai ni okeru Chōsenjin Gyakusatsu no Shinsō to Jittai (The True Facts Surrounding the Massacre of Koreans at the Time of the Great Kantō Earthquake)*, Tokyo, 1963.

Chōsenjin Kyōsei Renkō Shinsō Chōsadan (Group for the Disclosure of the True Facts Concerning the Forced Migration of Koreans), *Chōsenjin Kyōsei Renkō Kyōsei Rōdō no Kiroku – Hokkaidō – Chishima – Karafuto-Hen (Record of the Forced Migration and Labour of Koreans: Hokkaidō, Kuriles and Sakhalien)*, Tokyo, 1976.

Eguchi, Bokurō, et al, *Nihon Rekishi (The History of Japan)*, Vol. 19, *Gendai* (2) *(Modern)*, Vol. 2, Tokyo, 1963.

Gendai Nihon Chōsen Kankeishi Shiryō (Modern Japan, Historical Materials Relating to Korea), *Dai-sanshū* (Vol.3), *Zainichi Chōsenjin Taigū no Suii to Genjō (Changes in and the Present Treatment of Koreans in Japan)*, Tokyo, 1975. This compilation originally appeared in 1955 under the same title as *Hōmu Kenkyū Hōkokusho* (Judicial Affairs Investigative Report), Vol. 43, No. 3, Norita Yoshio, comp. This work covers the period 1910–1954 and draws upon numerous official reports and surveys compiled in Japan and Korea. Since no report cited in this book is reproduced in its entirety, this work is not listed as a compilation.

——.*Dai-goshū* (Vol. 5), *Chōsen ni okeru Nihonjin no Katsudō ni Kansuru Chōsa (Surveys Concerning the Activities of Japanese in Korea)*, Tokyo, 1977. This work contains extracts from official reports and surveys compiled during the colonial period.

Hatada, Takashi, *Nihonjin no Chōsenkan (The Japanese Image of Korea)*, Tokyo, 1972.

Hayashi, Shigeru, (et al), *Nihon Shūsen-shi (A History of the End of the War in Japan)*, 3 Volumes, Tokyo, 1962.

Imai, Seiichi, *Nihon no Rekishi (The History of Japan)*, No. 23, *Taishō Demokurashii (Taisho Democracy)*, Tokyo, 1978.

Inoue, Kiyoshi, and Watanabe, Tōru, *Kome Sōdō no Kenkyū (A Study of the Rice Riots)*, Tokyo, 1960–1964.

Ishikawa, Kammei, *Fukuzawa Yukichi Den (Biography of Fukuzawa Yukichi)*, Tokyo, 1932.
Iwamura, Toshio, *Zainichi Chōsenjin to Nihon Rōdōsha Kaikyū (Koreans in Japan and the Japanese Working Class)*, Tokyo, 1972.
Kada, Tadaomi, *Shokumin Seisaku (Colonial Policy)*, Tokyo, 1940.
Kang, Jae-on, *Chōsen Kindai-shi Kenkyū (A Study of Modern Korean History)*, Kyoto, 1970.
——.*Zainichi Chōsenjin no Nihon Tokō-shi (The History of the Crossing of Koreans to Japan)*, Takarazuka, 1976.
——.*Chōsen no Jōi to Kaika (Korea's Policy of Exclusionism and the Opening of the Country)*, Tokyo, 1977.
Kang Tŏk-sang, (comp.), *Gendai-shi Shiryō* (6) *(Source Materials on Contemporary History)*, Vol. 6, *Kantō Dai Shinsai to Chōsenjin (The Great Kantō Earthquake and Koreans)*, Tokyo, 1963.
——.*Gendai-Shi Shiryō* (26) *(Source Materials on Contemporary History)*, Vol. 26, *Chōsen* (2) *(Korea)*, No. 2, *San-ichi Undō* (2) *(March The First Movement)*, part 2, Tokyo, 1967.
Kang, Tŏk-sang, *Kantō Dai Shinsai (The Great Kantō Earthquake)*, Tokyo, 1975.
Kantō Dai Shinsai Gojū Shūsen Giseisha Chōsa Tsuitō Jigyō Jikkō Iinkai (The Standing Committee for Investigative and Memorial Enterprises, Fifty-Year Memorial for Victims of the Great Kanto Earthquake), *Kakusareteita Rekishi – Kantō Dai Shinsai to Saitama no Chōsenjin Gyakusatsu Jiken (The Hidden History – The Great Kanto Earthquake and the Massacre of Koreans in Saitama)*, Ōmiya, 1974.
Katō, Yūji, *Nihon Teikokushugi Ka no Rōdō Seisaku (Labour Policies Under Japanese Imperialism)*, Tokyo, 1973.
Keiō Gijuku, (comp.), *Keiō Gijuku Gojūnen-shi (Fifty-Year History of Keiō Gijuku)*, Tokyo, 1907.
Keiō Gijuku, (ed.), *Fukuzawa Yukichi Zenshū (The Complete Works of Fukuzawa Yukichi)*, Tokyo, 1958–1964.
Kim, Ch'an-jong, *Kaze no Dōkoku: Zainichi Chōsenjin Jokō no Seikatsu to Rekishi (The Lamentation of the Wind: The History and Lifestyle of Korean Factory Girls in Japan)*, Tokyo, 1977.
——.*Ame no Dōkoku: Zainichi Chōsenjin Dokō no Seikatsu-shi (The Lamentation of the Rain: The History of the Lifestyle of Korean Construction Workers in Japan)*, Tokyo, 1979.
Kim, Il-son, *Pak Yol*, Tokyo, 1973.
Kim, Tal-su, *Nihon no naka no Chōsen Bunka (Korean Culture in Japan)*, Vol. 1, Tokyo, 1970.
——.*Chōsen – Minzoku Rekishi Bunka (Korea: Its People, History and Culture)*, Tokyo, 1978.
Kim Tal-su, Kang, Jae-on, Yi Chin-hŭi, and Kang, Tŏk-sang, *Kyōkasho ni Kakareta Chōsen (Korea, As it Appears in Textbooks)*, Tokyo, 1979.
Kim, Tu-yong, *Chōsen Kindai Shakai Shiwa (A Historical Study of Modern Korean Society)*, Tokyo, 1947.
Ko, Chun-sŏk, *Minami Chōsen Gakusei Tōsōshi (A History of the Struggles of Students in South Korea)*, Tokyo, 1976.
——.*Ekkyō – Chōsenjin Watakushi no Kiroku (Crossing the Border – The Personal Record of a Korean)*, Tokyo, 1977.
Kondo, Ken'ichi, *Banzai Sōjō Jiken – San-ichi Undō – (The Manse Disturbances: March The First Movement)*, 3 vols., Tokyo, 1964.

Maeda, Hajime, *Tokushu Rōmusha no Rōmu Kanri (The Labour Management of Special Workers)*, Tokyo, 1943.
Matsuo, Hiroshi, *Chian Iji Hō: Dan'atsu to Teikō no Rekishi (The Peace Preservation Law: A History of Oppression and Resistance)*, Tokyo, 1976.
Matsuo, Takayoshi, *Yoshino Sakuzō – Chūgoku – Chōsen Ron (Yoshino Sakuzō: Essays on China and Korea)*, Tokyo, 1970.
——.*Taishō Demokurashii no Kenkyū (Studies on Taisho Democracy)*, Tokyo, 1978.
Miyata, Hiroto, *65 Man-nin – Zainichi Chōsenjin (650,000 People – Koreans in Japan)*, Tokyo, 1979.
Nagai, Michio, Tanaka, Hiroshi, and Hara, Yoshio, *Ajia Ryūgakusei to Nihon (Asian Students in Japan)*, NHK Bukusu, Tokyo, 1973.
Nakajima, Yōichirō, *Kantō Dai Shinsai (The Great Kanto Earthquake)*, Tokyo, 1973.
Nakamura, Hidetaka, *Nissen Kankei-shi no Kenkyū (Studies on the History of Japanese-Korean Relations)*, Tokyo, 1965–1969.
Nakamura, Shintarō, *Nihon to Chōsen no Nisen-nen (Two Thousand Years of Relations Between Japan and Korea)*, Tokyo, 1977.
Nanba, Nariakira, *Chōsen Gakusei no Gyōsho (The Dawn Bell for Korean Students)*, Tokyo, 1923.
Naoki, Kōjirō, et al, *Nihon Rekishi (The History of Japan)*, Vol. 1, *Genshi oyobi Kodai (Origins and Ancient Times)*, Vol. 1, Tokyo, 1975.
Nitchō Kyōkai Saitama Rengōkai (Japan-Korea Association Saitama Federation), *Kantō Dai Shinsai to Saitama ni okeru Chōsenjin Gyakusatsu Jiken (The Great Kanto Earthquake and the Massacre of Koreans in Saitama)*, Ōmiya, 1974.
Nishi, Junzō, Fujishima, Udai, and Suganuma, Masahisa, *Nihon, Uchi e no Sabetsu, Soto e no Shinryaku (Japan, Discrimination Within Aggression Without)*, Tokyo, 1972.
O, Lim-jun, *Zainichi Chōsenjin (Koreans in Japan)*, Tokyo, 1971.
Osaka Prefecture, *Osaka Hyakunen-shi (One Hundred Year History of Osaka)*, Osaka, 1968.
Ozawa, Yūsaku, *Zainichi Chōsenjin Kyōiku Ron* (A Study of Education for Korean Residents in Japan), Tokyo, 1977.
——.(ed.), *Kindai Minshū no Kiroku (Modern Record of the Masses)*, No. 10, *Zainichi Chōsenjin (Koreans in Japan)*, Tokyo, 1978.
Pak, Jae-il, *Zainichi Chōsenjin ni Kansuru Sōgō Chōsa Kenkyū (A Comprehensive Investigation Concerning Korean Residents in Japan)*, Tokyo, 1979.
Pak, Kyŏng-sik, *Chōsenjin Kyōsei Renkō no Kiroku (A Record of the Forced Migration of Koreans)*, Tokyo, 1973.
——.*Chōsen San-ichi Dokuritsu Undō (Korea, The March First Independence Movement)*, Tokyo, 1976.
——.*Tennōsei Kokka to Zainichi Chōsenjin (The Emperor System and Koreans in Japan)*, Tokyo, 1978.
——.*Zainichi Chōsenjin Undōshi: 8.15 Kaihōmae (A History of the Korean People's Movement in Japan: Before the Liberation of August 15, 1945)*, Tokyo, 1979.
Rōdōsha Ruporutaaju Shūdan (Labourers Report Group), *Nihonjin no Mita Zainichi Chōsenjin (Koreans in Japan, As Seen By the Japanese)*, Tokyo, 1959.
Shinozaki, Heiji, *Zainichi Chōsenjin Undō (The Korean People's Movement in Japan)*, Tokyo, 1953.

Takahashi, Kamekichi, *Nihon Sangyō Rōdō Ron (Industrial Labour in Japan)*, Tokyo, 1937.
Takahashi, Shin'ichi, (et al), *Rekishi no Shinjitsu: Kantō Dai Shinsai to Chōsenjin Gyakusatsu (History and Fact: The Great Kantō Earthquake and the Massacre of Koreans)*, Tokyo, 1975.
Tsuboe, Sanji, *Zainichi Chōsenjin Gaikyō (The General Condition of Koreans in Japan)*, Tokyo, 1965.
Watanabe, Manabu, *Chōsen Kindai-shi (The Modern History of Korea)*, Tokyo, 1968.
Watanabe, Sōzō, (comp.), *Hokkaidō Shakai Undōshi (A History of the Social Movement in Hokkaidō)*, Sapporo, 1966.
Yamabe, Kentarō, *Nikkan Heigō Shōshi (A Short History of the Japanese Annexation of Korea)*, Tokyo, 1978.
——.*Nihon Tōchika no Chōsen (Korea Under Japanese Rule)*, Tokyo, 1978.
Yi, Yu-hwan, *Zainichi Kankokujin Gojūnen-shi: Hassei-in ni okeru Rekishiteki Haikei to Kaihōgo no okeru Dōkō (A Fifty-Year History of the Koreans in Japan: Origins, Historical Background and Trends Since Liberation)*, Tokyo, 1960.
Yūbari Shiyakusho, *Yūbari-shi Shi (The History of Yūbari City)*, Yūbari, 1959.
Zainichi Chōsenjin no Jinken wo Mamorukai (Association for Protecting the Civil Rights of Koreans in Japan), *Zainichi Chōsenjin no Hōteki Chii (The Legal Status of Koreans in Japan)*, Tokyo, 1965.

2. *Articles (in Japanese)*

Abe, Hiroshi, '*Kyū Kan Matsu no Nihon Ryūgaku (III) – Shiryōteki Kōsatsu*' ('On the Documents Relating to Korean Students in Japan During the Late Yi Period (III)'), *Kan*, 3, 7, July, 1974.
——.'*Kaihōmae Nihon Ryūgaku no Shiteki Tenkai Katei to no Tokushitsu*' ('A Historical Review of Korean Students in Japan Before 1945: Development and Special Characteristics'), *Kan*, 5, 12, November, 1976.
Akaike, Atsushi, '*Dai Shinsai Tōji ni okeru Shōkan*' ('My Thoughts on the Period of the Great Earthquake'), *Jikei*, 51, November, 1923.
Akiyama, Onosuke, '*Senjin Rōdōsha to Shitsugyō Mondai*' ('Korean Workers and the Unemployment Problem'), *Shakai Seisaku Jihō*, 3, December, 1929.
Chang, Hyŏk-chu, '*Chōsenjin Shūraku o Yuku*' ('A Visit to a Korean Settlement'), *Kaizō*, July, 1937.
Etchuya, Riichi, '*Ichi Heisotsu no Shinsai Shuki*' ('Earthquake Diary of a Private Soldier'), *Kaihō*, August, 1927.
——.'*Kantō Dai Shinsai no Omoide*' ('My Recollections of the Great Kantō Earthquake'), *Nihon to Chōsen*, September, 1961.
Fujinuma, Eishiro, '*Kameido Jiken no Giseisha*', ('The Victims of the Kameido Incident'), *Rōdō Undōshi Kenkyū*, 37, July, 1963.
Fujishiro, Kazumi, '*Zainichi Chōsenjin Kenkyū to Kenkyūsha no Tachiba*' ('Studies of Koreans Residing in Japan and the Standpoint of Researchers'), *Kiyō*, 63, October, 1978.
Fuse, Tatsuji, '*Chōsenjin Sawagi*' ('The Korean Disturbances'), *Nihon Bengoshi Kyōkai Rokuji*, September, 1924.
Gotō, Chōtarō, '*Zainichi Gakusei ni tsuite*' ('Concerning Students in Japan'), *Chōsen Bunka no Kenkyū*, August, 1922.
Harada, Tamaki, '*Kim Ok-kyun no Kaika Sisō*' ('Kim Ok-kyun's Thoughts on Opening the Country'), *Sanzen Ri*, 9, February, 1977.

Hatada, Takashi, 'Nihonjin no Chōsen Kan' ('The Japanese Image of Korea'), *Sekai*, September, 1968.
Higuchi, Yūichi, '*Kyōwakai Zenshi*' ('The Early History of the Kyōwakai'), *Kaikyō*, 2, July, 1975.
——.'*Zainichi Chōsenjin Buraku no Sekkyokuteki Yakuwari ni tsuite*' ('The Positive Role of Korean Ghettos in Japan'), *Zainichi Chōsenjin-shi Kenkyū*, December, 1977.
——.'*Zainichi Chōsenjin ni taisuru Jūtaku Sabetsu*' ('Housing Discrimination Against Koreans Residing in Japan'), *Zainichi Chōsenjin-shi Kenkyū*, 2, June, 1978.
Hiraga, Makoto, '*Senjin Mondai ni tsuite*' ('Concerning the Korean Problem'), *Shakai Jigyō Kenkyū*, 11, 8, part 2, August 25, 1923.
——.'*Osaka ni okeru Senjin Hogo Shisetsu*' ('Protection Facilities for Koreans in Osaka'), *Chōsen*, 109, May, 1924.
Hirano, Takeshi, '*Nihon Tōchi Ka no Chōsen no Hōteki Chii*' ('The Legal Status of Korea Under Japanese Rule'), *Ōsaka Hōgaku*, 83, December, 1972.
Im, Kwang-chŏl, '*Chosen Minzoku Kaihō Undōshi*' ('A History of the Korean People's Movement'), *Rekishi Hyōron*, 28, 29, 1951.
Isomura, Eiichi, '*Roku Dai Toshi ni okeru Shitsugyō Kyūsai Jigyō*' ('Unemployment Relief Enterprises in Six Major Cities'), *Shakai Seisaku Jihō*, 118, July, 1930.
Iwamura, Toshio, '*Sekai Dai Kyōkōki no Zainichi Chōsenjin Rōdōsha no Tatakai*' ('The Struggles of Korean Workers in Japan During the Great Depression'), *Nihonshi Kenkyū*. 66, May, 1963.
Kang, Jae-on, '*Kantō Dai Shinsai to Chōsenjin Hakugai*' ('The Great Kantō Earthquake and the Persecution of Koreans'), *Chōsen Mondai Kenkyū*, 4, 3-4, September, 1960.
——.'*Ni Hachi Sengen to Tōkyō Ryūgakusei*' ('The February 8 Declaration and Korean Students in Tokyo'), *Sanzen Ri*, 17, February, 1979.
Kang, Tŏ-sang, '*Kempei Seijika no Chōsen*' ('Korea Under Military Police Government'), *Rekishigaku Kengyū*, 321, February, 1967.
Kim, Il-son, '*Zainichi Chōsenjin to Jiyū Hōsōdan*' ('Koreans in Japan and the Civil Liberties Legal Association'), 1-2, *Koria Hyōron*, 10, 93 and 11, 94, December, 1968, January, 1969.
Kimura, Eiichi, et al., '*Roku Dai Toshi ni okeru Shitsugyō Kyūsai Jigyō*' ('Unemployment Relief Projects in Six Major Cities'), *Shakai Seisaku Jihō*, 118, July, 1930.
Kushida, Tamizō '*Chōsen Rōdōsha no Inyū*' ('The Importation of Korean Workers'), *Kokka Gakkai Zasshi*, 366, 1917.
Matsumura, Takao, '*Nihon Teikokushugi Ka ni okeru Shokuminchi Rōdōsha*' ('Colonial Workers Under Japanese Imperialism'), *Keizaigaku Nenpō*, 10, 1967.
Matsuo, Takayoshi, '*Kantō Dai Shinsai Ka no Chōsenjin Gyakusatsu Jiken*' ('Massacres of Koreans at the Time of the Great Kantō Earthquake'), 1, 2, *Shisō*, 471 and 476, September, 1963, and February, 1964.
——.'*Yoshino Sakuzō to Yuasa Jirō*', ('Yoshino Sakuzo and Yuasa Jiro'), *Sanzen Ri*, 4, November, 1975.
Miki, Shōichi, '*Zainhan Chōsenjin ni tsuite*' ('Concerning Koreans in Osaka'), *Dai Ōsaka*, April, 1929.
——.'*Zaihan Chōsenjin no Jūtaku Mondai ni tsuite*' ('Concerning the Housing Problem for Koreans in Osaka'), *Dai Ōsaka*, January, 1930.
Mizuno, Rentarō, '*Jikeidan no Shimin no Jichi Kunren*' ('Vigilance Associations

and Training in Self Government for Citizens'), *Jikei*, 51, November, 1923.
Nakatsuka, Akira, '*Chōsen-no Minzoku Undō to Nihon no Chōsen Shihai*' ('The Korean Nationalist Movement and Japanese Rule in Korea'), *Shisō*, 537, March, 1969.
Nakajima, Chieko, '*Nikkan Heigō wo Meguru Sōgō Zasshi no Ronchō*', ('The Tone of Articles Dealing with the Annexation of Korea in General-Interest Magazines in Japan'), *Buraku Kaihō Kenkyū*, 3, September, 1974.
Nimura, Kazuo, '*Zenkoku Kōfu Kumiai no Soshiki to Katsudō*' ('The Establishment and Activities of the National Union of Miners'), 1–3, *Shiryō Shipō*, 159, 168, 185, February, 1970, January, 1971, August, 1972.
Nishida, Minoru, '*Hokkaidō Kōgyō no Shimpō*' ('Progress of the Hokkaidō Mining Industry'), *Shokumin Kōhō*, 97, July, 1917.
Nishikawa, Hiroshi, '*Zainichi Chōsenjin Kyōsantoiin: Dōchōsha no Jittai*' ('A Statistical Analysis of Korean Communists'), *Jimbun Gakuhō*, 50, March, 1981.
Ōtsuki, Bunpei, '*Hokkaidō ni okeru Chōsenjin Rōdōsha Mondai*' ('The Problem of Korean Miners in Hokkaidō'), 1, 2, *Shakai Seisaku Jihō*, 121 and 122, September and November, 1930.
Ozawa, Yūsaku, '*Senzen ni okeru Zainichi Chōsenjin no Seikatsu Jōtai no Ichi Dammen*' ('A Cross Section of the Living Conditions of Koreans in Prewar Japan'), *Kaikyō*, 8, December, 1978.
Pak, Kyŏng-sik, '*Nihon Teikokushugi Ka ni okeru Zainichi Chōsenjin Undō*' ('The Korean People's Movement in Japan Under the Rule of Japanese Imperialism'), 1–3, *Chōsen Geppō*, 2, 4, 6, 8–9, March, May, July, 1957.
——.'*Zainichi Chōsenjin Undōshi – 1920 Nendai no Minzoku Undō*' ('The Korean People's Movement in Japan – The Nationalist Movement During the 1920s'), 2, *Sanzen Ri*, 4, November 1975.
——.'*Chian Iji-Hō ni yoru Chōsenjin Dan'atsu*' ('The Suppression of Koreans Under the Peace Preservation Law'), *Gendai Shi*, 7, June, 1976.
——.'*Zainichi Chōsen Rōsō no Katsudō – Bira, Kikanshi, Taikai Hōkoku nado wo Yonde*' ('The Activities of the Federation of Korean Labour in Japan – Readings from Leaflets, Official Publications, Reports on Mass Meetings, etc.'), *Kaikyō*, 7, March, 1978.
——.'*Shisō Dantai: Hokuseikai, Ichigatsukai ni tsuite*' ('Thought Groups: Concerning the North Star Society and the January Society'), *Kaikyō*, 8, December, 1978.
Pak, Sŏng-t'ae, '*Zainichi Chōsenjin Undō Nenpō*', ('Almanac of the Korean People's Movement in Japan'), 1–3, *Buraku Kaihō Kenkyū*, 4, 6, 7, March, 1975, February and May, 1976.
Pak, Yŏl, '*Ajia Monrō Shugi ni tsuite*' ('Concerning an Asian Monroe Doctrine'), *Futei Senjin*, 2, December, 1922.
Sakai, Toshio, '*Chōsenjin Rōdōsha Osaka Torai no Ichi Gen'in*' ('One Reason Why Korean Workers Cross Over to Osaka'), *Dai Ōsaka*, December, 1929.
——.'*Chōsenjin Rōdōsha Mondai*' ('The Problem of Korean Workers'), 1–3, *Shakai Jigyō Kenkyū*, May, July, September, 1931.
Suzuki, Hideko, '*Zainichi Chōsenjin Undō to Nihonjin*' ('The Korean People's Movement in Japan and the Japanese'), *Chōsen Kenkyū*, 79, November, 1968.
Takatsu, Seidō, '*Chosen Undō Taikan*' ('An Overview of the Korean Movement'), *Kaihō*, July, 1925.

Takeda, Yukio, '*Naichi Zaijū Hantōjin Mondai*' ('The Problem of Peninsulars Living in Japan'), *Shakai Seisaku Jihō*, 213, 1938.
Tamura, Toshiyuki, '*Zainichi Chōsenjin Jinkō no Suikei: 1910–1945*' ('Estimates of the Korean Population in Japan'), *Kokumin Keizai*, 138, November, 1977.
Totsuka, Hideo, '*Nihon ni okeru Gaikokujin Rōdōsha Mondai ni tsuite*' ('The Problem of Foreign Workers in Japan'), *Shakai Kagaku Kenkyū*, 25, 1974.
Yamabe, Kentarō, '*San-ichi Undō ni tsuite*' ('Concerning the March First Movement'), 1–2, *Rekishigaku Kenkyū*, 184, 185, June–July, 1955.
——.'*Chōsen Kaikaku Undō to Kim Ok-Kyun*' ('The Korean Reform Movement and Kim Ok-Kyun'), *Rekishigaku Kenkyū*, 247, 1960.
Yamanaka, Hayato, '*Nikkan Heigō Toki no Shimbun Hōdō to Zainichi Chōsenjin-zō*' ('Newspaper Coverage at the Time of the Japanese Annexation of Korea and the Image of Koreans Residing in Japan'), *Zainichi Chōsenjin-shi Kenkyū*, 4, June, 1979.
Yi, Sun-ae, '*Zainichi Chōsen Josei Undō (1915–1926) – Joshi Ryūgakusei wo Chūshin toshite*' ('The Korean Women's Movement in Japan (1915–1926): Concentrating on Female Students'), *Zainichi Chōsenjin-shi Kenkyū*, 2, June, 1978.
Yoshino, Sakuzō, '*Chōsen Mondai ni Kanshi Tōkyoku ni Nozomu*' ('An Appeal to the Authorities Concerning the Korean Problem'), *Chūō Kōron*, February, 1921.
——.'*Chōsenjin no Shakai Undō ni tsuite*' ('Concerning the Korean Social Movement'), *Chūō Kōron*, 421, May, 1923.
——.'*Chōsenjin Gyakusatsu Jiken ni tsuite*' ('The Korean Massacre Incidents'), *Chūō Kōron*, November, 1923.
Yoshioka, Yoshinori, '*Chōsen Heigō to Nihon no Seiron (Ge)*' ('The Annexation of Korea and Japanese Public Opinion, part 2'), *Chōsen Kenkyū*, 72, April, 1968.
——.'*Shokuminchi Chōsen ni okeru 1918 nen*' ('The Year 1918 in Colonial Korea'), *Rekishi Hyōron*, 216, August, 1968.
Zensei, Eisuke, '*Chōsenjin no Naichi Tokō*' ('The Crossing of Koreans to Japan'), *Gaikō Jihō*, 607, March, 1930.

Unattributed, '*Naichi Chōsenjin Rōdōsha no Gaikyō*' ('A General View of Korean Workers'), *Chōsen Ihō*, 33, October, 1917.
Unattributed, '*Taishō Hachinen Hompō Rōdō Sōgi Ippan Gaikyō*' ('The General Condition of Labour Disputes in Japan in 1919'), *Kōjō Kenkyū*, September, 1920.
Unattributed, '*Hompō Rōdō Sōgi Gaikan Taisen no Zengo Hikaku*' ('A General View of Labour Disputes in Japan, Comparing the Periods Before and After the Great War'), *Kōjō Kenkyū*, June, 1921.
Unattributed, '*Zai Tōkyō Chōsenjin no Gaikyō*' ('A General View of Koreans Residing in Tokyo'), *Chōsen*, 88, July, 1922.
Unattributed, '*Chōsenjin Gyakusatsu*' ('The Massacre of Koreans'), *Tanemaku Hito*, October, 1923.
Unattributed, '*Naisen Kyōwakai Hakkaishiki*' ('Opening Ceremony of the Naisen Kyōwakai'), *Shakai Jigyō Kenkyū*
Unattributed, '*Osaka ni Hassen-nin no Senjin Rōdōsha*' ('Eight Thousand Korean Workers in Osaka'), *Dai Ōsaka*, January, 1931.

3. *Books (in English)*

Allen, G. C., *A Short Economic History of Modern Japan, 1867–1937*, (Revised Edition), London, 1972.
Allport, Gordon W., *The Nature of Prejudice*, New York, 1958.
Arima, Tatsuo, *The Failure of Freedom: A Portrait of Modern Japanese Intellectuals*, Harvard East Asian Series, 39, Cambridge, 1969.
Ashworth, Georgina, (ed.), *World Minorities*, Middlesex, England, 1977–1978.
——.*World Minorities In The Eighties*, Middlesex, England, 1980.
Aston, W. G., (trans.), *Nihongi, Chronicles of Japan from the Earliest Times to A.D.697*, Tokyo, 1972.
Ayusawa, Iwao F., *A History of Labor in Modern Japan*, Honolulu, 1966.
Beasley, W. G., *The Meiji Restoration*, Stanford, 1973.
Beckmann, George, and Okubo, Genji, *The Japanese Communist Party, 1922–1945*, Stanford, 1969.
Bellah, Robert N., *Tokugawa Religion: The Values of Pre-Industrial Japan*, Boston, 1970.
Betts, Raymond F., *Assimilation and Association in French Colonial Theory, 1890–1914*, New York, 1961.
Blacker, Carmen, *The Japanese Enlightenment: A Study Of The Writings Of Fukuzawa Yukichi*, Cambridge, England, 1964.
Bong, Choy-youn, *Korea, A History*, Rutland, Vermont and Tokyo, 1971.
Borton, Hugh, *Japan's Modern Century*, New York, 1957.
Castles, Stephen, and Kosack, Godula, *Immigrant Workers and Class Structure in Western Europe*, London, New York, and Toronto, 1973.
Cheng, Lucie and Bonacich, Edna, (eds.), *Labor Migration Under Capitalism*, Berkeley, Los Angeles and London, 1984.
Chesneaux, Jean, Bastid, Marianne, and Bergere, Marie-Claire, *China From The Opium Wars To The 1911 Revolution*, trans. Anne Destenay, Sussex, England, 1977.
Choe, Ching Young, *The Rule of the Taewon'gun, 1864–1873: Restoration in Yi Korea*, Cambridge, 1972.
Chung, Henry, *The Case Of Korea*, New York and London, 1920.
Cohen, Jerome B., *Japan's Economy in War and Reconstruction*, Minneapolis, 1949.
Cohen, Robin, Gutkind, Peter C. W., and Brazier, Phyllis, (eds.). *Peasants And Proletarians: The Struggles of Third World Workers*, London, 1979.
Conroy, Hilary, *The Japanese Seizure Of Korea: 1868–1910, A Study of Realism and Idealism in International Affairs*, Philadelphia, 1974.
Crowley, James B., (ed.), *Modern East Asia: Essays in Interpretation*, New York, 1970.
Cumings, Bruce, *The Origins Of The Korean War: Liberation and the Emergence of Separate Regimes, 1945–1947*, Princeton, 1981.
Davison, Charles, *The Japanese Earthquake of 1923*, London, 1931.
Deuchler, Martina, *Confucian Gentlemen And Barbarian Envoys: The Opening of Korea, 1875–1885*, Seattle and London, 1977.
DeVos, George A., and Wagatsuma, Hiroshi, *Japan's Invisible Race: Caste in Culture and Personality*, Berkeley, Los Angeles, and London, 1972.
Dore, Ronald P., *Land Reform in Japan*, London, 1959.
——.*Education in Tokugawa Japan*, London, 1965.
——., (ed.), *Aspects of Social Change in Modern Japan*, Princeton, 1973.
Dukes, Paul, *October And The World: Perspectives on the Russian Revolution*, London and Basingstoke, 1979.

Duus, Peter, *Party Rivalry and Political Change in Taisho Japan*, Cambridge, 1968.
Earl, David Magarey, *Emperor and Nation in Japan*, Seattle, 1964.
Fairbank, John K., Reischauer, Edwin D., and Craig, Albert M., *East Asia The Modern Transformation*, Boston, 1965.
Fairbank, John K., (ed.), *The Chinese World Order: Traditional China's Foreign Relations*, Harvard East Asian Series, 32, Cambridge, 1968.
Grajdanzen, Andrew J., *Modern Korea*, New York, 1944.
Griffis, William Elliot, *Korea, The Hermit Nation*, London, 1905.
Hackett, Roger F., *Yamagata Aritomo in the Rise of Modern Japan 1838–1922*, Cambridge, 1971.
Han, Woo-Keun, *The History of Korea*, Seoul, 1970.
Hane, Mikiso, *Peasants, Rebels and Outcastes: The Underside of Modern Japan*, New York, 1982.
Harada, Shuichi, *Labor Conditions in Japan*, New York, 1928.
Harootunian, H. D., *Toward Restoration*, Berkeley, Los Angeles, and London, 1970.
Harrington, Fred H., *God, Mammon and the Japanese: Dr. Horace N. Allen and Korean-American Relations, 1884–1905*, Madison, Wisconsin, 1944.
Hatada, Takashi, *A History of Korea*, trans. and eds. Warren W. Smith Jr. and Benjamin H. Hazard, Santa Barbara, 1969.
Henderson, Gregory, *Korea: The Politics of the Vortex*, Cambridge, 1968.
Henthorn, William E., *A History of Korea*, New York, 1971.
Holmes, Colin, *Anti-Semitism in British Society, 1876–1939*, London, 1979.
Hoshino, Tokuji, (comp.), *Economic History of Chosen*, Keijō, 1920.
Hulbert, Homer B., *The History of Korea*, Seoul, 1905.
——.*The Passing of Korea*, New York, 1906.
Ienaga, Saburo, *The Pacific War*, trans. Frank Baldwin, New York, 1978.
Ike, Nobutaka, *The Beginnings of Political Democracy In Japan*, Baltimore, 1952.
International Labour Office, *Industrial Labour In Japan*, Geneva, 1933.
Ishii, Ryoichi, *Population Pressure and Economic Life in Japan*, London, 1937.
Iwata, Masakazu, *Ōkubo Toshimichi – The Bismarck Of Japan*, Berkeley and Los Angeles, 1964.
Jansen, Marius B., *Sakamoto Ryōma and the Meiji Restoration*, Princeton, 1961.
——.*The Japanese and Sun Yat-sen*, Stanford, 1970.
——., (ed.), *Changing Japanese Attitudes Toward Modernization*, Princeton, 1972.
Johnston, Bruce F., *Japanese Food Management In World War II*, Stanford, 1953.
Kang, Younghill, *The Grass Roof*, New York, 1947.
Kawakami, K. K., (ed.), *What Japan Thinks*, New York, 1921.
Keene, Donald, *Landscapes And Portraits: Appreciations Of Japanese Culture*, London, 1972.
Kidder, J. E., Jr., *Japan Before Buddhism*, London, 1959.
Kim, C. I. Eugene, and Kim, Han-Kyo, *Korea And The Politics Of Imperialism 1876–1910*, Berkeley and Los Angeles, 1967.
Kim, C. E. Eugene, and Mortimore, Doretha E., (eds.), *Korea's Response to Japan: The Colonial Period 1910–1945*, Michigan, 1975.
Kim, Donguk, *History of Korean Literature*, trans. Leon Hurvitz, Tokyo, 1980.
Kim, Illsoo, *New Urban Immigrants*, Princeton, 1981.
Kim, Kwan Bong, *The Korea-Japan Treaty Crisis and the Instability of the Korean Political System*, New York, Washington and London, 1971.
Kim, San, and Wales, Nym, *Song of Ariran, A Korean Communist in the Chinese Revolution*, San Francisco, 1972.

Kuno, Yoshi S., *Japanese Expansion On The Asiatic Continent*, Port Washington, New York, 1967.
Kuznets, Paul W., *Economic Growth And Structure In The Republic Of Korea*, New Haven and London, 1977.
Lebra, Joyce C., *Ōkuma Shigenobu, Statesman of Meiji Japan*, Canberra, 1973.
Lee, Changsoo, and DeVos, George, *Koreans In Japan: Ethnic Conflict and Accommodation*, Berkeley, Los Angeles and London, 1981.
Lee, Chong-Sik, *The Politics of Korean Nationalism*, Berkeley and Los Angeles, 1963.
Lee, Hoon K., *Land Utilization And Rural Economy In Korea*, London, 1936.
Levenson, Joseph R., *Confucian China And Its Modern Fate: A Trilogy*, Berkeley and Los Angeles, 1965.
——.*Liang Ch'i-Ch'ao And The Mind Of Modern China*, Berkeley and Los Angeles, 1967.
Lockwood, William W., *The Economic Development of Japan: Growth and Structural Change (1868–1938)*, Princeton, 1961.
——., (ed.), *The State and Economic Enterprise in Japan: Essays in the Political Economy of Growth*, Princeton, 1965.
Marshall, Byron K., *Capitalism and Nationalism in Prewar Japan: the Ideology of the Business Elite, 1868–1941*, Stanford, 1967.
Maruyama, Masao, *Thought and Behaviour in Modern Japanese Politics*, ed. Ivan Morris, London, 1969.
Mayo, Marlene J., (ed.), *The Emergence of Imperial Japan*, Lexington, Mass., 1970.
McAleavy, Henry, *The Modern History Of China*, New York, 1969.
McCune, Shannon, *Korea's Heritage: A Regional and Social Geography*, Rutland, Vermont and Tokyo, 1963.
McKenzie, Frederick Arthur, *Tragedy of Korea*, London, 1908.
——.*Korea's Fight for Freedom*, (reprint), Seoul, 1969.
McLaren, Walter Wallace, *A Political History Of Japan During The Meiji Era 1867–1912*, London, 1965.
Melendy, H. Brett, *The Oriental Americans*, New York, 1972.
Mitchell, Richard Hanks, *The Korean Minority In Japan*, Berkeley and Los Angeles, 1967.
Mitchell, Richard H., *Thought Control In Prewar Japan*, Ithaca and London, 1976.
Moore, Barrington, Jr., *Social Origins Of Dictatorship And Democracy: Lord and Peasant in the Making of the Modern World*, Middlesex, England, 1974.
Morley, James William, (ed.), *Dilemmas of Growth in Prewar Japan*, Princeton, 1971.
Myers, Ramon H., and Peattie, Mark, (eds.), *The Japanese Colonial Empire, 1895–1945*, Princeton, 1984.
Nahm, Andrew C., (ed.), *Korea Under Japanese Rule*, Michigan, 1973.
Najita, Tetsuo, *Hara Kei and the Politics of Compromise 1905–1915*, Cambridge, 1967.
Nelson, M. Frederick, *Korea and the Old Orders in Eastern Asia*, Baton Rouge, 1946.
Norman, E. H., *Japan's Emergence as a Modern State*, New York, 1940.
Notehelfer, F. G., *Kōtoku Shūsui, Portrait of a Japanese Radical*, Cambridge, England, 1971.
Okamoto, Shumpei, *The Japanese Oligarchy and the Russo-Japanese War*, New York and London, 1970.
Osgood, Cornelius, *The Koreans And Their Culture*, Tokyo, 1966.

Passin, Herbert, *Society and Education in Japan*, New York, 1965.
Patrick, Hugh, (ed.), *Japanese Industrialization And Its Social Consequences*, Berkeley, Los Angeles, and London, 1976.
Pittau, Joseph, *Political Thought in Early Meiji Japan*, Cambridge, 1967.
Pyle, Kenneth B., *The New Generation In Meiji Japan*, Stanford, 1969.
Quigley, Harold S., *Japanese Government and Politics: An Introductory Study*, New York, 1932.
Reischauer, Edwin O., *The United States and Japan*, Cambridge, 1957.
——.*Japan: The Story Of A Nation*, Rutland, Vermont and Tokyo, 1971.
Reischauer, Edwin O., and Fairbank, John K., *East Asia The Great Tradition*, Tokyo, 1972.
Reischauer, Robert K., *Early Japanese History*, Gloucester, Mass., 1967.
Rex, John, *Race Colonialism and the City*, London, 1973.
Sansom, G. B., *Japan: A Short Cultural History*, Rutland, Vermont and Tokyo, 1975.
Sansom, George, *A History Of Japan 1334–1615*, London, 1965.
——.*A History Of Japan 1615–1867*, London, 1966.
——.*A History of Japan To 1334*, Stanford, 1969.
Scalapino, Robert A., *The Japanese Communist Movement, 1920–1966*, Berkeley and Los Angeles, 1967.
——.*Democracy And The Party Movement In Prewar Japan*, Berkeley and Los Angeles, 1975.
Scalapino, Robert A., and Lee, Chong-Sik, *Communism In Korea*, Berkeley, Los Angeles, and London, 1972.
Schumpeter, E. B., (ed.), *The Industrialization of Japan and Manchukuo, 1930–1940: Population, Raw Materials, Industry*, New York, 1940.
Shiba, Ryotarō, *The Heart Remembers Home*, trans. Eileen Katō, Tokyo, 1979.
Shindo, Takejiro, *Labor In The Japanese Cotton Industry*, Tokyo, 1961.
Shively, Donald H., *Tradition and Modernization in Japanese Culture*, Princeton, 1971.
Silberman, Bernard S., and Harootunian, H. D., (eds.), *Japan In Crisis: Essays On Taishō Democracy*, Princeton, 1974.
Skrzypczak, Edmund, (ed.), *Japan's Modern Century*, Tokyo, 1968.
Smethurst, Richard J., *A Social Basis for Prewar Japanese Militarism*, Berkeley, Los Angeles, and London, 1974.
Smith, Henry De Witt III, *Japan's First Student Radicals*, Cambridge, 1972.
Suh, Sang-Chul, *Growth and Structural Changes in the Korean Economy, 1910–1940*, Cambridge, 1978.
Takekoshi, Yosaburo, *Japanese Rule in Formosa*, trans. George Braithwaite, London, 1907.
Tanin, O., and Yohan, E., *Militarism and Fascism in Japan*, New York, 1934.
Totten, George O., III, *The Social Democratic Movement in Prewar Japan*, New Haven and London, 1966.
Tsunoda, Ryusaku, (et al), *Sources of Japanese Tradition*, New York, 1964.
Tsurumi, E. Patricia, *Japanese Colonial Education in Taiwan, 1895–1945*, Harvard East Asian Series, 88, Cambridge, 1977.
Tsurumi, Kazuko, *Social Change and the Individual: Japan Before and After Defeat in World War II*, Princeton, 1970.
Wagner, Edward W., *The Korean Minority In Japan, 1904–1950*, New York, 1951.
Ward, Robert E., (ed.), *Political Development in Modern Japan*, Princeton, 1973.

Wright, Mary Clabaugh, *The Last Stand of Chinese Confucianism: The T'ung Chih Restoration, 1862–1874*, Stanford, 1972.
Young, A. Morgan, *Japan In Recent Times 1912–1926*, Westport, Connecticut, 1973.

4. *Articles (in English)*

Abe, Hiroshi, 'Higher Learning In Korea Under Japanese Rule', *The Developing Economies*, 9, 2, June, 1971.
Abe, Yoshio, 'Development of Neo-Confucianism in Japan, Korea and China', *Acta Asiatica*, 19, December, 1970.
——.'The Characteristics of Japanese Confucianism', *Acta Asiatica*, 25, October, 1973.
Aoyama, Hideo, and Nishikawa, Toru, 'Business Fluctuations In The Japanese Economy During the Inter-War Period', *Kyoto University Economic Review*, 28, 1, April, 1958.
Ash, James K., 'The Tonghak Rebellion: Problems And Interpretations', *Journal Of Social Sciences And Humanities*, 30, June, 1969.
——.'Korea In The Making Of The Early Japanese State: Preliminary Survey to 815 A.D.', *Journal Of Social Sciences And Humanities*, 35, December, 1971.
Beardsley, Richard K., 'Japan Before History: A Survey of the Archaeological Record', *The Far Eastern Quarterly*, 14, 3, May, 1955.
Beasley, W. G., 'Self Strengthening and Restoration: Chinese and Japanese Responses to the West in the Mid-Nineteenth Century', *Acta Asiatica*, 26, March, 1974.
Bisson, T. A., 'Problems of War Production Control in Japan', *Pacific Affairs*, 16, 3, September, 1943.
Brudnoy, David, 'Japan's Experiment in Korea', *Monumenta Nipponica*, 25, 1–2, 1970.
Chang, Yunshik, 'Colonization as Planned Change: The Korean Case', *Modern Asian Studies*, 5, 2, April, 1971.
Chen, Edward I-Te, 'Japanese Colonialism In Korea And Formosa: A Comparison Of The System Of Political Control', *Harvard Journal of Asiatic Studies*, 30, 1970.
Choi Ho-chin, 'The Strengthening Of The Economic Domination By Japanese Colonialism (1932–1945)', *The Korea Observer*, 2, 4, July, 1970.
Clark, C. A., 'The Korean Church in Japan', *Japan Christian Quarterly*, 7, 3, July, 1932.
Colegrove, Kenneth, 'Labor Parties In Japan', *American Political Science Review*, 23, 2, May, 1929.
Conde, David, 'The Korean Minority In Japan', *Far Eastern Survey*, 16, February, 1947.
Cook, Harold F., 'Kim Ok-kyun's Second Visit to Japan', *Journal Of Social Sciences And Humanities*, 30, June, 1969.
——.'Pak Yong-Hyo: Background and the Early Years', *Journal Of Social Sciences And Humanities*, 31, December, 1969.
——.'Kim Ok-kyun's Early Career', *Journal Of Social Sciences And Humanities*, 35, December, 1971.
Farley, Miriam S., 'Korean Labor In Japan Depresses Wage Level', *Far Eastern Survey*, June, 1937.
Grajdanzev, A. J., 'Formosa Under Japanese Rule', *Pacific Affairs*, 15, September, 1942.

Hahn, Bae-Ho, and Hong, Sung-Chick, 'The Korean Minority in Japan: Their Problems, Aspirations and Prospects', *Korea Journal*, 15, 6, June, 1975.
Hatada, Takashi, 'The Significance of Korean History', *The Japan Interpreter*, 9, 2, Sum-Aut., 1974.
Hirano, Kunio, 'The Yamato State and Korea in the Fourth and Fifth Centuries', *Acta Asiatica*, 31, January, 1977.
Hunter, Janet, 'Japanese Government Policy, Business Opinion, and the Seoul-Pusan Railway, 1894-1906', *Modern Asian Studies*, 2, 4, October, 1977.
Idei, Seishi, 'The Unemployment Problem in Japan', *International Labour Review*, 22, 4, October, 1930.
Inoue, Mitsusada, 'The Ritsuryō System In Japan', *Acta Asiatica*, 31, January, 1977.
Jansen, Marius B., 'Ōi Kentarō: Radicalism and Nationalism', *The Far Eastern Quarterly*, 11, 3, May, 1952.
Jones, Hazel J., 'The Formulation Of The Meiji Government Policy Toward the employment of foreigners', *Monumenta Nipponica*, 23, 1, 1968.
Karasawa, Tomitarō, 'Changes in Japanese Education as Revealed in Textbooks', *Japan Quarterly*, 2, 1955.
Kawakami, K. K., 'Japan's Policy Toward Alien Immigration', *Current History*, 20, 3, June, 1924.
Kiley, Cornelius J., 'A Note On The Surnames Of Immigrant Officials In Nara Japan', *Harvard Journal of Asiatic Studies*, 29, 1967.
Kim, Yong-sop, 'Absentee Landlord System During The 19th-20th Century In Korea', *Journal Of Social Sciences And Humanities*, 37, December, 1972.
Kim, Young-ho, 'Yu Kil Chun's Ideal of Enlightenment', *Journal Of Social Sciences And Humanities*, 33, December, 1970.
Kishimoto Eitaro, 'The Characteristics Of Labour-Management Relations In Japan And Their Historical Formation', 1, 2, *Kyoto University Economic Review*, 35, 2, October, 1965, 36, 1, April, 1966.
Kublin, Hyman, 'The Evolution Of Japanese Colonialism', *Comparative Studies In Society And History*, 2, 1959-1960.
Large, Stephen S., 'The Romance of Revolution in Japanese Anarchism and Communism During the Taishō Period', *Modern Asian Studies*, 11, 3, July, 1977.
Ledyard, Gari, 'Galloping Along With The Horseriders: Looking for the Founders of Japan', *The Journal Of Japanese Studies*, 1, 2, Spring, 1975.
Lee, Hyoun-jong, 'Korean Influence On Japanese Culture', *Korean Frontier*, 19, November, 1970.
Lee, Kwang-rin, 'On the Publication Of The Independent By Suh Jae-P'il (Philip Jaisohn)', *Journal Of Social Sciences And Humanities*, 43, June, 1976.
McCune, George M., 'The Exchange Of Envoys Between Korea And Japan During The Tokugawa Period', *The Far Eastern Quarterly*, 5, 3, May, 1946.
McElroy, Robert, 'New Immigration Law Over Japan's Protest', *Current History*, 20, 4, July, 1924.
Matsumoto, Sannosuke, 'Yukichi Fukuzawa, His Concept of Civilization and View of Asia', *The Developing Economies*, 5, 1, March, 1967.
Matsuo, Takayoshi, 'The Development of Democracy in Japan', *The Developing Economies*, 4, 4, December, 1966.

——.'The Japanese Protestants in Korea', 1, 2, *Modern Asian Studies*, 13, 3 and 13, 4, July, 1979 and October, 1979.

Matsuzaki, Toru, 'Correcting Textbook Distortions: An Experimental Record of the Study of Korean History in Japan', *Bulletin of Peace Proposals*, 1979.

Mayo, Marlene J., 'The Korean Crisis of 1873 and Early Meiji Foreign Policy', *The Journal of Asian Studies*, 21, 4, August, 1972.

Minami, Jiro, 'Japanese-Korean 'Fusion' Said Vital To Creation of New Order in E. Asia', *The China Weekly Review*, 89, 12, August 19, 1939.

Mitchell, Richard H., 'Japan's Peace Preservation Law of 1925: Its Origins and Significance', *Monumenta Nipponica*, 28, 3, 1973.

Mizoguchi, Toshiyuki, 'Consumer Prices & Real Wages in Taiwan and Korea under Japanese Rule', *Hitotsubashi Journal of Economics*, 13, 1, June, 1972.

Mizuno, Rentarō, 'From Korea to Chosen', *Contemporary Japan*, September, 1933.

Mori, Katsumi, 'The Beginning Of Advance Of Japanese Merchant Ships', *Acta Asiatica*, 23, September, 1972.

Najita, Tetsuo, 'Restorationism In The Political Thought Of Yamagata Daini (1775–1767)', *The Journal of Asian Studies*, 31, 1, November, 1971.

Nelson, Beverly, 'Nationalism And Agrarian Populism In Modern Korean Literature – The Colonial Legacy', *Hitotsubashi Journal of Arts and Sciences*, 21, 1, December, 1980.

Newell, William H., 'Some Problems of integrating Minorities into Japanese Society', *Journal Of Asian And African Studies*, 2, 1967.

Ninomiya, Shigeaki, 'An Inquiry Concerning the Origin, Development, and Present Situation of the Eta in Relation to the History of Social Classes in Japan', *Transactions of the Asiatic Society of Japan*, 10, Second Series, December, 1933.

Norman, E. Herbert, 'The Genyōsha: A Study in the Origins of Japanese Imperialism', *Pacific Affairs*, 17, 3, September, 1944.

Ōbayashi, Taryō, 'The Origins of Japanese Mythology', *Acta Asiatica*, 31, January, 1977.

Odaka, Konosuke, 'A History of Money Wages in the Northern Kyushu Industrial Area, 1898–1939', *Hitotsubashi Journal of Economics*, 8, 2, February, 1968.

Okubo, Tadashi, 'The Thoughts of Mabuchi and Norinaga', *Acta Asiatica*, 25, October, 1973.

Ono, Kazuichiro, 'The Problem Of Japanese Emigration', *Kyoto University Economic Review*, 28, April, 1958.

Passin, Herbert, 'Untouchability in the Far East', *Monumenta Nipponica*, 2, 3, 1955.

Porter, Catherine, 'Korea And Formosa As Colonies Of Japan', *Far Eastern Survey*, 5, 9, April, 1936.

Saeki, Arikiyo, 'Studies on Ancient Japanese History, Past and Present', *Acta Asiatica*, 31, January, 1977.

Scalapino, Robert A., and Lee, Chong-sik, 'Origins of the Korean Communist Movement (III)', *Journal of Asian Studies*, 20, February, 1961.

Shunzō, Yoshisaka, 'Labour Recruiting In Japan and its Control', *International Labour Review*, 12, 4, October, 1925.

Tahara, Tsuguo, 'The Kokugaku Thought', *Acta Asiatica*, 25, October, 1973.

Raira, Koji, 'The Characteristics of Japanese Labor Markets', *Economic Development and Cultural Change*, 10, 2, 1962.

Tashiro, Kazui, 'Tsushima han's Korean Trade, 1684–1710', *Acta Asiatica*, 30, February, 1976.
Totten, George O., 'Labor And Agrarian Disputes In Japan Following World War I', *Economic Development And Cultural Change*, 9, 1.2, 1960.
Tsurumi, E. Patricia, 'Education and Assimilation in Taiwan under Japanese Rule, 1895–1945', *Modern Asian Studies*, 13, 4, October, 1979.
Tsurushima, Setsure, 'Origins of the Prejudice and Discrimination against Koreans in Japan as seen from a Historical and Social Background', *Kansai University Review of Economics and Business*, 5, 1, June, 1976.
——.'Korean Immigrants in Kando in 1920's', *Kansai University Review of Economics and Business*, 7, 1–2, December, 1978.
Wantanabe, Manabu, 'The Concept of Sadae Kyorin in Korea', *Japan Quarterly*, 24, 4, October–December, 1977.
Wray, Harold J., 'A Study in Contrasts, Japanese School Textbooks of 1903 and 1941–1945', *Monumenta Nipponica*, 28, 1, 1973.
Yanaihara, Tadao, 'Problems of Japanese Administration in Korea', *Pacific Affairs*, 11, 1938.
Unattributed, 'A War of Coal', *The Oriental Economist*, 11, 4, April, 1944.

5. *Unpublished Theses*

Baldwin, Frank Prentiss, Jr., *The March First Movement: Korean Challenge And Japanese Response*, (Ph.D., Columbia University), 1969.
Bang, Hung-kyu, *Japan's Colonial Education Policy In Korea* (Ph.D., University of Arizona), 1972.
Choe, Ching Young, *The Decade of the Taewon'gun: Reform, Seclusion, and Disaster*, 2 vols. (Ph.D., Harvard University), 1960.
Chon, Dong, *Japanese Annexation Of Korea: A Study Of Korean–Japanese Relations to 1910*, (Ph.D., University of Colorado), 1955.
Dong, Chon, See Chon Dong.
Collick, R. M. V., *Labour and Trades Unionism in the Japanese Coal Mining Industry, 1850–1935*, (Ph.D., Oxford University), 1970.
Dong, Wonmo, See Wonmo Dong.
Durkee, Travers E., *The Communist International and Japan*, (Ph.D., Stanford University), 1953.
Fuccello, Charles Joseph, *South Korean–Japanese Relations In The Cold War: A Journey To Normalization*, (Ph.D., New School For Social Research), 1977.
Han, Sang-Il, *Uchida Ryōhei And Japanese Continental Expansion, 1874–1916*, (Ph.D., Claremont Graduate School), 1974.
Im, Kwan Hwang, *The Korean Reform Movement Of The 1880's And Fukuzawa Yukichi*, (Ph.D., Washington University), 1975.
Kim, Bernice B. H., *The Koreans In Hawaii*, (M.A., University of Hawaii), 1937.
Kim, Han-gu, *Tonghak: Revitalization Movement in Korea*, (Ph.D., University of Toronto), 1970.
Lin, Jung-shun, *Popular Movements in the Taisho Era (1912–1926)*, (Ph.D., University of Pennsylvania), 1960.
Sabey, John Wayne, *The Gen'yōsha, The Kokuryūkai And Japanese Expansionism*, (Ph.D., University of Michigan), 1972.
Tatara, Toyori, *1400 Years of Japanese Social Work From Its Origins Through The Allied Occupation*, 2 vols., (Ph.D., Bryn Mawr College), 1975.
Tipton, Elise Kurashige, *The Civil Police In The Suppression Of The Prewar Japanese Left*, (Ph.D., Indiana University), 1977.

Weems, Clarence N., Jr., *The Korean Reform and Independence Movement (1881–1898)*, (Ph.D., Columbia University), 1954.
Wonmo, Dong, *Japanese Colonial Policy And Practice In Korea, 1905–1945: A Study In Assimilation*, (Ph.D., Georgetown University), 1965.

Index

Aichi, 64, 80, 180
Akaike Atsushi, 36, 77, 169,170,186,187
Akamatsu Katsumaro, 104
Akashi Motojirō, 31, 32, 34
Annexation
  Proclamation of, 32, 52
  Treaty of, 21
Aoki Shūzō, 17
Aoyama Gakuin, 134
Arahata Kanson, 147
Ashio and Besshi Copper Mines, 99
Asō Hisashi, 100

Black Wave Association *see* Kokutōkai

Chang Tŏk-su, 127, 151, 225
Chiba, 150, 165, 172, 174, 175, 178, 180
Chientao, 74
Ch'oe Kap-ch'un, 150
Chōfu, 167
Ch'okhudae (Scouting Party), 150
Chon Yong-t'aek, 134
Chŏng Han-gyŏng, 133
Chŏng T'ae-song, 179
Chŏng Un-hae, 105
Chōsen Gakkai (Korean Learned Society), 128
Chōsen Joshi Ryūgakusei Shimbokkai (Friendship Association of Korean Women Students in Japan), 128, 134, 145
Chōsen Ryūgakusei Shimbokkai (Fraternal Association of Korean Students in Japan), 128
Chung, Henry *see* Chŏng Han-gyŏng
Ch'ungch'ŏng Province, 11
Chūō Kōron (Central Review), 132, 140, 192
Chūsūin (Central Council), 33-4
Comintern, 144, 146, 147
Communist Party, Japanese, 101, 105, 108, 150, 190-1
Company Regulations 1911, 40
Congregational Church, Japanese, 21, 131, 132, 141
Cosmos Club, 106, 144, 146
Chrysanthemum Incident, 122

Dai Nippon Rōdō Sōdōmei Yūaikai (Greater Japan Confederation of Labour-Fraternal Society), 100
Datsu-A-Ron, 16

Demokurashii, 139, 140
Dōmei Gōshikai (Joint Fund Society), 215
Dōyūkai see Tōkyō Chōsen Kugakusei Dōyūkai

Eguchi Kiyoshi, 176
Enomoto Takeaki, 13
Etchūjima, 169
Etchūya Riichi, 176, 177

Fukuda Masatarō, 175
Fukuda Tokuzō, 126
Fukugawa, 169
Fukuoka, 54, 63, 64, 66, 71, 84, 89
Fukuzawa Yukichi, 11-16, 117-9
Funabashi Naval Transmission Station, 172, 175, 184
Fuse Tatsuji, 106, 151, 191
Futei Senjinsha (Company of Korean Malcontents), 109, 111, 151, 179

Gakuyukai see Zai Tōkyō Chōsen Ryūgakusei Gakuyukai
Gen'yōsha (Black Ocean Society), 13
Gifu, 63, 64, 168
Gotō Fumio, 172
Gotō Shimpei, 32, 76, 175
Gumma, 168, 174, 180, 188
Gyōminkai (Dawn People's Society), 106

Hanabusa Yoshimoto, 10, 13, 21
Hansong, Treaty of, 15
Hasegawa Yoshimichi, 31
Hideyoshi, 18
Hiraga Makoto, 110
Hirohito, Crown Prince, 184
Hiroshima, 63, 64, 71, 180
Hokkaidō, 52, 63, 64, 66, 71, 167
  Steamship and Colliery Company, 60-2, 75, 84, 89, 104
Hokuseikai (North Star Society), 107-9, 145, 150, 151, 179
Honjō, 179
Hōten, 175, 176
Hwanghae Province, 72, 73, 218
Hyōgo, 63, 64, 66, 71, 125, 130, 180, 215

I.A.R.A. see *Teikoku Zaigo Gunjinkai*
Ibaraki, 174, 180
Ichigatsukai (January Society), 108
Iida Sanji, 118
Ikebukuro, 189

Ilchinhoe (Renovation Society), 20
Imai Seiichi, 177
Inchon, 10, 14
Independence
  Declaration of, 134-6, 148, 149, 219-24
  Movement, 56, 101, 123, 131-40, 146, 186
  Resolution, 135, 222
Inoue Kakugorō, 118, 119
Inoue Kaoru, 10, 15, 16
Ishikawa Kōfudai, 178
Ishimitsu Maomi, 170
Itagaki Taisuke, 10, 13, 15
Itō Hirobumi, 14, 15, 19, 20
Itō Miyogi, 172
Iwakura Tomomi, 9, 13
Iwasa Sakutarō, 107, 144, 149, 150
Izome Rokurō, General, 183, 187

Japan Greater Korea Association of Students, 122
Jiji Shimpō, 13, 20, 21, 138
Jikeidan, 174-9, 181, 183, 184, 187-9, 191
Jimbohara, 179
Jimmu, Emperor, 17
Jiyū Hōsōdan (Civil Liberties Legal Association), 191

Kagoshima, 215
Kagurazaka, 167
Kamato Eikichi, 119
Kameido Incident, 176-7
Kanagawa, 63, 164, 174, 175, 180, 182, 189
Kanasugi, 164
Kanda, 105, 122, 136
Kaneko Ayako, 151
Kang Kum-san, 168
Kanghwa, Treaty of, 10
Kangwŏn Province, 72, 73, 218
Kansai, 80, 107, 185, 202
Kansai Rōdō Dōmeikai, 107
Kantō, 167, 175, 176, 181, 182, 202
  Great Earthquake, 4, 152, 164-200, 203
Kantō Rōdō Dōmei (Kantō Labour League), 150
Kashiwagi Gien, 131, 132
Katayama Sen, 99, 150, 191
Kato Tomasaburō, 169
Katsu Rintarō, 7, 8
Katsura Tomokazu, 120, 121
Kawaguchi, 173
Kawai Eizō, 104

Kawasaki, 101, 165, 167
  Dockyard, 101
  Shipyards, 58
Kawasaki Katsumi, 138
Keijō, 73 see also Seoul
  Imperial University, 38
Keiō Gijuku (Keiō University), 12-14, 117-21
Kenseikai, 138, 139
Kido Kōin, 8, 9
Kikka Jiken (Chrysanthemum Incident), 122
Kim Ch'ŏl-su, 134
Kim Chong-bŏm, 106, 107, 109
Kim Chun-yŏn, 133
Kim Hong-jip, 118
Kim Kwang-bŏm, 151
Kim Ok-kyun, 12, 14, 15, 117-9
Kim Yak-su, 105, 107, 108, 149, 150
Kiryū, 168
Kishiwada Cotton Spinning Company, 59
Kitahara Tatsuo, 151
Kōbe, 25, 75, 87, 201, 209, 215 see also Osaka-Kōbe Steelworks, 58
Koji Taira, 49
Kojong, Emperor, 20, 56, 118, 134, 137
Kokuryūkai (Amur River Society), 13, 20, 173
Kokutōkai (Black Wave Association), 107, 108, 145, 149, 150
Kokuyūkai (Black Friends Society), 107, 145, 150, 151
Kondō Eizō, 147
Korean Youth Independence Corps, 134, 136
Kōtoku Denjirō, 99
Kōtoku Shūsui, 19
Kuboyama, 165
Kugakusei Dōyūkai, 106, 149
Kugakusei Keisetsukai (Self-Supporting Student Association for Diligent Study), 145
Kuni, Imperial Prince, 167
Kuroda Hisao, 106
Kuroda Kiyotaka, General, 10
Kyŏnggi Province, 72, 73, 218
Kyŏngsang Province, 11
Kyōtō, 64, 117, 125, 130, 180, 215
Kyōtō Chōsenjin Rōdō Kyōsaikai (Kyōtō Mutual Aid Society of Korean Labour), 103, 215
Kyushū, 52, 62, 85, 89

Li Hung-chang, 15
Li-Itō Convention, 15
Li O-gen, 168

Maebashi, 168
Maeil Sinbo (Daily News), 33, 137
Manchuria, 20, 35, 52, 74, 76, 132, 182

Maruyama Tsurukichi, 77, 141
Matsuo Takayoshi, 177-8, 191
Meguro, 189
Meiji period, 1, 2, 8, 12, 34, 51, 117, 201
Meiji University, 127
Mie, 63
Miike mine, 62
Min, Queen, 119
Minami Senjū, 164
Miners, National Union of, 104
Mizuno Rentaro, 31, 36, 76, 142, 169-71, 186, 187
Moji, 86
Moriya Konosuke, 139
Moriyama Saneyoshi, 173
Moriyama Shigeru, 9-10, 21
Motono Ichirō, 20

Nagano, 63, 64, 180, 188
Nagasaki, 63, 64
Nagoya, 215
Nakabashi Kisaburō, 189-90
Nakamura Masanao, 118
Nakano, 167
Nankatsu Labour Association, 177
Narashino Division, 173, 176-7
National Congress, Petition for the Calling of a, 135, 222
National Youth Association see Seinendan
Nihon Rodo Sodomei (Japan Confederation of Labour), 100, 106-9, 190
Niigata, 64, 105
Nishi-Nari County, 88, 209
Nishio Suehiro, 107
North Chŏlla Province, 72, 73, 218
North Ch'ungch'ŏng Province, 72, 73, 218
North Hamgyŏng Province, 72, 73, 218
North Kyŏngsang Province, 72, 73, 218
North P'yŏngan Province, 72, 73, 218
North Star Society see Hokuseikai

Odawara, 164
Oi Kentarō, 13
Oishi Masami, 32
Oita, 63, 64
Okayama, 168, 180
Okubo Tosimichi, 9
Okuma Shigenobu, 21
Omori, 167
Osaka, 56, 57, 62-6, 69-71, 74, 75, 84, 86-8, 90, 101, 103, 107-10, 110, 125, 130, 150, 180, 185, 186, 190, 201, 208-10, 215
Osaka Asahi Shimbun, 22, 83, 86, 109
Osaka Chōsen Rōdō Dōmeikai (Osaka League of Korean Labour), 107-9
Osaka-Kōbe, 77, 78

Osaka Mainichi Shimbun, 57, 62, 137, 138, 168, 184, 189
Osugi Sakae, 107, 144, 146, 147, 149, 150, 177, 188
Otsuka, 167, 173
Oya Shōzō, 107

Paek Mu, 105-7
Pak Jae-il, 212, 214
Pak Kyŏng-sik, 182
Pak Un-sik, 127
Pak Yŏl, 105-7, 149-52
Pak Yŏng-hyo, 12, 117
Paris Peace Conference, 133, 135, 137, 146
Preservation of Public Order, Imperial Ordinance for, 183, 185
Protection, Treaty of, 12
Provisional Government, Korean, 123, 127, 143, 148, 149, 225
Pusan, 8, 9, 60, 62, 66-8, 77, 117, 185, 202, 209, 214
Pyŏn Hŭi-Yong, 179

Reimeikai (Dawn Society), 132, 139
Revolutionary Corps in China, Korean, 127
Rhee, Syngman see Yi Sŭng-man
Rice Riots 1918, 100, 101, 139, 186
Rinji Shinsai Kyūgo Jimukyoku (Emergency Earthquake Relief Bureau), 169
Rōdō Kumiai Dōmeikai (League of Labour Unions), 100
Rōdō Shimbun, 108, 109, 111
Rōdōsha Shimbun, 109, 111
Russo-Japanese War 1904, 18
Ryokō Shōmeisho (Certificate of Travel), 56

Sada Hakubo, 8, 9
Saigō Takamori, 9
Saitama, 168, 173-5, 179, 180, 184, 186, 188
Saitō Makoto, 35, 36, 141, 186
Sakai Toshihiko, 19, 144, 147
Sakamoto, Sergeant, 178
Sangenjaya, 167
Sano Manabu, 104
Sanyō Shimpō, 168, 175, 184
Seinendan (National Youth Association), 187, 188, 190
Senyū (Comrades in Arms), 188
Seoul, 10, 12, 18, 21, 35, 56, 105, 119, 136, 137, 203 see also Keijō
Seoul-Inchon railway, 18
Setagaya, 167
Settsu Cotton Spinning Company 56-7, 58
Shakai Minshutō (Social Democrat Party), 100
Shanghai, 133, 134, 143, 147, 151, 225
Shibuya, 167
Shiga Shigetaka, 17
Shimizu Ikutarō, 178

INDEX

Shimonoseki, 57, 66-8, 202, 212, 214
Shinagawa, 167
Shinano River Incident, 105
Shinjin (New Man), 141
Shinjinkai (New Man Society), 103-4, 132, 133, 139, 144
Shinjuku, 189
Shinozaki, 178
Shinyūkai (Faithful Friends Society), 100
Shizuoka, 64, 164, 180, 186
Sino-Japanese War 1894-5, 17, 18, 119
Sinsa Yuramdam (Gentlemen's Touring Group), 12, 118
Sŏ Kwang-bŏm, 12, 117
Sōaikai (Mutual Love Association), 76-7, 179, 181
Sōdōmei see Nihon Rōdō Sōdōmei
Song Chang-bŏk, 107
Song Chin-u, 129
Song Kye-baek, 131, 222, 224
South Chŏlla Province, 69, 72, 73, 218
South Ch'ungch'ŏng Province, 72, 73, 218
South Hamgyŏng Province, 72, 73, 218
South Kyŏngsang Province, 72, 73, 208, 218
South P'yŏngan Province, 72, 73, 218
Student Supervisor, Korean, 121, 123, 126, 142
Suehiro Shigeo, 139-40
Suihei Undō (Levellers Movement), 90
Suzuki Bunji, 100, 106

Taishō period, 49, 126, 164
Taiwan, 31, 32, 76
Taiyō (The Sun), 139, 140
Takashima mine, 52
Takatsu Seidō, 144, 147, 150, 151
Takekoshi Yosaburō, 31
Tanahashi Kotora, 100
Tanaka Giichi, General, 187
Tasaka Sadao, 191
Teikoku Zaigō Gunjinkai (Imperial Army Reservist Association), 187-8
Terada Motoyoshi, 117, 118
Terashima, 167
Terauchi Masatake, 21, 31-4, 49, 101
Tientsin, 15
Treaty of, 15
Tochigi, 174, 180
Tokotomi Sohō, 17
Tokugawa Ienobu, *Shōgun*, 7, 8, 11, 51, 122
Tokutomi, 18
Tokyo, 15, 19, 62-4, 71, 77, 87, 88, 100, 105, 107, 109, 120-2, 124, 125, 129-36, 141, 144, 146, 147,
149-51, 164-87, 201, 215
Tōkyō Asahi Shimbun 20, 190
Tōkyō Chōsen Kugakusei Dōyūkai (Comradely Association of Self-Supporting Korean Students in Tokyo), 145, 147
Tōkyō Chōsen Rōdō Dōmeikai (Tokyo League of Korean Labour), 106, 107, 109, 150
Tōkyō Mainichi Shimbun, 19-21
Tōkyō Nichi Nichi Shimbun, 19, 137, 138, 176, 181, 184, 188
Tomizaka, 167
Tonga Ilbo, 105, 151
Tonghak movement, 11, 18
Toyama, 64
Tōyō Keizai Shimpō (Asia Economic Bulletin), 18
Tōyō Kyōkai (Oriental Institute), 76, 142
Tōyō no Meishu (Leader of Asia), 12

Uchida Kōsai, 169, 172
Uchida Ryōhei, 173
Ŭibyŏng (Righteous Army), 20
Ŭiyŏldan (Righteous Fighters Corps), 151

Wakayama, 57, 64, 80, 215
Washington Conference, 143, 147-9
Wilson, Woodrow, President, 56, 126, 133, 143, 149
Wonsan, 60

Yamabe Kentarō, 40
Yamagata Aritomo, 9, 16, 17, 20, 31
Yamagata Isaburō, 31, 138
Yamaguchi, 63, 64, 71, 172, 180
Yamaguchi Seiken, 165, 188
Yamakawa Hitoshi, 109, 146, 147, 150
Yamamichi Jōkichi, 139
Yamamoto Gombi, 169, 175, 176, 181
Yamanote-Honmachi, 165
Yamazaki Kesaya, 191
Yasuda Tametarō, 104
Yi Ch'un-suk, 146, 225
Yi Chŭng-nim, 147
Yi Kwang-su, 126, 127, 134, 222, 224
Yi period, 9, 11, 38, 40
Yi Sŭng-man, 133
Yi Tal, 131, 136
Yi Tong-hwi, 127
Yi Tong-in, 117, 118
Yi Tong-ji, 179
YMCA see *Zai Tōkyō Chōsen Kirisutokyō Seinenkai*
Yodobashi, 167, 173
Yokohama, 87, 164, 165, 167, 172-4, 183, 184, 188
Yokohama Shinsai Hogodan (Yokohama Earthquake Protection Association), 165

Yomiuri Shimbun, 18, 104, 105
Yorozu Chōhō, 138, 190, 192
Yosano Hiroshi, 18
Yoshida Shōin, 7, 8
Yoshino Sakuzō, 21, 104, 126, 131, 132, 139-41, 182, 192
Yoshisaka Shunzō, 56, 57
Yōshisatsu Chōsenjin Shisatsu Naiki (Internal Regulations for the Observation of Koreans Requiring Surveillance), 129, 141
Yu Kil-chun, 12, 118
Yūaikai (Fraternal Society), 100, 103
Yüan Shih-K'ai, 12
Yūbari mine, 60, 104
Yun Ch'i-ho, 12

Zai Tōkyō Chōsen Kirisutokyō Seinenkai (Korean Young Men's Christian Association in Tokyo), 122, 127, 128, 133-6, 141, 144, 146, 147
Zai Tōkyō Chōsen Ryūgakusei Gakuyūkai (Fraternal Association of Korean Students), 128, 131, 133, 135, 144, 146, 147
Zaihan Chōsen Shimbokkai (Korean Friendship Society of Osaka), 128, 215
Zen Chōsen Seinen Dokuritsudan (All Korean Youth Independence Corps), 219
Zen'ei (Vanguard), 105, 108

DS 832.7.K6W45 1989

circ The origins of the Korean community in J
Bergen Community College Library

**Library and Learning
Resources Center
Bergen Community College**
400 Paramus Road
Paramus, N.J. 07652-1595

Return Postage Guaranteed